Merthyr Historian

Merthyr Riverside area, 1960.
(Photo courtesy Mrs. Eira M. Smith)

MERTHYR HISTORIAN

— *VOLUME TEN* —

MERTHYR TYDFIL HISTORICAL SOCIETY
SOUTH WALES
1999

Financial assistance from the
Welsh Church Act Fund 98/99,
administered by the
Rhondda Cynon Taff County Borough Council,
is gratefully acknowledged.

Learning Resources
Centre

ISBN 0 953055 4-0
1999
Printed and Bound in the UK by WBC
Book Manufacturers Bridgend
Mid Glamorgan
Typeset by
Keith Brown & Sons Ltd.
Cowbridge (01446) 774490

INTRODUCTION

The Committee authorised the production of Merthyr Historian, Volume Ten, to celebrate and mark the twenty fifth anniversary (1972-97) of Merthyr Tydfil Historical Society.

The first offering is an Illustrated History of Merthyr Tydfil Historical Society, produced by Honorary Secretary Hugh Watkins, who has held Office continuously for twenty five years.

The second item, another chapter in an on-going autobiography by Professor Sir Glanmor Williams, gives an account of his time as a teacher at County School, Merthyr Tydfil, about 1942.

On 2nd December 1996 Professor Brynley F. Roberts travelled from Aberystwyth to lecture the Historical Society on "Welsh Scholarship at Merthyr Tydfil", his essay is based on that lecture.

Our fourth paper "George Martin Maber, Rector of Merthyr Tydfil", was written by Revd. Roger Lee Brown, The Vicarage, Welshpool. Roger used different sources and his essay complements that of Barrie Jones, published on the same topic in Merthyr Historian, Volume Nine. Revd. Brown contributed an essay "The Wealthiest Place and the Poorest Ministry" to Merthyr Historian, Volume Eight.

"Child Emigration from Merthyr Tydfil Workhouse" is the title and substance of Professor Muriel Chamberlain's essay. This topic was the subject of a talk by Professor Chamberlain to the Historical Society on 4th March 1996.

Our sixth contribution, a detailed account of the Merthyr Tydfil National Eisteddfod, 1881, by Professor Hywel Teifi Edwards, was the topic of a lecture to the Society on 5th June 1995.

The seventh essay was contributed by Professor J. G. Jones, School of History and Archaeology, University of Wales Cardiff, "Reflections on some sixteenth-century East Glamorgan Gentry". Professor Jones lectured the Society on this topic on 2nd June 1997.

Item Eight, "Reminiscences of Dr. Emanuel Gross, a Prisoner of War in Siberia, 1914-18", is the second part of a three-part story, translated from his father's German language account, by Historical Society Founder Member and President, Dr. Joseph Gross.

A. Lloyd Hughes, Archivist, Museum of Welsh Life, St. Fagans, has edited letters sent to Merthyr Tydfil and Swansea from the Great War, to produce Item Nine.

"Life in the Lamb" by Mrs. Rosina Hughes (born Walsh) is an illustrated account of the daily life of her family (from 1928) when living in that famous old Merthyr Inn, THE LAMB.

Item Eleven is a brief history of Tabernacl Chapel, Bryant's Field, precursor of present day Tabernacl, Brecon Road, by Fred Holley. Thanks are due to Dr.William Linnard for translations from the Welsh. Some very scholarly pastors served at Tabernacl, Bryant's Field, three are mentioned in *Eminent Welshmen*, Volume One. T.R.Roberts, 1908:—

1. R. D. Roberts, Llwynhendy, pp.475-76.
2. Dr. J. Emlyn Jones, Ioan Emlyn, p.254.
3. J. Ceulanydd Williams, p.574.

Item Twelve, an account of the first forty years of Merthyr Tydfil Soroptimists, was contributed by Mrs.Sydney Jones. Thanks are due to Mrs. Dorothy Kertesz for acting as an intermediary.

"Abercanaid, Some Remembered Yesterdays", Part Five, by Edward Rhys-Price, gives an account of the author's travels in Australia and America and a business venture in London. Rhys-Price died a rich man in 1993, leaving £40,000 in trust for the benefit of the National Eisteddfod of Wales, to provide an annual prize to an author of a book about Wales and £40,000 to provide two annual scholarships at University of Wales Cardiff to students attending the College.

Educated in the University of Hard Knocks, but a scholar at heart, Mr.Rhys-Price's life story provides an interesting contrast to that of Professor Sir Glanmor Williams, a calm ascent of the Academic Ladder.

"Twenty five Years of Pleasure" is a brief History of the Treharris Male Voice Choir, by A. A. James. Thanks are due to Mr. Connolly, Brondeg, for procuring this essay and pictures.

Item Fifteen, "A Visit to Joseph Edward's Studio, 1854" was transcribed by the Editor. Two works from Graig Chapel, Abercanaid, by Edwards, recently found a new secure home in The Cellars, Cyfarthfa Castle Museum and Art Gallery. WELL DONE.

"Visit of a Maori Princess to Merthyr Tydfil, 1903" by Fred Holley, tells the story of a vocalist who, like Dame Kiri Te Kanawa, in recent times, performed in the presence of Royalty.

"The Way We Were, 1929-39", by Mrs. Rosina Hughes (born Walsh) gives an account of everyday life in Merthyr prior to the second World War.

Merthyr Historian, Volume Nine, contains some account of the musical activities of the Merthyr-born sculptor, MYNORYDD, William Davies. In Item Eighteen we reproduce a biography of Mynorydd's daughter, "Dr. Mary Davies, Sweet Singer, Great Lady".

Item Nineteen gives some account of nine nineteenth century Merthyr-based artists, not studied in the Merthyr Historian Series previously.

Barrie Jones contributed an account of the Keir Hardie Estate, Twynyrodyn, Merthyr Tydfil. His essay on the Revd. George Martin Maber, M.A., Rector of Merthyr, 1795-1844, appeared in Merthyr Historian, Volume Nine.

Item Twenty one, "William Evans, Ironmaster" by J. Brynmor Jones and T. F. Holley, is one of a series on Dowlais Works General Managers.

See "The Martin Family of Dowlais", M.H.,Volume Six.

"William Menelaus of Dowlais", M.H.,Volume Seven.

Item Twenty Two is an account of a talented Merthyr watchmaker and enthusiast for the Eisteddfod, David Jones, Senior, 1766-1842.

In Item Twenty Three Huw Williams has studied an example of internal migration. Credit drapers from Scotland descended on Merthyr to trade and banded together to form the long-lived MERTHYR TYDFIL CALEDONIAN SOCIETY. Initiated as a debt-collecting agency, the Society matured into a respected dining club, patronised by Members of Parliament.

Item Twenty Four, reminiscences by T. F. Harvey, long-serving surveyor to Merthyr Corporation, INTEGRATES, UNIFIES AND PLACES IN PERSPECTIVE many of the essays which have appeared in previous volumes of the Merthyr Historian series, and provides new insights to happenings in Merthyr Tydfil in the period 1870-1925.

The last essay, by Exmouth resident Raymond Jones, is a personal view of the history of Aberfan. Born and reared in Aberfan, Raymond attended Pantglas Junior School, Quaker's Yard Grammar School, University of London (B.Sc.Botany), University of Durham

(M.Sc.). He taught in Dorset and in Western Nigeria, then settled in Devon and had a distinguished career at Rolle College of Education (now the University of Plymouth).

Retired, Raymond is active as a freelance lecturer and writer. He contributed an essay "Ladies of Letters" to Merthyr Historian, Volume Eight.

The Editor thanks the authors for placing their essays at the disposal of the Historical Society, for publication.

VERY SPECIAL THANKS IS OFFERED TO THE MANY LECTURERS WHO HAVE GIVEN TALKS AT THE MONTHLY MEETINGS OF MERTHYR TYDFIL HISTORICAL SOCIETY OVER THE LAST TWENTY FIVE YEARS. DIOLCH YN FAWR.

The Staff of Merthyr and Dowlais Libraries, including Mr. James, Mrs. Carolyn Jacob, Mr. J. Downey, Mrs. Cynthia Roberts and ever-cheerful Beverley, are thanked for help willingly given.

John David Holley has voluntarily produced for the Historical Society an abundance of Newsletters and Promotional Material, on his computer.

Finally thanks is due to Colin Mawer, Commercial Director, W.B.C. Book Manufacturers, for invaluable help with Volumes Five to Ten.

Publications of M.T.H.S. may be purchased from
W.H.Smith, Merthyr.
Merthyr Central Library.
Dowlais Library.
Cyfarthfa Castle Museum.
HMSO Oriel, Cardiff.
Dillons Bookshop, Cardiff.
Whitchurch Bookshop, Cardiff.
Cowbridge Bookshop, 72 Eastgate.
Lockyer's, Abergavenny.
Probert, Newsagent, Pontmorlais, Merthyr.

FRONT COVER.
Merthyr riverside area, 1960.
Photo courtesy Mrs. Eira M. Smith.

BACK COVER.
Fountain, Cyfarthfa Castle Park. Inscription reads :
PRESENTED TO THE TOWN OF MERTHYR TYDVIL BY Mrs. T. J. JONES OF GILSANWS, CEFN COED AND HER DAUGHTERS OLIVE AND VIOLET AND LT.COL. AND Mrs. JONES, FRONHEULOG, CEFN COED, 1918.

T. F. Holley. Ph.D. T.C.D.
Chairman and Editor.
52, Chester Close,
Heolgerrig. Merthyr Tydfil.
CF48 1SW.

Some members, Treharris Male Voice Choir, 1997.

CONTENTS

Merthyr Historian

SHAPE THE FUTURE AROUND THE PAST
MERTHYR TYDFIL HISTORICAL SOCIETY, 1972-1997

by

HUGH WATKINS

As Secretary of the Merthyr Tydfil Historical Society for the past twenty five years, I am dedicating this essay as a tribute to a stalwart, dedicated band of men and women and to the memory of those now deceased, who have over the past twenty five years freely given of their time, through conservation, historical research and protest, in preserving the rich past historical culture of Merthyr Tydfil.

MERTHYR TYDFIL IRON HERITAGE TOWN.
TREF TUDFUL DREFTADAETH HAEARN.

These brown imposing signposts greet the traveller, tourist, visitor today and inform them that they are entering the confines of Merthyr Tydfil, the world famous IRON HERITAGE TOWN.

This was not always the case, the decade 1966-75 saw Merthyr Tydfil in the throes of re-development. Many people at the time expressed concern that the town of Merthyr Tydfil was throwing away her right of heritage and history. THE GREAT TOWN DETERIORATED OR DESTROYED IN THE NAME OF SO CALLED "ADVANCEMENT".

Dowlais and Penydarren, sites of early ironworks, buildings and places of historic value to our nation, had been destroyed. Merthyr Tydfil, home of invention, the town of iron and steel, that helped build an empire, DYING IN HISTORY'S HOME. The cry was "build our new houses by all means, but do not allow the real town to die in its dirt. Do something NOW and help preserve the very little that remains of the real town! It is our right and heritage handed down for safe keeping by our fathers".

An article appeared in the *Merthyr Express* of Friday 9th.June 1972, in which the late Mr.Vince Harris, licensee of the Penydarren Inn, a keen local historian, stated that there was an urgent need for the formation of a PRESERVATION SOCIETY IN MERTHYR TYDFIL. This was brought about by a decision of the Merthyr Tydfil Borough Council to demolish the main entrance gates at Cyfarthfa Park. Mr.Vince Harris invited all persons interested to a 7.30pm meeting on Monday 12th June 1972. The meeting took place at the Narrow Gauge Inn, Glebeland Street, Merthyr Tydfil, where it was agreed to form a Society known as the Merthyr Tydfil Historic Preservation Society. The aims of the Society were to PRESERVE the PAST, PROTECT the PRESENT, PROPAGATE the FUTURE, historical, social, cultural and industrial achievements of Merthyr Tydfil.

Eleven interested persons attended the first meeting, and the following Officers were elected:—

Chairman	Mr.Vince Harris	
Vice Chairman	Mr. Fred Vaughan	
Treasurer	Mr. R. Phillips	
Secretary (temporary)	Mr. T. Grant	
Committee (temporary)	Dr. Joseph Gross	Mr. W. Wilson
	Mr. R. Cremin	Mr. V. Wilding
	Mr. Hugh Watkins	Mr. John Owen
	Mr. Clive Thomas	

1

The first meeting took place at the Narrow Gauge Inn, Glebeland Street, on the 26th June 1972, when the aims and objectives of the Society were discussed, namely:—

1. Preservation of historic and cultural relics.
2. Creation of an Industrial and Cultural Museum, as a tourist attraction in Merthyr.
3. Liaison with the Merthyr Tydfil Borough Council and other interested bodies for the promotion of tourism and other facilities.
4. Prepare schemes for the utilisation of Cyfarthfa Park.
5. Formation of a section to encourage interest of apprentices at the College of Further Education and young people generally.
6. Representation on and liason with the various interested bodies.
7. Formation of a Finance and Social Committee to deal with subscriptions, appeals, lectures and social activities.

In 1972 one thousand two hundred tourist attractions, buildings and structures, including seventeen ancient monuments, had been identified as requiring protection and conservation in Merthyr Tydfil.

Merthyr Tydfil was the world's iron metropolis and one of the first towns of the industrial revolution, where modern industrial society began. Artefacts listed for preservation included old cast iron milestones which once marked the route for the old stage coaches between Merthyr and Abergavenny and Merthyr's most prestigious building, CYFARTHFA CASTLE, designed by Robert Lugar for William Crawshay The Second, it was completed within twelve months in 1825. At a cost of £30,000 it invoked yet another series of quarrels between William Crawshay the Younger and his father, William Crawshay The First, who had paid for the building.

The castle occupied a site of nearly an acre surrounded by eighteen acres of land which was soon transformed into plantations, shrubberies, greenhouses, lawns and gardens.

The late Dowlais-born Professor Gwyn Alfred Williams also expressed concern that Merthyr Tydfil was losing its past heritage. He stated that Merthyr need no longer be bulldozed into dust and blown away by the winds of history. Merthyr Tydfil must grow out of its past and shape itself to the future around its past. The total eradication of the known, as in Dowlais, would mean that the people of Merthyr Tydfil were completely disinherited. There was a need for the people of Merthyr to take a hand in making their own future.

Professor Williams used the example of Cyfarthfa Castle which, he said, "certain prominent local citizens wanted people to believe was the symbol of their servitude to the Iron Masters. If they had their way, Cyfarthfa Castle would be bulldozed away, the trees cut down, and the lakes filled in. A bright regimented housing estate would then be built to be filled with all the consumer goods the television adverts tell people they must have."

PRESERVATION

Cyfarthfa Castle Park Gates
The Society in 1972 approached Merthyr Tydfil Borough Council to preserve these gates for their historical and aesthetic value. While agreeing with this, the Council of the day were concerned about access dangers for buses taking children to Cyfarthfa Castle High School. They were also worried about the condition of the gates and railings, and the expense of necessary repairs.

3. Cyfarthfa Park Gates: on the move?

4. Gates and Lodges, Cyfarthfa Castle Park.

Engineering expert, the late Mr. John Owen, President of the Historical Society and the Works Manager at the British Steel Corporation Dowlais plant, offered to save the one hundred and fifty four year old historic gates and railings. The gates had been forged in 1820. They were made of cast iron not wrought iron. Mr. John Owen in his survey stated that any repairs could not be carried out unless they were done *in situ*, because he was afraid the gates and railings would fall apart if moved. He put a price of £3,375 on the work and in addition to this there would be extra work done by direct labour, total cost would be in the region of £5,000. 1976 saw the gates in the same condition, now the cost of repairing and renovating the iron gates and railings had risen to £11,000. Eventually the restoration was carried out.

The Iron Bridge.

The most emotive souvenir of all, for Merthyr people, was the Old Iron Bridge, the second oldest of its kind in the world. Merthyr's bridge was made in 1798 and erected in 1800 over the River Taff to service the old Ynysfach Works and the Penydarren Tramroad. It stood for one hundred and sixty three years spanning the mottled history of Merthyr Tydfil through prosperity, disaster, depression and prosperity again.

In 1963 the Iron Bridge was dismantled and taken to the kitchen gardens of Cyfarthfa Park. In October 1972 a deputation from the Society approached the Council with respect to an undertaking given by the M.T.B.C. in 1963, that the Old Iron Bridge would be re-erected in a suitable spot after it had been removed from its original position spanning the River Taff. From 1963-72 the bridge had lain in Cyfarthfa Park in a dismantled condition.

One suggestion put forward by M.T.B.C. was that the bridge was likely to be re-erected near the birthplace of musician, Dr. Joseph Parry. It had been examined by Professor M. K. Lloyd, then Professor of Metallurgy at University College, Cardiff, and by his colleagues, Dr. J. L. Taylor and Dr. D. L. Carpenter. In their report, they stated that the Old Iron Bridge although mainly of cast iron was in a reasonable condition and corrosion had been limited. They stated that no interim protective measures were necessary, but when the bridge was re-erected it should be sandblasted, zinc sprayed and treated with black zinc paint. They further stated that the methods of joining the various sections of the bridge were likely to be the most difficult and costly and would require special consultants and contractors.

In 1972, nine years after the dismantling of the bridge, a further inspection by Mr. John Owen estimated the cost of re-erecting the bridge at £15,000, some sections of the bridge were now completely missing and the cost of replacing them meant a realistic estimate of £25,000.

In 1974 the bridge was in a sorry state, large sections by then had disappeared. Although many suggestions were put forward, it was however too late, and the famous OLD IRON BRIDGE passed into obscurity.

On the 13th February 1974 the then Town Clerk for the M.T.C.B. Mr. Selwyn Jones, submitted to the Society a list of buildings of architectural and historical importance within the County Borough. Mr. L. E. L. Davies, at the Welsh Office, then based at St.David's House, Wood Street, Cardiff, also submitted a list, as the Society was anxious to assist when the Merthyr C.B. Council area was to be resurveyed.

On the 9th. April 1974, Mr.D.Morgan Evans, Inspector of Ancient Monuments, Department of the Environment, Central Office for Wales, visited Merthyr Tydfil to see first

5. The Iron Bridge, Merthyr. Forged 1798, erected 1800, dismantled 1963.

hand what Industrial Monuments remained in Merthyr. Concern was expressed by the Society that demolition had already taken place namely:—

1. Plymouth Arms, Bridge Street.
2. Gwaelodygarth Cottage.
3. Penydarren House.
4. Lodge to Penydarren House.
5. Cast Iron Bridge, dismantled, lying in Cyfarthfa Park.
6. Three Lodges to Cyfarthfa Castle.
7. Dowlais House, home of Lady C. Guest, translator of the Mabinogi.
8. Dowlais Central Schools.
9. Iron Bridge over Canal.
10. Bargoed House, Treharris.

The Department of the Environment did offer a fifty per cent grant towards the cost of re-erecting the Canal cast iron bridge and the Ynysfach Engine House was scheduled as an ancient monument, also the Penydarren Tramroad was under consideration for scheduling.

On the 8th April 1974 the Chief Leisure Service Officer for Merthyr approached Chairman Mr. Vince Harris for any relevant information to be included in a brochure to be produced by the newly formed Leisure Services Committee in respect of local historical interest regarding Merthyr Tydfil and surrounding area.

Merthyr Council set up a Sub-Committee to discuss the ancient monuments and buildings of historical interest in the Borough. The setting up of the Committee was moved by Councillor Albert John. The then Mayor of Merthyr Tydfil, Coun. John Reddy, commented "I think there is need for a Committee which could give specific thought to the problems that can arise as the result of re-development and involve buildings which may be of some significance and give some character to the Borough".

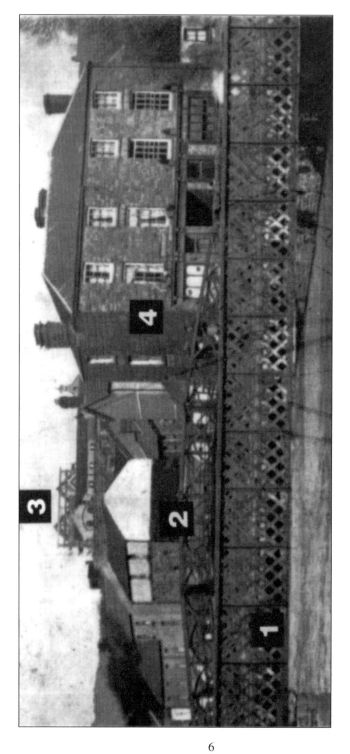

6. 1. New Iron Bridge, Merthyr, erected 1879.
   2. Old Iron Bridge, made at Cyfarthfa Works.
   3 Abermorlais Schools.
   4. Former Headquarters, Halifax Building Society, Merthyr.

The Mayor stated that immense benefits could be gained by the Borough if such buildings were protected. The Sub-Committee set up comprised the Mayor and a member from each ward. They were Coun. Bill Healy (Dowlais), Coun. John Reddy (Penydarren), Coun. Leon Stanfield and Coun. Gareth Foster (Park), Coun. John Gamlin (Cyfarthfa), Coun. Gerry Donovan (Town), Coun. Jack Handley (Plymouth), Coun. Bill Tudor (Merthyr Vale), Coun. Albert Gurney (Treharris), Coun. Joseph Bromley (Bedlinog) and Coun. Morgan Chambers (Vaynor).

In November 1975, the Conservation and Tourism Sub-Committee decided to co-opt representatives of local amenity societies to advise it in its deliberations. The recommendation was made following a meeting between the Sub-Committee and representatives of the M.T. Historical Society, the M.T. Civic Society and the Wales Tourist Board.

Mr. Vince Harris, Chairman, M.T.H.S., stated that his organisation was always prepared to give the local authority all the help and advice it could. He hoped that in return, efforts would be made to preserve some of the town's notable old buildings.

The then Secretary of the Civic Society, Miss Meryl Davies, stated that her organisation also wanted to give practical help to the Sub-Committee in an attempt to achieve aims that were shared both by the Council and the Civic Society.

The Merthyr Tydfil Civic Society was formed to help in the planning of Merthyr's future, to work with the authorities to help make "the best of the past" the basis of the future, while accepting the financial difficulties of the present. Its first Chairman was Community Councillor Morgan Chambers, Vice Chairman Mr. Alun Morgan, Secretary, Miss Meryl Davies. Executive Committee:—Mr. Phillip Griffiths, Mr. Emrys Roberts, Mr. Elwyn Bowen, Mr. Terry Strachan, Mrs. Margaret Jones, Mr. Gwilym Jones and Mr. Mansel Williams.

A representative of the Wales Tourist Board, Mr. Gwyn Jones, also promised full support for the kind of schemes that the Sub-Committee had in mind. He stated that if they reached fruition, they would prove a great tourist attraction for the town. The Wales Tourist Board was starting a new campaign to publicise the great tourist potential of the South Wales Valleys and Merthyr Tydfil had more to offer tourists than virtually any other valley town.

Richard Trevithick and the Tramroad Tunnel.

In 1973, members of M.T.H.S., including Chairman, Mr. Vince Harris, Vice Chairman Mr. Fred Vaughan, Explorations Organiser Mr. Clive Thomas, President Dr. Joseph Gross and his son John Gross, Mr. Ossie Bevan (Headmaster), Mr. Ken Gunter and four students from Afon Tâf High School History Research Unit, excavated the Tunnel.

The group walked fifty yards into the Tunnel which was some twelve feet high by fourteen feet wide. The party was prevented from going any further by the presence of silt and mud.

The Tunnel is situated in the lower Merthyr Tydfil area in the tip complex behind a number of garages on Pentrebach Road. The Historical Society had received permission from the agents of the Plymouth Estate, owners of the land, to make this entry into the Tunnel, which had to be resealed. Despite the fact that the visit did not produce any conclusive evidence (because of the presence of quantities of silt and mud), members were still of the opinion, that the Tunnel covered the area of the old Trevithick Tramroad.

The only things that the group came across on this, their initial survey, were stalactites and several manholes. They were convinced that the deep layer of silt was hiding relics of

7. Richard Trevithick Tramroad Tunnel. Built in 1803.

the old tramroad which was covered over by waste material from a coal level being operated in conjunction with the old Plymouth Furnaces.

At this time the Society was in communication with Ryan Industrial Fuels, Ltd., in the hope that the Company, which was already working the tip site, would be able to assist in the task of making a more effective survey of the Tunnel on the next occasion.

M.T.B.Council gave a commitment, that they would save the Tunnel, if the engineers decided it was feasible. The CWMBLACS TIPS LAND RECLAMATION SCHEME had threatened the Tunnel which had been sealed at both ends. The Tunnel had been built to serve the Penydarren Tramroad, which ran from Merthyr to Abercynon. The tramway was used by Richard Trevithick on his pioneering steam train journey, when he drove the first steam locomotive and train through the Tunnel in 1804.

The Merthyr Tydfil Heritage Trust, under its Chairman, Dr. J.Gross, had outlined plans to preserve the Tunnel. The entrance would be excavated and it would be turned into a tourist attraction. Dr. Gross presented plans for the project to the M.T.B. Council's Conservation and Tourism Sub-Committee.

In October 1976 Mid-Glamorgan County Council gave permission to J. E. JONES (Design) Ltd., of High Street, Blackwood, to remove coal and coke breeze from the tips at the rear of Baker's Garage, Pentrebach Road. The plan to extract coal near the world's first railway tunnel worried the Merthyr Historical Society.

The Merthyr Tydfil Borough Council at the time decided not to oppose an application to extract coal at the rear of Plymouth Street, subject to safeguards for the Tunnel. The Society expressed its concern and stated at the time "This Tunnel is unique and we fear that this excavation work could destroy it. Adequate precautions must be taken to preserve it, and we as a Society would like to see this as one of the conditions by which planning permission was granted".

MERTHYR TYDFIL BOROUGH COUNCIL

TREVITHICK'S TUNNEL &
Plymouth Ironworks

THESE WORKS ARE BEING CARRIED OUT AS PART OF A CONTINUING PROGRAMME TO
DEVELOPE AND INTERPRET THIS SITE AS A VISITOR ATTRACTION AND HERITAGE FEATURE
ON THE IRON TRAIL. THIS SCHEME IS FUNDED BY THE WELSH OFFICE VALLEYS
INITIATIVE OF MERTHYR TYDFIL BOROUGH COUNCIL.

| CHIEF EXECUTIVE & TOWN CLERK | LANDSCAPE ARCHITECT |
| ROGER V. MORRIS LLB (Wales) | Merthyr Tydfil Groundwork Trust |

THIS IS A VALLEYS INITIATIVE SCHEME FOR MERTHYR TYDFIL

Councillor Jack Handley, Chairman of Merthyr Planning Committee, stated "The firm concerned are going to extract coal about forty feet away from the Tunnel and we have established as a Planning Committee, that they will not touch it. They own the land and I will be negotiating with them to ask if they will make a gift of the Tunnel to the Council. We, too, believe the Tunnel is of historical importance".

The Tunnel was built in 1803 to allow the Penydarren tramroad traffic to pass through the Plymouth Ironworks. In its heyday trains were carrying seventy tons of iron a journey down to Abercynon. The Tunnel fell into disuse after the closure of the Plymouth Ironworks.

A £160,000 scheme was carried out by Mid-Glamorgan County Council's Land Reclamation Unit and Ashbank Construction for the Merthyr Council. This ambitious project to renovate the Tunnel was completed in 1987. It is now one of the Borough's tourist attractions, with a landscape picnic area, car park and commemorative plaque. A fitting memorial to Richard Trevithick.

Ynysfach Engine House.

The Society's next concern was the preservation of the Ynysfach Engine House and furnace area. The Action Committee at the time pressed for the buildings to be listed as ancient monuments and wanted them incorporated in any future development. Mr. John Beale, then Director of Education for Merthyr Tydfil, had written to the Council, that he and the College Governors were concerned about the condition of the Engine House and the retaining walls at the rear of the college workshops. He added that it had been suggested that the Engine House might be of some historic significance and that the Council might want to keep it in good condition.

One councillor of the day suggested that it was "A monument to the slavery of the working class, twelve hour days and starvation wages—is this what we want to preserve?—Pull it down!"

Alderman Mrs. Glenys Lambert stated that the Engine House "was an example of first class craftmanship, generations might forget in the future what craftmanship is".

The Ynysfach Ironworks were founded in 1801, by Richard Crawshay, as a subsidiary to the Cyfarthfa Ironworks. In that year, two furnaces were erected to plans submitted by Watkin George, the engineer who constructed Merthyr's famous Iron Bridge. The building work was undertaken by one Thomas Jones, a native of Merthyr Tydfil.

The Ynysfach Works operated as an adjunct to the vastly successful Cyfarthfa Works, where Crawshay's grandson William was achieving relative production figures that would make the modern industrialist weep with envy. In 1821, for example, Cyfarthfa turned out more iron than the whole of Britain had produced in the decade 1740-50. As Cyfarthfa grew, so did Ynysfach. In 1836 two more furnaces were built and alongside appeared the remarkable four-storey Engine House. It was built from pennant sandstone with white-ash-lared limestone quoins forming the corners. The doors and windows are all surmounted with circular arches. The Historical Society stated that it was a fine example of early industrial architecture and would seem an ideal structure to utilise perhaps as an industrial museum. The keystone on one of the furnaces was surmounted by an iron plate bearing the inscription "W.C.1836". This W.C. stamp was known as the "COMBE MARK" and became recognised throughout the world as the mark of a superior grade of iron. It was a valuable and jealously guarded trademark for William Crawshay, but the Penydarren Iron Company, employing unethical but profitable sleight of hand, began to use a mark that was so similar

10. Ynysfach Engine House and Furnaces. Built in 1836.

to Crawshay's that the indignant gentleman brought a court action against them for imitating his mark.

The sway of the "Combe Mark" was so wide that when Crawshay won the court case he had the report published in Russian, Turkish and several other foreign languages.

The Ynysfach furnaces however went out when the Bessemer technique came in. Mr. Charles Wilkins, eminent Merthyr historian, wrote that by the spring and summer of 1903, there was no more than a suggestive picture of past industry at Ynysfach. He wrote "The seeds of wild flowers have settled there and germinated. The purple phlox and pimpernel and the yellow bedstraw with great marqueriotes gather on the top like a crown and even in the dark shadows there lurk infant ferns nigrum and spleen wort".

The Borough Engineer at the time, Mr. Cledwyn Jones, felt that the building should not be demolished but preserved. He also stated that the furnaces should be investigated, as they were in his opinion of greater historical importance than the Engine House. Wheels were set in motion of an ambitious plan to develop the CYFARTHFA PROJECT, an imaginative scheme to renovate and rebuild a trail of Merthyr iron and steel industry sites linked with the CYFARTHFA WORKS and the Crawshay ironmasters. The task was undertaken by Mrs. Jane Pearson, then Director of the Merthyr Tydfil Heritage Trust, with fifty six workers, costing £100,000. The work was carried out by COWLIN private contractors and funded by the Welsh Office.

Dr. Joseph Gross, President of the M.T.H.S. and Chairman of the Heritage Trust, stated at the time that the site would be as popular as the Ironbridge Museum in Shropshire. "It will show peoples lives in the nineteenth century, the conditions in which they lived and worked and their social and political conditions. The Ynysfach Heritage Museum and Centre was officially opened by Sarah, The Duchess of York, on 31st July 1989.

11. Visit of Prince of Wales to Dowlais Stables, July 1981.

The Dowlais Stables.

The Borough's one hundred strong Historical Society presented proposals to the Town Clerk for Merthyr Tydfil, Mr. Selwyn Jones, to preserve the historical façade of the Dowlais Stables. Roman numerals above main entrance archway reveal date.

The Stables were built in 1820, having been commissioned by the Guest family. The ground floor buildings were used as stables for the horses owned by the Dowlais Ironworks. The upper floor was used as a school. The first in Dowlais, this school catered exclusively for boys, one hundred and thirty five in five classes. THOMAS JENKINS was the first headmaster, a girls school was opened at a later date at nearby GWERNLLWYN FARM (now demolished).

Until 1844 the boys school was run by one headmaster, with assistance from senior pupils. There was a regular attendance at the school of over two hundred pupils. In 1844 the boys school was completely reorganised and staff increased to three masters, with MATTHEW HIRST, a Talygarn native, appointed as Headteacher. Among the subjects taught were:—

SCRIPTURE, READING, WRITING, ARITHMETIC, GRAMMAR, GEOGRAPHY, ANCIENT AND MODERN HISTORY, MUSIC AND MECHANICS.

Children in the upper school paid the princely sum of two pence (old money) a week, writing materials were provided. Those in the lower school paid one penny, with no materials provided.

Lady Charlotte Guest also opened it as a night school for domestic servants.

The school closed in 1854 with the opening of the Dowlais Central School. This building was commissioned by Lady Charlotte Guest as a memorial to Sir John Guest and designed by Sir Charles Barry who designed the Palace of Westminster.

The Stables themselves were closed in the 1930s with the shutdown of the local collieries. Mr. Vince Harris, then Chairman of the Historical Society, stated "We want to retain the façade and believe that the back of the building could be developed". He further stated "In America, they retain anything that is more than a hundred years old, so I cannot see why we in Merthyr Tydfil should not do the same. There are so many people in Dowlais with memories of the Stables that it would be a disaster if they were ever pulled down. Our Action Committee's proposals on the Stables have been sent to the Town Clerk and we think the District Council should go into the matter closely. We are prepared to liaise with them and assist them in whatever way possible".

Unfortunately the controversy over the historic Dowlais Stables went on, until the question was asked "What future lies in store for the Stables, rapid renovation, demolition or sudden and possibly tragic collapse?"

1975 saw the Stables threatened by demolition. A Borough Council Sub-Committee after considering a report from the then Chief Technical Officer, Mr. Idris Williams, recommended that they be pulled down, he stated "Consideration should be given to the preservation of Dowlais Stables and House which are Class Two listed buildings. In my opinion buildings should not be preserved for preservation sake and any building can be saved at a cost. Partial preservation of Dowlais Stables could be achieved as part of a housing project".

Dowlais ward members at the time wanted the Stables demolished because of their condition.

The Georgian stables at Dowlais which the Victorian Society recommends should be preserved.

12. Dowlais Stables. Built 1820.

13. Dowlais Market as Stables, Strike, 1875.

14

Councillor Leon Stanfield stated at the time, that he was in favour of saving the Stables as they were of unique value, "Certainly it is a building of wonderful proportions and is still standing proudly as a living memorial".

1976 saw further deterioration of the Stables, the Historical Society agreed that there was now a certain amount of danger with falling masonry and that this should be obviated with the small amount of money being spent, temporary repairs could be carried out on the façade to make it safe for twelve months. If this was done proposals could be drawn up to permanently safeguard the façade. The Society felt that it was important to preserve the memory of the great part Dowlais played in the early industrial life of THE WORLD AS A WHOLE. Dowlais had already lost several impressive buildings, notably Dowlais House. On 3rd July 1981 H.R.H. Prince Charles visited the Dowlais Stables.

In December 1981 the M.T.Heritage Trust acquired the Stables. The W.D.A. contributed £50,000 towards the restoration of the listed Stables. Contributions were also received from the Wales Tourist Board, the Historic Buildings Council, Julian Melchett Fund, the Monumental Trust, the United Kingdom Housing Association and Form Structure Ltd. The completion of the renovation took several years, but the restored Stables with its Georgian façade is now a fitting memory to Dowlais's historical past.

Cefn-Coed Viaduct.

In 1972 the Society decided to fight to save the one hundred and six year old Viaduct at Cefn Coed which was threatened with demolition. The Society's Secretary, Mr. Hugh Watkins, wrote to the Department of the Environment and to the Secretary of State for Wales, asking for any request to demolish the Viaduct to be carefully considered. The Society claimed that the Viaduct was listed as being of historical interest and architectural beauty, regarded as one of the finest in the world. The Society estimated that the cost of demolition would be in the region of thirty thousand pounds.

The then Vaynor and Penderyn R.D.C. decided not to support any plans to save the structure and Breconshire County Council stated that they would raise no objections to its demolition.

Mr. Alun Rogers, then Reclamation Officer for the Monmouthshire Land Reclamation Joint Committee, of which Merthyr was a member, stated at the time that he was negotiating with British Railways for the acquisition of all surplus railway land in Merthyr. This would include the Viaduct at Cefn Coed and that as soon as these negotiations were completed, plans would be drawn up for its demolition.

The Viaduct was built in 1866 by Savin and Ward at a cost of £25,000, to carry the old Brecon to Merthyr line. The Viaduct stands one hundred and fifteen feet high and seven hundred and twenty five feet long with fifteen arches.

Alexander Sutherland employed three hundred and fifty stone masons on the two viaducts. The PONTSARN VIADUCT was built entirely of limestone from railway cuttings. The Cefn Coed Viaduct was built on a graceful curve, a feat of engineering which adds much to its beauty. The joints between the coarse stone blocks in the massive piers fit exactly as to be almost invisible. It was said that mortar, although used, was unnecessary because the stones, weighing several hundredweight each, were so truly laid that the stability of the piers could depend upon the laws of gravity.

The masons were not only versatile and inventive but they had great faith in their own craftsmanship. In February 1866, when only piers and abutments had been completed, the

14. Vince Harris (left) with D. M. Evans, H. M. Inspector of Ancient Monuments, Cefn Coed Viaduct, 9th April 1974.

stone masons from both viaducts came out on strike. They objected to the employment of nineteen men who would not join their trade union, though they were admittedly "good and sober workmen". The strike went on for several weeks of bitter weather when roads and hedges were under deep snow, but hunger and hardship eventually sent the strikers back on the old terms. Within a week, however, nearly all of them were sacked.

The employers arranged to buy eight hundred thousand bricks from HIRWAUN and WELSHPOOL and employed bricklayers to build the fifteen arches, instead of using stone. This is why one sees bricks lining the underneath of the arches, whilst the remainder of the structure is of stone. Work then went ahead quickly and on 27th August the last arch was keyed in by the architect's estimable wife "using a mahogany mallet and silver trowel".

On 12th January 1973 the then District Estate Surveyor, D. W. Baird, F.R.I.C.S., for British Railways Western Region, wrote to the Society about the Cefn Coed Viaduct. He stated that the question of preservation of this structure had been discussed with representatives of the Welsh Office, the County Council and the Department of the Environment, and although it was desirable to keep certain structures of historical value it was an inescapable fact that massive structures such as these were very costly to maintain.

The Viaduct is built of limestone which develops cracks into which water penetrates and when this freezes it forces the gap gradually wider and results in large pieces of stone falling to the ground. The Viaduct has to be descaled at intervals, the descaling of one arch costs about £1,500 and there were fifteen arches to consider.

Dr. Joseph Gross, President of the Society, stated that it would be an act of vandalism to demolish the Viaduct and that the Society would fight the proposal all the way. He added that the Society felt that the Viaduct was an outstanding example of Victorian engineering and architecture and is of great technical, historical and aesthetic interest. It is an amenity that could attract tourism if properly used and the Historical Society felt that demolition

Viaduct and Morlais Rocks, Pontsarn.

would be costly out of all proportion compared to maintenance of the structure. He stated that the Viaduct was as sound today as when it was built.

Objections to demolition were voiced by both Merthyr's M.P., Rt. Hon. Ted Rowlands and Douglas R. Hague, for the Royal Commission on Ancient and Historical Monuments, in Wales and Monmouthshire.

After lengthy and voluminous correspondence by all concerned, the Cefn Coed Viaduct was designated a Grade Two listed building by the then Secretary of State for Wales, Rt. Hon. Peter Thomas. M.P. . The Viaduct stands today in all its majesty, no one at the time realised that the building of the new A470 road extension would have given such an unobscured view of its grandeur.

The Pentrebach Triangle.

The Historical Society also gave its support to the Civic Society over the question of the rehabilitation of the historic TRIANGLE at Pentrebach. Chairman Mr.Vince Harris was also present at the Court of Inquiry set up by Rt. Hon. John Morris, P.C.,M.P., then Secretary of State for Wales.

Merthyr Tydfil's famous TRIANGLE was demolished after the Society's three year fight to save it. Despite objections from the Civic Society, the Historical Society, the Merthyr Tydfil Liberal Association, Ancient Monuments Society, the Association of Industrial Archaeology, the Council for British Archaeology, the Civic Trust, the European Architectural Heritage Year Committee, and the Save Our Heritage Campaign.

The TRIANGLE at Pentrebach was built in 1853 by the ironmaster Anthony Hill of the Plymouth Ironworks to house his workmen from the Plymouth Ironworks. It was to be a "model community", in the form of a triangle. Anthony Hill was the most personally attractive of the Merthyr Ironmasters. He provided a total of two hundred houses for his workmen. The seventy nine houses which formed the TRIANGLE were stark stone built cottages which were noticeably taller than the cottages of the same period built in Georgetown and Dowlais.

There were three identical blocks arranged around an open court with two parallel rows (LONG ROW and CHURCH STREET) situated at the rear. The grouping of the houses, and its central "village green" succeeded in giving the TRIANGLE a close, communal atmosphere.

The settlement must have looked peculiarly attractive with its unusual layout and peaceful setting. Although it took four years to try to save the Triangle, it only took two hours to bulldoze it to the ground in 1977.

Joseph Parry's Birthplace.

The Merthyr Tydfil Civic Society launched a campaign to ensure that the Chapel Row birthplace of Merthyr's famous composer, Dr. Joseph Parry, be preserved. Representatives of M.T.H.S., the Civic Society, represented by its secretary, Miss Meryl Davies, and the Wales Tourist Board met councillors to discuss their co-option on the Sub-Committee. Councillors agreed that the three organisations should each have a representative on the Committee, although they would have no voting rights.

The M.T.B.C. approved a £40,000 scheme to improve five cottages in Chapel Row, Merthyr.

Dr. Joseph Parry, who died, aged sixty two, in 1903, was a pit-boy at nine and an ironworker at twelve. He left Merthyr with his family for Danville, Pennsylvania, USA, when he was thirteen. When he returned to Wales, Dr. Parry became head of the Department of

17. The Triangle at Pentrebach—a 'model community' of the Industrial Revolution.

18. The Triangle, Pentrebach.

Music at University College, Aberystwyth, and also gained a doctorate of music. He was the composer of more than four hundred hymns and nine operas, wrote about three hundred songs and a further three hundred tunes mainly anthems, choruses and orchestral works.

The work on restoring Chapel Row won a Prince of Wales Award for Cyfarthfa High School and M.T.B.C. The School carried out clearance work on the bed of the old Glamorganshire Canal at Chapel Row, designed a commemorative plaque for Dr. Parry's birthplace, prepared a booklet on the life of the composer and cleared undergrowth in the area.

The architect of the Chapel Row Project was Mr. Mansel Richards, B.A., then Head of History at Cyfarthfa High School. More than one hundred pupils from Cyfarthfa High took part and the art work on the plaque and booklet was done by Head of Art, Mr. Dewi Bowen.

On Friday 22nd September 1978 Dr. Joseph Parry's birthplace, No.4, Chapel Row, Georgetown, was officially opened by the Mayor of Merthyr Tydfil, Coun. Mrs. Mary John and by Miss Elizabeth Parry, great grand daughter of the composer. In attendance were representatives of both the Historical and Civic Societies.

In 1981 H.R.H. Prince Charles visited Chapel Row to see the restoration.

Pentrebach House.
1974 saw the Society's campaign to try to save PENTREBACH HOUSE, once the home of ironmaster Anthony Hill, from being demolished. In 1974 Pentrebach House was an old people's home and the Council decided that it was to be demolished because of its age, and it was not entirely suitable for use as an old people's home. The proposal was to demolish the House and replace it by a custom built home for the aged.

The Society felt that Pentrebach House, a substantial building at one of the entrances to Merthyr Tydfil, which had a long historical association with the development of coal in the Borough and built on the site of an ironworks, should be preserved.

The Historical Society suggested that Pentrebach House, built in Georgian style, long and low with the façade broken by two square bays, could be registered as a Grade Two ancient monument.

Dr. Joseph Parry, the Merthyr pit-boy who became Wales' first Professor of Music, was born in 1841 at No. 4, Chapel Row, Georgetown, the cottage that is second from the right.

19. Dr. Joseph Parry, the Merthyr pit-boy who became Wales' first Professor of Music, was born in 1841 at No. 4, Chapel Row, Georgetown, the cottage that is second from the right.

20. Visit of Prince of Wales to Joseph Parry's birthplace, July 1981.

Pentrebach House was built in 1850 by Anthony Hill, one of the famous Hill family who were renowned for their iron and coal interests, he lived there until his death in 1852.

Anthony was the youngest son of Richard Hill, who established the Plymouth Ironworks at the end of the 18th. century. He introduced a pension scheme for his workmen, built homes for some of them at the Triangle and founded schools in the area.

Later Pentrebach House became the home of Mr. Norman Frederick Hankey, owner of the Plymouth Collieries. He was a member of a family of London bankers, who had loaned money to the Colliery Company. The Company was unable to pay off the loan, so Mr. Hankey came along to take over. He entered into the community life of Merthyr Tydfil and eventually became a councillor for the Plymouth Ward. Keen on private enterprise, he disapproved of the Merthyr Corporation taking on the "bus services". He thought it should have been given over to a Mr. Snow who was already operating a bus service in the Borough. When Mr. Hankey married it was almost like a Royal occasion. He gave a tea-party for all the school children in the Plymouth Ward. It was held in the open on the field near the late famous Dr. Ryce's home.

In 1974 feelings in the Borough were running high that another of the Borough's notable historic buildings was due for the demolition hammer. To quote "Does the building of a new home to replace Pentrebach mean that this fine house has to disappear? Surely it is not beyond our wit to find a use for the building? Or must it go the way that so many of Merthyr's landmarks have gone, sacrificed in the dubious cause of 'progress' and 'economic expediency'?"

Today, retaining its original façade, Pentrebach House is a reputable restaurant and hotel of the Brewers Fayre Co.

Dic Penderyn Memorial.

On Saturday 12th February 1977 officers and members of the Historical Society attended the ceremony, when Mr. Len Murray, the then Secretary of the T.U.C. unveiled a plaque, in memory of DIC PENDERYN, at the Central Library.

It was while the late popular novelist, Alexander Cordell, was visiting Merthyr in 1975 to promote his book "The Fire People" that he suggested there should be a memorial to Dic Penderyn in Merthyr. The idea was sponsored by Coun. Gerry Donovan, who was at the time the Mayor of Merthyr Tydfil. The memorial's inscription in both Welsh and English, stated:—

"I, Dic Penderyn, Ganed Richard Lewis ym 1808 yn Aberafan, Crogwyd yng ngharchar Gaerdydd ar Awst 13.1831 ar ol y terfysg ym Merthyr yr un flwyddyn Merthyr gweithwyr Cymru".

In English it reads:—

"Dic Penderyn, Born Richard Lewis in 1808 in Aberavon and hanged at Cardiff Goal on August 13.1831, following the Merthyr Insurrection of that year, A martyr of the Welsh working class".

Dic Penderyn, whose last words were "O, Arglwydd dyma gamwedd" (O Lord what an iniquity), had no justice at all being condemned on the perjured evidence of the two witnesses Shoni Crydd and James Abbott, both of whom had sworn to fix him for personal reasons, the judge's partisanship. An emigrant in America, on his death bed, confessed to the crime for which Dic was hung.

21. Pentrebach House. Built 1850. Home of Anthony Hill, Plymouth Ironmaster.

Mr. Murray unveiled the plaque made of Welsh slate on the wall of the town's Central Library in High Street near the place where soldiers confronted the rioting iron workers protesting against low wages and poor working and living conditions.

Mr. Murray said of Dic Penderyn "He was a true son of Wales, who gave his life for trade unionism in the face of exploitation and injustice. He set a standard making it the duty of all trade unionists to be ever vigilant in the representation of their members".

As Mr. Murray unveiled the plaque a thunderstorm burst over the town as one did according to history, when Dic Penderyn (Richard Lewis) mounted the scaffold steps at Cardiff.

Among those present at the ceremony were Welsh miners' leader, Mr. Emlyn Williams, the Chairman of Wales T.U.C., Mr. Ivor Davies, the Deputy Mayor of Merthyr Tydfil, Coun. Mrs. Linda Foster, Merthyr's M.P., The Rt. Hon. Mr. Ted Rowlands, Mr. Dewi Bowen (who designed the plaque). Mr. Bill King, Mr. Terry Strachen (Press Officer Merthyr Trades Council), Revd. Bill Morgan, Mr. Idris John.

Dic Penderyn was one of the leaders of working class people who fought against slashing cuts in wages imposed by the ironmasters in 1831 and also against the evils of the Company Shops, the Truck System and the tyranny of the Court of Requests. Though innocent of the charge of wounding a soldier, Dic Penderyn presented a convenient scapegoat for the Merthyr Riots of 1831.

1979 saw the Merthyr Tydfil Civic Society, which had fought vigorously to save the ironworkers cottages at the Triangle, pass into history. After five years campaigning for the retention of Merthyr's heritage, the Civic Society amalgamated with the Merthyr Tydfil

22. Len Murray, Secretary, TUC, unveils plaque to the memory of Dic Penderyn. 12th February 1977.

Historical Society. It was the Civic Society which led the protest against the planned demolition of the Triangle at Pentrebach. After a public inquiry a Welsh Office Inspector found in favour of preservation only to be over-ruled by the Secretary of State for Wales. Finally the Triangle was demolished in 1977.

Among the achievements of the Civic Society was the renovation of Bethesda Chapel, Georgetown, now demolished. "The Civic Society members decided that their aims were in accordance with ours" stated M.T.H.S. President, Dr. Joseph Gross.

1980 saw the unveiling of the Adrian Stephens Memorial. Stephens, the inventor of the STEAM WHISTLE, died at his home on the Brecon Road in 1876 and was buried in the Cefn Coed Cemetery. He had invented the steam whistle in 1832 while working for the Dowlais Iron Company. The Merthyr Tydfil Heritage Trust had arranged for a plinth of dressed sandstone blocks supporting the original gravestone to be erected at the entrance to the cemetery. The plinth was unveiled by the only surviving relative of Adrian Stephens, a Mrs. Laura Cribb of Cardiff, in the presence of the Mayor, Coun. Gareth Foster, Dr. J. Gross and a small party of about two dozen people, on a very rough day of snow and sleet.

1980 saw the twinning of Merthyr Tydfil with CLICHY-LA-GARRENE, a suburb town of Paris. This French town had a very similar economic and cultural background to Merthyr Tydfil.

Also in 1980 Merthyr Tydfil celebrated fifteen hundred years of its past history, tracing its origins to 480 A.D., to Tydfil, daughter of the Welsh chieftain, Brychan. The Society

23. The Court of Requests, Georgetown. Presided over by Joseph Coffin, 1831.

24. Medal presented to Founder Chairman Mr. Vince Harris.

took part in the town's festivities with an organised Historical Exhibition and in the many other functions connected with the Tydfil Festival.

On Friday 21st March 1980 Mr. Vince Harris retired as Chairman of the Merthyr Tydfil Historical Society. A Dinner was held to mark his retirement as Chairman after eight years service. Guests included the Mayor, Coun. Dave James and the Mayoress, Mr. Ted Rowlands, M.P., and his wife Mrs. Janice Rowlands.

Dr. Joseph Gross, President of the Society, presented Vince with a silver medallion which had been especially made for him. Mr. Ted Rowlands, M.P., presented him with a book written by Bernard Cox, on the history of the Houses of Parliament. Mr. John Owen, Works Manager of the Dowlais Works, presented Mr. Harris with a plaque.

1986, in his letter to the Rt. Hon. Nicholas Edwards, M.P., Secretary of State for Wales, Dr. Gross stated that the heritage of Merthyr Tydfil was a heritage well worth preserving. He wrote "Members of the Merthyr Tydfil Historical and Civic Society and of the M.T. Heritage Trust particularly welcome that you singled out the development of the industrial past of Merthyr Tydfil as offering unique opportunities to provide both immediate employment and tourist attractions.

Members of these two groups have long been convinced that Merthyr's potential in this respect is second to none in the Principality and have for many years worked hard towards the preservation and enhancement of our heritage.

"The M.T.H. and C.S. has actively supported the study of Merthyr's heritage by fostering research, arranging monthly lectures, exhibitions and competitions. The M.T. Heritage Trust was set up in 1979, with the active support of the M.T. Borough Council to secure the preservation and restoration of buildings and features of historical and industrial interest in the Borough".

25. Launch of Volume One, Merthyr Historian. Friday 28th May 1976. L to R Mr. Vince Harris, Rt. Hon. T. Rowlands, Mr. Hugh Watkins, Miss M. S. Taylor, Dr. Joseph Gross.

Lectures and Publications.

Established in 1972, to preserve the past, protect the present and propagate the future, the Society has aimed high in its efforts to bridge the massive gap between the popular but out of print old histories of Merthyr Tydfil with their sometimes suspect scholarship and the most up-to-date of modern learning on subjects linked with the town's industrial, social and religious past.

For the past twenty five years a series of monthly lectures have instructed and entertained audiences, through the Society's meetings.

1976 was a momentous year for the Society when under the auspices of Dr. Joseph Gross the Society published Volume One, Merthyr Historian. Friday 28th.May 1976 was the historic day when the launch was held at St. David's Hall, by kind permission of the Rector. The excellent arrangements were by the Society's Social Secretary, Mrs. Maureen Protheroe. Copies of this Merthyr Historian were presented to the lecturers who had lectured the Society during the previous three years, by the Society patron, the M.P. for the Constituency of Merthyr Tydfil and then Minister of State at the Foreign Office, the Rt. Hon. Ted Rowlands. Mr. Rowlands praised the Society as well as the authors of the lectures, as an outstanding example of local initiative and imagination. The Society praised Dr. J. Gross, for his hard, untiring work in bringing this publication into being. Speaking as someone who has been trained as an historian, Mr. Rowlands commented "When one reads these fascinating essays, digs out the nuggets in an ancient WILKINS or envelops oneself in the authoritative essays on Merthyr politics by Professor Glanmor Williams, one wonders why we still haven't an authoritative and definitive history of our Borough. Its history is the history of Britain's first industrial revolution and the pains and passions of that revolution".

Contents. Merthyr Historian. Volume One.

Successive volumes of the Merthyr Historian followed, first under the Editorship of Dr. J. Gross and now under the present Editor and Chairman, Dr. T. F. Holley. Volume One was reprinted in 1976.

The contents of Merthyr Historian, Volumes Two to Nine, are listed in the Appendix which terminates this essay.

Four successive books of photographs, "VIEWS OF MERTHYR TYDFIL AND DISTRICT", were assembled by Mr. John Owen, Works Manager, B.S.C. Works, Dowlais, with considerable personal financial sacrifice. They were published by the Historical Society, Volume One in 1986, Volume Two in 1990, Volume Three in 1994 and Volume Four in 1997.

Volumes One to Six, Merthyr Historian, are out of print, at the present time (1999). Volumes Seven, Eight, Nine and Ten are available.

Volumes One to Three "VIEWS OF MERTHYR TYDFIL AND DISTRICT" are out of print, Volume Four is still available.

In 1978 the M.T.H.S. offered a series of prizes for original research into certain aspects of Merthyr's history. A competition was open to the general public, pupils in the local Comprehensive Schools, University students. A prize of £250 was offered for an essay of original historical research for the period 1801-1945, dealing with various topics, such as language, education, social history or religion, relating to Merthyr's past.

In view of the success of the 1979 competition when the standards were very high and the winning entries spread widely over the contributory schools, a second competition was held in 1981 which was also highly successful.

Cyfarthfa Castle Museum.

Concern was expressed in 1974, over the state of Cyfarthfa Museum. It was badly publicised, grossly outdated, not even signposted. Many visitors came to the Museum from all over the world and could not even purchase a set of postcards, depicting Merthyr's history. In many other towns, visitors could purchase sets of black/white or even coloured trans-

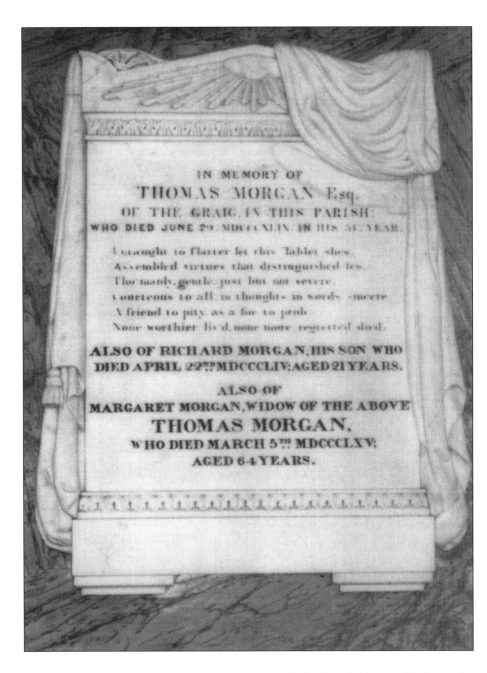

IN MEMORY OF
THOMAS MORGAN Esq.
OF THE GRAIG, IN THIS PARISH;
WHO DIED JUNE 29, MDCCCXLIX; IN HIS 51 YEAR.

Untaught to flatter let this Tablet shew,
Assembled virtues that distinguished few.
Tho' manly, gentle; just but not severe;
Courteous to all, in thoughts, in words, sincere;
A friend to pity, as a foe to pride;
None worthier liv'd, none more regretted died.

ALSO OF RICHARD MORGAN, HIS SON WHO
DIED APRIL 22ND MDCCCLIV; AGED 21 YEARS.

ALSO OF
MARGARET MORGAN, WIDOW OF THE ABOVE
THOMAS MORGAN,
WHO DIED MARCH 5TH MDCCCLXV;
AGED 64 YEARS.

26. A Joseph Edwards sculpture. Formerly housed at Graig Chapel, Abercanaid. Acquired by Cyfarthfa Castle Museum and Art Gallery in 1998. Now displayed in the Cellars there.

parencies. The guide book to the museum was antiquated. The Historical Society felt that something should be done with the wealth of material available at the Museum.

In 1975 Merthyr's Development and Planning Committee received formal notice from the Welsh Office, that Cyfarthfa Castle, the Park gates and railings had been listed as being of special architectural and historical interest. Chief Executive Officer, Mr. Selwyn Jones, stated that Cyfarthfa Castle had been listed in the Grade One category and the gates and railings in Grade Two, no one could now take any action to demolish them.

Cyfarthfa Castle and grounds were purchased by the Merthyr Corporation from W. T. Crawshay for the sum of £18,000, and opened to the public in 1909 by Mayoress Mrs. Andrew Wilson.

The Cyfarthfa Castle Museum was opened in 1910, two years later, 1912, the year R.M.S. TITANIC sank in the North Atlantic, SIXTY THOUSAND PEOPLE visited the Museum and Park. In 1967 forty five thousand people visited the Museum.

Today Cyfarthfa Castle Museum is considered to be one of the finest provincial museums in Wales and is one of Wales's premier visitor attractions, attracting thirty thousand visitors a year. New galleries in the cellars of the Castle were opened in 1988, by the Australian B.B.C. entertainer and broadcaster, Mr. Rolf Harris, in memory of his grandfather, Charles Harris, a celebrated Merthyr photographer and painter.

The cellars tell the unique story of Merthyr Tydfil, entitled "The Merthyr Story", outlining three thousand years of Merthyr's history. Seventeen different galleries or areas, each illustrating a different aspect of life in Merthyr Tydfil, from Early Beginnings, Tydfil the Martyr, the Romans, the Roman Road, Penydarren Fort, Early Industrialisation, the famous reconstructed Welsh Kitchen and Dairy, Dic Penderyn and the Merthyr Riots in 1831, Merthyr as a Boom Town with the Ironworks at Cyfarthfa, Dowlais, Penydarren and Plymouth, the evolution of the Labour movement from Chartist days to Keir Hardie, impact of coal mining on Merthyr, to present day Merthyr.

The 1991-96 renovations of the Castle rooms themselves with the restored original wallpaper today gives an authentic flavour of the Castle origins as a grand house of the Regency period. One can step back into the elegant surroundings of this family house complete with authentic Regency decor including handblocked wallpaper, unique curtains and blinds created by young Welsh designer Cefyn Burgess.

1976 saw a change in Local Government, when Plaid Cymru defeated the sitting Labour Council. Policy also changed, also the attitude of the Council to the conservation of the remaining historical relics within the Borough. Mr. Vince Harris, Chairman, and President, Dr. J. Gross, were elected as members of the new Conservation and Tourism Committee, representing the M.T.H.S.

In 1976 Merthyr like the rest of the country experienced a severe drought and we were no longer able to use Cyfarthfa Primary School to hold our monthly lecture meetings. Dr. J. Gross was successful in approaching Mr. E. Roberts, area Divisional Education Officer and obtained the use of a room at Merthyr Technical College, with the kind permission of Principal, Mr. J. Taylor. We remained at the College for many years, until overcrowding there made us seek another venue namely the renovated Ynysfach Iron Heritage Centre.

Visits.

On 8th July 1973 members of M.T.H.S. visited Llanfair Court, Usk, to take tea as guests of Sir William and Lady Crawshay. Also in 1973 the Society was entertained at the Dowlais Foundries, as guests of John Owen, Works Manager.

On Wednesday 29th May 1974, the members of the M.T.H.S. left local concerns behind them for a visit to the London County Council Archives on the South Bank of the Thames. The visit was made at the suggestion of Mr. Illtyd Harrington, J.P., the Merthyr born Deputy Leader of the Greater London Council, and Miss E. Mercer, they spoke on the value of preserving documents. The thirty members who made the trip were shown a specially mounted exhibition of the Archives, the documents, maps, prints and photographs. The exhibition showed that from seemingly uncompromising sources such as Council minutes, Court Rolls and sewerage reports, it was possible to gain a great deal of historical information, and a colourful insight into the social life of the past.

Certain examples from the Court Lists detailed the rowdy exploits of Welshmen who followed Henry VII to London in the late fifteenth century, and who showed a remarkable talent for recording their presence, in the Court Rolls.

Also on view were extracts of Council minutes of various London Boroughs which showed their widely differing reactions to the HUNGER MARCHES, with details of the sympathetic reception they received in the Borough of Bedford.

The Historical Society was able to see the extent of the London Archives, thousands of documents were received and catalogued each year. The major achievement was that these documents are permanently available to the public and cover a comprehensive range of subjects.

The party was also shown the Caradoc Cup, the choral trophy which failed to make its way to Aberdare, home of the Cup winners.

Mr. Harrington stated that Merthyr was "a town which had NEGLECTED ITS HISTORY, Merthyr Council having allowed (the town's) heritage to be forgotten or abused and distorted to their own image or likeness". The history of a community was its collective "memory" and as such belonged to the whole community.

When documents are destroyed, the community stands in danger of becoming a faceless place. Mr.Harrington dealt with Merthyr's past, and the documents which tell us some surprising stories of the town. He pointed to the coroners reports as being "quite likely the nastiest and most bloodthirsty set of coroners reports in the world", telling as they did of frequent murders of Irishmen by Welshmen and vice-versa for jobs during the nineteenth century. The finding of the Royal Commission on Public Health, held in 1834 after the Cholera epidemic in Merthyr, not only noted that sixteen Irishmen were living in one room, but also that under their beds were found between two and three hundred pounds of explosives.

On Friday 9th April 1976 the Society visited the Bridgend Police Museum.

By kind permission and invitation of Sir Hugo Boothby, on 21st May 1976 Society members visited FONMON CASTLE in the Vale of Glamorgan.

On 19th April 1977 an excursion was made to visit the home of Sir Leslie Joseph at Porthcawl, to see his famous collection of Swansea China and Porcelain.

On Thursday 22nd April 1982 the Society visited the Houses of Parliament as guests of our M.P.

Many of the Society's visits were arranged by Social Secretary, Mrs. Maureen Protheroe, to whom we are indebted.

A series of successful Dinner Dances were also held between 1974 and 1986. These were also arranged by Mrs. Maureen Protheroe, ably assisted by her husband, Deri Protheroe, then Head of Music at Cyfarthfa High School.

1987 saw the end of an era when the famous Dowlais Works (1759-1987) ceased operations.

Patrons

The Historical Society in 1972 extended invitations to eminent men with Merthyr Tydfil connections to become honorary patrons of the Society. Other prominent persons were also approached. Those who accepted were:—

The Rt. Hon. The Earl of Bessborough, Stansted Park, Hants.

The Rt. Hon The Viscount Wimborne.

The late Lord Merthyr, Saundersfoot, Pembs.

The late Lord Brecon, Talybont on Usk.

Rt. Hon. Anthony Berry.

The late Colonel Sir William Crawshay.

The Rt. Hon. Mr. T. Rowlands, M.P.

Mr. C. N. D. Cole, Managing Director, Thomson Regional Newspapers Ltd.

Mr. William G.Tasker Davies.

Dr. Sydney Jones, designer of the High Speed Train & Advanced Passenger Train.

Mr. John Lloyd, Welsh Sports Editor, Daily Express.

Professor Sir Glanmor Williams.

Mr. Stewart Williams, Publisher.

Miss Sylvia Crawshay.

Officials

Many of the following have faithfully served and are still serving the interests of the M.T.H.S., over the past twenty-five years.

President
    Mr. John A.Owen, 1972.   Dr. J. Gross, 1974-98*.

Chairman
    Mr. V. T. Harris, 1972.   Mr. John Owen,1984.
    Mr. Ron Jenkins, 1985.   Mrs. Maureen Protheroe, 1986.
    Dr. T. F. Holley, 1993-98*.

Vice-Chairman
    Mr. F. Vaughan, 1972.

Hon.Secretary.
    Mr. Hugh Watkins, 1972-98*.

Treasurer
    Mr. T. Grant, 1972.   Mr. D. Barlow, 1976-83.
    Mr. Barrie Jones, 1986.   Mrs. Susan Harris, 1990.
    Mr. Ron Jenkins, 1996-98*.

Minute Secretary
    Miss Meryl Davies, 1975.

What of the Future???

With the approach of the MILLENIUM, Merthyr Tydfil like the rest of the world will enter the twenty first century. Merthyr is now much more tourist orientated than in 1854, when a visitor, Anna Treliving, writing to her sister, Georgina Lean, from Aberdare on 25th October 1854, wrote:—

"You must be expecting to hear from me, I am sure, by this time, but then getting about so very much there seems to be but little time for writing. John is gone over to Aberammon. It seemed likely for rain when he started. We arrived here yesterday afternoon from Merthyr where we spent our Sunday. The CHOLERA still rages there, not as they hoped on the decrease. I do not like the town. It is so dirty but a large place, and in the streets you hear nothing but Welsh spoken and the inhabitants look dirty, plain people, with their high hats.

Sunday we attended the English Baptist Chapel. We had some trouble to find it. It was some distance from the Royal Hotel and we found it very little use asking in *English* of the passer by to direct us, the common people very rarely speak anything but Welsh. It will be quite a break to see a neat lace cap on women's heads. They all wear thick muslin with two wide borders and the girls heads are all terribly untidy - all the hair is combed back in one great rough twist at the back of the head. The scenery here is lovely. We have travelled a good deal (all by rail of course) after dark and oh how I have wished for you many a time to see the fires from the ironworks. They are just like immense furnaces close together reaching for sometimes half a mile from that to a mile and a half in length and there they blaze away. John says he fancies nothing can nearer approach the idea one forms in their own mind of the bottomless pit. At night tis really awful and in Merthyr on Sunday the people were as busy with their horses and carts as on any other day at the Works.

I saw less of Merthyr Tidvil than any other place on account of the dreadful disease there and John did not like me to go out without him".

Years ago the only visitors to Merthyr Tydfil were relatives, who left during the Depression, coming back for a funeral or holiday. The idea of regarding the scarred towns like Merthyr as tourist attractions would have aroused laughter in many a valley pub.

People have now become more aware of the uniqueness of the Valleys as a tourist potential. Merthyr has more to offer than many of the other valley towns. It was the original melting pot of the Industrial Revolution and the beginning of the iron and steel trade.

Merthyr Tydfil Today.
1987 saw the opening of a purpose built Tourist Information Centre. Now a lively busy centre, Visitors can book accommodation through a bed booking service, and obtain informative leaflets about the town and surrounding areas. Craft objects such as Welsh love spoons and walking sticks are stocked. A wide range of books of local interest is available and PUBLICATIONS OF THE MERTHYR TYDFIL HISTORICAL SOCIETY ARE STOCKED. The address is 14A, Glebeland Street, Merthyr, CF47 8AU. Telephone No. 01685 379884.

Local Heritage Sites.
Cyfarthfa Castle.	The grandest ironmaster's house in South Wales.
	PUBLICATIONS of M.T.H.S. ARE STOCKED.
Chapel Row.	Birthplace of famous composer Dr. Joseph Parry.
Dowlais Stables.	Imposing façade, stables housed Guest Dowlais Works horses.
St.Tydfil's Parish Church.	Site of Martyrdom of St.Tydfil.
Iron Heritage Centre.	Ynysfach.
Court of Requests.	Georgetown.
Richard Trevithick Tunnel.	The world's first Railway Tunnel.
Trevithick Monument.	Pontmorlais.
Viaducts.	Cefn Coed and Pontsarn.
The Brecon Mountain Railway.	Pant.
The Lucy Thomas Fountain.	

Merthyr Tydfil Heritage Trails
The TAFF TRAIL from Cardiff to Brecon, Section Four, Pontypridd to Merthyr.
Merthyr Tydfil Iron Trail.
Step into the Past, a Walk at the Heads of the Valleys.

From 1999 residents and tourists alike will be able to take tours through selected areas of the Borough to see what has been preserved. Key buildings will be marked with colour coded plaques with fact filled historical details enabling the visitor to walk back in time.

Merthyr Tydfil used to be regarded as an eyesore, now like the valleys themselves, people can look upon Merthyr Tydfil and its surrounding areas as interesting and in many ways beautiful.

From its simple beginnings, the Merthyr Tydfil Historical Society has over the past twenty five years striven to preserve what is left of Merthyr's cultural and historical heritage, for its future citizens, the generations to come.

THE FOUNTAIN
MERTHYR

WE can just make out the name "Berni Bros." on the
back of the cart to the left of the Fountain.

Our more knowledgeable staff say that the firm
was famous for its fish and chips which were served
from carts like the one above.

This fine picture of St. Tydfil's Fountain dates
from the turn of the century and shows the monument
complete with troughs for horses.

APPENDIX

Contents. Merthyr Historian. Volume Two. 1978.

Contents. Merthyr Historian. Volume Three. 1980.

28. Members of the M.T.H.S. meet to discuss plans for Merthyr Historian, Volume Four. Executive members are, front row, L to R, Josh Powell, Fred Holley, Hugh Watkins, Ann Lewis, Ron Jenkins.

Contents. Merthyr Historian. Volume Four. 1989.

Contents. Merthyr Historian. Volume Five. 1992.

Contents. Merthyr Historian. Volume Six. 1992.

Contents. Merthyr Historian. Volume Seven. 1994.

Contents. Merthyr Historian. Volume Eight. 1996.

Contents. Merthyr Historian. Volume Nine. 1997.

28A. Mr.Tom Jones, B.A., Latin Master, County School.
(Photo courtesy Sister G. Jenkins)

THE "COUNTY" SCHOOL

by

GLANMOR WILLIAMS

In the summer of 1942 the time had come for me to leave Aberystwyth - however reluctantly. I freely admit that I should have much preferred to stay there and go on with research for a post graduate degree. I had a subject all ready in my mind: 'Bishop Richard Davies and the Reformation'. That had presented itself to me as an ideal introduction to the Protestant Reformation in Wales, the subject with which I'd become more and more fascinated as an undergraduate. Davies himself was an interesting individual; he embodied in his own career many aspects of the Reformation in Europe, England and Wales; and he was a considerable figure in the development of Welsh thought and literature. I made one last desperate effort to stay on in Aberystwyth. A friend of mine in the department of Agricultural Economics told me that it was looking for a young assistant. I had no formal qualifications in Economics, of course, but I thought I could lose nothing by trying for the job. I was actually interviewed and even offered a post but the only wages they could manage were those paid to a lab. boy of sixteen. I couldn't possibly have contrived to live in lodgings—not even student digs.—on such a pittance, and I wasn't prepared to ask my parents for money which I knew perfectly well they couldn't afford. So it was no use my hankering any longer after research in Aber, however desirable. The authorities had made it plain to me that while I had been allowed an additional year to complete teachers' training, that was all I should get. There was nothing for it now but to look for a job as a school-teacher.

I made applications for the comparatively few jobs I saw being advertised. Fairly early on in July I was interviewed for two posts; the one in Newcastle-under-Lyme, and the other in Dolgellau. There was no question that the former was the better school, with superior buildings and facilities; but I didn't care overmuch for the area, which was completely strange to me and where I knew no one. I liked the school at Dolgellau much better and sensed that I would almost certainly be happier there, though I had to admit to myself that Newcastle-under-Lyme would offer the better opportunities. I'd been offered both these jobs but had asked for a few days to think things over. I was tending to come down in favour of Dolgellau, but while I was uneasily turning both over in my mind, my dilemma was unexpectedly resolved for me, when I was suddenly offered a post at the Merthyr Intermediate School (the 'County School'). I need hardly say that I was particularly pleased to have the opportunity of living at home. I knew it would give my parents great delight; it would be infinitely more congenial than having to live in war-time digs.; it would enable me to keep up many old acquaintances—not least, I should be reasonably near my girl-friend; and I also considered that it would give me a better prospect of carrying on part-time research. The then director of Education for Merthyr, W. I. Owen, a Gelli-deg man by origin, was an administrator of rare ability. He was keen that I should take on the job, and I confess that I didn't need much pressing. After a short and friendly interview with the Chairman and members of the Education Committee and the Headmaster, W. P. Morrell, I was duly appointed to teach Welsh and a bit of History. If the truth be told, however, I had some slight misgivings about going to the County School. Faint residual traces of the years of schoolboy rivalry between 'County' and 'Castle' still lingered. I also had an unworthy suspicion that the County School was in most respects inferior to Cyfarthfa. Finally, having been educated in a boys-only secondary school myself, I was somewhat uncertain how I should make out in a mixed school of boys and girls. I needn't have worried; what I discovered in a short space of time was that these doubts were entirely groundless and were speedily dispelled. I was so warmly welcomed by the staff and pupils of the school I had now joined that I might well have been a former pupil and not an intruder from a rival establishment. I was soon to learn that, far from being inferior to Cyfarthfa, the County was at the very least its equal. As to finding it difficult to settle down in the atmosphere of a mixed school, it did not take long to become evident to me that a mixed school was decidedly more conducive to friendlier and more civilized behaviour, especially on the part of the boys. I was only to spend about two and a half years at the school, but I can truthfully say that they were among the happiest years of my life.

At first sight, the County School might not inspire too much confidence. Perched on a hillock a short distance above the Merthyr General Hospital, its buildings were small, old-fashioned, and over-crowded for the school population it was by then intended to house. Nor did the rather ramshackle temporary buildings, irreverently known as 'the Huts', do much to ease the situation. The area around the school, in sharp contrast to the broad green acres of Cyfarthfa Park, was cramped and afforded little scope for exercise and recreation. Yet the atmosphere within the school completely belied its somewhat uninspiring premises; it was that of an unusually friendly and good-natured community.

To this, the lady members of the teaching staff contributed in no small measure. My opportunities for getting to know them were somewhat limited, but even so a number of them made a highly favourable impression on me. The senior mistress, Miss Tydfil Thomas, was one of whom I went in great awe. She was a small, spare lady in her late fifties or early sixties, I should think. She wore her skirts unfashionably long, just above her ankles, and her greying hair was drawn tightly into a prim Victorian 'bun'. The daughter of the Revd. John Thomas, an eminent minister of Zoar Chapel in late-Victorian and Edwardian Merthyr, she carried about her much of the ascetic, Puritan flavour of her early upbringing. I'm sure that I was altogether too young and frivolous to meet with her approval, but I could nevertheless admire her as an excellent example of the strict and methodical teacher of the old school. As the senior French teacher, she took the risk of putting me in charge of the newly-recruited Second Formers. At the outset she impressed on me the absolute necessity of getting my charges away to a good start. 'Remember', I recall her saying, 'you can make or break them in this first year'. I never forgot her admonitions; indeed, I worked so hard to make a success of the French classes that I learned an enormous amount about the essentials of the art of teaching in consequence. At the end of the first year, when Miss Thomas paid me the less-than wholehearted compliment, 'Well, you don't seem to have done them any harm at all events', I felt quite irrationally flattered.

Among the other ladies I remember well were Miss Gardiner, a relaxed, genial, mildly-spoken and amply-proportioned lady, who taught Geography and got on very well with her pupils and everyone else who came in contact with her. Miss MacDonald who taught Biology, was also a very amiable person. Then there was the rather terrifying Miss Knight, she of the rubicund face and a very sharp tongue, who was in charge of cookery and catering, and Miss Margaret Hughes, tall, angular and somewhat strait-laced, a lady from Dowlais whom I knew pretty well. Secretly, I was more than a little bit scared of her, all the more so because she taught quite a lot of junior Welsh—theoretically under my direction.

44

There were also a number of younger ladies who were easy and pleasant colleagues: Miss Nesta Jones, who taught History and was always very affable to me; Miss May Treharne, who taught a miscellany of junior subjects and was a relative of Professor R. F. Treharne and also had a shock of black curly hair in common with him. Miss Megan Davies taught Needlework and Miss Rhoda Thomas Art; both of them were very good sorts with whom I remained in occasional touch after leaving the County. Miss Thomas later married Dr. Joseph Gross, a very good friend of mine who will need no introduction to the readers of *The Merthyr Historian*. The lady whom I got to know best was Miss Myra Bowen James, a young English graduate who started her career in the County about the same time as I did. Like me, she had a taste for amateur dramatics, and jointly producing a school play with her brought us into close and enjoyable association.

The man who had the task of holding us all together and directing our efforts was our headmaster, W. P. (Bill) Morrell. He had previously taught Mathematics in the school and was the son of a leading Merthyr councillor, Enoch Morrell, a man of Scottish antecedents. Bill Morrell himself, though born in Merthyr, retained a faintly Scottish tinge to his speech; for instance, he was frequently given to using Scots dialect words like 'lassie' or 'muckle'. He was a jovial, extrovert character, much given to wearing colourful clothing and bow-ties. I couldn't honestly say that he was the greatest of headmasters; but it would be less than just of me not to recognize how encouraging he always was to me. When, for example, he discovered that I was engaged on postgraduate research, he always took care to ask regularly about its progress and constantly urged upon me the need to persevere with it.

The men teachers' common room—at the opposite end of the school from the womens'—was small, spartanly-furnished, and hardly big enough for us all to squeeze into. Yet it was a most agreeable place, and I always looked forward to the breaks at mid-morning and lunch-time. The senior master, Wilson Jones, an old bachelor in his early sixties and something of a cynic, was basically a good sort, if not inclined to exert himself overmuch. Then there was A. J. (Pop) Saunders, the Physics teacher and in some ways the most remarkable individual on the staff; a character of Dickensian proportions. He was a portly, aldermanic figure, usually very jovial but on the odd occasion given to 'blowing his top'. His most striking characteristic was his fondness for using the word 'bloody'. I shall never forget him saying of one good-looking but conceited sixth former, 'that boy thinks he's a Rudolf Val-an'-bloody-tino'. Yet the remarkable thing was that if a member of the opposite sex was present, the word 'bloody' never crossed his lips! The man in charge of P.E. was H. S. ('Monty') Warrington, an off-beat Yorkshireman, who had a wry sense of humour and was much given to curious anecdotes about out-of-the-way characters like Arabs and their susceptibilities if any infidel so much as trod on their prayer-mats.

The man whom I admired most was the Latin master, Tom Jones ('Tommy Oil'), a Welsh-speaker from Heolgerrig, who regularly spoke to me in our native tongue. Like many classicists, he was a strict disciplinarian and could at times be acid in manner. But he was a superb teacher and a man of broad cultivation, who kept up a wide range of reading. I learnt a great deal from him; more by observing how he set about his task than from anything he said to me. He and Leslie Bernstein ('Bernie'), who taught English, had the sharpest minds on the staff, and I believe that both contributed more to my intellectual and personal development than anyone else at this stage. Bernstein, a member of a very well-known family of Jewish drapers in Merthyr, was possessed of a witty tongue and a wicked sense of humour. He came into the staff room one morning just before Christmas and vented a complaint about having been woken up the previous night by carol-singers. 'To make matters worse', he complained in mock indignation, 'they added insult to injury by bawling out, "*Christians awake, salute the happy morn*".'

Another senior member to whom I became greatly attached was the Chemistry master, Gilbert Horton, a notable games player in his youth and still an athletic figure, who was later to become a very successful headmaster of the school.

The French master was known as 'Taddy' - so called because as a young man he was known as 'Tadpole' or 'Taddy', being too young to be a fully-fledged 'Froggy', and he was the best-dressed and most smartly groomed of all the staff.

Ernie Hughes, in charge of woodwork, was a temporary master and a non-graduate, but he was a most engaging man, whom I got to like enormously. However, the man to whom I was closest was a junior Maths. master, Elwyn Thomas, some years older than I but who had been at Cyfarthfa for part of the time that I was there. He began teaching at the County when I did, and I found him to be a staunch friend and colleague. He was an assured teacher and personality; and, by his advice and still more his example, gave me much more confidence than I should ever have had if left to myself.

A part-time teacher, who came in once or twice a week, was the well-known Merthyr musician and choral conductor, W. J. Watkins. A good-looking man, he was always well turned out and elegantly sported a rose in his button-hole. We discovered at an early stage that, as a boy, he'd known my mother's father very well. It appeared that he'd accompanied my grandfather on the piano regularly and had a high opinion of him as a singer and a man. That put us on a very good footing with one another—slightly to my mother's disgust, because she always regarded W. J. Watkins as something of an arch-enemy, he being the conductor of the Merthyr Choral Society, bitter rivals of her own beloved Dowlais United Choir. The remaining member of the staff who greatly endeared himself to me was the school caretaker, Dai (I can't now remember what his surname was; not that anyone ever used it anyway!) He was an ex-collier and a Welsh speaker, as my father and both my grandfathers had been, so this gave us a lot in common. He seemed to enjoy talking to me in Welsh as much as I did to him. Dai was typical of the down-to-earth, no-nonsense style of the old collier, and his comments were spiced with a salty, mischievous humour. However, the characteristic about him which still stands out most vividly in my memory was the unfortunate disfiguring growth which had spread over his mouth and part of his chin. From the nickname which the pupils gave him I realized how devastatingly apt, but cruel, children can be. They called him—behind his back, of course—'Kissproof'.

During the lunch-hour at the County the particular joy of those of us who stayed in school for lunch, as most of us did, was to resort to the gymnasium and there indulge in fast and furious games of table tennis. We always played 'doubles', and the choice of partners, and the relations between them, could be very amusing. The winning pair had the privilege of staying at the table and challenging any other combination that fancied its chance. The good-natured badinage that passed between us could be as devastating as some of the fore-hand drives!

Looking back on my colleagues at this time, I suppose that as a group they were pretty typical of the staff of an old-style grammar school of the period. Nearly all of them were university graduates; most of them with sound second-class degrees or better. They cared about their pupils and were concerned to do their best for them, though they had no illusions that some among them needed pretty firm control applied to them if they were to be brought up to the mark. I couldn't help noticing that some of the older ladies who were, it goes without saying, unmarried - a lady teacher couldn't keep a job and a husband at that time - were especially devoted to their profession. Their pupils often seemed to me to be like a substitute family for some of them. Nearly all the staff seemed to elicit a good response from their classes; and I was impressed by the friendly relationship existing in general between teachers and taught.

For my part I found the teaching hard going at first. I was young, inexperienced and nervous; and I hadn't much idea of how best to establish a satisfactory *rapport* with my classes. Some of the more mischievous lads in the fourth forms, not surprisingly perhaps, were inclined to 'take the mickey' out of me, though on the whole I had few disciplinary problems. It wasn't that sort of school. What I soon came to realize was that most children like a sense of humour in a teacher, especially if he's willing to take a joke as well as to give one. What I did appreciate early on was that if you're going to teach anything successfully you really have to master the subject beforehand. It's only when you come to try to put it over to others that you discover how much more thoroughly you have to be on top of your material. So I quickly learnt how essential it was to work hard beforehand to get to grips with the content of your lessons if you were to make a success of teaching. Oddly enough, it was the experience of teaching French that taught me most. My own studies of French had not taken me much beyond School Certificate level—hardly an adequate preparation for teaching the subject to others. As a result, I had to buckle down and master it as thoroughly as I could. Then, remembering what Miss Thomas had emphasized to me about how vital it was that those bright young people in Form Two should get away to a good start, I also gave a lot of thought to the question of how best to convey the subject to them. I came to the conclusion that first, I must try to make sure it was clear in my own mind. Without that I should never be able to make it clear to those at the receiving end. I also believed that I must at all times make it interesting; to infect the youngsters if I could with my own enthusiasm for what I was teaching. To do so I was convinced that I'd got to be as patient and as good-humoured as I could with them. I found that one of the best ways of appealing to them was to set aside ten or fifteen minutes at the end of every lesson to play competitive games, sing songs, and perform playlets and sketches with them. They always seemed to enjoy this greatly, but unbeknown to themselves they were in addition revising what they'd learnt and committing it to memory. I found these techniques effective in the French lessons and soon extended them, where appropriate, to other subjects I taught. Looking back after many years, I readily confess that these were the groping and uncertain efforts of a new and very raw if enthusiastic teacher. I'm sure that I committed some awful blunders at first, but as time went on things began to improve, especially as the pupils and I got to know each other better and both sides entered into the spirit of the relationship wholeheartedly. I wouldn't claim to have had outstanding gifts as a teacher, but I'm deeply grateful for those years in the County School which taught me more than anything else about the basic arts and skills required for teaching. I wouldn't deny that in the first years of teaching one is likely to be more enthusiastic, less disillusioned, and nearer the children in generation and outlook. Experience can certainly sharpen the technique, but it may conceivably make the individual more cynical and less willing to experiment with new methods and ideas.

One of the features of life in the County which gave me a good deal of pleasure was the extra-curricular activity which went on. I liked taking my turn occasionally at looking after sporting teams as they fulfilled their away fixtures. Taking part in some of the after-school society meetings and groups was also agreeable. But I think the greatest delight was to join in the end-of-term parties. I had always taken part in plays and sketches and I continued to do so. One of the 'turns' that always went down well, I remember, was a skit which I used to do to 'take off' the then very well known South American actress, Carmen Miranda. I used to wind a school scarf around my head in imitation of the towering fruit head-dress that the redoubtable Carmen wore, and the pupils roared out the choruses of her songs with tremendous gusto. Producing Welsh performances for St. David's Day was another aspect which gave me a lot of pleasure and also enabled me to get to know many of the children that much better. The highlight in this respect, however, was the school play which Miss Myra James and I jointly produced. It was a performance of Eden Philpotts's well-known comedy, 'The Farmer's Wife', and the members of the cast were boys and girls drawn from the upper forms.

Miss James herself was an accomplished actress and, though young, a skilled producer. We worked hard but to little effect in the early stages because the actors were painfully slow in learning their lines. Just when we were beginning to despair of ever getting it into shape, it suddenly dawned on the cast that there was very little time left before the performance and they began to respond nobly. At that point one of the actors was taken quite ill and I was drafted in to take his place in the role of a very old man. 'Just be yourself, sir', was the jocular adjuration I got from one of the young hopefuls taking part. The performances were held on three nights in the school hall and were surprisingly successful. 'The Farmer's Wife' might have laid the foundations for a flourishing acting tradition, but alas, was to be the only play I had the chance to produce.

In the mean time, I hadn't forgotten my obligations to get started on postgraduate research. I was sure that I must set aside some of my somewhat scanty leisure hours to press on with my work. Mother and Dad were very supportive and made things as convenient for me as possible. Even in the air-raid wardens' post at Pant School nearby, where I was carrying out some duties, they were very encouraging and gave me many opportunities to read. My severest handicap was that I had no research supervisor. My former professor, Dr. E. A. Lewis, had died in 1941 and no successor to him had been appointed. Professor Treharne was sympathetic and encouraging, but as he himself admitted, he knew little or nothing about my subject. He put me in touch with two people whom he thought should have been able to help me, and indeed ought to have been, but not to put too fine a point on it, both turned out to be quite hopeless. 'No names, no pack drill'. There was nothing for it but to make my own way to the best of my ability. The staff of the Merthyr Public Library were exceedingly helpful in borrowing books for me through the Inter-Library Loan Scheme, which was a godsend to me. I was amazed by the extent and range of the books they were able to obtain for me. I read voraciously and took copious notes. I still have those notes, written in my rounded and rather boyish handwriting, but neat and clear. I'm happy to say that after more than fifty years I find them still legible and useful, and I was able to incorporate much of the material into a book recently published. (Glanmor Williams. *WALES and the REFORMATION*, University of Wales Press, Cardiff, 1997. T.F.H.).

I should never have guessed when I first compiled these notes that I would be making use of them after such a long interval.

My biggest headache, though, was having to work on manuscripts from the sixteenth century. This entailed learning to read the rather difficult 'Secretary' handwriting in which most of them had been written. Having no one to instruct me I had to pick up this skill for myself. It wasn't easy, and I can still recall all too painfully the disaster of my first experience of trying to read Tudor documents in the National Library of Wales. I had asked to see a bishop's register dated 1554 to 1565. When it arrived, the text was in Latin, was heavily abbreviated, and was written—scrawled perhaps I should say—in an abominable handwriting which would have shamed any self-respecting spider. After spending a whole morning laboriously wrestling with it to little purpose, I should think I'd managed to decipher about 20 or 30 individual words scattered here, there, and everywhere on the pages. I was plunged into despair and had more or less come to the conclusion that I should never manage to read such handwriting and would be well advised to change to a different field of study where the sources were likely to be much more legible. Fortunately, Fay, my wife-to-be, was in Aberystwyth. She met me as I came out of the Library, utterly crushed and feeling almost suicidal. With that fund of calm common sense she's always possessed, she talked me round. 'This is your first stab at it. Give yourself time. It will come.' she said. Her words were very comforting and they proved perfectly true. It *did* come—with time, patience, and persistent slogging. I always think that learning to read old manuscripts is like learning to ride a bicycle: for some time it seems as if you will never get the hang of it; then once you really get started, you move forward surprisingly quickly. I suppose that having to learn the hard way, by my own unaided efforts, with no one to warn me against mishaps and pitfalls, it was a slow and painful process, but in the long run a valuable one. Never-the-less, I can't help feeling that I should have saved myself endless time and trouble and gained a great deal from having a research supervisor. I know from conversations with friends and colleagues how indebted many of them feel themselves to be, to the inspiring scholars who guided their earliest faltering steps on the road to research.

Still, I felt I was progressing reasonably well in the circumstances. At least, I had, so to speak, got my teeth into the business of research. I was sure that I liked the taste of it and didn't think that I should lose my craving for it. I had reason to be grateful that as things were turning out it was possible for me to gain experience of holding a teaching post and undertaking research simultaneously. It was to prove an invaluable apprenticeship for the kind of occupation that would take up most of my working life.

About the end of 1944 there was a completely unexpected turn of events. Fay, who was now teaching in Gowerton, wrote to tell me that she'd had it on good authority that there was likely to be a temporary assistant lectureship in History going in the Univesity College of Swansea. I wrote to Professor Treharne asking him whether he thought I should try for it. He replied urging me strongly to do so. I believed I should put in for it, even though it was only a temporary job. If I got it, it would at the very least give me invaluable experience and it might lead to something better.

All the same, the prospect of leaving the County School was decidedly unwelcome to me. I was extremely happy there; I was getting on well with my colleagues and my pupils; and I had a permanent job. Every time I look back to those days and those with whom I was associated, I think of them with genuine warmth. That was undoubtedly one of the happiest phases of my life. For years afterwards, whenever I saw the school or encountered one of my former colleagues or pupils, I felt a distinct pang of hiraeth. When the County School closed down, I must have been only one of the thousands who had passed through its portals who heard the news with profound regret. A fine old educational institution had finally served its time.

Yours truly,

Thos. Stephens

WELSH SCHOLARSHIP AT MERTHYR TYDFIL

by

BRYNLEY F. ROBERTS

The large industrial town of Merthyr Tydfil in the first half of the nineteenth century, "the birthplace of the Welsh working class", with its pulsating radicalism and industrial empires, may appear to be an unlikely environment where scholarship and research into the history and literature of Wales could thrive. But Merthyr, through its busy Welsh societies, Cymreigyddion, Cymrodorion, Gomerians and others, was very much part of contemporary Welsh cultural life, so much so that it is a microcosm of the way in which Welsh scholarship faced its crisis in the mid-nineteenth century and of the success with which it overcame it. The scholarly careers of three leading figures in Merthyr society encapsulate the development of Welsh scholarship in those crucial years before the founding of the university colleges between 1872 and 1884.

The leaders of the eighteenth-century cultural revival were copyists, literary historians and antiquaries: Lewis Morris, Evan Evans (the most scholarly of all), Edward Richard, and the immensely learned but wayward genius, Edward Williams, "Iolo Morgannwg". These men and others associated with them, by collecting and transcribing manuscripts, by their own enquiries and more especially by their founding of literary societies in London— Cymmrodorion, Gwyneddigion, and later, Cymreigyddion—were able to inspire and organize research which led to the publication of two important collections of medieval Welsh literature, *Barddoniaeth Dafydd ab Gwilym* (1789) and *The Myvyrian Archaiology of Wales* (1801-1807), a collection of prose and verse in three volumes, edited by Owen Jones ("Owain Myfyr"), the main sponsor, Edward Williams and William Owen (later Owen-Pughe). These collections were, for many years, almost the sole published remnants of early and medieval Welsh literature.

Many of the scholarly aspirations of these societies, especially the ambition to continue to publish literary texts, were taken up in the nineteenth century by a group of literary-minded, antiquarian clerics, "the literary parsons", and the provincial and local Cymreigyddion societies and their *eisteddfodau*, which were established throughout Wales under the leadership of such sound but sometimes over-enthusiastic scholars as Walter Davies, "Gwallter Mechain", John Jenkins, "Ifor Ceri", W. J. Rees, of Casgob, Thomas Price, "Carnhuanawc" and others.

These men kept the study of Welsh culture and the search for the past alive but their scholarship was not of the highest order. Furthermore, their work was hampered by the lack of availability of original texts and nothing came of their many efforts to continue *The Myvyrian Archaiology*.

Iolo Morganwg, (1747-1826) was an inventor of literary traditions and forger of texts of such skill that he was not fully revealed as such until the twentieth century. His additions to *Barddoniaeth Dafydd ab Gwilym* and to *The Myvyrian Archaiology*, and the forged poems which he composed, deceived almost all his contemporaries, but they are, nevertheless, only the tip of his remarkable creative energy. Iolo's knowledge of early Welsh literature and history, perhaps even more his insight and "feel" for the tradition, enabled him to produce chronicles, legends and documents of an apparently authentic character and he was able to

51

create a spurious bardic and quasi-religious/druidical history for Welsh poetry, a bardic tradition with its own records and alphabet, *Coelbren y Beirdd*, which had been preserved and transmitted to his own day in Glamorgan. His creations naturally found fertile ground in the uplands of Glamorgan, in the growing industrial valley-communities where local literary societies and *eisteddfodau* were becoming ever more popular from the 1820s onward. This cultural life was based on poetry, song and harp music; and by and large it was grounded in the Iolo-tradition of Welsh literature.

This was, however, not the only element in the cultural life of Glamorgan in the first half of the nineteenth century. The Cymreigyddion Society of Abergavenny began holding their series of *eisteddfodau* in 1833-34, and they became the crucial means of combining the revival of popular Welsh writing and more critical historical attitudes. Cymreigyddion y Fenni had the support of powerful patrons in the Halls of Llanover, perhaps over-enthusiastic and romantic in their zeal for Welsh tradition but members of the gentry class with influential friends. They, and the Cymreigyddion, wholeheartedly supported patriotic historians like Thomas Price, "Carnhuanawg", (1787-1848), and they held traditional Welsh poetry and singing in high regard, but they also introduced serious academic subjects as eisteddfod competitions which were to develop themes in Welsh literary and social history, e.g. Breton-Welsh links, relationships between medieval Welsh literature and continental romance. The *eisteddfodau* were the means of bringing amateur archaeologists, and antiquaries and local historians among the gentry and clergy into contact with contemporary Welsh cultural life and learning so that men like J. M. Traherne of Coedriglan, Octavius Morgan of Tredegar Court and others brought their academic attitudes into discussions of Welsh culture.

The Llanover circle and the Abergavenny *eisteddfodau* touched the cultural life of south Wales in a special way but they were mirrored to some degree in the interests of the Williams family of Aberpergwm. Maria Jane Williams's pioneering and influential *Ancient National Airs of Gwent and Morgannwg* (1840) had its genesis in an Abergavenny eisteddfod competition and is another aspect of gentry involvement in local culture.

Lady Charlotte Guest's active interest in Welsh literature is well known, as is the assistance which she received from native scholars; nor was she alone among the new industrialists in her support for and knowledge of current issues in Welsh life. The Society which symbolizes this rich tapestry of cultural activity is the Welsh Manuscripts Society, established in 1837 directly as a result of discussions at an Abergavenny eisteddfod with the purpose of preparing and publishing editions of primary documents of Welsh history. The Society brought together representatives of all strands of Welsh cultural life—the antiquarian-minded gentry, the leaders of the provincial *eisteddfodau* and some of the prime figures in Welsh-language culture.

The Welsh Manuscripts Society was one of the signs of changing attitudes in Welsh scholarship in the 1840s and 1850s as the battle developed between imaginative Iolo-based views of the past and factual, dispassionate and critical research. The easiest way to illustrate the change is to personalize it and to see it at work in a sequence of Merthyr scholars.

Jonathan Reynolds, "Nathan Dyfed" (1814-91), wheelwright and self-taught poet, typical of those who came to Merthyr Tydfil early in the nineteenth century from rural areas, was "graduated" a bard by Taliesin Williams, "Taliesin ab Iolo" (1787-1847), staunch defender of his father's bardic tradition: Thomas Stephens (1821-1875), bitter critic of all that was dis-honest in Welsh scholarship and "the brightest intelligence of his day", a friend of Llywarch Reynolds (1843-1916), the Oxford-educated son of "Nathan Dyfed". The chronology is clear, as are the inter-relationships, for these men lived within a few miles of one another and they shared a wide circle of acquaintances. Thomas Stephens serves as a bridge between the old school—Nathan Dyfed, Taliesin ab Iolo—and the new—Llywarch Reynolds and Charles Wilkins (1831-1913). These inter-relationships over the whole of the nineteenth century make Merthyr Tydfil uniquely revealing in the history of Welsh scholarship.

Taliesin Williams was born in 1787, perhaps at Cardiff while his father, then aged forty, was in the debtor's prison. There is no doubt that Taliesin was marked out from birth to be his father's interpreter and successor. His name, Taliesin, is significant for this is the period when scholars were rediscovering the works of the oldest Welsh poets. The premier poet of ancient times was Taliesin, historical poet and also the subject of bardic myth and legend, and it is no coincidence that Iolo should have named his son Taliesin. "I hope my *Taliesin* will live to be the Editor and Translator of the works of his ancient name's sake", wrote Iolo when the boy was born. Nor was Iolo the only scholar to reveal a father's aspirations for and through his son. Iolo's contemporary and fellow-editor of *The Myvyrian Archaiology*, William Owen (-Pughe), named his son Aneurin after another sixth-century poet, and even the lowly Nathan Dyfed was to call his son after another, supposed, old Welsh poet, Llywarch Hen.

Tally was brought up in the family cottage in Flimston in the Vale of Glamorgan, and after his father's return from London where he had spent an unsettled period, he learned his father's craft as a stone-mason, stone-cutter and "letterer", in stone, wood and paint. Father and son worked together as a family firm in local churches and farms and they must have spent hours in each other's company, so that it is inconceivable that Iolo did not share with this chosen son his latest ideas and 'discoveries'. The years 1789 and on into the 1790s saw Iolo developing his phantasies and inventions into some sort of order and structure and there must have been hours of conversation, or monologue, as Iolo expounded his ideas to his son. Taliesin listened, and watched his father at work in the evenings in the cottage, reading, transcribing, writing, but without any hint that most of this activity and these testimonies to ancient bardic rites and usage stemmed from Iolo's fertile imagination. Nor is there any suggestion that Taliesin doubted what he heard and, perhaps, read.

Ab Iolo also received a more conventional education, probably at Cowbridge. About 1811-12 he turned to school-teaching, firstly at St. Athan's, and then, 1813, as an assistant to David Davies who kept an "academy" at Neath. Davies came from a notable family of unitarian ministers and schoolmasters. His father, David Davis, of Castell Hywel, Ceredigion, kept an academy of genuinely high standards and another son, Timothy, was a minister at Evesham. Iolo was himself a leading unitarian and Taliesin, who had been among the first members of the unitarian association of south Wales in 1802, was drawn into the orbit of unitarian church life and radicalism. Taliesin must have learned a great deal about teaching and the school curriculum at Neath, but Davies and Taliesin fell out in 1815.

The issue appears to have been a trivial matter and attempts were made to patch up the quarrel but Davies was a schizophrenic and his illness may have been a factor in the affair. Taliesin resigned his post but spent a very unsettled few months as he sought to continue his career. He considered a place in Bridgend where he could combine a school with a stationer's shop, or, as so many other unitarians did, a school and a church: Taliesin thought of London, then of emigrating. By the end of the year he had decided to set up his own

Commercial School at Merthyr Tydfil which opened its doors on 1st February 1816. Taliesin, twenty nine years of age, was an experienced teacher and his advertisement in *The Cambrian*, 20th January, 1816, promised a high level of instruction in English, Arithmetic, commercial subjects and a host of other useful attainments.

Taliesin quickly took his place in municipal life at Merthyr. An influential middle-class was developing in the swiftly growing industrial town—shopkeepers, ministers, doctors, lawyers, works managers and the like, many of whom were themselves radicals and unitarians. Gwyn A. Williams has described how this inter-related group created the ethos of the new society which was being formed in Merthyr and which reached its crisis in 1831. Taliesin, the schoolmaster of the sons of many of these families, married into the group and shared their ideals. As early as 1817 he had spoken against the re-rating of workmen's cottages and he was to be active in the Reform Bill meetings of 1830 and in the aftermath of the 1831 rising. Throughout his thirty or so years at Merthyr until his death in 1847 Taliesin was a well-known and respected figure in the town.

Iolo kept in close contact with Taliesin during the years at Neath and later in Merthyr. They corresponded regularly: Iolo advised Taliesin, chided him, kept him informed with news of his work. He visited Taliesin frequently. The bond between father and son persisted and Iolo's tutoring continued. Taliesin may have been slow responding for he may have been overwhelmed and overawed, standing in the shadow of a father who was increasingly being acknowledged as the ultimate authority on Welsh tradition. Nor must it be forgotten that Taliesin was himself a busy man engaged in establishing his new school. But about 1814, while he is still in Neath, there are signs that he is becoming part of his father's world. He seeks Iolo's help as he tries to compose *englynion*; he comments on the work of those near-contemporary poets, whom Iolo had described as the sole survivors of ancient bardic practice as it had been preserved in Glamorgan. For his part, Iolo declares that he intends sending Taliesin a monthly letter on ancient Welsh literature, a serial history of Welsh literature based on his own papers.

Like so many other plans which Iolo claimed were in preparation, these letters were never written, but the intention to continue to educate Taliesin in his father's faked traditions is clear and was to continue.

Taliesin was an apt pupil. From the 1820s his horizons broadened, though he never doubted the unique value of what he saw in his father's papers, now transferred to him at Merthyr where he tried to impose order upon them and to bind them into booklets. In January 1821 he visited John Jenkins, "Ifor Ceri", at his rectory in Montgomeryshire, the cradle of the new vitality in popular Welsh culture through the provincial societies and the *eisteddfodau*. The Montgomeryshire clerics knew of the bardic grammar which Iolo had "discovered" and they wished to see it published. Taliesin met the group (in place of Iolo) and though *Cyfrinach Beirdd Ynys Prydain* did not appear until 1829, there is no doubt that coming into personal contact with these leaders of Welsh cultural life inspired Taliesin. He was encouraged to write an awdl for the Powys eisteddfod of 1823-24, some of his poetry was published and he began to discuss bardic matters in his correspondence as he studied Iolo's papers. Increasingly Taliesin takes on the role of Iolo's interpreter and he acts out his *gorsedd* and bardic order creations in the local Welsh society, the Cymreigyddion.

There were over a hundred such societies in Wales by the 1820s. Their general aim was to safeguard and to further Welsh literary and musical culture by bringing together poets and musicians to discuss their work and matters of common interest and to hold *eisteddfo-*

dau. Inspired by the eighteenth-century London-Welsh societies, the origins of local societies were, nevertheless, varied. Some of the Free Enquirer (or Philosophical) societies of the early nineteenth century became literary societies and it is no surprise that the earliest recorded eisteddfod at Merthyr was held at The Patriot inn in 1820, the tavern where, said Charles Wilkins, "liberal minds and respectable tradesmen" came together to discuss "the politics of the day and advanced subjects of thought in the religious and scientific world".

This can be read as a description of a Free Enquirers' society, or of the Gwladgarwyr (Patriots') society which continued to meet at the Patriot in 1824: but it is equally a description of a middle-class radical, unitarian group, albeit with literary leanings. That a Cymreigyddion society should have been established in Merthyr early in the 1820's is not unexpected for here, more than almost anywhere else in Wales, there was a direct link or even identity between Iolo's *gorsedd* and Bardic Chair on the one hand and radical unitarianism on the other.

Were not the Merthyr and Aberdare valleys the land of Edward Evan (1716-98), unitarian minister and, claimed Iolo, "the only one besides myself remaining in Wales of these genuine Ancient Welsh Bards"? If the prime aim of Cymreigyddion societies was to safeguard the literary tradition, in Merthyr Tydfil, under the guidance of Iolo and Taliesin, this could only mean establishing, not merely a Cymreigyddion society, but rather Cymdeithas Cadair Merthyr Tudfyl, the Chair of Merthyr Tydfil. Taliesin ab Iolo personifies the integration of those social, religious and literary ideas which were at work in the first part of the nineteenth century creating the ferment which was to lead to a new urban and industrial society.

Taliesin strived to make the Cymreigyddion society which was founded in the Boot inn in 1823, "as conformable as possible to genuine ancient usage", and he described the early years in the selection of eisteddfod poetry which he edited in 1826, *Awenyddion Merthyr Tydfil*. This society was Taliesin's base as he became increasingly involved in the literary scene in south Wales, as a poet, president of the *gorsedd* at Pontypridd, medalist at *eisteddfodau* at Cardiff and Pontypridd, a leading figure at the Abergavenny *eisteddfodau* from their inception, and prize-winning essayist at *eisteddfodau*. Further afield Taliesin was recognized as the leading authority on the Welsh literary tradition (Iolo's version) and he was called upon to answer queries and to provide translations.

From our point of view the most important example of Taliesin's role as the authority on Welsh poetics is the part which he played in the preparation of Maria Jane Williams's *Ancient National Airs of Gwent and Morgannwg* which won a prize at the 1837 Abergavenny eisteddfod. As the book of folk songs, claimed to have been taken from the lips of singers, was being edited for publication, Taliesin was caught in the crossfire between two very determined ladies. Miss Williams of Aberpergwm, the collector, had less interest in the words than the music and had an eye on the middle-class English market. Lady Hall of Llanover, the sponsor of the eisteddfod, was determined that the words of the songs, whether traditional, newly written or translated, should be "appropriate and authentic". Augusta Hall appealed to Taliesin as "the *only* person whose opinion will have any weight". He succeeded in suitably editing the Welsh words or supplying new ones and he prevailed upon Maria Jane Williams to accept traditional words for the music which she had noted. Part of the success and of the value of this pioneering collection which appeared in 1840 can be attributed to Taliesin. The respect paid to his knowledge of the folk poetry of Glamorgan was not misplaced in this instance.

But Taliesin achieved the fullest contemporary recognition of his standing and of the presumed value of his father's papers when he was commissioned by the Welsh Manuscript Society to prepare an edition of a selection for publication. This he would have seen as the fulfilment of Iolo's great ambition and one which his father had encouraged Taliesin to undertake several times.

Taliesin began work in January 1840 and was paid £100 (out of an agreed £200) in May 1841, but ill-health and his inability to complete any large scale project prevented the continuation of the work. He did, however, prepare a long section on Welsh history and other sections on church history, folktales, bardic miscellanies and a collection of poetry. Taliesin translated and annotated much of this material but failed to progress beyond page 494 of the printed text. He resigned the editorship in August 1845, leaving the work to be completed by others who, significantly, made a point of commenting that they did not wholly agree with ab Iolo's views.

Iolo Manuscripts, a volume of 708 pages which appeared in 1848, was intended as a selection "in prose and verse from the collection made by the late Edward Williams, Iolo Morganwg, for the purpose of forming a continuation of the Myvyrian Archaiology; and subsequently proposed as materials for a new history of Wales". It was viewed as a serious contribution to research, a partial fulfilment of the long standing ambition to make more primary sources of Welsh literature and history available. Iolo had already been able to include some of his forged chronicles and triads in Volume Three of The Myvyrian Archaiology but the publication of a comprehensive collection of his papers under the imprint of the Welsh Manuscript Society gave them unwarranted and unfortunate authority both at home and further afield.

Taliesin ab Iolo was totally loyal to his father's reputation and blind to any criticism or doubts. For all his interest in Welsh literary history he seems to have read very little outside his father's papers which are the basis of all his work. Even at his most creative, Iolo's papers are the stuff of his popular poetry. Following the fashion for historical ballads and lays in the style of Sir Walter Scott, Taliesin composed two narrative poems, "Cardiff Castle" and "The Doom of Colyn Dolphyn", but even these are based on Iolo's spurious history of Glamorgan and on his forged history of the Stradling family and Taliesin clearly laid as much emphasis on the "historical" notes as on the poems themselves.

This is where Taliesin's significance lies, for he is Iolo's most level-headed interpreter, quite unlike some of his uncritical and bizarre adherents. Taliesin's status and his ability to present his material clearly and logically are prime factors in the reception of Iolo's phantasies by a wide audience of scholars.

His projected biography of his father was another of his unfulfilled aims, and Taliesin's productive life was comparatively short, from the mid 1820s to about 1840. He died aged fifty nine in February, 1847. According to Thomas Stephens, a fellow-member at Twynrodyn unitarian church and one who appears to have respected Taliesin personally,

"Ten years ago he was a great man in this district, but he has of late years shut himself up very close, and has died and been buried 'unhonoured and unsung'."

This is not wholly true for the bards mourned his loss and Joseph Edwards sculpted his bust but in broader terms Stephens was correct. The days of what Taliesin represented in Welsh scholarship were passing.

The years 1847-1870 have been described as years of "crisis in Welsh Studies", as the battle developed between a romantic and essentially imaginary view of Welsh history and a stand for factual, unprejudiced research. The weakening of the scholarly tradition and the absence in Wales of a strong college or academic base—"no cultural urban centre where people meet naturally" in Lord Aberdare's words—made the critical evaluation of Iolo's inventions almost impossible and there was no check on the more bizarre flights of imagination of men such as John Williams ab Ithel, and Iolo's disciple, "Myfyr Morgannwg". The struggle for Welsh scholarship, whether it was to be "scientific", i.e. based on the evaluation of evidence, self-critical and logical, or romantic, imaginative and conjectural, was real during the years between the founding of the new antiquarian and archaeological journal *Archaeologia Cambrensis* in 1847 and the birth of the movement for a university, a national library and a national museum in the 1870s. Had ab Ithel, his *Cambrian Journal* and Cambrian Institute gained intellectual control of the county history societies, their journals and of the literary societies, Wales would not have been able to take advantage of the new educational movements which led to the university colleges and intermediate schools and Welsh scholarship would not have flowered so swiftly when the Chair of Celtic was established in Oxford and Sir John Rhŷs's pupils began to occupy Chairs of Welsh in the university colleges in Aberystwyth, Bangor and Cardiff.

Thomas Stephens's role was of prime importance during these years and it was fitting, perhaps, that he died in 1875, the year the college at Aberystwyth opened.

Born in 1821 in Pontneathvaughan, Thomas Stephens belongs to the amateur tradition of Welsh studies, amateur in the sense that these were a leisure activity quite different from his daily profession. In Welsh history and literature he was self-taught but his scholarly work is only part of his publicly inspired labours. Stephens came from a well-established unitarian family and was educated at a school at Neath kept by the Revd. John Davies, a nephew of the David Davies to whom Taliesin ab Iolo had been an assistant and who had been obliged to give up school teaching in 1824. Stephens would have received a good education in English and mathematics, probably some Latin, Greek and science also, but equally important would have been the attitudes encouraged in him to seek to be led by his own intellect and honesty of investigation. It is ironic that this critic of Iolo Morganwg should, nevertheless, share his *gorsedd* motto, *y gwir yn erbyn y byd* (truth, above all). In 1835 Stephens was apprenticed to a chemist in Merthyr Tydfil and following the completion of his period, he became his own master a few years later. He became a successful businessman and one of Merthyr's prominent public figures. Stephens was motivated by religious and social conscience to improve the lot of those who needed help, "a friend of the working classes, using his exertions untiringly towards their improvement, elevating and ameliorating their lot".

Thomas Stephens was High Constable in 1858, an active charitable worker and leader of many social reforms in the fields of sanitation, temperance, Board of Health, cemeteries. He was equally concerned with improving minds, as managing director of *The Merthyr Express* and especially as one of the main founders of the library and reading room. Such an institution, which would bring within the reach of young working men the best authors in literature, history and science and where lectures could enlighten and guide them, had been proposed by Stephens as a young man, no doubt he had realised how it might have contributed to his own education, and he was unfailing in his support even in the face of criticism. His biographer referred to him as a "philosophical reformer": abstract theories had to be worked out in specific circumstances and lead to specific actions, a recipe for apparent contradictions. Never one to shirk the consequences of his personal opinions Stephens evoked from time to time considerable unpopularity when his logic led him to views which were out of line with those of his peers as in the argument over the voluntary system in education where Stephens was at odds with dissenters.

Politically, too, Stephens was caught between his belief that power resided in the professional middle class and his support for the workers.

Stephens could not support the Chartist cause and urged the workers to ally themselves with the old regime. In 1868, when Fothergill and Henry Richard gained the parliamentary seats, Stephens remained loyal to the ousted member, Bruce, having failed to appreciate the changes which were occurring in society.

Stephens views on Welsh literature were equally robust. "He loved (Wales) too well to be blind to her failings" and he consistently wrote and spoke out against any inflated opinions about the achievements of Welsh tradition. His honesty of enquiry led to criticism but his commitments to Welsh studies and to encouraging Welsh culture both nationally and locally was too great for us to believe that he was not motivated by a high regard for the history and literature of Wales. His attitudes towards the Welsh language may appear ambiguous today but in his own time they were conventional in many circles.

Stephens did not share the contemporary arrogant opinion which held the eisteddfod up to ridicule, for Stephens's most powerful channel for many of his essays was eisteddfod competitions and he was particularly active in the local Cymreigyddion society, but he chose to write his major works in English. One reason was "to ensure obtaining attention to the just claims of the Principality" but he also referred to "the prevelant cant upon the importance of the preservation of the language" and like some of his contemporaries in Wales he advocated an English utilitarian education, restricting Welsh to eisteddfod and chapel. Nevertheless, in the furore following the publication of the Reports of the Commission of Inquiry into the State of Education in Wales in 1847 and 1848 (the "Treason of the Blue Books") Stephens took the opportunity as president of an eisteddfod at Merthyr on Christmas Day 1847 to voice strong opposition to "the notion . . . of the great inferiority of the Welsh people" arising "from the tenacity with which they clung to the language of their country", and in an essay which he later wrote on "the morality and literature of the Cymry" he again attacked the conclusions of the Commissioners.

It is difficult to trace Stephens' first involvement in popular culture and then in more serious study. Presumably he progressed along the established paths of literary debates, papers in chapel societies, letters to the press and Welsh societies. Throughout his life in Merthyr he was involved in the Cymreigyddion society serving as its president in 1847, and it is appealing to imagine the established Taliesin ab Iolo taking the young chemist and fellow member of Twynrodyn unitarian church under his wing, however greatly their ideas subsequently diverged.

While he was learning his craft as a chemist, Stephens was able somehow to lay the basis for a remarkable range of close reading of published texts of the history and literature of Wales together with some of the critical studies. The vehicle for his studies was the eisteddfod essay though he also contributed regularly to scholarly and literary journals in both English and Welsh.

Though Stephens composed essays on social and educational themes, e.g. *Addysg grefyddol i blant* ("Religious education for children"), *Buddioldeb arfer rheswm* ("The value of the use of logic"), History of human civilization, his first major prize on an historical subject was an essay on Glamorgan history at the Liverpool National Eisteddfod in 1840 when he was only nineteen. Thereafter, almost every year, there appeared an essay, sometimes two or three, or a series of articles on Welsh history, (Glamorgan and Cardiff history, Caerphilly castle, Druids, the Welsh language—though he showed little sign of his critical faculties here—biographical dictionary, trial by jury), archaeology, Welsh law, and Welsh literature (heraldry, bardic order, early Welsh poetry, bardic alphabet, chronicles), as well as essays on place-names.

The labour involved in his reading, planning and writing essays and proof reading for this businessman and social reformer was enormous. The sum and range of his work from 1840 until about 1863 are remarkable but his significance lies in his critical attitude, especially in the field of Welsh Literature where he is at his best in a series of works on heraldry and Welsh poetry (1845); *The Literature of the Kymry* (1848, 1876); the poems of the sixth-century poet Taliesin (1851); the sixth-century *Gododdin* poem by Aneirin (1853, 1888); *Madoc* (1858, 1893).

If the young Stephens enjoyed the company and guidance of older scholars, they do not appear to have influenced him in any way: and if ab Iolo had shown him his father's papers, they had been firmly rejected. He published a long essay on heraldry in Welsh poetry (which had gained the prize at the 1845 Abergavenny eisteddfod) in the unitarian journal, *Yr Ymofynydd*, in 1849-50. The essay reveals a great deal of close, intelligent reading of four-teenth and fifteenth-century poetry, familiarity with the literature on the subject and access to reference works. He is already a master of literary Welsh. Stephens, at twenty four years of age, making his way professionally and already active in public life, is conversant with the history of heraldry and he knows, or is prepared to speculate intelligently, about differ-ent grades or types of poets in medieval Wales. It is an essay which none of his contemporaries could have written. It was this kind of sustained reading of difficult prose and verse and consideration of their context and meaning which made possible Stephens's best known book.

The Literature of the Kymry, a prize essay of 1848, was published the following year through the generosity of Sir John Guest. This is an extremely well organized description of Welsh literature and music from 1080 to 1350 and it is one of those books which merits being termed "pioneering" or "seminal". It is the first attempt to write a history of Welsh lit-erature from a "scientific" approach, based on an interpretation of texts without any preconceived ideas or theories. For almost the first time early Welsh poetry, court poetry and the medieval prose tales are critically evaluated in their historical context. Not only is a chronology of Welsh literature set out (6th.c.-11th.c.; 1080-1350; to 1650; to the 19th.c.) but the analysis of texts permits the development of orthographical, linguistic and other cri-teria for their dating, so paving the way for their authenticity or otherwise to be established. Stephens was attracted to the difficult poetry written in the courts of the Welsh princes in the twelfth and thirteenth centuries and he enjoyed the prose tales, but one senses that his main interest was in the historical value of these texts, so that he was insistent on the need to recognise them as genuine relics or late fabrications.

The Literature of the Kymry, "a revolution in Welsh literary history", established Stephens as the premier literary historian of Wales of his day and gained for him a national and international reputation. He continued to revise his compositions and notes throughout his life and his best work, the second edition of *The Literature of the Kymry*, the books on the Gododdin and the Madog legend, all appeared after his death. Following the success of the 1848 volume Stephens began to pay increasing attention to the earliest Welsh poetry in a series of important articles on the poet Taliesin in *Archaeologia Cambrensis* in 1851. Here, as in his study of the Gododdin, he reveals himself as the only serious fore-runner of the twentieth-century scholars of the calibre of Edward Anwyl, John Morris-Jones and Ifor Williams.

The 'honest and searching criticism" which characterized Stephens's work marked a new beginning in Welsh scholarship. The academic chasm which separated Taliesin Williams and Thomas Stephens is revealed in their essays on Iolo's bardic alphabet, *Coelbren y Beirdd*. Taliesin had submitted an essay on the antiquity of this supposed bardic script for the Abergavenny eisteddfod of 1838. It won the prize and was published in 1840, endorsed by the patriotic historian Thomas Price, "Carnhuanawg", but with some reservations by the Oxford cleric John Jones, "Tegid".

In his essay Taliesin acknowledged the comparatively recent discovery, and publication of the bardic alphabet and confessed that some had attributed its composition to Iolo. In response Taliesin listed eight points of doubt and produced a counter argument for each. It appears to be a comprehensive and scholarly rebuttal of Iolo's critics until it is realised that the counter arguments are, in fact, themselves based on Iolo's papers and his idiosyncratic readings of lines from medieval poetry. Taliesin's methodology is convincing enough: what is lacking is knowledge of the broader context of Welsh literature and familiarity with a wide range of text.

Stephens voiced his doubts in a letter to *The Cambrian* in 1843 but his devastating response came in an article in *Archaeologia Cambrensis* in 1872. He praised Taliesin for the clarity of his presentation but utterly destroyed his material, and showed clearly that the so-called bardic alphabet was a late invention which had "the same parent" as the bardic Chair of Glamorgan.

The Cymreigyddion society, which Stephens had actively supported, had been set up by Taliesin to be Cadair Merthyr Tydfil, "conformable" to the old usage of Cadair Morgannwg. Stephens finally lays the claim and the intention to rest, fiercely critical of the blind patriotism which had prevented scholars from seeing the truth. In *Archaeologia Cambrensis* of 1858 he had subjected Iolo's forged chronicle, Brut Aberpergwm, to a detailed analysis and showed that it could not have been written in the twelfth century. These texts, Stephens said in 1872, had "falsified the history of bardism, corrupted the genealogies of Glamorgan, vitiated the chronicles of Glamorgan and Morgannwg, and had deluded the weak minded with specious absurdities". His righteous indignation is that forgeries hinder scholarship. If he was to go wherever the facts led, life was too short for him to be taken up blind alleyways by invented traditions and spurious texts.

Nevertheless Stephens appears chary of following his own logic and he never actually accuses Iolo of fabricating these texts which he believed were sixteenth-century compositions. Stephens seems never to have questioned the sources of these texts in the abundant papers which Taliesin ab Iolo had kept so carefully and which Stephens may have seen.

It was inevitable that much of Stephens' work was motivated by the need to correct the errors of others in a search for truth. His study of the legend of the discovery of America by the twelfth-century Madog ab Owain Gwynedd typifies his own integrity as a scholar and as a man but the reaction to his work also reveals the shallowness of what passed for scholarship in some circles.

The sorry affair of the 1858 Llangollen eisteddfod symbolizes "the crisis in Welsh Studies" referred to above. "The discovery of America in the Twelfth Century by Prince Madoc ap Owen Gwynedd" was one of the essay subjects set at the eisteddfod. Six essays were submitted and read by the adjudicators—Silvan Evans, a leading Welsh scholar, Thomas James, "Llallawg", a respected antiquary and Evan Davies, "Myfyr Morgannwg", an archdruid obsessed with druid-mania and Iolo's bardic system.

Stephens examined the evidence in his usual critical and unbiased way and came to the conclusion that there was no historical basis for the legend. There was no doubt that his essay was the best but it was held to be *ultra vires* in that it did not address the discovery, but rather the non-discovery, of America by Madog. It could not, therefore, be awarded the prize. Silvan Evans reiterated his former judgment and there were dramatic scenes at the eisteddfod, but Stephens did not receive his prize. Half of the prize was awarded to John Williams ab Ithel who was one of the eisteddfod secretaries and who together with other eccentric and romantic cultural historians—Môr Meirion, Myfyr Morgannwg, Dr. William Price—was one of the organisers.

Stephens's essay was not published until his friend Llywarch Reynolds brought it out in 1893. Reading it and comparing it with ab Ithel's essay which appeared in The Cambrian Journal in 1859, we can admire once again Stephens' masterly review of the evidence and his logical analysis and conclusions.

The Llangollen eisteddfod is a watershed in the history of the eisteddfod movement, for from this corrupt shambles there came, in sheer disgust, a resolve for reform which gave birth to the modern national eisteddfod. But it was also a milestone in the history of Welsh scholarship. The phantasists won the day but it was a pyrrhic victory for the clear injustice suffered by Stephens ensured that the war would be won by him, Silvan Evans and Llywarch Reynolds.

Thomas Stephens's books were bequeathed to Merthyr library (a catalogue reveals what a fine scholar's collection it was), but his papers and correspondence were preserved by his younger friend Llywarch Reynolds (1843-1916). He and Stephens worked closely together and had discussed these literary problems but Reynolds's background was more advantageous. His father, Nathan Dyfed, was a literary figure, a poet and secretary of ab Iolo's Cymreigyddion society, so that Llywarch was brought up in a cultured household, albeit of the old, romantic and less formally educated school. But Llywarch himself was educated at Llandovery College and Jesus College, Oxford and returned to practice as a solicitor at Merthyr Tydfil. He became part of the literary scene at Merthyr and competed in *eisteddfodau* on essay subjects and translations: he worked closely with his father on literary themes. But there are interesting differences between Llywarch and Stephens. Reynolds is nowhere near as productive a writer as Stephens and he is less involved in eisteddfod competitions. His range of interests is narrower and he does not have essays on the social subjects which are typical of Stephens's generation of eisteddfod competitors.

As a scholar Llywarch Reynolds is more closely focused, working in detail on a few texts: transcribing and preparing editions of medieval prose (Charlemagne legend), and poetry (Gwalchmai, Thomas Prys of Plas Iolyn, Siôn Cent) and copying the work of Glamorgan poets from a seventeenth-century manuscript that he had acquired. His correspondents also reveal a different circle of fellow workers who include Sir John Rhŷs and Prof. Thomas Powel of Cardiff, and Reynolds' acceptance as a member of the new academic community is seen in his articles and reviews in Y Cymmrodor and his translations (with his wife) of articles in French and German by the emerging generation of Celtic scholars in Europe. Through Reynolds' good offices Stephens's Gododdin was edited by Thomas Powel and published as a Cymmrodorion monograph in 1888.

Llywarch Reynolds is more recognizably a modern researcher. Thomas Stephens, whose scholarly instinct was keener and whose achievements were greater, developed along the path of eisteddfod competitions, the accepted way of Victorian young men seeking self-improvement and education. Stephens used the eisteddfod essay to produce high-quality research, he became part of the scholarly community through his *Archaeologia Cambrensis* articles, but his roots are in the amateur, non-university group of researchers. Llywarch Reynolds, through his father and his own associations, worked within the same ambience, but far more he prefigures the renaissance in Welsh scholarship which followed the election of Sir John Rhŷs to the Jesus college, Oxford, Chair of Celtic in 1877, a whole world removed from Taliesin ab Iolo's defence of his father's invented tradition.

References.

For the history of Merthyr Tydfil in this period see the relevant chapters in Glanmor Williams, ed., *Merthyr Politics* (1966) and Gwyn A. Williams, *The Merthyr Rising* (1978).

All the persons referred to in the article are noted in *The Dictionary of Welsh Biography to 1940* (1959).

For Nathan Dyfed see A. Huw Williams in *Merthyr Historian*, vol. 6 (1992).

For Thomas Stephens see the biography by B. T. Williams in the second edition of *The Literature of the Kymry* (1876), Mair Gregory in *Yr Ymofynnydd* (1949), Mair Elvet Thomas, *Afiaeth yng Ngwent* (1978) on Stephens and the Abergavenny *eisteddfodau*, Havard Walters in *Y Genhinen*, vol. 20 (1970), vol. 21 (1971), *Llên Cymru*, vol. 10 (1968-69).

The papers of Taliesin Williams, Thomas Stephens, Llywarch Reynolds and Nathan Dyfed are preserved at the National Library of Wales, Aberystwyth.

A. J. Perman has useful comments on Taliesin Williams's poetry in *Merthyr Historian*, vol. 8 (1996).

For the crisis in Welsh Studies see Ben Bowen Thomas in *Archaeologia Cambrensis*, vol. 127 (1978).

GEORGE MARTIN MABER,
RECTOR OF MERTHYR TYDFIL.

by

ROGER L. BROWN

It is not surprising that George Martin Maber, rector of Merthyr Tydfll from 1795 until his death in 1844, has had a bad press. For much of that time he was an absentee from his ever increasing parish, paying a pittance to his curate from his substantial income, yet pleading poverty throughout. Bishop Copleston, his diocesan, found it hard to be sympathetic to him, while the people of Merthyr relayed various stories about him which were hardly to his credit. Gwyn Alf Williams, a contemporary writer, noted the tradition that all that his parish could remember of its rector was that he could polish off a whole goose at one sitting.[1] A correspondent of the *Morning Chronicle*, writing in the early 1850s in a series on the conditions in the large manufacturing towns, wrote that the rule that one should not speak ill of the dead only applied to their private lives, and thus proceeded to castigate Maber for causing the decline of the Church and the growth of nonconformity in Merthyr. He noted a tradition that Maber, having left his parish permanently in about 1812, only revisited it once thereafter. He then arrived in a post-chaise in order to vote for a church rate, his vehicle proving as great a curiosity to the inhabitants as his person. The truth of this one visit is questionable, as is his assertion that the congregation of the church "fell away" almost to the clerk and sexton.[2] Charles Wilkins, writing in his *History of Merthyr Tydfil*, is equally critical. He records further traditions that Maber had assumed on his appointment that Merthyr was a picturesque village rather than a grim industrial town, over-populated and inefficiently policed or managed. Keeping himself aloof from the people, and having put down the use of the churchyard for games, his conduct was resented and tricks were played on him, such as the tithe cheeses being produced without salt and thus rapidly decaying. It is for these reasons that Wilkins alleges that Maber soon migrated to Swansea.[3]

Recently, the correspondence of Bishop Copleston of Llandaff has become available to scholars, and the Bute correspondence at the National Library of Wales has been catalogued. These indicate all too clearly the truth of many of these criticisms.

Nevertheless, a case can be made out for Maber in the initial years of his ministry. Maber was born in or about the year 1766 in London. Educated at St Paul's School and St John's College, Cambridge, he became chaplain to the first marquess of Bute when he was ambassador to Spain. The friendship that resulted led to his appointment to Merthyr.[4] In 1798 he married Mary Moser, who has been identified as the daughter of Richard Crawshay's sister, Elizabeth. She was to receive £1,000 in his will.[5] It might be argued that Maber endeavoured to reform his new parish, evidenced by his desire to end the practice of churchyard games, while in 1806 he rebuilt the parish church. In 1802 he promoted a private parliamentary bill, Maber's Estate Bill, which permitted him and his successors to grant building leases on the glebe, so adding considerably to the income of the living. It is not surprising that he also served as a county magistrate.[6]

By 1812, after a ministry of nearly seventeen years in the parish, Maber obtained a licence of non-residence and went to live at Swansea "for the benefit of his health"[7]. It does not appear that he had any other living, but managed to live comfortably on the income of his parish and possibly on inherited money. The income of that parish was returned in a parliamentary enquiry of 1832 as £884 gross and £675 net, from which he also had to pay his curate.[8] But what was left was still a substantial sum for those days. Although Maber's contemporaries appear to have regarded his "ill health" as an excuse for leaving the fumes of Merthyr for the then quiet watering place of Swansea, it does appear to have been a genuine reason. We find this from a letter written by Bishop Richard Watson's son, another Richard, to the second marquess of Bute in 1818. "The disparaging accounts of Mr Maber's health", he wrote, will probably render the living of Merthyr Tydfil vacant. It appears that some years earlier, at a time when Maber's health was thought to be precarious, Lord Bute had offered Bishop Watson of Llandaff the disposal of the next presentation to the parish. With some delicacy his son suggested that his lordship might possibly still feel bound by that offer and therefore presented himself as the preferred candidate, though he had the goodness to acknowledge that if he became the successor to Maber he would feel it necessary to make himself "acquainted" with the Welsh language.[9] Maber was to live for another 26 years, however, and there is no evidence that he ever spoke Welsh, which would be another reason why he felt alienated from his parish. Those years, however, were still accompanied with ill-health. His bishop, Copleston, writing to Bruce Knight, his archdeacon and resident in the diocese (Copleston was also dean of St Paul's), noted in December 1836 that Maber had asked for a renewal of his licence of non-residence, but thought it would be his last application for "his health is much broken".[10]

Copleston's criticism of Maber was not so much about his non-residence, for that was an accepted custom at the time when there was little or no provision for retirement, but for his refusal to provide any more than one curate for his ever-increasing parish. He wrote: " . . . I own this is one of the most unsatisfactory cases in my diocese. He lives an easy life at Swansea, & leaves this enormous load of duty to an underpaid curate."[11] Others may well have argued that a resident incumbent would be able to give relief to the poor and assist parochial charities, whereas a non-resident incumbent might be unaware of the needs.

For many years Maber's resident curate at Merthyr was one John Jones, whom Wilkins suggests came from Barmouth. Wilkins was much impressed by Jones, whom he described with other curates as "really noble-minded men, who swept away the prejudice existing against the Church, and showed how worthy it was of the people's love, and how easily it might be made a powerful means of improvement in the parish." Jones, he notes, "was a model for even modern days. He did the Church excellent service", brought back into her service a number of people who had seceded to the Welsh Methodists, and with them established a Welsh Sunday School which attracted seven to eight hundred children and adults, a Sunday evening prayer meeting, and a society meeting which Jones presided over.[12] It was not a problem that a curate ran the parish, however, for it is clear that being Welsh speaking and "nonconformist" in tone Jones was far more effective than ever Maber could be. The problem was that the poor curate had to exist on a pittance, while Maber, an absentee, took the riches of the parish elsewhere; riches, which some might have emphasised, were intended to provide for a ministry in the parish itself. And in spite of the fact that a parish the size of Merthyr needed additional assistance, Maber was not prepared to even offer a small contribution to the stipend of an assistant curate. The law decreed that he had to supply one substitute, and this was sufficient for Maber.

Copleston, at the beginning of his episcopate, thus visited Merthyr and noted with disgust the arrangements made by Maber for the spiritual care of his parish. He wrote as follows to Bruce Knight in September 1828:

> The drive from Llandaff to Merthyr Tidvill was delightful . . . Of the scene itself . . . [the works] I shall say nothing—except that the effect on my imagination was more like enchantment than anything I have yet experienced. For after spending three hours in this Tattarean region, led by my faithful conductor from one group of grisly shapes to another, amidst deafening roar of furnaces, rattling wagons, gleams of liquid fire, gigantic machinery, apparently in full muscular exertion deriding the puny efforts of man, at the close of the day the scene suddenly shifted—a sumptuous banquet was prepared for myself alone—the windows of my apartment looked on a spacious green adorned with flowers & so planted as to exclude all view of the sordid objects I had been examining . . . and here I was left to the enjoyment of every thing which the most fastidious taste could devise.
>
> The next day was employed in visiting the Church & Dowlais Chapel & in conversing with Mr John Jones & Mr Jenkins on the circumstances & conditions of the parish.
>
> They appear to me to be both excellent men—but both sadly underpaid. Mr Maber allows £75, and £15 for a house —but if the living is worth £600 or £700 a year, which I am told is the value, surely an addition might be made. He also allows £30 to Mr Jenkins—but here there is some difference of opinion as to the terms of that grant. Mr Jones understands that Mr Jenkins is to take part of the surplice duty, in consideration of it, but this is not done, nor understood by Mr Jenkins to be the object of the grant. I think of settling it by requiring Mr Maber to give all the fees to his curate, & by letting them (i.e. Messrs Jones & Jenkins) make an arrangement between themselves as to this portion of duty . . . [13]

Jenkins was the minister of the district church of Dowlais, formed the previous year out of the parish of Merthyr, under the auspices of Sir John Guest, the Dowlais ironmaster. Under such arrangements the surplice fees belonged to the incumbent of the mother parish as a life interest, so that Maber collected the fees from Dowlais and seems to have allowed Jenkins some payment in lieu. Copleston was hoping that additional churches could be provided by other iron-masters, and in subsequent correspondence condemned their mercenary interests, refusal to help, and "unpardonable . . . lukewarmness", especially in a place which was as volatile and dangerous as Ireland itself![14] Behind such criticisms was an understanding of the Church as a means of policing and pacifying society.

From the experience of this visit as well as his concern for the well-being of the Church and society in that parish, Copleston was well aware of the need for assistance for Jones. In December 1830 Copleston, sensing the parish was too much for Jones, wished to offer him Llantillio, but when he discovered that the duty of that Gwent parish of two morning services and an evening service during the summer months would be too heavy for him, wondered about offering him a parish in the diocese of Bangor put at his disposal by the Lord Chancellor.[15] This plan did not materialise, and in 1833 Jones was made a surrogate for the issuing of marriage licences, Lord Bute's "kind intentions" towards Jones securing this appointment.[16]

During the following year Copleston wondered if Maber could be prevailed upon to give his curate at Merthyr an assistant, and whether Lodwick Edwards could be placed there.[17] In the event Edwards went to Cadoxton by Neath, and one Mr James came to Merthyr, Copleston receiving a very satisfactory character about him from the principal of St David's College, Lampeter, Dr Lewellin. James was said to be 30 years of age, and was required in order to start a 6.00 pm service, which Copleston accepted was "absolutely necessary for the interest of the Church" at Merthyr. But Maber was not prepared to contribute towards his stipend, which Copleston fixed at £50. As Copleston wrote to Bruce Knight on 10 May, 1834: "Maber tells me he has seven children entirely dependent on him—that he has broken in upon his settled property for their support—that he cannot even keep a gig, though recommended for his health. I believe he is a liberal minded man. I cannot however expect aid from him. A letter from the bishop to Lord Bute indicates that Jones, the curate, had offered £10 from his own meagre stipend towards this second stipend, which Copleston was not prepared to accept. Although the claims of the parish were stronger upon him as bishop than upon Bute, Copleston continued, yet as Bute was patron of the living and a large proprietor in it, and the claims upon his purse from all parts of his diocese substantial, he thought that something less than half the stipend should come from his episcopal income. Were it in his power he would most certainly charge the whole £50 to Maber. Thankfully Lord Bute rose to the hint and offered £30 while Copleston found £20, and James also assisted in the private classical school run by Jones. For the good of the church Copleston permitted a private ordination at his home in Llansanfraed and made it clear that a nomination from Maber as curate was not required. As a result of his appointment the times of services in Merthyr were altered to allow Welsh services at 9.00 am and 3.00 pm, and English services at 11.00 am and 6. 00 pm.[18]

Within 18 months, however, Jones and James were on bad terms with one another, and for some reason, not specified, James had lost the good opinion of the church people in the parish. As a result Copleston placed him in Michaelston, hoping that he would profit by his experience in a new place.[19] This meant that a new assistant had to be found for Merthyr. Joseph Hughes (possibly *Carn Ingli*, who was appointed as Welsh chaplain at Liverpool in the following year) was sounded out for the position, and told that James had managed to augment his income to £100 a year by his school-mastering. He was not interested, and Copleston felt that unless the school post was included in the curacy it would be difficult to attract anyone to it. He certainly did not feel disposed to increase his own share of the stipend, feeling that Maber ought to be made to provide entirely for the second curate out of his own substantial parochial income. Eventually John Williams, curate of Blaengwrach, applied for the position and was found acceptable by Jones the curate.[20]

The 1842 *Clergy List* indicates that a Thomas Williams was curate of the parish, assisted by John Lloyd as assistant curate and Jeffrey Davies as lecturer (though he also served as curate of Dowlais). It is not known what or by whom they were paid, but it is doubtful if Maber contributed to the stipends of any but his "official" curate.[21] Copleston's last letters relating to the parish speak of his despair regarding it. In September 1840 he wrote that it was in a deplorable state "as to church matters". The curates of Merthyr and Dowlais were feuding with one another, "and I really know not what to do."[22] In April 1843 he was concerned about the feuding going on regarding the building of the new church (St David's), writing that it had been "most vexatiously delayed by the very persons who ought most to have promoted it."[23] It appears from a previous letter that Guest and Anthony Hill had withdrawn their subscriptions "on the pretence that they had not the choice of an Architect", even though they knew that without the grant of £1,000 from the Commissioners for

Building New Churches, who had made it a condition that the architect Wyatt was employed, no church could be built. The bishop added, in his exasperation, "What the meaning of the word *honour* is in these gentlemen's dictionary I am at a loss to conjecture." An appeal would have to be made to the county, for their combined subscriptions only totalled £450, and he felt the full circumstances ought to be made public.[24] The church was eventually opened in 1847.

As these rows and disputes were going on, George Martin Maber breathed his last. The news was conveyed to Lord Bute by Bruce Knight in a letter of 8 January 1844. Maber had died earlier that day. Knight was already aware that it had been Bute's wish that he be appointed to succeed Maber, following a request of Bute's grandfather, and while he was grateful for this act of confidence he felt at his time of life that he would be unable to adequately discharge "the arduous duties of so populous a parish". Furthermore his appointment to the deanery of Llandaff had given him a sufficient stipend, and presumably time, to enable him to pursue various studies which he hoped would be of benefit to the Church. Without wishing to be presumptuous, he recommended James Colquhoun Campbell, then vicar of St Mary's, Cardiff, for the incumbency, "notwithstanding Mr Campbell's connection with your family" (he was a distant relation). His appointment would benefit not only Merthyr but the diocese, while he could testify to his learning, piety, humility, discretion, good sense and exact conduct. He was all that a Christian, a minister and a gentleman should be, and was an honour to his calling. To lose him to another diocese (Campbell was contemplating a move) would be "nothing less than a public calamity."[25]

Another letter reached Bute the same day. This was from Thomas Williams, the curate of Merthyr, who had heard from the son "of the Venerable Rector of this Parish", John Maber, that his father was in a dying state with no hope of recovery. His concern was more personal. Bute's interest was solicited with whoever he appointed to the living to retain him in his curacy. He had been in the parish for eight years and, after "making allowances for human infirmities to what all are liable in this sinful state", he hoped that he had discharged his duties faithfully for it was his chief desire "to spend and be spend in the service of our common Lord and Redeemer."[26] Two days later Williams had changed his tune. If it was his lordship's intention to divide the parish, he hoped it would not be considered presumptuous in him to solicit his appointment to a portion of it. Though he had no claims on his lordship, yet he had the testimony of his conscience that he had endeavoured to faithfully discharge his duties faithfully to "my God and people."[27]

Similar letters from other clergy, soliciting the rectory, soon arrived for his lordship. Few were unaware of the value of the living. Richard Pendril Llewelyn, rector of Llangynwyd, also wrote to Bute on the 10th of January, two days after Maber's death. Though he was a stranger to his lordship, yet he would not have ventured to apply unless he had testimonials of the highest order as to his moral character and literary attainments. Although he was a Welshman he possessed "a sound and perfect knowledge of the English language", and had received the degree of M.A. from the archbishop of Canterbury in 1838. Were it not for the inadequacy of his present living to support his young and increasing family he would be content to remain in his existing parish.

Mrs Charlotte Rickards, wife of the vicar of Llantrisant (who was too infirm to write), wrote in favour of her son Hely. She reminded Bute of his promise to her some years back that he would present her son to a living "whenever it might be in your favour". After eight years in orders the only preferment he had had was that of the living of Michaelston, valued at £100 only. The whole family were looking naturally to his lordship for his future advancement, and if he had the goodness to present him to the living "you will confer a great obligation on Mr Rickards and myself." Hely too wrote, stating that the announcement of Maber's death was his apology for intruding himself upon his lordship's notice. He continued: "From a kind promise made to my mother some years ago, I have been led to look forward to your lordship for some advancement in my profession". Having been nearly eight years "in the church", he was anxious to be settled in a parish of his own. From some time he had been taking great pains to obtain a knowledge of the Welsh language, and if he was appointed neither zeal nor fidelity would be wanting on his part "to fulfil to the utmost of my power and ability the duties of so responsible a situation."

A further letter came from William Leigh, vicar of Eglwysilan. His lordship's well known benevolence would excuse any charge of presumption in his application for the vacant living, for it was not from a sense of ambition that he applied. Rather it was from the duty he owed to his numerous family of twelve children, "for whose decent maintenance and education the preferment I now hold, which was given to me, unapplied for, by my worthy Diocesan, is quite inadequate." For the previous twelve years he had occasionally performed divine service at Merthyr in both English and Welsh, and if he were appointed, he hoped that by the grace of God he would be "able to demonstrate it was not misapplied."[28]

Bute as an evangelical, however, was not impressed that the argument of begetting a large family was sufficient to justify the care of a large parish, nor was he impressed by the apparent assumption of a promise made some years before. Instead he took the advice of Bruce Knight and offered the living to Campbell. Campbell, a comparatively young man, had very mixed feelings about the offer. While he was gratified by this proof of Bute's approbation (as well as Knight's opinion), "my heart sunk within me when I thought on the extent of the field of duty thus presented, and the awful responsibility which must accompany so vast a charge." A conference with one Mr Jones about the parish, and a letter from Leigh Morgan, who was to follow him at St Mary's and make that parish into an evangelical stronghold, encouraging him to accept the offer, especially as he knew the wants of the place so well, had persuaded him to accept the offer. His one anxiety, besides the "large cure of souls", was to have sufficient income as to retain the services of the two efficient curates. It seems that he had not been fully briefed about the value of the parish. He concluded that he trusted that Bute would have no cause to regret his kindness.[29] It was Campbell who gave the parish the leadership it required, being the first resident incumbent for almost two generations. His willingness to learn Welsh, and his care for the parish during the 1849 cholera epidemic, won him the devotion of his parishioners, and his hard work in caring for it and building it up won him a reputation which led to his appointment as bishop of Bangor in 1859.[30]

Maber's non-residence was possibly not the disaster it has been depicted. The accounts of the decline of the church at Merthyr were certainly exaggerated, and one wonders from whom the unknown correspondent of the *Morning Chronicle* gained his evidence that the church had been deserted by the population. It may have been nonconformist rhetoric. The curates who served as *ipso facto* incumbents were certainly able men, and managed to build up the church in that town to the best of their ability and within the limitations of a state church. While they were able to attract or retain substantial Welsh congregations these men lacked one thing. This was the education and background necessary to influence the ironmasters and local gentry in favour of the established Church, and to persuade them to give from their substantial profits the financial assistance the Church required in order to build new places of worship and fund additional curacies. Essentially such men were unable to offer leadership to those in the higher echelons of society. On the other hand as even Bishop Copleston was unable to persuade these ironmasters to support his enterprises, this may be an unfair judgement. The real issue with Maber was that he retained far too much of the income of his living for himself, and declined to support the very parish which gave him that substantial living beyond the bare minimum the law required. The problem of Merthyr during Maber's years of non-residence was its rector's avarice, rather than his non-residence. And even that was partly discounted by the generosity of others.

END NOTES

This article was written before I was aware of Barrie Jones' article, "The Reverend George Martin Maber, M.A., Rector of Merthyr, 1795-1844", which appeared in this journal, volume 9, pages 1-14. I am grateful to the editor for allowing me to read the article before publication, and for his acceptance that as I and Mr Jones have approached the subject in different ways the articles are complementary to each other.

CP Copleston Papers in the Archives of Llandaff Cathedral [the number is of that of the letter in the collection]
BP Bute Papers, at the National Library of Wales both used by kind permission

1   In Glanmor Williams [ed], *Merthyr Politics* [Cardiff 1966], p 9.
2   J Ginswick [ed], *Labour and the Poor in England and Wales 1849-51* [London 1983],III 68f.
3   C Wilkins, *The History of Merthyr Tydfil* [Merthyr Tydfil 1908], pp 307f. His assertions that Maber was a tutor to Lord Bute and later master of St Paul's School, London, were incorrect.
4   *Cardiff and Merthyr Gardian*, 20 July 1866, p 5; CP 260, Copleston to Bruce Knight, 22 March 1836, notes that Maber had been chaplain to the then Lord Bute's grandfather and a personal friend of him.
5   C Evans [ed], *The Letterbooks of Richard Crawshay* [Cardiff 1990], pp 168, 188. He notes that Maber acted as a middle-man between Crawshay and Lord Bute.
6   Wilkins, *Merthyr Tydfil*, p 307; Jones, "Maber", p 8.
7   Cardiff and Merthyr Guardian, 20 July 1866, p 5; Jones, "Maber", p 4 notes an infant son Henry buried at Merthyr the previous year.
8   See my article, "The Wealthiest Place and the Poorest Ministry" in *Merthyr Historian*, 8 [1996] 63.
9   BP, L5/11, Richard Watson to Lord Bute, 7 [ ] 1818.
10 CP 314, Copleston to Bruce Knight, 20 December 1836. The value of the living is stated here as £930, through an increase in surplice fees and the determination of the glebe leases, though there had been a high increase in the poor rates.
11 CP 260, Copleston to Bruce Knight, 22 March 1836.
12 Wilkins, *Merthyr Tydfil*, p 308. Problems sometimes resulted because of the absence of the incumbent. One related to the appointment of the parish clerk, whose dismissal was upheld as he had been appointed by the curate, not the rector, and thus did not possess a valid parochial office [CP 160 and 163, Copleston to Bruce Knight, 28 January, 1 February 1834]. There were also difficulties about the provision of a burial ground for cholera victims, required for use before it had been consecrated [CP 1, Copleston to Bruce Knight, 22 August 18(36?)].
13 CP 7, Copleston to Bruce Knight, 30 September 1828.
14 CP 145, 184-5, Copleston to Bruce Knight, 22 November 1833, 2 and 4 April 1834.
15 CP 25, Copleston to Bruce Knight, 16 December 1830.
16 CP 105, 107, 119, Copleston to Bruce Knight, 7 February, 6 March, 14 May 1833.
17 CP 184, Copleston to Bruce Knight, 2 April 1834.
18 CP 191, 198, 201-2, 204, Copleston to Bruce Knight, 10 May, 5, 9, 20, 31 July 1834; BP L77/75, Copleston to Bute, 4 June 1834.
19 CP 241, Copleston to Bruce Knight, 8 February 1836.
20 CP 245, 247, 249, 252, 257, 260, Copleston to Bruce Knight, 1, 24 & 26 February, and 1, 17 & 22 March 1836.

21 Jones, "Maber", p 7, suggests from an item in the February 1840 *Cambrian* that Maber had agreed to support three curates and that two new churches were to be built in the parish, and adds the quotation from the paper, "Both the Marquis of Bute and the Bishop of Llandaff expressed their high approbation of his example of liberality." As the additional churches were not built in Maber's lifetime it is doubtful he held to his promise.

22 CP 89, Copleston to J M Traherne, 5 September 1840.

23 CP 113, Copleston to J M Traherne, 16 October 1843.

24 CP 109, Copleston to J M Traherne, 24 September 1842. Copleston wrote to Bruce Knight that "It is painful to be obliged to talk courteously to such men" when he heard that Guest had proposed that on Maber's death Knight should be appointed to Merthyr, and would be required to give a liberal salary to the incumbent of Dowlais so that he, Guest, could withdraw his own assistance [CP 311, 12 December 1836].

25 BP L89/12, Bruce Knight to Bute, 8 January 1844. See also L5/11, Richard Watson to Bute, 7 July 1818, who notes Bute's grandfather's wish that Knight should succeed Maber, and also CP 311, Copleston to Bruce Knight, 12 December 1836, and 113, Copleston to J M Traherne, 16 October 1843.

26 BP L89/13, Thomas Williams to Bute, 8 January 1844. John Maber kept a private academy in Swansea, advertising himself as educated at Cheltenham and Cambridge [*Western Mail*, 26 October 1874, p 6]. One of Maber's daughters, Mary, became a member of Prince's infamous and freelove community called the "Abode of Love". She left the sum of £1,700 to the community after she committed suicide in 1856 [Jones, "Maber", p 10].

27 BP L89/14, Thomas Williams to Bute, 10 January 1844.

28 BP L89/16, Richard Pendril Llewelyn to Bute, 10 January 1844; L89/18, Charlotte Rickards to Bute, 12 January 1844; L89/19, Revd Hely Rickards to Bute, 12 January 1844; L89/20, William Leigh to Bute, 12 January 1844. All three remained in their parishes until their deaths, though Rickards obtained, in plurality, the parishes of Llandough and Leckwith in addition to that of Michaelston-le-Pit.

29 BP L89/22 & 28, J C Campbell to Bute, 15 & 18 January 1844. He had been offered by Lord Bexley in the previous year the incumbency of a new church in the parish of Sidcup, Kent, and was inclined to accept the offer. This was because he felt inadequate to serve St Mary's Church at Cardiff which needed "a great compass of voice and strength of lungs", and which left him with feelings of exhaustion and fatigue [L88/78, Campbell to Bute, 29 March 1843, and L89/79, Bruce Pryce to Bute, 29 March 1843].

30 For an appreciation of his ministry at Merthyr see Wilkins, *Merthyr Tydfil*, pp 308f

CHILD EMIGRATION FROM MERTHYR TYDFIL WORKHOUSE[1]

by

MURIEL CHAMBERLAIN

Seventeen children, all girls, were sent from Merthyr Tydfil Workhouse to Canada in the 1870s.

Geographers speak of 'push' and 'pull' factors in migrations. The 'pull' factors from the Canadian side are easy to determine. In 1867 the British North America Act established the Confederation of Canada, consisting originally of Ontario, Quebec, Nova Scotia and New Brunswick. In 1869 the Hudson Bay Company surrendered its vast territories in the north and west to the British Crown and in 1870 Manitoba, the first western province, was carved out of the Prairies. From that time on the Canadians were actively looking for new immigrants. Ideally, they wanted farmers and farm labourers but domestic servants were also in demand. The 'push' factor from the British side was the growing depression in both industry and agriculture, characteristic of the 1870s, which replaced what economic historians sometimes call the period of mid-Victorian prosperity. The problem of orphaned or abandoned children was a perennial one in Victorian England but girls were considered more difficult because they could not be apprenticed to trades as boys could.

Merthyr Tydfil Workhouse had been set up in 1836, under the terms of the Poor Law Amendment Act of 1834. A Union workhouse had been built at Thomastown in 1853 and, after 1863, covered the parishes of Aberdare, Gelligaer, and Merthyr Tydfil in the then county of Glamorgan and of Rhigos, Penderyn and Vaynor in Breconshire. Its affairs were administered, under the terms of the 1834 Act, by an elected Board of Guardians.

In the early 1870s a crisis point was reached, in particular about the large number of little girls in their care. Their School Committee reported that there were 68 girls aged from two to sixteen, far too many for the solitary school mistress to cope with. They tried the experiment of appointing what they called a 'trainer' to teach the girls sewing and laundry work but it was not a success. The 'trainer' could not maintain discipline and the House Committee reported that the girls had learnt only the simplest sewing and nothing at all about washing and ironing. Perhaps the fact that, even by the not very exacting standards of the day, the room they had to use could only be described as 'cold, draughty and uncomfortable' made learning seem even less attractive.[2]

It must have seemed very tempting to the Guardians when, in the summer of 1872, they received a circular from Maria Rye, inviting them to send suitable children to Canada under her care. Miss Rye was a highly respectable woman from a professional family—several of her male relatives were well-known lawyers—and she had influential connections. She was also a very remarkable woman for her time. Although, rather curiously, she opposed women's suffrage, she was passionately interested in providing employment opportunities for women so that they could support themselves. Her original concern was for middle class women and she set up several enterprises run by women, notably a 'law stationers' in London and a 'telegraph school' to train women as telegraph clerks. In 1861 she founded the Female Middle Class Emigration Society and spent the next seven years escorting parties of women and girls to the British colonies of settlement, Canada, Australia and New Zealand.[3]

In 1869 she turned her attention to the emigration of children—still predominantly girls—and children of a very different class in society. In March she wrote a letter to The Times, proposing taking out what she termed the 'gutter children' of London, Manchester, Birmingham, Bristol and Liverpool to a new life in Canada and the western United States. Similar work was being pioneered at about the same time by a formidable Scotswoman, Annie Macpherson, who was literally collecting the waifs and strays, sleeping rough in the streets of London and other big cities. Annie Macpherson continued her work with the street children but Maria Rye generally preferred to draw her young emigrants from the 'pauper' children of the workhouses. She arranged for children from several Poor Law Unions to go out to Canada in 1868-9 and, in 1870, she received the official blessing of the Poor Law Board. She had already bought a converted gaol and courthouse, 'our Western Home', at Niagara-on-the-Lake, near Niagara Falls, to act as a staging post and distribution centre.[4]

Nevertheless the Merthyr Guardians hesitated whether to accept her offer. By chance the meeting was attended by a highly respected civil servant, the Local Government Board Inspector, Andrew Doyle, who had come to discuss a question of public health. Doyle later recalled, 'Objections were made by some of the guardians, but, upon the whole, they consented, and looking to the fact that the system had been approved by the Local Government Board, I expressed myself in favour of the application being acceded to.' An 'Emigration Committee', as it came to be called, was set up, consisting of five local worthies, the Rev. John Griffith, William Harris, Rees Lewis, John Williams and Arthur Jones.[5]

The Committee reported to their fellow Guardians at the meeting on 7 September 1872. They had examined 'all the children of suitable age' and selected six 'fit to emigrate'. The six were Elizabeth and Mary Thomas, sisters, aged eleven and nine respectively; Mary and Anne Griffiths, also sisters, aged thirteen and eleven; Mary Ann Lewis, aged ten; and Elizabeth Aubrey (given elsewhere as Aubery), aged eight. The sort of children selected can be gauged from the other comments. By the Thomas sisters' names was written, 'Deserted by the father 2 years ago; there is a warrant out against him but he cannot be found. Mother is dead some years. They have been in the House more than two years. No friends can be found. The Guardians examd. the children and they gave their consent to go & seemed pleased with the proposition.' The Griffiths sisters were in a similar situation. It was recorded, 'Deserted. Their father and mother are alive but not married. The mother has separated from the father 5 years, and the children have been living with him during the whole of that time. He is now in our Workhouse for the last 6 weeks, owing to a bad leg. The reputed father is a very drunken character, 72 years old and shattered in health. They seemed very willing to go.' Mary Ann Lewis was a slightly different case. She was an orphan. Of her it was written, 'Has been 2 years in the House and has no relations. The Guardians examd. her and she expressed herself very pleased to go. A very intelligent child.' The youngest, Elizabath Aubrey, does not seem to have been asked whether she wished to go but the reasons for their decision are clear in the Guardians' notes, 'has been in the House between 2 & 3 years. Has a sister who is a prostitute and it is very desirable to separate them.' The children's 'creed' also had to be recorded. The Griffths and Thomas sisters were all Baptists, Elizabeth Aubrey, an Independent, and Mary Ann Lewis, Church of England. Mary Ann Lewis came from Merthyr Upper parish, the rest from Merthyr Lower.

The Medical Officer, at this time J. Jones Gabe, testified that they were all in good health. Elizabeth Aubrey had been suffering from ringworm but was now cured. Money was tight because the statute limited the expense which could be incurred for each child to £10 and 'the passage fee will be £8, we putting the children on board.' Nevertheless, they budgeted for some clothing to be provided for each child. Finally William Harris moved and David P. Davies seconded what became the standard motion when sending children off: 'That the several Indoor Pauper children whose names are hereunder written residing in Merthyr Tydfil Union being desirous of emigrating to Canada, the necessary steps be immediately taken to effect the emigration, and that a sum not exceeding Ten Pounds be expended for each person to be charged upon the Common Fund.'[6]

When they said 'immediately', they meant it. The children left the Workhouse on Wednesday, 18 September 1872, recorded in the Discharge Book as 'Sent to Niagara Canada, under care of Miss Rye.'[7] On 15 March 1873 they received a Report from Miss Rye, telling them how the children had been placed. It read:—

'Merthyr Girls leaving England 19 Sep. 1873 in S.S. Sarmatian.

Name	Name & Occupation of employer	Residence
Elizabeth Aubrey Adopted	Mr Keys Labr. & Sexton no children	Lewiston, New York State, U.S.
Eliz Thomas Adopted	Mr Hamply Farmer 25 yrs there	Peel Drayton Post Office Ontario
Mary Thomas Bound [i.e. indentured]	Mr Rd. Logan Farmer. 1 ch[ild] 30 yrs there	Thorndale P. Office Ontario
Mary Ann Lewis adopted	Mr Dalton Post Offe. Dept 13 [?months] there	Carling St. London, Ontario
Mary Griffiths Bound [i.e. indentured]	Mr Jno Brown Druggist - mcht. [merchant] 11 yrs there	Thorold Ontario
Ann Griffiths [no status given]	Mr Harman—Hosteller [?Hotelier] Farmer 11 yrs there	Virgil Ontario

Even as an interim report it would seem to have many weaknesses but the Guardians were obviously satisfied. Apart from asking why Elizabeth Aubrey had gone to the States (an enquiry to which there is no record that they ever received an answer) they seem to have asked no questions. Instead they ordered the Workhouse master to report by the next Board meeting as to children in the House suitable for emigration to Canada.[8]

As a result six more children were identified—Mary Lewis, aged 13, an orphan; Elizabeth Morris, aged 12, an orphan; May A. Mcinnes, 12, 'Deserted'; Sarah A Jones, 8 'Deserted'; Martha Bowen, 13, 'Deserted, and Mary Ford, 11, 'Deserted'. The motion to send them to Canada was proposed by Mr Rees H. Rhys[9] and seconded by Mr Arthur Jones and the approval of the Local Government Board sought. This was obtained and the formal resolution passed on 5 April 1873. The Board now required that children proposed for emigration should be either orphans or 'deserted' and this is recorded but, unlike the earlier group, no further details are given in the Minutes. The children were supposed to give their consent before two magistrates but there is no formal record of this. The matter was now obviously regarded as routine. The children left on 30 April. The Workhouse Admission and Discharge book only adds the information that Mary Lewis and Elizabeth Morris came from Aberdare parish, Martha Bowen, Mary Ann McInnes and Sarah Jones from Merthyr Upper and Mary Ford from Merthyr Lower.[10]

Once again the Guardians were well pleased with what they had done. At their meeting on 3 January 1874, a letter from Miss Rye (the details of which, unfortunately, are not recorded) was read, reporting on the children who had sailed the previous May. The Guardians resolved 'that the Clerk be instructed to thank Miss Rye for her very satisfactory report.' On 21 March they instructed the Master to prepare, by the following Saturday, a list of girls in the House thought suitable for emigration to Canada. It was presumably to pay for this group that on 23 May they authorised the payment of a cheque for £64 to Miss Rye for the passage of the children to Canada. The formal motion was put to the Board, proposed by R. H. Rhys and seconded by Arthur Jones, on 6 June 1874. On 27 June they received the permission of the Local Government Board in respect of five more girls, Elizabeth Driscoll, aged 13; Sarah Ann Salsbury, 13; Margaret Haddocks, 12; Sarah McInnes, 8; and Rachel Williams, also 8. The first three were orphans. There is a note beside the name of Sarah McInnes, 'Deserted by Father. Sister in Canada'—this was presumably the Mary Ann McInnes, who had gone with the previous group. Rachel Williams is described as 'Deserted by mother. Father in America'. This time all the girls came from Merthyr Upper, except Rachel Williams, who came from Merthyr Lower.[11]

Miss Rye's intentions may have been of the best but the supervision in Canada was lax, as the vagueness of her 1873 Report to the Merthyr Guardians would suggest. Disquieting rumours began to spread. Andrew Doyle was particularly uneasy because he felt that his voice had been decisive in persuading the Merthyr Guardians to subscribe to the scheme. In 1874 he was near retirement but he felt strongly that the children in Canada should be visited and he went out on an official mission of enquiry. He travelled to Canada with the last group of Merthyr children in the summer of 1874.[12]

Andrew Doyle was no ordinary middle-ranking civil servant. As his name suggests, he was of Irish extraction, being born in Dublin in 1809. He studied at Trinity College, Dublin, before proceeding to Lincoln's Inn and being called to the Bar in 1842. (In his later controversies with Maria Rye, she accused him of being a Roman Catholic, prejudiced against her because she was a strong Protestant. In fact, Catholics were forbidden by their Church to attend Trinity at this time and Doyle was an Anglican.) As a young man he was an influential newspaper editor. From 1843 to 1848 he edited the *Morning Chronicle*, then a Whig newspaper and, in the opinion of many, second only to *The Times* in influence. He was the son-in-law of the proprietor, Sir John Easthope, and when Easthope sold his interest in the paper and it changed its politics, Doyle left the paper and joined the Civil Service as a Poor Law Inspector in February 1848. His title subsequently changed to Local Government Inspector.[13]

He had a huge district to cover, including most of Wales and a swathe of the border counties. In 1852 he took up residence in the parish of Llandulais in Denbighshire. In 1868 he bought Pendarren Cottage in Llangenny near Crickhowell and developed his estate there over the next two decades, building a large new house, Pendarren, which was completed in 1876.[14]

He was a man of formidable energy. His Reports as a Poor Law Inspector were notable, not least for their pioneering use of statistics, and he also wrote important Reports on Vagrancy in 1849 and 1865 and on pauper education in 1860 and 1862. In 1870 he was sent on an official mission to Germany to enquire into the German system of poor relief. Later between 1879 and 1882 he played an important role as an Assistant Commissioner on the Royal Commission on the Depressed Condition of the Agricultural Interests.[15]

Merthyr Workhouse was only a small part of his responsibilities but it must have been kept in the forefront of his mind by a long-running enquiry he had to conduct in 1872-3 into a dispute between the Master and the Medical Officer, which culminated in the resignation of Dr Gabe Jones.[16]

Doyle seems to have approached his 1874 assignment very much in the spirit of a modern investigative journalist. He wrote a very detailed Report, which was subsequently to be published as a Parliamentary Paper. He thought that the arrangements for sending out the children were somewhat *ad hoc*. When a sufficiently large party, usually 100-200, had been collected, the notice of the departure day would be sent out. Some assembled in London but those from 'remote Unions' came directly to Liverpool. The Merthyr children were numbered among the latter and Doyle records, 'The children from the Merthyr Tydfil Union were delivered by the Master to one of Miss Rye's attendants.' He thought the children were well dressed and looked healthy and cheerful. They then embarked on the *Sarmatian,* one of the Alban steamers. Miss Rye herself accompanied the children, as she usually did, and the accommodation on the ship seemed satisfactory, although there was no means of isolating some children who developed measles on the voyage.[17]

It was when they got to Canada that, in Doyle's opinion, the disorganisation began to show. They arrived in Quebec and went through immigration. Some children were immediately despatched to families in New Brunswick and Nova Scotia but Miss Rye's main party embarked on the Grand Trunk Railway to Niagara. Doyle agreed that 'our Western Home' was clean and in good order. (For a former gaol, its photographs seem to show it as a pleasant, even gracious building, at least from the outside.) His only serious complaint concerned the washing facilities, which he regarded as inferior even to English workhouse standards. Some children complained that the food was bad or inadequate but he had to concede that the children looked healthy enough.[18]

The real problem was the lack of supervision and proper inspection both before and after the children were placed with families. Miss Rye distributed children over a wide area of Ontario, Nova Scotia and New Brunswick. Applicant families were expected to fill in a detailed questionnaire about their occupations and how long they had been in a particular location. They were also expected to name referees, one of them preferably a minister of religion. It was impressed upon them that they must provide for both the secular and religious education of the children. But, as Doyle discovered, the children were rarely visited to find out what conditions were really like.

The youngest were generally adopted by the families to whom they went and, on the whole, they were the ones who fared best. Older children might be apprenticed or 'indentured to service'. Some simply went into domestic service with no special form of agreement. Where there were agreements, they were often verbal and not enforced. Doyle doubted the legal force even of many written agreements.[19]

Some children, of course, did very well but others were badly and oppressively treated. Recent accounts (especially television programmes) have perhaps dwelt too exclusively on the horror stories. One of the most balanced of modern studies is also one of the first, Phyllis Harrison's *Home Children*,[20] based on the accounts of immigrants or their immediate descendants, which presents a convincing cross-section of their experiences in what was still in many areas a very harsh environment. When things did go wrong, the faults were not all on one side. Miss Rye complained in despair, 'In Canada the workhouse child exhibits the most frightful and disheartening obstinacy and deceit.'[21] Many Canadians came to distrust the children. The feeling is well expressed in that children's classic, Anne of Green Gables, when Marilla tells Mrs Lynde, 'At first Matthew suggested getting a "Home" boy. But I said "no" flat to that. "They may be all right—I'm not saying they're not—but no London street arabs for me," I said. "Give me a native born at least. There'll be a risk, no matter who we get. But I'll feel easier in my mind and sleep sounder at nights if we get a born Canadian".[22]

How did the Merthyr children fare? Unhappily, the only one whose fate can be traced in detail, Mary Ford, was one of the very unlucky ones. Miss Rye told Doyle that Mary was with a Mrs Dallas of Wellington Street, Hamilton, Ontario. Doyle records, 'Walking up Wellington-street, Hamilton, in quest of Mrs Dallas's house, I asked a coloured man whom I met if he could direct me to it, and, to assist him in doing so, told him that I was looking after a little English [sic] child who was there in service. "Oh!", he replied, "I am glad that anybody has come to look after her: I have seen that child flogged worse than a slave; but don't mention me as telling you, for I do all the white-washing of the house." Upon visiting Mrs Dallas, who, I was informed, kept a boarding house for young men, she told me that she had been frequently obliged to punish the child severely; that she was a thief and a liar; she stole money and anything else she could lay her hands on; there was no believing a word she said. She further described the way in which the child had been sent to her by train, with a label pinned upon her breast, "as if she was a parcel of goods". More than once, she told me, she was on the point of turning the child out of the house. "Why", I asked "did you not write to Miss Alloway?" (Miss Rye's assistant.) "I did write to her and she took no notice of my letter." "But Miss Rye is in the country, why did you not write to her?" "I did write to Miss Rye asking her to change the child. But she has taken no notice of my letter." From the time the child was placed in service no person had been to see her or inquire about her.'

Doyle goes on to say that Mary left the workhouse in Merthyr with a very good character. 'With this child I had a long conversation apart from her mistress. She admitted quite frankly some of the offences with which she was charged; but there was no mistaking her character—that of an affectionate and impressionable child. It may seem a trivial thing to mention, but when I spoke of her former teachers and associates, of whom I knew something, her eyes filled with tears.' He was persuaded that 'the visit at an early period of a judicious friend, who took an interest in her, might have saved that child from the trouble that I greatly fear is in store for her, as such visits might have saved Annie McMaster and other children from the fate that has befallen them.' (Annie McMaster, who had come from Chichester workhouse, had had an illegitimate child, probably by the son of the family with whom she was placed.)

Doyle, writing at a later stage in his controversy with Miss Rye in 1877, published Miss Rye's 'synopsis' of Mary Ford; 'Mary Ford, 15. Bound [i.e. indentured] for service, 1st place, Mr Dallas, Wellington-street, Hamilton, returned; girl unmanageable, mistress impertinent. 2. Mrs Sorby, Rice Lake, Ontario: girl returned, absolutely unmanageable; ran away from the "Home" [i.e. at Niagara], returned to Mrs Sorby, who sent her back (some 60 miles) by a confidential servant: replaced. 3. Mrs Bayly, Oakville: returned to the "Home" since my return to England: an unmanageable, ill-conditioned girl, who ought never to have been sent abroad. Illegitimate. One-year-and-half in workhouse school. Doing very badly in 1875.' Doyle added, 'That case in all its circumstances, is not an unfair illustration of the methods and consequences of Miss Rye's system of supervision.' He noted with contempt that Miss Rye did not even know where the girl came from and mistakenly listed her among the Bristol children.

But his real *coup-de-grace* was to contrast Miss Rye's synopsis with a letter which Mary had written to her brother, Edward, still in Britain. 'Dear Edward,—I take the greatest pleasure in writing to you these few lines, as I suppose that you have long been expecting a letter from me, but you must please pardon my neglect; give my best love to darling Willie [presumably another brother], and tell him that I feel very anxious about him: but I hope that both of you may see better days to come; I hope my dear sister Jane has been to see you, and I hope, dear, that you are improving in your lessons, as I feel very anxious about you. I have been very sick for a long time, as the winter has been very cold, but summer has been very warm, and I hope in time to come, that I may be able to take you both out of the poorhouse, but I can think nothing more now, but perhaps, in my next letter, I may have more to say.' Doyle says that there follow some childish verses, of which he quotes only a little,

'My pen is bad, my ink is pale,
My love for you will never fail.
Your affectionate Sister,
Mary Ford.'[23]

Battle raged between Andrew Doyle, and Maria Rye for several years. Almost the whole Ontario press united to denounce him and support Miss Rye. He was accused of seeking a lucrative job 'inspecting' the immigrant children (hardly likely at his age) and the canard that he was a Roman Catholic, denouncing a Protestant enterprise, found a ready ear in 'Orange' Ontario. But the main thrust of the indignation was against the suggestion that the Canadians were exploiting children, whose prospects could hardly have been worse at home.[24] In fact Doyle never suggested that all the children fared badly but he was adamant that an adequate system of supervision and inspection must be established. In Britain Maria Rye had powerful supporters, including Lord Shaftesbury and the Archbishop of Canterbury but the government could hardly ignore Doyle's cogent criticisms. The Local Government Board suspended all emigration of workhouse children to Canada in 1875, although Miss Rye continued to send out destitute children, not under Poor Law control. The emigration of workhouse children was allowed to resume in 1883 but under tighter regulations and, in 1888, the Canadian government agreed to the setting up of an inspection system under its control. Children were sent out under this system until 1924.[25]

The Merthyr Guardians obviously felt that they had burned their fingers in the 1870s. When a new official communication came to them in 1887, they let it lie on the table.[26] The pressures had eased somewhat by this time. The workhouse was extended in the 1870s and an 'Industrial School' (later called a Training School) established at Trecynon, Aberdare, in

1877. The discharge books from the workhouse in the 1880s show a fair number proceeding to Aberdare.[27]

The Training School was superseded by the building of the cottage homes at Llwydcoed between 1912 and 1919. But the story of child migration to Canada was not quite concluded. The *Democrat's Handbook to Merthyr*, published in 1912, had a section on the Poor Law administration. It recorded that Merthyr Parish had 'the lowest type of children under our care . . . We have sent two boys to Canada, and find them doing well there. We are sending some more, who, we are certain, cannot be kept from their old ways, except by putting them far enough away from their old haunts.'[28] In 1923 William Price, whose father had been killed in the colliery at Aberfan, was sent to Canada from Llwydcoed at the age of 13. He recorded his experiences in a book, *Celtic Odyssey*.[29] His fortunes in Canada had been mixed but his memories of Llwydcoed were not happy ones.

Perhaps, if they had written them, the memoirs of the 1870s child immigrants would have been much the same. We have one tantalising, possible, later glimpse of Mary Ford. In October 1911 a new editor took over the 'Home Pages' of the *Grain Growers' Guide*, a weekly journal which circulated widely in the west. She was a campaigning journalist with a powerful pen. She wrote in favour of women's suffrage and the right of women to become 'homesteaders' and claim their 160 acres like men. She also campaigned for women's education, especially on health, and for sex education for children. Some of her writing was startling even by modern standards. In February 1912 she published statistics showing that during the previous 27 months, 600 children under 12 had been treated in hospital for venereal disease; 20 per cent as the result of assaults, 20 per cent inherited from parents, 60 per cent contracted from others.[30] Perhaps it was too strong meat for the journal. She did not last long in the job. But her name was Mary Ford. Did she originate from Merthyr Tydfil? Her age would seem to be about right. We know that she could write remarkably well for an uneducated child. Did she choose to emulate the campaigning journalism of her would-be saviour, Andrew Doyle?

References

1. An earlier version of this paper was published as 'The Sad Case of Mary Ford' in *The Welsh in Canada* (ed. M. E. Chamberlain), CSWG, 1987.
2. Glamorgan Record Office (hereafter GRO). U.M. 1/17. Merthyr Tydfil Union, Poor Law Guardians, Minute Books, Minute 154, Meeting of 27 May 1871, Report of School Committee, 25 May; Minute 708, Meeting of 4 May 1872, Report of House Committee, 29 April.
3. GRO. U.M. 1/17, Minute Book, Minute 933, 17 Aug 1872; *Dictionary of National Biography, Supplement, 1901-1911*. Maria Susan Rye; G.Wagner, *Children of the Empire*, Weidenfeld & Nicolson, 1982, pp.39-40.
4. Wagner, pp.36-47.
5. GRO. U.M. 1/17, Minute Book, Minute 933, 17 Aug 1872, Minute 952, 24 Aug 1872, Minute 967, 31 Aug 1872; *Parliamentary Papers*, LXXI (1877) 8, Reply of Mr Doyle to Miss Rye's Report on the Emigration of Pauper Children to Canada.
6. GRO. U.M. 1/17, Minute Book, Minute 983, 7 Sept 1872.
7. GRO. U.M. 28/3, Admission and Discharge Register of Merthyr Tydfil Union, 18 Sept 1872.
8. GRO. M.U. 1/17, Minutes. Minute 1369, 15 March 1873
9. Although not on the original 'Emigration Committee', R. H. Rhys was now playing a leading role in the emigration policy. A man of substance, he is accorded the title 'Esq' in all attendance registers, the only one who is.
10.GRO. U.M. 1/17, Minute 1453, headed 'Emigration of children to Canada', 5 April 1873; U.M. 28/3, Admission and Discharge Register, 30 April 1873.

11.GRO. U.M. 1/18, Minute 139, 3 Jan 1874, Minute 183, 21 March 1874, Minute 225, 9 May 1874, Minute 240, 23 May 1874, Minute 256, 6 June 1874, Minute 276, 27 June 1874. U.M. 28/3 Admission and Discharge Register, 30 June 1874.

12.*Parliamentary Papers*, LXIII (1875) 255. Report by Andrew Doyle, Local Government Inspector, to the President of the Local Government Board, as to 'The Emigration of Pauper Children to Canada'. Dated Llandulas, Abergele, 1 Dec 1874. Parlt. Papers, LXXI (1877) 8. Reply of Mr Doyle to Miss Rye's Report on the Emigration of Pauper Children to Canada. Andrew Doyle to the President of the Local Government Board. Dated from Plas Dulas, Abergele, 14 May 1877.

13.A. Raymond Hawkins, *The Doyles of Pendarren* (copy kindly supplied to author by Dr T. F. Holley); *The Times*, 25 December 1888, obituary; *Dictionary of National Biography, Supplement 1901-11*, entry for his son John Andrew Doyle; S. Koss, *The Rise and fall of the Political Press in Britain*, Hamish Hamilton, 1981, pp.38, 75.

14.Hawkins, pp.3-7.

15.*The Times*, 25 Dec 1888; Hawkins, pp. 3-5.

16.GRO. U.M. 1/17, Minute Book, *passim*.

17.*Parliamentary Papers*, LXIII (1875) 255, Report by Andrew Doyle, Local Government Inspector, to the President of the Local Government Board as to the 'Emigration of Pauper Children to Canada'. Dated Llandulas, Abergele, 1 December 1874.

18.*Parlt. Papers*, LXIII (1875) 261-3

19.*Parlt Papers*, LXIII (1875) 263-5; Parlt. Papers LXXI (1877) 107; see also examples of documents given in Wesley Turner, 'Miss Rye's Children and the Ontario Press', *Ontario History*, 68:3 (1976) 201-3.

20.P. Harrison, *Home Children*: their personal stories, Watson & Dwyer, Winnipeg, 1979.

21.*Parlt Papers*, LXXI (1877) 7.

22.L. M. Montgomery, *Anne of Green Gables*, Harrap, 1943, p.11.

23.*Parlt. Papers*, LXXI (1877) 8-9.

24.A Select Committee of the Canadian House of Commons also refused to accept most of Doyle's criticisms of the system. The subject is thoroughly explored in Wesley Turner, 'Miss Rye's Children and the Ontario Press, 1875', *Ontario History*, 68:3 (1976) 169-203.

25.W. A. Carrothers, Emigration from the British Isles, P.S. King, 1929 (reprinted Cass, 1965), pp. 278-82. See also J. Parr, *Labouring Children: British Immigrant Apprentices to Canada, 1869-1914*, McGill-Queens University Press, Montreal, 1980.

26.GRO. U.M. 1/21, Minute 422, 9 July 1887.

27.GRO. U.M. 4/1, Industrial Training School, 1876-1883; U.M. 28/5, Admission and Discharge Register, 1883-6, *passim*.

28.*The Democrat's Handbook to Merthyr*, Education Publishing Co., 1912, p. 85.

29.William R. Price, *Celtic Odyssey*, Dorrance & Co., Philadelphia, 1970.

30.*Grain Growers' Guide,* Winnipeg. See particularly issues of 7, 21, 28 February 1912. Mary Ford had become editor of the Home Pages in October 1911. She disappears without explanation soon after the February articles.

29A. Eos Morlais, Robert Rees. (1841-92)

THE MERTHYR TYDFIL NATIONAL EISTEDDFOD, 1881

by

HYWEL TEIFI EDWARDS

The National Eisteddfod was launched in Aberdare in 1861 and relaunched in Merthyr twenty years later following almost identical preliminaries. The 'modern' eisteddfod movement, first set in motion in 1789 when the Gwyneddigion Society in London assumed a patron's rôle, had grown apace since 1819 when the Dyfed Cambrian Society held the first in a series of Provincial Eisteddfodau in Carmarthen and by the 1850s the eisteddfod stood unrivalled as a cultural institution on whose platform the Welsh disported themselves and invited what they hoped would be the approving scrutiny of 'onlooking nationalities'. Its importance as a cynosure of national merit was considerably heightened by the onslaught on Welsh cultural and moral failings published in 1847 by the three English commissioners appointed by parliament to report on the educational provision—particularly the teaching of English—made for the children of the working class. Their Reports, which became lodged in Welsh memory as the treacherous 'Blue Books', by and large told a very sorry tale and the Victorian eisteddfod, in playing a major part in the work of rebuttal and reinstatement, would fix its attention closely on English expectations much to the detriment of the Welsh language and its literature.

It should be stressed, however, that the 'Blue Books' did not trigger the anglicization of the eisteddfod; it simply increased the bias which had earlier disillusioned the promoters of the Provincial Eisteddfodau between 1819 and 1834 and was to continue uncorrected in the Cymreigyddion Eisteddfodau held in Abergavenny under the aegis of Lady Llanover between 1834 and 1853. What triggered the process was the necessity, so perceived, of securing the support of 'our best people' for the eisteddfod movement which in turn necessitated the liberal use of English as the language of their éclat. The central, sobering fact in the history of the major *eisteddfodau* from 1819 to the 1930s is that they happily countenanced the dominance of the English language while professing a commitment to the celebration and advancement of Welsh culture. They provided a national stage for a 'reasoned' Victorian response to Wales's so-called 'bilingual difficulty' in which can be found the roots of the complexes and fatuities which today, in letters to the Welsh press, still coil about the 'language problem'. A student of Welsh psychology would do well to study the history of the eisteddfod.

In the 1850s, in the deep shadow of the 'Blue Books', Welsh progressives, aware that *eisteddfodau* were attracting increasing attention from the English press,began to berate recurring irregularities and improprieties. The inadequacies and vagaries of local committees and the vulgarity of unsuccessful competitors—choleric poets and musicians would confront adjudicators and continue their altercations for weeks on end in the press—made clear the need for some kind of reform which would rid the eisteddfod of 'the curse of the local'. The creation of an annual National Eisteddfod organized and regulated by a properly constituted national body was mooted and in 1858 events at the epochal Llangollen Eisteddfod led to rapid action.

Promoted by the Reverend John Williams (Ab Ithel), an entrepreneurial clergyman who saw a National Eisteddfod following inevitably in the train of the railway age, the Llangollen venture was to prove decisive. Ab Ithel and his supporters were devotees of Iolo Morganwg who had introduced his Gorsedd of Bards into the eisteddfod movement at

Carmarthen in 1819, hugely embarrassing the bishop of St. David's, Thomas Burgess,who found himself released from the mystic circle on the lawn of the Ivy Bush hostelry a bemused, beribboned druid. From then on the Gorsedd would be a continuing source of unease—not to say shame—for worthy progressives who feared the ridicule of 'onlooking nationalities', but Ab Ithel was a thorough-paced Ioloite intent on celebrating the druidic myth and insisting on the Gorsedd's 'age-old' right to prevail in eisteddfodic matters. In Llangollen, the Gorsedd appeared in its true colours, supported by a magnificently psyche-delic Dr. William Price with his daughter on horseback, and the eisteddfod programme showed a contempt for 'mere usefulness' by favouring subjects of an antiquarian, historical and romantic hue. Ab Ithel's Llangollen Eisteddfod reflected the aspirations of the clergy-men who had promoted the Provincial Eisteddfodau and its backward look at former glories was bound to antagonize would-be modernisers.

In the event, Ab Ithel gave them the best of opportunities to attack. A prize of twenty pounds and a silver star was offered for an essay on Prince Madog ab Owain Gwynedd's 'discovery' of America in the twelfth century. That written by Thomas Stephens of Merthyr, the acclaimed author of *The Literature of the Kymry* (1849),was adjudged the best but in dismissing Madog's claims out of hand Stephens, according to Ab Ithel, had defeated the object of the competition. He could not be given the prize. In the ensuing uproar in the Cambrian Tent, Stephens demanded to be heard; one of Ab Ithel's lieutenants commanded the band to deafen the audience which then insisted on Stephens's right to speak. His argu-ments in favour of his scholarly approach to the Madog myth were irrefutable but his prize was still denied him. The treatment meted out to one of the few Welsh authors of the day to achieve British renown outraged the progressives who were further incensed when it tran-spired that Ab Ithel was the author of the second-best essay in the competition and that his children were also unexpectedly winning prizes. To rob Thomas Stephens and feather one's own nest at the same time was taking eisteddfod chicanery a step too far.

A hurriedly convened 'reform meeting' in the Cambrian Tent concluded that it was time to act and two years later, before the close of the Denbigh Eisteddfod,there was in being a national body—'The Eisteddfod'—and an elected executive—'The Council'—who in 1861 held the first officially designated National Eisteddfod in Aberdare. Another seven followed before 'The Eisteddfod' foundered on debts in 1868. Merthyr did not host one of them despite its having been a particularly lively centre of eisteddfod activity since the 1820s and having held, as recently as September 1859, under the auspices of the Cymmrodorion Temperance Society, an eisteddfod deemed sufficiently superior in character to be called a 'National'. Be that as it may, in the person of the ill-done-by Thomas Stephens, Merthyr can claim to have had its finger on the trigger of reform.

The constitution of 'The Eisteddfod', as drawn up by William Thomas (Gwilym Tawe), saw its prime duty as the promotion of the Welsh language and its culture, but it immediate-ly succumbed to the forces of anglicization. When Hugh Owen (1804-81), a powerful civil servant at the helm of the Poor Law Commission in London and an unstinting campaigner for the creation of a comprehensive system of education in Wales, introduced his 'Social Science Section' at the Caernarfon National Eisteddfod in 1862, he provided a conduit for English utilitarianism. Invited 'savants' would urge the study of geology at the expense of poetry and the advancement of English at all costs. Welsh poets wilted in the high noon of usefulness and found themselves marginalized on the eisteddfod stage where the concert favourites flaunted their metropolitan sophistication. Squeezed between Hugh Owen's determination to provide Wales with an 'educational edifice' that would equip it for a British rôle and the growing realization that England might stomach the image of Wales as 'The Land of Song', the Welsh language counted for very little during 'The Eisteddfod' 's reign. As the quintessential self-made man, David Davies, Llandinam, told the Cardiganshire 'gwerin' at the Aberystwyth National Eisteddfod in 1865, they should continue to speak Welsh if they were content with brown bread but if they craved white they would have to speak English. In 1867, Rector John Griffiths, the Council president, was happy to assure the mocking English press that 'The Eisteddfod' could not afford 'to spend all our time in the perpetuation of the Welsh language. The language is very well able to take care of itself. I think our time might well be better employed than in bolstering up a language that may be of a questionable advantage'.

When a combination of poor management and parochial obduracy broke 'The Eisteddfod' in 1868, Hugh Owen, in appealing to the nation for assistance, admitted that perhaps they had been too dismissive of the traditional 'eisteddfodwr''s predilections, remarking that it was 'the common people—the many—who had done almost everything in Wales that was really worthy of the country'. His contrition fell on deaf ears and together with Rector John Griffiths he had to go deep into his own pocket to keep 'The Eisteddfod' out of the courts. He would not again assume a prominent rôle as an eisteddfod reformer until 1878 when he sought, at the Birkenhead National Eisteddfod, to reintroduce his 'Social Science Section' ambitions through the meetings of the Cymmrodorion Society which he had been instrumental in reviving in London in 1873.

During the 1870s, major *eisteddfodau* held mainly in North Wales kept alive the image of the 'National' fashioned in the 1860s. They were, however, essentially local affairs and as such susceptible to local imperfections. Hugh Owen made clear once again at Birkenhead that Wales needed a clearly defined National Eisteddfod with a properly constituted national body to plot its course and regulate its proceedings, and on 16 March 1880 he read a paper on 'Eisteddfod Reform' before a Cymmrodorion Society meeting chaired by Professor John Rhŷs in the Freemasons' Tavern in London, in which he argued for the creation of a permanent 'National Eisteddfod Association' with an executive Council 'appointed for the purpose, among others, of co-operating with the local committee and assisting in rendering the eisteddfod arrangements in all their parts such as may still further increase the popularity and extend the usefulness of our national institution'.

Hugh Owen's paper, prepared with the characteristic thoroughness of an accomplished civil servant, was very well received and it but remained to present his scheme for approval at the Caernarfon Eisteddfod in August, 1880. That it needed to be adopted quickly was made clear when the Swansea Eisteddfod, held a fortnight in advance of that at Caernarfon, also claimed 'National' status, occasioning bitter wrangling in the press. On 25 August it was put before a meeting of the Cymmrodorion, some twenty-seven members in all, six of whom were recognised poets, and after another well-argued paper on 'The best means of improving the eisteddfod' had been read by Mrs Anne Thomas (Morfydd Eryri) of St.Ann's Vicarage, Llandygái in which she urged 'the incorporation of the Eisteddfod as a society under a Royal charter', and its endowment by State Funds, it was subsequently decided to support Hugh Owen's scheme.

The Welsh language did not figure prominently in it; on the contrary he made no specific reference to its importance. The Gorsedd 'with its mystic rites and high claims to veneration' would be upheld but its 'degrees' should not be given without proper examination.

Ridicule was not to be invited. The proposed 'National Eisteddfod Association' should co-operate with the local committees to 'still further increase the popularity and extend the usefulness of our national institution', and the Council should seek to make it 'the upholder of public virtue as well as the promoter of excellency in literature, poetry, music, art, manufacture and handicraft'. The stamp of Victorian moral earnestness was to be firmly imprinted on all its works, the Council intent at all times on 'excluding from the eisteddfod proceedings whatever may be deemed low, vulgar, or in bad taste; as this highest court of the nation ought to be characterised in all respects by propriety, decorum, and even dignity, while its decisions ought to be marked by soundness of judgement and integrity of aim'.

When Dr. Cadwaladr Davies proposed at Caernarfon:

> 'That this meeting of bards and literati and friends of the Eisteddfod begs to invite the Honourable Society of Cymmrodorion to consider the various suggestions contained in the papers read by Mr. Hugh Owen and Mrs. Thomas, and prepare, in conjunction with twelve gentlemen to be elected by this meeting a scheme for the reform and future management of the Eisteddfod',

he was opposed by J. Owen Griffith (Ioan Arfon) who proposed:

> 'That the question of Eisteddfod reform should be considered, not by the Cymmrodorion Society, but by the bards and literati in Eisteddfod assembled'.

A poet, trade unionist and geology enthusiast who remembered well the reign of 'The Eisteddfod', Ioan Arfon resented London-Welsh dominance, but to no avail. Cadwaladr Davies's proposition carried and the Cymmrodorion agreed to meet at the Raven Hotel in Shrewsbury on 17 September 1880 to create the necessary machinery for action.

Anxious to appear conciliatory from the beginning, some twenty-seven prominent poets and musicians, including Ioan Arfon, were invited to the Shrewsbury meeting to act in conjunction with the Cymmrodorion as a provisional committee 'to define the scope and functions of the Association', and the degree of suspicion—or indifference—can be gauged from the fact that only four attended. Ioan Arfon, who died in 1881, was not one of them. All seventeen who did attend, with one exception—the Reverend John Eiddon Jones—were exiles and J. H. Puleston, the Tory MP for Davenport who chaired the meeting, was at pains to emphasise that it was the wish of the proposed Association 'to co-operate with the eisteddfod, and not to be the eisteddfod itself', they did not want to 'arrogate to themselves the position of dictators . . . ' Hugh Owen, on the other hand, foresaw the time 'when it would swallow up the eisteddfod, and the eisteddfod would merge into this association' . . . an expression of imperious intent which prompted disclaimers from both Lewis Morris and Puleston, the former maintaining that 'so long as the eisteddfod consisted chiefly of poetry and music, the bards must have a considerable voice in it'. A descendant of the famous Lewis Morris of Anglesey (1701-65), Morris, who was knighted in 1895, made a name for himself as an educationist and a poet who aspired to succeed Tennyson as 'Poet Laureate'. His ambition far exceeded his talents but as the author of *The Epic of Hades* (1876-77) and an influential campaigner for higher education in Wales, he would figure largely in National Eisteddfod affairs until his death in 1907.

At the Shrewsbury meeting it was finally resolved to establish 'The National Eisteddfod Association' and the annual subscription fee was set at half a guinea. Sir Watkin Williams Wynn, Bart., MP, was offered the presidency—which he subsequently accepted—and all the Welsh peers, bishops and Members of Parliament representing Welsh constituencies, together with J. H. Puleston, MP, Major Cornwallis West and Archdeacon John Griffiths were to be vice-presidents. The Council was not to exceed fifty members, its chairman would be Lewis Morris and every chaired poet would be an 'ex officio'member. With T. Marchant Williams, BA, acting as honorary secretary, J. H. Puleston was appointed treasurer and an executive committee with equal representation for both poets and Cymmrodorion members was to ensure continuing progress and would report to the first annual meeting of the Association at the National Eisteddfod in 1881. It did so at the Castle Hotel in Merthyr on 31 August when David Griffiths (Clwydfardd), long since recognized as the Archdruid, acted as chairman.

The executive committee had by then established a sub-committee to secure the services of a permanent secretary and before the end of the year (Sir) Vincent Evans was appointed to the post which he filled until his death in 1930. When he was also appointed secretary of the Cymmrodorion Society in 1887, again filling the post until his death, the London-based exile from Merionethshire held the reins of two institutions with the capacity to contribute greatly to the well-being of Welsh culture. Regrettably, Evans's autocratic manner and over-long reign were to prove a considerable obstacle to a new generation of reformers after the First World War who wanted a genuinely Welsh National Eisteddfod. In 1881, however, Evans's appointment was much welcomed and with the statement of accounts at the Merthyr meeting showing a sum of £103.7.6. in the bank, there were grounds for optimism. Sir Hugh Owen—he was knighted in August 1881—was too ill to travel to Merthyr and he died in November much mourned by his countrymen. He left behind him, however, a revived National Eisteddfod cast very much in his own image and his utilitarian,anglicizing influence would pervade it for many years after his death. English, for him, was the essential language of eisteddfod reform and when Lewis Morris, whom Owen nominated at the Shrewsbury meeting in 1880, thought it inappropriate that he, as a non-Welsh speaker, should be appointed chairman of the Council, he was assured by the nation's favourite Welsh poet, Ceiriog, that his appointment would preclude accusations of 'clannishness' and Professor John Rhŷs was rewarded with ready laughter when he wittily observed, 'Who cannot speak English?' Sir Hugh Owen's eisteddfod work had been done and he could rest content in 1881.

The Merthyr National Eisteddfod, 30 August-2 September 1881, had many expectations to fulfil and not a few suspicions to allay. The local committee appointed David Rosser as its chairman, Rhys T. Williams as its secretary and W. Merchant as its treasurer—the three having had experience of organizing the Cardiff and Swansea *eisteddfodau* of 1879 and 1880. Both Rosser and Merchant lived in Pontypridd, Merchant as manager of the town branch of the Bank of Wales, and Williams's home was in Treherbert where he would continue to live until some three months before the eisteddfod when he would move into temporary accommodation in Merthyr. The committee in appointing their chief officers could scarce have foreseen the problems that would arise when the time came to dispose of 'the surplus'. Not even the appointment of the High Constable of Merthyr—David Williams and subsequently Gwilym James—as Rosser's vice-chairman served to prevent an unsavoury squabble over the division of the spoils as we shall see.

After deciding as late as the beginning of August that the Market Hall would not answer the needs of a National Eisteddfod, the committee hired Wingfield and Company of Gloucester to erect a pavilion in Penydarren Park—a skeletal construction of wood and canvas, 205 by 80 feet—with seating for some six thousand people and a gallery provided by James Bros., Cowbridge. A proposal to site the pavilion on the Post Office field was defeated by 18 votes to 7 on the grounds that it was too small; some of the objectors also argued that its location in the rougher quarter of Merthyr would expose the town's 'moral sores' to public view. Rhys T. Williams ensured that railway excursions from near and far would bring the crowds to Merthyr for a reasonable fare—the GWR and the LNW, for example, set the return from Liverpool, Birkenhead and Warrington at 9s.6d, from Chester and Wrexham at 8s and from Oswestry at 7s.6d—and in the press he boasted that a large contingent of Welsh Americans had already crossed the Atlantic bound for Merthyr, with still more to follow. He implored South Walians to behave in a manner that would give North Walians no cause to flaunt their moral superiority as 'eisteddfodwyr', emphasizing that the sale of alcohol was forbidden in the Park and warning that no 'unsteady' competitors would be allowed to appear on stage. All poets, in particular, were expected to do their duty by the 'National'.

Monday, 30 August, was a depressing day. Heavy rain ensured a large expanse of glutinous mud which appears to have followed the 'National' around ever since, the pavilion had not been finished and one 'eisteddfodwr' was to have a narrow escape when three supports were blown down by a high wind which, like the mud, has regularly made its presence felt since 1881. Clwydfardd, the Archdruid, found to his horror that the Gorsedd circle located at the Market square was not such as to inspire awe!: 'A small kerb stone had to do duty for the sacred altar and the circle was composed of ordinary stones and bricks picked up from the streets, and placed in an irregular manner on the square at considerable distances from each other'.

Gwilym Cowlyd, the singularly quixotic bard from Llanrwst who had been appointed by the committee to attend to the 'correctness' of the Gorsedd ceremonies, was later observed directing a labourer with a barrowload of redemptive stones towards the 'irregular' circle, and the Reverend William Thomas (Glanffrwd), vicar at St. Asaph, a native of Ynys-y-bŵl, poet and one of the eisteddfod conductors sought to make good the Gorsedd's shabbiness by making the most extravagant claims for its sacerdotal antiquity when expatiating on 'The Gorsedd in its Relation to Christianity; or, The Past of the Celts and the Future of the World'. It would have made Iolo Morganwg blush. He happily speculated that it probably originated with Adam naming all creatures, insisted that it had been a fount of all knowledge throughout the ages from which the bards continued to draw and proclaimed that in its present state it was indeed a Christian institution wherein 'we swear an oath of fidelity to its "Hu" (God), of honour to our country, of loyalty to our Queen, of love to our fellow-countrymen, of zeal towards the language of our fathers—in the name of God and all Goodness —we are at the gorsedd, in the face of the Sun and in the Eye of Light—here dieth dissimulation and perisheth ignorance; prejudice cannot live in the light of this gorsedd . . . ' It was an address to contort the features of all progressives in a collective wince.

Tuesday brought its share of woe. A mere thousand or so occupied the pavilion, a bitterly disappointing audience which, it was claimed, was more the result of 'the depression of trade' than the wretched weather. Particularly upsetting was the failure of the pavilion lights during the opening evening concert, for they were not the customary gaslights. The inaugural National Eisteddfod of what is a continuing series was symbolically lit by electricity, six lamps having been obtained from the Cardiff representatives of the 'Brush Electric Light' patentees at a cost of £50, the power for driving the dynamo supplied by the engine of the

Merthyr Local Board's road roller stationed on a pathway. When the two popular singers, Marian Williams and Martha Harries, were about to launch into duet, 'Trust her not', five of the six lamps went out, prompting a wag in the audience to point dramatically at the sixth, and shout, 'Trust "her" not!' No sooner had they finished and Joseph Parry had appeared on stage than it failed, leaving the pavilion in darkness. One hundred years later, during the first morning session of the Machynlleth National Eisteddfod, a power cut again brought proceedings to a stop, but as in 1881 it was to prove no more than a temporary hindrance. The show went on and still goes on.

There was a palpable desire that the first official Merthyr 'National' should do Wales proud and it was a severe blow when the Prince of Wales declined an invitation to preside at one of the meetings and further refused, along with his brother, the Duke of Edinburgh, to let his name be included in the list of patrons. Not even Tennyson's appearance on a lengthy list of honorary vice-presidents could ease the hurt and the Welsh-language press in particular inveighed against the Prince's philistinism, his wantonness and sheer disregard for Wales. The Eisteddfod, in future, should not demean itself by trying to entice him from his fleshpots. In mitigation of the Prince, *The Times* stated that he had been warned by the government against accepting the invitation because the National Eisteddfod was 'a relic of the old Welsh constitution' and the Prince in supporting it would be endangering the Union! It was a comment worthy of the 'Say No' campaigners of 1997.

More weird proof of the nation's obsession with its moral standing came in May, 1881, from Cardiganshire where the Reverend Dr. T. C. Edwards, Principal of the University College at Aberystwyth outraged the Methodist Sanhedrin by supporting the Athletics Club's sportsday careless of the fact that alcohol could be bought on the field. He was found wanting, a conclusion which triggered a slashing anonymous defence of his conduct in the Methodist weekly, *Y Goleuad*, its author gleefully taunting the 'Cardis' with tales of their animal lusts. The furore attracted the mocking English press and an enraged David Davies, MP, the Llandinam Midas, thundered in the Methodist Association meeting at Llanidloes that he was prepared to spend his last penny to unmask the wretch who had so embarrassed him and his friends. London's journalists so blackened Wales that they had to hide their heads in shame—a sorry plight for one who had long since discarded brown bread for white.

The matter was still sufficiently painful for Archdeacon John Griffiths to revert to it anxiously when he opened the Cymmrodorion Section on Monday evening, 30 August. He was primarily concerned to convince 'eisteddfodwyr' that they had nothing to fear from the Cymmrodorion who had no intention of destroying the character of the old institution. On the contrary, they were benefactors who sought 'by their labours to add to the usefulness and stability of the old institution' as they were 'impressed with the belief that it can be made capable of producing more practical good to their fellow-countrymen than it has hitherto done, and of becoming a more beneficial institution in the land'. Nothing would better illustrate the value of the Cymmrodorion Section than its practical concern for the moral welfare of the working class and its encouragement of domestic reforms that would preclude the kind of lowering comment which the anonymous writer in *Y Goleuad* had subjected them to. What mattered was that the National Eisteddfod became 'an institution of real lasting good'; that was what its enlightened supporters most wanted and Archdeacon Griffiths as he had done in the 1860s when President of the 'The Eisteddfod', was eager to tell 'eisteddfodwyr'—the character of whose eisteddfod the Cymmrodorion had no wish to change!—what they should straight away accede to:

The day has long passed when 'Yr Eisteddfod' can move in a narrow groove of selfishness or national exclusiveness. Let 'Oes y Byd i'r Iaith Gymraeg' be written on its banners, but let it not be forgotten that 'Iaith y Saeson' has become the great vehicle of thought, of information, and of culture, and that we Welshmen dare not dispute it, or live in ignorance of it, if we would occupy our right place amongst the nationalities that compose the great English nation.

Viscount Tonypandy could not have put it better and it was fitting that the Archdeacon was thanked by C. H. James, MP, who earlier on Whit-Monday, during the Mountain Ash Chair Eisteddfod, had urged the Welsh to accept philosophically the imminent death of their mother tongue.

Of the four invited Day Presidents, only Henry Richard, MP, appeared. Lewis Morris substituted for Sir Hugh Owen on Tuesday, the Reverend John Griffith, Rector of Merthyr, did likewise for Sir Watkin Williams Wynn, MP, on Wednesday as did Archdeacon John Griffiths for Sir Edward J Read, KCB, MP, on Friday. Henry Richard alone saw fit to speak Welsh, remarking that it was 'rather inconsistent that the proceedings at an eisteddfod—an institution so closely connected with the music, poetry, literature, and history of Wales, should be conducted in a foreign language'. He recognised that the over-use of English reflected Welsh apprehension of metropolitan mockery but the eisteddfod no longer had to fear the slings and arrows of outrageous journalism. As an institution for the elevation of working people, England could put nothing in the field to compete with it: its detractors had been made to eat humble pie. Furthermore, there was no denying its influence on a strikingly loyal people who did not aspire to home rule—they merely expected fair treatment. The eisteddfod had no sinister, hidden political agenda and Richard quoted, to much laughter and applause, the comment of a distinguished member of the government who, when passing through the lobby for yet another vote on the Irish question, said, 'What a pity that Ireland is not inhabited by the Welsh'. The eisteddfod was a gushing mouthpiece for British Wales.

The Western Mail, which never forgave him for ousting Lord Aberdare leave alone his persistent censure of Toryism,found Richard's speech abrasive and self-serving, choosing to ignore the fact that the Rector of Merthyr the day before had been just as critical of disparaging English journalism and even louder in his claims for the cultural benefits accruing to the Welsh people from their eisteddfod exertions. It seemed that in 1881 the Reverend John Griffith hoped at last to eradicate the memory of his testimony in 1847 before R. R. W. Lingen, one of the three ill-famed commissioners of the 1846-47 enquiry, which on account of the harshness of its condemnation of the moral laxity of the womenfolk in his Aberdare parish, marked him out for unremitting Nonconformist enmity. Both in tone and content his testimony in 1881 could not have differed more from that of 1847 and it chimed with Richard's sentiments the following day as sweetly as it did with Archdeacon Griffiths's presidential address on the closing day. He even echoed the Archdeacon's insistence in 1867 that the eisteddfod was not concerned to safeguard the Welsh language because it did not need supporting: 'They spoke now the very language that was spoken 2,000 years ago, and they did not allow it to sink into a state of corruption—they spoke the language in which Taliesin wrote in the sixth century, and they did not intend to give it up'. From year to year in the 'Nationals' after 1881 the Welsh language was fed a diet of like-sounding English assurances of its secure position in the people's affections. It did not need to be heard as often as English.

The Wednesday and Friday meetings of the Cymmrodorion Section were determinedly earnest, well-intentioned affairs and thoroughly consistent with the 'raison d'être' of the 'Social Science Section' of the 1860s. The worker's best interests were targeted by the Reverend T. D. Jones, Tonyrefail and David Jones (Dafydd Morganwg) in papers on 'The Collier's Home Life' and (in Welsh) 'Coal and Collieries'. On Friday, 2 September, Dr. Humpidge from the University College at Aberystwyth read a paper on 'Wasted Energy and Materials in Wales' in which he stressed the huge importance to Wales of converting its abundant water resources into sources of motive power—particularly electricity It was a paper that anticipated an exciting future and its arguments, in retrospect, highlight so many lost opportunities. Dr. Humpidge was followed by Mr. W. Davies who read a paper by Mr. T. Fawcett, MA, headmaster of Merthyr Tydfil Proprietary School on 'Education in the Merthyr District'—a paper which elicited a peppery response because it found the education provided by the Board schools for 'the boys of the middle classes in the hill districts of Glamorganshire', as it put it, 'lamentably deficient', contrasting 'most unfavourably with that of the middle classes not only in England but also in the Colonies'. And as if that were not enough he also scorned the calls for intermediate schools as a blatant ploy by people who could well afford to pay the fees of a good middle-class school 'to get their children educated, to a great extent, at the expense of the ratepayers'. Needless to say, Mr. Fawcett's views were opposed, politely by Archdeacon Griffiths and hotly by T. Marchant Williams and the Reverend Dr. Thomas Rees who thought that he was simply intent on advertising his school.

Education had been the prime subject of concern in the National Eisteddfod since the inception of the 'Social Science Section' in 1862 and it was again centre stage at Merthyr in 1881 where Lewis Morris and Henry Richard in their presidential addresses and T. Marchant Williams in his paper on 'Higher and Intermediate Education in Wales' before the Cymmrodorion, explained the nature and significance of the Report of the Departmental Committee—the epochal Aberdare Report (1880)—and urged its acceptance by the nation. (Interestingly, the Sunday Closing Act was not debated or celebrated in the Merthyr National—victory having been assured—Archdeacon Griffiths in his closing speech contenting himself with a plea for 'the resuscitation of the Sunday Schools, which had been of so much value to Wales'; he hoped 'that the old spirit of interest in this noble institution would be revived').

Morris and Richard had served as members of the Departmental Committee for the preceding twelve months which Morris believed had been 'the happiest, and I think the most useful of my life'. His only regret was that the Cymmrodorion Section had not been in place earlier to assist the Committee in its deliberations. They had discovered that there was higher education provision for a mere 3,000 boys in Wales and of those available places a mere 1,570 were taken up. The committee had considered how best to provide an educational ladder so that 'there is nothing to prevent a Welsh boy, or Welsh girl, of promise and ability to climb to the very top'. The Aberdare Report showed the way forward and its proposals merely required a little financial sacrifice by the Welsh people to make them bear fruit. They did not have to beg for government support:

It rests with the people to consider whether by any small sacrifice they may make they cannot do something to make the history of our country better than it has yet been in the past—of the God-fearing, the law-abiding, the devout, the often-gifted,and the always—intelligent men and women who form the population of Wales.

Henry Richard in calling on the country to unite behind the report echoed Morris's sentiments and it was left to T. Marchant Williams to enter into its details which he did at length and with relish, leaving Lewis Morris to bewail the fact that time did not permit a proper discussion of his presentation. One can sympathize with him for Marchant Williams had been dealing with the future of education in Wales in a way that bore comparison with the famous 'Social Science Section' meeting at the Swansea National in 1863 when Dr. Thomas Nicholas and Hugh Owen instigated a debate on 'Higher Education and a University for Wales' which led directly to the opening of the University College at Aberystwyth in 1872.

The enthusiasts of the Cymmrodorion Section signalled their determination in Merthyr to focus serious attention on issues of national importance to Wales, believing that their meetings would have a large part to play in securing a proper recognition of legitimate Welsh aspirations further afield. Indeed, the revived National Eisteddfod saw itself from the outset as the authentic voice of Wales and the decision to send a telegram of commiseration to Mrs. Garfield and the American people, expressing the hope that President James A. Garfield would recover from the attempt to assassinate him, was loudly applauded when it was read out by Lewis Morris, the Council chairman:

> The National Eisteddfod of Wales desires to express its sympathy with Mrs Garfield and the people of America in their very great trouble, and its hope for the President's speedy recovery.

Morris, together with C. H. James, MP, emphasized the strong ties between Wales and America, and 'the vast company, at the request of the chairman, stood up, and uncovered, the proposition being agreed to unanimously'. President Garfield died and in 1882, at the Denbigh National Eisteddfod, the poets in contention for the Crown had to write in praise of him. He became one of the many foreign figures of renown whom the National Eisteddfod, seemingly as proof of its readiness to relate to the world at large, has over the years seen fit to commemorate. The fact that Dafydd Rhys Williams's eulogy of Garfield in 1882 was a somewhat leaden poem did not render the exercise futile. It was the intent that mattered.

Literature, in either language, was not well served in the first Merthyr National. The prize-winning compositions were not published so that one of the National Eisteddfod Association's primary objectives was not realized. The 'surplus', even had it not been lost in a thicket of wrangles, had been earmarked for the promotion of music—music being the food of Welsh satisfaction. Rhys T. Williams excitedly announced in the press that a body of competitive literature—385 compositions weighing as much as 93lbs—had been submitted for adjudication, but its quality was to prove somewhat lighter. The 'eisteddfodwyr' enjoyed the Gorsedd razzle-dazzle as two popular poets, namely Evan Rees (Dyfedfab, later shortened to Dyfed) was chaired for his 'awdl' on 'Cariad' (Love)—he also won prizes for a satirical poem on 'Collfarnwyr yr Eisteddfod'(The Eisteddfod's Detractors) and a descriptive poem on 'Y Newyddiadur'(The Newspaper)—and the Reverend Watkin Hezekiah Williams (Watcyn Wyn) was awarded £20 and a gold medal for his 'pryddest' on 'Bywyd' (Life). The Reverend Rowland Williams (Hwfa Môn) delivered an oration 'on the undying character of the Welsh nation' which 'roused the audience to a pitch of excitement seldom witnessed . . . He seemed to assume, before one's very eyes, the character of a kingly priest of the Druids'. Dyfed and Watcyn Wyn, both young and former colliers, were lionised. Dyfed was subsequently to serve as Archdruid for twenty-one years and Watcyn Wyn was to achieve the status of a 'national character', but their exploits in 1881 were not long remembered.

Not even a ten-guinea epic on 'Duc Wellington'(The Duke of Wellington) by Morgan Rees Williams of Cefncoedycymer lived to tell its tale after the passing of the Merthyr National, no more than did the two-guinea poem to 'Tydfil Ferthyres'(Tydfil the Martyr) by Miss Parry of Llandudno in a competition 'restricted to females'. The ladies were castigated for their imperfect grammar. And subjects which might have been expected to inspire poetry of lively interest—for example, ten guineas and a gold medal were offered for a poem on 'Iolo Morganwg' and Dame Edith Wynne-Agabeg (Eos Cymru—the Welsh Nightingale), offered six guineas for an 'awdl' on 'Cadeirio'r Bardd' (Chairing the Bard), pointing out its stimulating influence on the people'—failed to do so. If subjects of such a 'congenial' nature proved less than fruitful it was hardly surprising that five guineas and a silver medal for a 'cywydd' on 'Haearn'(Iron) failed to spark inspiration. The poets of the Victorian eisteddfod by and large had very little to say to industrial Wales and a subject of splendid relevance in Merthyr, of all places, wrought only cast iron cynghanedd, the prize being shared by two poets from North Wales. 'Plain John' 's complaint in *The Merthyr Express* on reading the Eisteddfod programme was indeed justified: 'No coal, or iron, or steel worker has been thought worthy of being invited to give his mite of practical wisdom respecting what digging and delving has suggested to them. It seems that all this is of no account in this gorsedd of celebrated bards and trombone blowers'.

The essays submitted, if not remarkable for their literary distinction, could at least be welcomed on the grounds of usefulness, not that all the subjects set bore fruit. It must have been a great disappointment to the committee when a prize of £10 offered for an essay on 'The Genius of the late Thomas Stephens' had to be withheld as neither of the two competitors deserved it. Their disappointment must have been the greater in knowing that sixteen essays (not exceeding twenty pages) had been written on 'The Life, Character, and Achievements of Sir William Jones' for a prize of three guineas which was won by Mr. William Evans, barrister, of Merthyr. Professor John Rhŷs had also to withhold a prize of twenty guineas for an essay on 'The Orthography of the Welsh Language' and the Rector of Merthyr's five guineas for an essay (Welsh or English) on 'The Sports, pastimes and amusements of the Welsh people in the last century, with a view of showing the effect they had upon the national character', likewise went a-begging.

Of the subjects that bore fruit, the Welsh essay by Robert Pryse (Gweirydd ap Rhys) on 'The History of Religion in Wales from 500 AD to 1280' was adjudged the best of the four submitted and worthy of the prize of ten guineas. Five lengthy essays were submitted on 'The History of the Literature of Monmouthshire and Glamorganshire from the earliest period to the present time', the prize of twenty guineas and a gold medal being awarded to Charles Wilkins, Merthyr Tydfil's literary postmaster who was seen locally as Thomas Stephens's successor. Wilkins would incorporate his eisteddfod writings in *The History of the Literature of Wales from 1300 to 1650* which he published in 1884 and along with Gweirydd ap Rhys he is a good example of the way in which *eisteddfodau* enabled talented, industrious 'amateurs' to make valid contributions in fields of study which to date had attracted very little academic attention.

The emphasis placed on usefulness from the outset by the National Eisteddfod Association was very well illustrated by three other prose competitions, the first offering a prize of sixteen guineas for an essay (Welsh or English) on 'The Advantages and

Disadvantages of Incorporating Merthyr Tydfil', which was won by D. J. Rowlands, an accountant at the Brecon Old Bank in Merthyr who wrote in Welsh; the second offering a prize of ten guineas for a Welsh essay on 'The Cause or Causes of Periodical Panics, which bring about the prosperity and depression of trade, and is it possible to avoid it', which was divided between the Reverends J. R. Thomas (Ap Tydfil) of Narberth and Owen Jones, MA, Newtown; and the third offering another prize of ten guineas (one of the donors was Mr. Frank James, president of the Merthyr Chamber of Trade) for an essay (Welsh or English) on 'The adaptability of Merthyr for the establishing and carrying on of other trades than those already carried on there', which was divided between Mr. John Howells, St.Athan and the Reverend William Thomas, Gwynfe. These essays of 1881, unfortunately, were not made available to a wide readership in an official eisteddfod publication but after the Cardiff National in 1883 the Association published an annual volume of prize-winning compositions and adjudications which constitute a primary research source of undeniable value to students of Welsh culture.

The National Eisteddfodau of the 1860s had shunned the novel, fiction having no part to play in the Council's plans to elevate the life of the nation. Much to their credit, the promoters of the 1881 venture saw fit to follow the lead given by the *eisteddfodau* of the Merthyr Temperance Cymmrodorion in the 1850s when the novel was welcomed, admittedly for propaganda purposes, and in 1855 brought into prominence when two novels depicting the life of the reformed drunkard were published. Lewis Lewis (Llew Llwyfo) of Anglesey took the prize with his tale of *Llewelyn Parri* but it is generally agreed now that Richard Roberts's *Jeffrey Jarman* was the better novel. Llew Llwyfo's work was essentially a moral fable and no doubt fashioned to satisfy the organizers's expectations. Probably the most versatile and certainly not the most abstemious 'eisteddfodwr' of his day, Llew Llwyfo would have had no difficulty in championing temperance for the sake of his thirst.

The fact remains that the Welsh novel was given its first eisteddfod boost in Merthyr in 1855 and it was in keeping with the town's radicalism that a prize of three guineas, donated by Mr. Walter Lloyd, the proprietor of the popular Welsh weekly, *Y Gwladgarwr*, should be offered in 1881 and won by Isaac Craigfryn Hughes, a collier from Quaker's Yard whose novel, *Rhys Trefor*,was published that same year along with his more successful *Y Ferch o Gefn Ydfa*—yet another retelling of the Ann Maddocks melodrama. *Rhys Trefor*, sad to say, soon disappeared without trace but Merthyr had again made plain that the 'National' had a duty to the Welsh novel. It was a duty that would be grudgingly recognized but a start had been made.

There was, however, nothing grudging in the 1881 National's recognition of music, in particular vocal music, as its 'sine qua non'. It had been so since the first major eisteddfod choral competition in the Swansea National in 1863 and the feats of Caradog's 'Côr Mawr y De' in the Crystal Palace in 1872 and 1873 had released a gush of triumphalism which showed no sign of abating in 1881. Commanding the wonder of all on the front of the platform with the display of flowers and plants sent from Cyfarthfa Castle Gardens was the huge Crystal Palace Challenge Trophy. There could be no more palpable proof of the epiphany of 'The Land of Song'.

A self-assuring array of native talents was assembled to reinforce the image of a people singing to command approving attention. On the panel of adjudicators Dr. Joseph Parry, Caradog, Ivander Griffiths, Dr. William Frost and the Reverend Edward Stephen (Tanymarian) were considered every bit as authoritative as J. Spencer Curwen of the Tonic

Sol-fa College in London, and of the soloists who came to Merthyr to be feted a number of them, such as Mary Davies, Martha Harries, Lizzie Williams, Ben Davies and James Sauvage had distinguished themselves at the Royal Academy of Music and were accomplished professional performers. Lewis Thomas, of Welsh parentage although born in Bath, had been one of Britain's greatest bass singers since the 1850s and Robert Rees (Eos Morlais) had emerged in the 1870s as the first in a long line of Welsh tenors who became household names. He did not opt for a professional career contenting himself with giving unstinting support to such as Megan Watts of Dowlais and Ben Davies of Pontardawe in their efforts to succeed professionally, but he captivated Welsh audiences in a way that no other tenor, excepting David Lloyd, ever succeeded in doing. Born and bred a miner in Dowlais, together with Joseph Parry, the harpist William Frost and David Bowen who accompanied Caradog's 'Côr Mawr', he incarnated the passion for music which made Merthyr, together with the Cynon, Rhondda and Swansea valleys, one of the powerhouses of 'The Land of Song' on the threshhold of the 1880s. As if in response to his presence, sixteen tenors competed for a prize of two guineas for singing 'The Sorrow's of Death' (Mendelssohn's *Hymn of Praise*), the adjudicators failing to separate David Davies, Treherbert, Thomas Felix, Treorchy and David Howells, Aberaman—three 'eminent tenors' who were rewarded with a guinea each.

It had long been established before 1881 that the financial success of the National Eisteddfod depended on the drawing power of concerts and choral competitions. The comparative neglect of instrumental music had been a cause of concern for musicians who demanded more from the 'National' than 'big lung contests', but progress was slow. In 1881 Joseph Parry was glad to see Merthyr giving a lead by offering a prize of seven guineas for the orchestral band (not less than eight in number) who would give the best performance of 'Le Calife de Baghdad'. Two bands from Merthyr and Treherbert competed, the prize being awarded to the Merthyr band whose playing showed more promise than finesse in a competition which Parry wanted to see encouraged. Indeed, he was to seize his opportunity to draw attention to the fact that there was no institution in Wales for instructing and educating would-be musicians who for a variety of reasons could not progress to London. The Aberdare Report gave the wants of Welsh music scant regard and Parry feared 'that unless some efforts be made for higher culture in music we shall have a certain low standard of mediocrity without a sufficient number excelling'. His determination to make good the deficiency by establishing the 'Musical College of Wales, Swansea' proved that he was not merely fishing for eisteddfod applause.

The competitions for fife and drum bands and brass bands (not less than twelve in number) also aroused much interest. The Llantrisant and Penydarren fife and drum bands shared the first prize of five guineas for playing any three Welsh airs, and the famed Cyfarthfa Brass Band, conducted by George Livesey, won the twenty guineas and gold medal for playing Handel's 'We never will bow down', defeating the Morriston Artillery Band, The Neath Volunteer Band, and the bands of Corris, Merthyr and Tredegar. Corris won the second prize, a baby trombone valued at eighteen guineas, and they were loudly cheered if only because not a single choir from North Wales saw fit to compete in the Merthyr National. In his adjudication, Ivander Griffiths, who had made his home in Workington, compared the six brass bands unfavourably with the standard of playing achieved by the bands of Yorkshire and Lancashire, thereby antagonizing many of Cyfarthfa's admirers whose resentment was voiced by *The Merthyr Express*. Given the intensity of the support for bands and choirs it is not surprising that adjudicators were wont to lavish superlatives before giving their decisions. It was often good practice to mollify losers before putting them in their place.

Of the individual instrumentalists who took prizes in 1881, one fourteen year old in particular was to enjoy a considerable professional reputation as a flautist. Frederic Griffith, born in Swansea in 1867, won first prize for playing the piccolo and by 1896, when he edited *Notable Welsh Musicians (Of To-day)*, he had established himself in London, had toured with Melba and been appointed solo flute at the Royal Italian Opera, Covent Garden. He was to triumph again at Cardiff, 1883, Liverpool, 1884 and Aberdare, 1885, before entering the Royal Academy of Music and subsequently receiving further tuition in Paris from Paul Taffanel, 'the greatest of all flautists'. Not since the young Merthyr harpist, William Frost, an adjudicator in 1881, had won Pencerdd Gwalia's harp scholarship at Swansea in 1863, had the National Eisteddfod unearthed such a talented instrumentalist—and Griffith was to eclipse Frost's accomplishments.

The 1881 National also gave further prominence to a young North Walian composer of songs by the name of R. S. Hughes, dubbed 'the Arthur Sullivan of Wales' before his death at the age of thirty-eight in 1893. At the South Wales Eisteddfod in Swansea in 1880, two of his songs, 'Y Dymestl' for the bass-baritone voice and 'Arafa Don' for the tenor voice, had won him acclaim and remain to this day firm favourites with Welsh audiences. 'Y Dymestl' was the test-piece for baritones in 1881 and in a competition which attracted thirty-four entrants, the prize was shared between Dan Price of Dowlais who would go on to excel as a professional singer, and Gwilym Thomas, one of the three legendary heroes of the Tynewydd pit rescue in April 1877. Thomas was also to win the competition for bass voices outright and his presence on the Merthyr stage was seen as powerful proof of the uplifting influence of music on the Welsh working classes. R. S. Hughes took two first prizes, three guineas for the best baritone song to English and Welsh words and five guineas for the best soprano song suitable to be sung at the 'chairing of the bard', and before his untimely death he would be in the front rank of native composers who emerged in the 1870s and 80s to fuel an unprecedented pride in the nation's God-given gift of song.

That pride, as many a fracas following a choral competition illustrates, could be an unlovely thing to hear and see. The choirs in 1881 behaved impeccably—perhaps the absence of a challenger from North Wales in the chief choral competition helped—but an unlikely clash between North and South which rumbled on in the press for weeks after the Merthyr National saw the Reverend Edward Stephen (Tanymarian) disagreeing violently with Joseph Parry and J. Spencer Curwen over the withholding of the prize for a cantata on 'Cantre'r Gwaelod'. Tanymarian, whose oratorio 'Ystorm Tiberias' and concert appearances as a 'fashionable' ballad singer had endeared him to audiences since the 1850s, was convinced that Parry and Curwen had colluded to deprive his fellow-North Walian, W. Jarrett Roberts,of the prize he believed he fully merited and the ensuing furore did nothing for the image of a reformed eisteddfod, given that the three adjudicators could have been expected to be above such a wretched business. It proves, however, that the premium attaching to the status of 'National Winner' in a small country long starved of attention could have lowering results.

According to Tanymarian's account, he and Curwen had agreed that Roberts's cantata deserved the prize and Roberts went to Merthyr to receive it—Tanymarian subsequently denying that he had anything to do with informing him of the adjudicators's decision! Parry decided that none of the competitors was worthy of the twenty guineas and gold medal offered by the London Welsh Choral Society and the Merthyr Eisteddfod committee, particularly since it was intended to perform the successful work in London. On being told by Parry in Merthyr that they had the right as adjudicators to withhold the prize, Curwen concurred with him, and on announcing their joint decision the storm broke. It did not help that Roberts had been at the receiving end of a similar decision at the Conway Eisteddfod in 1879, when Joseph Parry and Dr. Roland Rogers disagreed with Tanymarian and gave the prize for a motet to W. T. Rees (Alaw Ddu)—a South Walian. When Roberts solicited Sir Julius Benedict's opinion on the two compositions, he sided with Tanymarian, which did little for Roberts's equanimity. The Merthyr affair was enough to convince him that he was the victim of prejudice.

It was a dismal experience for Parry whose probity—unjustly—was called into question by sections of the Welsh press, Llew Llwyfo in particular giving a vengeful, North Walian view of things in the leading Welsh weekly, *Baner ac Amserau Cymru*. It is to his credit that he continued to adjudicate in major *eisteddfodau* without ever being subjected to another such assault on his character—his competence was never in doubt—but it was a sore trial so soon after his rancorous departure from his post at Aberystwyth University College, to find himself the target of detractors in the first of the revived National Eisteddfodau at Merthyr, his home town, of all places.

And no less bitter an experience must have been what he considered the disastrous performance of his oratorio, *Emmanuel*, by the Merthyr Harmonic Society. The Eisteddfod committee, anxious to display its progressive intentions, staged a first performance of David Jenkins's cantata, *David and Saul*, by the Rhymney United Choir with orchestral accompaniment, on the Wednesday evening, to be followed by *Emmanuel* on Thursday. Jenkins's intensive preparations saw the choir and artistes—Martha Harries, Marian Williams, Ben Davies and James Sauvage—under his baton give a performance that was well received, but *Emmanuel,* an exacting oratorio with some twenty-five choruses, was a laborious business for all concerned. It lasted for three and a half hours without intermission! First performed at St. James's Hall in London in May, 1880, Joseph Parry had high hopes for it in the Merthyr National. He had written to the committee requesting that English artistes should sing the chief solo parts—the subordinate parts could be entrusted to 'secondary' artistes—because he wanted the work to make an impression in England. The committee agreed but in the event Parry had to make do with Welsh singers,namely Mary Davies, Lizzie Evans, Lizzie Williams, Lewis Thomas, Ben Davies and Eos Morlais. A late attempt to replace the local conductor, Lewis Morgan, by Parry himself, saw the choir of some 280 voices threaten to go on strike and what followed, in his own words, was a fiasco: 'Silence is golden, and therefore I will say nothing at this point—it is better to bury it in the bottomless cauldron of all the dreadfuls of the past'. The general response to the performance was more appreciative—notwithstanding the patchy playing of the 'pro tem' orchestra assembled from Merthyr, Bristol and Gloucester and conducted by E. G. Woodward—but as the ambitious composer Parry felt badly let down and no amount of 'local boy' lionising would appease him.

Friday brought the 1881 National to a mighty choral conclusion when six mixed choirs, numbering between them some 1452 choristers, contested the prize of £100 and a gold medal for the conductor before a huge audience of some ten thousand people. Twenty-six railway excursions in all brought supporters in their thousands to witness the competition and the 'takings' at the gates say more than enough about the magnetism of the 'Chief Choral'. Tuesday's receipts amounted to £124.0.6; Wednesday's to £222.14.10; Thursday's to £509.15.11/2 and Friday's to £812.5.101/2. Penydarren Park was awash with some thirteen thousand 'eisteddfodwyr', all of whom seemed intent on seeing and hearing the choirs. It was a scene worthy of the talents of William Frith:

> From early morning the immense pavilion was crowded, and as the members of the various choirs came in hundreds, the operation of "stretching the cords of the tents" had to be gone through, and the canvas at the sides was lifted so that those outside could hear, and the breeze clear the heated atmosphere of the eisteddfod. For some time prior to this competition being commenced there was some little noise consequent upon the crowding, but, considering that there were in the tent its full complement of about 6,000 people, and that others were walking about outside, and that the majority of those were bent upon one of two objects—taking part in or hearing the choral contest, the only wonder is that matters went on so orderly.

Between Tuesday and Thursday, two competitions for male voice parties and two for congregational choirs had whetted the appetite for the 'Chief Choral'. In the first competition for male voice parties numbering twenty-five singers, the Taibach and Aberavon Glee Party conducted by Leyshon Davies had shared with Maesteg Minstrels, conducted by Evan Jenkins, the prize of five guineas and twenty-five copies of Curwen's *The Standard Course* (doubled by J. S. Curwen as a result of the draw) for singing 'The Tyrol' (Ambroise Thomas). In the second competition they were joined by the Morriston Glee Party, The Ton Glee Party and the Quarrymen of Glan Morlais in contesting another prize of five guineas and twenty-five copies of *The Standard Course* for singing David Jenkins's 'Cydgan y Chwarelwyr' (The Quarrymen's Chorus), which this time was won outright by the Morriston Glee Party conducted by David Francis, a Merthyr musician whose Merthyr Choir in winning all four choral competitions at the Chester National Eisteddfod in 1866 had caused a sensation, prompting *The Sunday Times* correspondent to say, 'That such a man should be compelled to work underground is . . . anything but creditable to his fellow-countrymen, and ought to be looked to forthwith'.

J. S. Curwen expressed himself well satisfied with the singing of the male voice parties and the congregational choirs likewise pleased the adjudicators. In the first competition for choirs numbering not less than sixty voices, a prize of £25 and a gold medal for the conductor was offered for singing the first part of John Ambrose Lloyd's sacred cantata, 'Gweddi Habacuc' (Habakkuk's Prayer). No choir was permitted to appoint a conductor from outside its own particular congregation but it was permissible to go outside for a soloist. Three choirs competed: David Francis conducted the Tabernacle Choir (Morriston), D. Coleman conducted the Caegarw Choir (Mountain Ash) and John Evans conducted the Bethania Choir (Dowlais)—Bethania was the chapel where the talents of Eos Morlais and Megan Watts had flowered under the encouragement of Abraham Bowen but on this occasion it had to yield to David Francis's Tabernacle singers. It is doubtful that his Merthyr roots made it easier for Bethania to succumb!

The second competition, under the same rules, for congregational choirs numbering not less than thirty voices, offered a prize of £10 and a silver medal for singing John Thomas's chorus, 'Yr Arglwydd sydd yn Teyrnasu' (The Lord reigns). Five choirs competed: Gellideg (Merthyr); Bethesda (Merthyr); Salem, Penyrheolgerrig (Merthyr); Soar (Hirwaun) and the victors, Siloh (Tredegar) conducted by David Jones. Joseph Parry found enough to praise in both competitions and thought that the three choirs contesting the prize of £25 could well have coped with a more difficult test. On the evidence of what they had heard the quality of Welsh congregational singing was quite justifiably a cause for national pride, its standard having improved dramatically over the past twenty years.

Six choirs each numbering between 150-300 voices, were primed after months of intensive preparation to sing the two test pieces, Mendelssohn's chorus, 'Ye nations, offer to the Lord' and D. Emlyn Evans's 'Haleliwia, Amen'. The six were: Rhondda Choral Union (240 voices), conducted by M. O. Jones; Ebbw Vale, Beaufort and Brynmawr Choir (220), conducted by Thomas Davies; Rhondda Philharmonic Society, Treorchy (250), conducted by D. T. Prosser (Eos Cynlais); Ebbw Vale Choir (287), conducted by David Bowen; Taibach and Aberavon United Choir (285), conducted by Leyshon Davies and Cardiff United Choir (170), conducted by D. C. Davies.

The anticipation of the audience was intensified by the knowledge that the Taibach and Aberavon Choir under Leyshon Davies should have been conducted by Silas Evans who had prepared them, as well as the male voice party, for the Merthyr National. A week before the actual competition he died at Swansea when rehearsing the choir that was to sing for the royal party at the opening of the Prince of Wales Dock in October, leaving behind a widow and six children with very little to support them. The Rector of Merthyr and Joseph Parry in alluding to his passing urged the setting up of a fund in recognition of Evans's contribution to the development of a Welsh choral tradition, noting that none had played a more significant part in the 50s and 60s in putting Aberdare and the Cynon valley at the heart of 'The Land of Song'. And the presence as adjudicator of Ivander Griffiths, who had led his Swansea Valley Choir against Silas Evans's Aberdare United Choir in that momentous competition at the Swansea National in 1863, served to deepen the poignancy of his early death.

But in delivering the adjudication Joseph Parry was happy to announce that 'the most important choral competition held in Wales to date' had been clearly won by the Rhondda Philharmonic Society, a result which highlighted the emergence of Treorchy as a centre of choral excellence which would, under the influence of 'Prosser bach' and his illustrious successors, assume almost mythical proportions. Prosser's choir excelled 'in control, and in attack, and smoothness, and finish, and harmonious melting and blending of the voices', and as was to happen regularly after 1881, the victorious conductor was greeted with tremendous cheering which lasted for many minutes. The great Victorian choirs provided the earliest opportunities for displays of national celebration following exploits on the fields of popular culture and 'eisteddfodwyr' certainly made the most of them. Martha Harries had sung 'The Lost Chord' with thrilling effect for her audience on Tuesday. 'Prosser bach' sent the thousands home on Friday content with the resonating glory of a Treorchy 'Hallelujah'.

The Merthyr committee in the immediate aftermath of the 1881 National breathed more than a sigh of relief. They 'anticipated' a surplus of some £600 and felt that a little self-congratulation would not be amiss. The press, by and large, saw little to censure and even the leading Welsh weekly *Baner ac Amserau Cymru,* after insisting on the superior North Walian way of organizing *eisteddfodau,* was ready to acknowledge the good start made in Merthyr. *The Western Mail* took *The Pall Mall Gazette* to task for penning what was, by London standards, an innocuous satire of the proceedings, accusing it of adopting 'a tone of contemptuous superiority' and indulging in 'Pecksniffian sneers'. The Eisteddfod, in so far as it satisfied 'a genuine need of the Welsh people', would 'successfully repel ridicule and opposition in the future'.

Local pride in what had been achieved was, however, best expressed in the editorial columns of *The Merthyr Express*. Comparing the National Eisteddfod with the Olympic Games of the ancient Greeks, 'we are decidedly disposed to award the highest honours to the Eisteddfod. The Eisteddfod is one of the grand moral agencies which promote conquests on the fields of peace'.

While the Games encouraged physical and martial prowess,

> . . . our Eisteddfod soars high above the animal nature and addresses itself exclusively to the culture of the intellectual faculties, the elevation of the moral and religious char- acter, and the ennobling of human nature, by diverting its highest and best energies from fields of blood and strife into the happier rivalries which make the victors con- querors indeed, but leave the vanquished themselves gainers in only an inferior degree.

Untroubled by the thought that not a few adjudicators and participants might have demurred at such a rosy account of competition, the editor also rhapsodized on the Eisteddfod as an institution which 'has been the rallying point of Welshmen, and the great bond of brotherhood between them during centuries of vicissitudes, sometimes bright and glowing, oftener dark and gloomy, and nothing can tear it from their hearts'. Its future was assured as long as it rejected 'much which provoked the smile of pity or the loud explosive laughter of ridicule'—a shaft directly aimed at the Gorsedd of Bards—and welcomed the kind of progressivism advocated by the Cymmrodorion which would attract 'the wealthy and educated classes from their reserve' to mix 'with their humbler countrymen and women upon a platform intended, and calculated under proper management, to work an immense amount of good for the Welsh nation at large'. Its value should inhere in its genuine worthi- ness, free of all gasconade, 'so as to defy the assaults of malevolent criticism and command the respect of the majority—the good will of all'.

When the Merthyr committee began to discuss the use to which the surplus should be put, good will was found to be in short supply and David Rosser, in particular, became the object of much suspicion. It had been obvious from the beginning of 1881 that there were two issues which troubled members of the committee. Rosser, Rhys T. Williams and W. Merchant, as chairman, secretary and treasurer respectively, had organized the South Wales Eisteddfod in Cardiff and Swansea in 1879 and 1880. The Swansea venture had left a debt of some £300 and it was known that the Cardiff surplus had been set against it. The Merthyr committee was adamant that should the 1881 National leave a surplus it would not be used to clear the Swansea debt, members declaring their unwillingness to sign a bond for a guar- antee fund unless they were assured of a voice in the disposal of the surplus, should there be any. Rosser, as chairman, insisted that the Swansea debt would not swallow up any Merthyr surplus, because although initially conceived as the third South Wales Eisteddfod, the Merthyr Eisteddfod of 1881 had assumed the status of a National Eisteddfod in accordance with the wishes of the reformers who deliberated at Caernarfon. It then followed that the surplus of a national venture could not be misappropriated to pay off local debts. At the end of February,1881, the Merthyr committee signed the bond.

It then remained to decide how the anticipated surplus should be properly put to national use and in the same meeting that saw the signing of the bond it was proposed: 'That the sur- plus of the eisteddfod be devoted to the foundation of musical scholarships for Welshmen in the Royal Academy of Music, London, and that the amount be invested in the names of the trustees to be hereafter appointed'. An amendment was moved that the word 'London' be omitted so that the University College at Aberystwyth might be open for candidates and appears to have been carried. Rosser was certainly of that opinion as his subsequent implacable opposition to boosting the Pencerdd Gwalia scholarship at the Royal Academy of Music shows.

In a letter which was read out in his absence at a committee meeting held at the Temperance Hall on 22 September, he complained that the total gate receipts amounting to £1,666.16.4. had not been transferred to the treasurer, W. Merchant. It transpired that sums had been withheld by the High Constable, Gwilym James, and his predecessor, David Williams, and it was decided that T. Howard and Henry Lewis be appointed to audit all the eisteddfod monies before any more should be released. It was felt that too much had been paid out already without the committee's sanction. The anticipated surplus of some £500 had already, according to the secretary, been halved, and it was obvious that the committee had no intention of being hurried along by Rosser.

In the October meeting a letter from Pencerdd Gwalia was read out, in which he entreated the committee to contribute to his fund for establishing 'A Permanent Scholarship for Wales at the Royal Academy of Music'. It then stood at £700 and his target was £1,000. They postponed their decision but voted by ten votes to four against Gwilym James's proposal to reward David Rosser's work as the committee chairman with a gratuity of £20, remarking that the honour accorded him was reward enough. So much for good will, leave alone generosity.

In November, the storm broke. A letter from Gwilym James informed the committee that he had met Pencerdd Gwalia in London and should he receive £200 of the Merthyr surplus he could launch his scholarship in January 1882. James urged the committee to support him but Rosser was not prepared to accept a motion to that effect, maintaining that they should adhere to their 'initial' proposal to establish a scholarship for the benefit of South Wales. In view of his intransigence, a motion that Rosser should vacate the chair was put, and on being lost by fourteen votes to twelve he promptly closed the meeting.

A letter to the press from Pencerdd Gwalia denied that he had put pressure on Rosser in anyway. He had merely reminded him that he was still waiting for the £10 Rosser had promised him for his fund after the Cardiff Eisteddfod in 1879. When the Merthyr committee met for the thirtieth time in December, 1881, Rosser was voted into the chair whereupon W. Thomas proposed that the surplus should be entrusted to a treasurer and four trustees, namely Gwilym James, David Williams, T. J. Webster and John Jones. An amendment proposing Rosser as a fifth trustee was put—and lost. Dan Evans, a Merthyr man, was appointed to replace the much praised Rhys T. Williams as secretary for the duration of the committee's life and Rosser found himself at the receiving end of a vote of thanks which he sardonically acknowledged.

Twenty years later the 'National' returned to Merthyr Tydfil. Of the 1881 surplus in excess of £200 it was said that some £50—what remained of it after pointless litigation between the Pontypridd and Merthyr factions—had been banked in the names of Gwilym James and Dr. T. J. Webster. By 1901 it had doubled in value so that Merthyr's second 'National' benefitted from the rancour which in 1881 frustrated Pencerdd Gwalia and left aspiring young musicians in South Wales without a compensatory scholarship. In the history of the National Eisteddfod 'the Merthyr squabble' is no more than one among many and no matter how regrettable they may have been in the view of earnest reformers and image-makers they all of them testify that the 'National' has been seen as crucial to the survival of a fraught culture. In 1881, Merthyr posed the question of how best to make use of it—a perennial question which has ensured the continuation of the 'National' as a boisterous, moveable feast to this day. May it soon return to Merthyr for the third time.

29B. W. Cadwaladr Davies

REFLECTIONS ON SOME SIXTEENTH-CENTURY
EAST GLAMORGAN GENTRY

by

J. GWYNFOR JONES

In the dedication of *A Breviat of Glamorgan* in 1596 to his kinsman Thomas Morgan of Rhiw'r Perrai (Ruperra), a descendant through a cadet branch of the famous Morgan family of Tredegar and steward to Henry Herbert, second earl of Pembroke, Rice Lewis, himself declared 'that syth it hath pleased God by his providence to make you a Glamorganshire man, and there withall to bringe you to the Credite of Authority with his honour who is greatest Lorde there', he was to be informed about 'the estate of that Countrey'. He doubtless regarded Glamorgan-born men of repute as being of the highest order. It was an age when emphasis was placed on locality and regional loyalty as much as on service to the Tudor monarchy. About the same time George Owen, that redoubtable squire of Henllys, had pleasant comments to make. His praises of that monarchy in 1594 was remarkably overt. He wrote in considerable detail on legal and administrative features of the government structure of Tudor Wales, and his applause for that dynasty was recorded in long passages which described how the accession of Henry Tudor to the throne and the policies adopted by his son Henry VIII to assimilate Wales with England had, in his view, created a new Wales:

> No country in England so flourished in 100 years as hath Wales done since the government of Henry VII to this time in so much that if our fathers were now living they would think it some strange country inhabited with a foreign nation, so altered is the country and countrymen, the people changed in heart within and the land altered in hue without, from evil to good and from bad to better.

In view of what Owen had to say it is evident that he and his contemporaries were writing exclusively as men of their time who had benefited substantially from the Tudor settlement and, even more, from the consequences of that remarkable social phenomenon which historians have generally labelled the 'rise of the gentry', which can be traced broadly over the previous two centuries. The Tudor myth, which historians have identified with the appearance of the 'son of prophecy', was publicized in the writings of social commentators because they possessed a distinct sense of loyalty to the dynasty by virtue of their ancestral affinities. It was enshrined in the belief that Henry Tudor had fulfilled the needs of Wales at the battle of Bosworth and had emancipated the Welsh nation. In reality, however, the gentry supported Henry chiefly because he was the only contestant to the throne in 1485 who could meaningfully fulfil their needs in the unstable social and economic circumstances of the time. As political leaders themselves their eyes were cast firmly on his policies and on the benefits that they could derive from them. Henry's more personal appeal, as illustrated by Owen needs, therefore, to be viewed with caution since it reflects a subjective view of sixteenth-century Wales. Despite his enthusiastic outburst, Owen, however, did have something positive to say about Wales of the Tudor period. It was certainly the era when the gentry 'came of age'. Landowners claiming Welsh ancestry, who had settled upon land or had inhabited towns and who dominated life in rural and urban Wales were known as *uchel-*

wyr (men of high birth), and their origins could be traced back for at least two centuries before the Tudor period. Their forebears emerged out of the declining social and economic order of the later Middle Ages, a process that was accelerated by the Owain Glyndŵr revolt. Many of them overcame the disabilities imposed by the anti-Welsh laws of Henry IV. They prospered chiefly through the acquisition of land rather than kindred relations and held administrative offices in the Principality and the old Marcher lordships. They also gradually broke down social and racial barriers through intermarriage between native Welsh and Anglo-Norman or English families. Despite the penal laws of Henry IV imposed chiefly on privileged individuals they strengthened the bonds with other members of powerful families, and it is evident that 'the age of the gentry' had been well established before the Acts of Union (1536-43) were enacted.

This study is designed to examine the landed gentry in one part of the old lordship of Glamorgan which, in 1536, was formally created a shire, together with Pembrokeshire, and five other new shires including Monmouthshire. It needs to be understood that both lordships of Glamorgan and Pembroke had for many years before 1536 been regarded as counties since they were under royal government and possessed the same administrative structure as English shires and those of the old Edwardian Principality in west and north Wales. Like other shires in Wales Glamorgan, stretching from Gower to the old cantref of Senghennydd (Also known as Cantref Breiniol), with its centre at Cardiff Castle, contained a large group of gentry families, varying in their material means and estates, whose proprietors served as administrators and leaders of their communities. A large amount of source material has survived enabling historians to study their backgrounds and activities, usually in the form of estate and family records, local government files and a miscellany of other materials which reflect the cultural and other interests of these privileged families. It is unfortunate that it is by means of such record evidence that historians largely learn what sources are available about the lower orders; historical sources relating to the underprivileged in Glamorgan society are therefore often seen through the eyes of others, and are limited and inadequate.

Any examination of the socio-economic history of east Glamorgan in the sixteenth century, for example, needs to take account of the prestige and authority enjoyed by the middle layers in society, between the aristocracy at the top end of the scale and the underprivileged at the other end. To the most prosperous of families land meant wealth and wealth gave them power and influence. They not only cared for their own individual interests but were also responsible for maintaining peace and good order in their localities, particularly at shire and parish levels. Indeed, it was by serving the government as administrators that they were best able to advance their fortunes as private landowners and tenants. They often used local offices to feather their own nests and to maintain the continuity of family interests. Public service, however, should not be regarded necessarily as the prime method of advancement but rather as one among a number of factors which assisted in building up the gentry order. Their milieu emerged through the blending of ancient lineage, ownership of land, administrative skill, prudent marriage alliances and business acumen.

Another aim in this chapter is to examine some aspects of gentry activities in east Glamorgan comprising broadly the upland and lowland region extending from the eastern edge of the vale of Glamorgan to the boundary at the river Rhymni between the old lordship of Glamorgan and the cantref of Gwynllwg. In this area, as elsewhere, there appeared families of mixed origins, different social status and background claiming gentility. They all formed distinct parts of the hierarchical structure that was normally accepted in those days. People usually knew to what social order they belonged, their assumptions based mainly on lineage and landed inheritance, and they were sensitively aware of the privileges and obligations appertaining to their rank. Society was also patriarchal whereby the head of the household, invariably the father, would assume a dominant role within the family and the region. As leader of his community, landed proprietor and head of his household he was aware of his responsibilities, and they, within the social structure, varied according to birth and lineage as well as occupation. The gentry of east Glamorgan were basically property owners or tenants who earned their living almost entirely off the land. Their incomes, most of which were very modest, were derived mainly from tenants' rents, the yield of agricultural produce and, where they existed, minerals on their estates. The most prosperous could afford to employ bailiffs or stewards to maintain their estates, thus enabling them to attend to other private and public affairs such as litigation and shire administration. Taken as a composite social group, however, the gentry were not sufficiently prosperous to be able to leave such estate duties to others, and normally they themselves, as farmers, would attend to their own needs and conduct their own business.

References have already been made to ancestry and status. These two basic factors are essential in any evaluation of the social standing of a squire or gentleman. Geographically and racially the gentry of east Glamorgan were divided into two broad sections, namely those of the upland (*Blaenau*) and lowland (*Bro Morgannwg*), Welsh and English or native and alien. Some of the English families could trace their ancestry back to the *advenae* who entered the lordship following the Norman Conquest. In this context attention needs to be given to the socio-economic background extending back to Norman times for the uplands or Welshries were occupied almost exclusively by native freeholders who practised a stock-rearing economy and who adhered to their own legal customs based on the laws of Hywel Dda. In the Englishries, on the other hand, marcher legal customs prevailed alongside a mixed agrarian economy practised in the fertile lowlands. This social and economic division survived into the sixteenth century and a distinction existed between native Welsh gentry emphasizing the merits of lineage as opposed to material wealth, and the anglicised gentry of the more progressive lowlands. By the Tudor period, however, many land proprietors had adopted English methods of landowning and were generally better off. Tombs and effigies in country churches, such as the Basset-Mansel monument at Llantrithyd church, and the Morgan chapel at Lower Machen church, country houses and elsewhere, as well as manuscripts containing pedigrees and bardic adulation, have survived to demonstrate the importance placed on a person's status within his community. This was a dominant feature which characterized all gentry families whether they were elevated to high status or not, but even the more modest freeholders claimed gentility. It was in such a situation that proven ancestry would secure for them, of whatever rank, the status which they claimed. Indeed, the battle to maintain and defend status in an age of social mobility brought the traditional *uchelwr*, like his peers in the lower regions, to the forefront as the defender of the existing social order. Economic or personal circumstances could adversely affect the standing of an individual or family and a fortuitous turn of events could raise or lower status and within the social order a new virile group of landowners and businessmen—*the nouveaux riches*—emerged to assume predominance and to cause resentment among some heads of the more conservative families.

Three major aspects of gentry life and activity in east Glamorgan in the sixteenth century need to be addressed briefly:

(i) The gentry and their environment;
(ii) The gentry in public affairs;
(iii) The gentry as cultural leaders of their communities

(i) Rice Merrick, that assiduous antiquary and country gentlemen of Cotrel near Bonvilston, in his *Book of Glamorganshire Antiquities* (1578) referred joyfully to the major impact of the Tudor settlement of Wales:

> Now, since Wales was thus, by gracious King Henry VIII enacted that the laws of England, and thereby united to the same, and so brought to a monarchy . . . they are exempted from the dangers before remembered . . . Thus unity engendered friendship, amity, love, alliance . . . assistance, wealth and quietness, God preserve and increase.

Despite this fulsome appraisal of the social and political order of Merrick's day his intention was to explain the degree to which stability had been achieved in community life and how much prosperity families of gentry rank had enjoyed. As agencies of the government these successful families were largely responsible for maintaining that equilibrium which Tudor government and society had achieved in Wales. They were certainly not paragons of excellence but through their landed power, they were regarded as key persons in their respective regions.

Who were these families in east Glamorgan between c. 1536 and c. 1600? At the top end of the social scale, towering above the most substantial of gentry families, were the two aristocratic houses which had close connections with the shire namely the earls of Worcester and earls of Pembroke, of whom the latter were the more prominent. The Somersets were English, and it was through the marriage of Charles Somerset, created earl of Worcester, in 1492 to Elizabeth, daughter and heiress of William Herbert, 2nd earl of Pembroke of the first creation, that the Welsh connection was established, leading to a marked increase in his power based largely on public office, and this was also the trend with regard to his successors, Henry Somerset (d. 1548) and William Somerset (d. 1589). The latter half of the sixteenth century, however, saw the ascendancy of the Herberts, a family stemming, on the female side, from the stock of Einion Sais and Bleddyn ap Maenyrch. After William Herbert became earl of Pembroke of the second creation in 1551 most of the offices held by the Worcesters fell to him and his successors, and the Pembroke influence was felt strongly, particularly in Cardiff and Swansea. William Herbert, first earl, was a grandson of William Herbert, first earl of Pembroke of the first creation, during whose time the Pembroke family extended its hold over territory in south-east Wales. It was this grandson who, in 1551, was also created Baron Herbert of Cardiff, and his son Sir Henry Herbert was to become one of the richest men in the realm and served as Lord President of the Council in the Marches in 1586 in succession to Sir Henry Sydney.

Among the more prosperous gentry were the Stradlings of St. Donat's Castle, of whom Sir Edward Stradling ranked as the dominant personality in Glamorgan in Elizabethan days. They claimed descent from the *advenae* as did the Turbervilles of Pen-llyn and the Bassets of Beaupre. The Stradlings were a powerful east Glamorgan family, and the connection with St. Donat's dated from the end of the thirteenth century. Sir Edward possessed lands on both sides of the Bristol Channel, and was lord or part owner of eleven manors in Glamorgan. Despite his efforts to trace the family's early history to the Norman invaders of Glamorgan they were in fact incomers from England, the first to settle in the lordship being Sir Peter de Stradling who married the heiress of St. Donat's. The Turbervilles, who were ardent Catholic recusants in the Elizabethan period, may have had connections with Robert fitz Hamo's invasion of Glamorgan and settled at Coety in the vale, but by the sixteenth-century, although they were divided into several branches at Tythegeston, Pen-llyn, Llanilltud and Llantrisant, they all appeared to be illegitimate and not of the direct line. The Bassets of Beaupre also had relatives at Bonvilston and Llantriddyd, and although this family also claimed descent from the Normans their ancestors in Glamorgan cannot be traced earlier than the reign of Henry IV. Other families claiming *advenae* descent and who settled in the eastern part of the lordship were the St. Johns at Fonmon and the Kemeys family of Cefn Mabli, descendants of one Stephen de Kemeys in the mid-thirteenth century.

Of the native families claiming descent from Gwaethfoed of Ceredigion were the Mathews of Llandaf and Radyr and their offshoots the Thomases of Llanbradach, the Lewises of Y Fan and the Prichards of Llancaeach. From Bleddri ap Cadwgan sprang a few Monmouthshire families, some of whom, such as the Morgans of Rhiw'r Perrai and Rhiwbeina, settled in Glamorgan. The famous Morgan family of Tredegar claimed descent from Cadifor Fawr, lord of Cil-sant, and from him descended Ifor ap Llywelyn (Ifor Hael) of Gwern-y-clepa, patron of the celebrated fourteenth-century poet Dafydd ap Gwilym. The Carne family of Nash and Ewenni were descended from the obscure Ynyr Fychan ap Meurig ab Ynyr, Prince of Gwent.

Of these families brief references need to be made to the Lewises of Y Fan near Caerphilly and the Prichards of Llancaeach. Edward Lewis was described by John Leland in 1539 as the only gentleman in all Senghennydd. His residence at Y Fan, also impressed Leland who described it as a 'fair place'. Edward Lewis was the first to adopt the family name, as was customary in the mid-sixteenth-century. The family was well-known for acquiring monastic and secular property, his power lying in the extension to his landed possessions. He purchased the manor of Roath-Keynsham in Cardiff, strengthened his position by marrying into the Morgan family of Pen-coed in Monmouthshire and served as sheriff of Glamorgan on three occasions. His son Thomas Lewis extended Y Fan and built the house known as Lewis House in St. Mary Street, Cardiff. It was Edward Lewis's grandson and namesake who purchased the manor of St. Fagan's from William Herbert and moved the family seat to that site.

The Prichards of Llancaeach stemmed from the Lewis family, David Richard, being described by John Leland as one of only two 'gentilmen of any fame' in Uwch Caiach. The family became more prominent in the public life of Glamorgan in the late sixteenth century when his son and heir Edward Prichard I served as a justice of the peace and sheriff in 1599. He established good matrimonial connections in each of his three marriages, linking him with the Carne family of Nash, the Lewises of Y Fan and the Morgans of Bedwellty. His son and heir, David Prichard, continued the family tradition in public office, followed by his son Edward Prichard by his second marriage to Mary Carne of Nash. He was Edward Prichard II, better known as Colonel Prichard, a man of Puritan tendencies, whose title probably derived from a commission which he received as colonel of the militia under the lord lieutenant of Glamorgan. He was appointed sheriff in 1637, and it is said that Charles I dined in his house on 5 August 1645 on his way to Brecon. The impressive and by now popular mansion at Llancaeach Fawr, which is open to the public, bears witness to the relative prosperity enjoyed by the Prichards in the middle years of the seventeenth century.

The Thomases of Llanbradach and Ystrad Mynach, a minor gentry family claiming descent from Gwaethfoed, was to achieve prominence in the eighteenth-century. Rice Merrick referred in 1578 to John ap Rhys Thomas ab Ieuan who owned Blaen Bradach. The main seat was Llanbradach demesne in Llanfabon and John ap Thomas improved his social status through his marriage into the Morgan family of Bedwellti and Penllwyn Sarth. Further developments occurred when his son, William Thomas, married the heiress of Rhydlafar, thus extending its landed possessions.

Thus the landowning order in Glamorgan was a mixture of old and new, native and foreign and prominent and moderately placed families. Those who had settled in the hinterland of the eastern borderlands of Glamorgan were usually of native origin, and modest though they were through their matrimonial connections were the mainstays of their communities. Humphrey Llwyd, the well-known mid-sixteenth-century scholar and antiquary, referred to the gentry of his age as being 'somewhat high-minded and in extreme poverty, acknowledging the mobility of their family [and] are given more to culture . . . than to riches . . . and being very apt to learn courtly behaviour'. This was evidently a generalization that needs qualification but there is no doubt that even the most modest of Welsh gentry were aware of their status and role in society. It was after all the age when the privileged were given publicity and regarded as the leaders of community life.

(ii) Performing public service was not new to the Glamorgan gentry after the Acts of Union. Their forebears had served in the government of the Marches long before Thomas Cromwell decided to create the office of justice of the peace in Wales in 1536. It is evident, however, that the office added a significant dimension to the role of the gentry in regional affairs. The gentry became the rulers or governors of the regions placed in their care, and were constantly involved in running affairs as sheriffs, magistrates, deputy-lieutenants and members of parliament. A survey of the shire's public records—where they exist—reveals how eager individual members of prominent and less distinguished families were to acquire office. Among the most powerful were the Lewises of Y Fan who, along with other dominant houses, provided members of the commission of the peace, which was regarded as pivotal in county government and a source of immense prestige. The office of sheriff, held on an annual basis after 1543, was also a prime position, as was the deputy-lieutenancy, traced in Glamorgan from 1579, when Sir William Herbert of Swansea and Thomas Lewis of Y Fan shared the post. Membership of parliament, especially for the shire, was equally prestigious. According to the Act of Union, one knight of the shire and one member for the county borough were to be elected and, in due course, shire representation, in particular, became the source of much rivalry between families.

The holding of office was regarded as a prime task and responsibility and the gentry, although they often abused their positions as public servants, usually attended seriously to their responsibilities to the government and their own communities. The linchpin of local government was the office of the Justice of the Peace, and the gentry who were commissioned to serve met in the courts of Quarter Sessions, the active headquarters of county life, held at Cardiff or Cowbridge. Not only was it a court of law but also an institution responsible for dealing with a multitude of legal and administrative matters concerning county affairs. It is hardly surprising, therefore, that some families clung steadfastly to the office; Edward Lewis of Y Fan, for example, served as magistrate from 1542 to 1575, and his son Thomas from 1564 to 1594. Likewise, Edward Kemeys of Cefn Mabli remained continually in office from 1573 to 1608 and was, in that period, four times chosen sheriff of the shire. Other less-known families also served in local government, such as the Mathews of Castell-y-mynach, Pentyrch, the Morgans of Rhiw'r-perrai and the Prichards of Lancaeach Fawr. Most of the public-spirited families came from the lowlying areas of the shire. Indeed, in the uplands of East Glamorgan only four major families were prominently engaged in administration, namely the Lewises of Y Fan and Rhiw'r-perrai (a branch of the Llanbradach family), the Morgans of Rhiw'r-perrai (which came to prominence in the seventeenth century) and the Prichards of Llancaeach (which was the only family of the four firmly established in the hinterland of the Blaenau). Other families were not continually represented on the bench although they proved to be powerful agents of government in the locality. Among them appeared the Bassets of Beaupre, the Kemeys of Cefn Mabli and the Mathews of Llandaf and Radyr. The East Glamorgan families who were honoured with seats in parliament at various intervals were the Mathews, Stradlings, Bassets and Herberts who dominated membership of shire and borough constituencies for most of the latter half of the century. Government at county level lay exclusively in the hands of the landed gentry, and lower offices such as high and petty constableships, were normally reserved for substantial yeomen-freeholders who were themselves powerful individuals and the backbone of the agrarian community in commote and parish.

The hierarchy of legal institutions and officialdom, extending downwards from the Council in the Marches to the courts of Great and Quarter Sessions, the County Court, the Petty Sessions and several manorial courts, represented a mixture of both old and new systems adopted to establish a stable form of government. According to Rice Lewis, in the early sections of *A Breviat of Glamorgan*, it was Henry VIII who

> gave all the subiectes there [Wales] the whole freedom of the lawes of England, in a large and ample manner as any subject in England hath. To the eternal renoun of that most famous King and continual comfort of all subjects there.

That may well have been so in theory but in practice, as Lewis might well have been aware, he was writing at a time when a marked instability and rivalry marred the fortunes of several prominent Glamorgan families intent on advancing their own interests. Faction was evident in Glamorgan politics and often corrupted the administration of local government and perpetuated animosities. Early on after the Acts of Union rivalry was centred mainly on relations between the earl of Worcester and the Carnes of Ewenni and their satellites, between the Carnes and the Herberts, William Herbert of Cogan Pill and Sir Thomas Stradling, the Herberts and Mansels and, in the 1560s and 1570s between the Stradlings, Turberviles, Bawdrippes and Mathews on one side, and the Mansels, Carnes and Bassets on the other. The Cardiff bridge dispute in 1575, for example, concerning the payment for its rebuilding, caused much bad feeling between the town's people and the county gentry, and further quarrels occurred in the 1580s between the supporters of the Pembroke faction and Mansel. A contest also took place for the hand of Barbara Gamage, during which the Pembroke influence was felt mainly in the background. All this contention did not end the rivalries for, in 1593-8, the Cardiff Riots occurred involving Sir William Herbert of Swansea and many local gentry. Other clashes might also be cited which illustrate that the main factor responsible for these upheavals was the conscious desire on the part of privileged families to protect their status in county society.

Local government was an essential aspect of county life since it not only drew the gentry together but also identified their common interests. It can be said that a feeling of county identity had gradually developed by the mid-sixteenth-century although that must not be taken too far. Cardiff, the shire-town, and Cowbridge, to a lesser extent, had become the hub of activity for the gentry of all ranks; and it was there that the major institutions were established. Thus emerged a semblance of unity among the governing families, and despite the vicious contests which often rent them apart it was this growth in corporate awareness that eventually became the prime feature of social life in Glamorgan. The institutions of government established by the Act of Union survived, there was greater attention given to litigation rather than to open feuds, and the offices grasped by the gentry gave them added initiatives to improve their standing and to maintain Tudor rule in periods of war and threats of invasion, especially after 1585 when war broke out with Spain. Although inefficiency and self-interest marred the smooth running of the defence system, and although piracy, which again involved self-interest, sorely affected the communal life of the county, in the last resort it was the landed gentleman utilizing its resources who served the Crown and maintained order. Most of the gentry allied themselves fervently with the Crown in government and religion and accepted the Protestant faith in the reign of Elizabeth. Although full commitment to that faith was not universal, and despite prevalence of Roman Catholic recusancy in parts of the shire, especially among the Turbervilles and individuals like Sir Edward Carne of Ewenni and Sir Thomas Stradling, overall the structure of the Tudor settlement in government and religion was maintained.

(iii) The previous section on county government has indicated that leadership was a basic feature of the lives of the gentry. They were the natural leaders of their communities, their responsibilities having derived from ancient customs which identified their predecessors with kindred stocks and clan leaders who were men of military prowess. Such ties determined their attitudes towards their superiors and dependents. Common bonds tied them to the soil and often, usually through intermarriage, they strengthened their links with region or neighbourhood. Thus their loyalties ran deep in the areas where they resided, and their mansions or plastai became prime centres of power and authority. They cherished twin loyalties, to the Crown and the locality. Where tensions arose between them it was usually their local associations or affinities that proved the stronger force which enabled them to maintain their cultural identity. They were rooted locally and, in addition to the deep-seated bonds of family relations which attached them to native ways of life, they, in line with their peers among the English families adapted newer and more exciting avenues of development, particularly in educational establishments and settlement in the border English towns and London. Courtly etiquette became the order of the day in many gentry houses, the chief representative being Sir Edward Stradling of St. Donats, who is regarded generally among historians as the prime symbol of the Renaissance gentleman in Wales. The impact of the 'new gentleman', influenced by contemporary ideas on polite behaviour, became the norm for an increasing number of Glamorgan gentry. Into such houses as Cefn Mabli, Rhiw'r-perrai, Y Fan, Greyfriars House, Cardiff, and later Llancaeach Fawr were introduced the habits and customs of educated society and a new urbane culture.

Governed by the strict conventions of their ancient craft the traditional Welsh bards continued to visit the homes of English and native families alike at specific intervals (a tradition known as *clera*), extolling their virtues and emphasizing the prime features which identified them as worthy benefactors, but the decline in the standard of composition, compared to standards in other parts of Wales, was particularly marked. The gentry who patronized the bards in east Glamorgan were becoming much thinner on the ground, the chief centres of hospitality being the Mathew residences at Llandaf, Llanishen, Meisgyn, Radyr and Rhoose, Y Fan near Caerphilly (where Dafydd Benwyn, Meurig Dafydd and Rhisiart Iorwerth contested with each other for patronage) and Rhiw'r-perrai, all of which claimed descent from Gwaethfoed. Among the English families, some of whom were familiar with the Welsh language, a little patronage is discovered, especially among the Bawdrems of Penmark and Splott, Buttons of St. Nicholas, St. Johns of Fonmon, Butlers of Dunraven, Gibbons of Cefn-tre-baen, Thomases of Wenvoe and Vans of Marcross. Other families who supported the bards were the Kemeyses of Cefn Mabli, Herberts of Cardiff and Stradlings and Turbervilles in the Vale.

Apart from bardic patronage some gentry also indulged in writing or supporting other more varied forms of literary activity, usually antiquarian or historical. Sir Edward Stradling wrote 'The winning of the Lordship of Glamorgan or Morganiae', purporting to claim descent from Robert fitz Hamo and the twelves knights. It was he who financed the Latin grammar of the Welsh language by the famous Catholic humanist scholar Dr. John Davies (Siôn Dafydd Rhys) in 1592, and his contribution to the study of antiquity was of enormous benefit to others including Rice Merrick, who compiled *The Book of Glamorganshire Antiquities*. Other antiquaries and copyists were Rice Lewis, who compiled, as noted above, *A Breviat of Glamorgan*, and Anthony Powell, the gentleman-genealogist of Llwydarth in the parish of Llangynwyd, who according to Iolo Morganwg, copied several rare Welsh manuscripts including a copy of *Brut y Saeson*. Among the bards and professional scribes, Lewys Morgannwg (fl. 1520/65), Dafydd Benwyn (second half of the sixteenth-century), Llywelyn Siôn (1540/1602), Sils ap Siôn (late sixteenth-century) and Meurig Dafydd (1510/95) were the most conspicuous. The quality of their verse varied, the most prolific among them, but not necessarily the most skillful, being Dafydd Benwyn. Sils ap Siôn came probably from Radyr or Llandaf and is sometimes associated with the commote of Maesgyn. He, along with other bards, held a convivial literary meeting with William Evans, treasurer and chancellor of Llandaff, and Thomas Lewis of Llandaff 'I gany ar wawd am y vaistrolaeth' ('To sing in verse for the mastery'). Meurig Dafydd came from Llanishen and served forty years as household bard for the Lewis family of Y Fan.

It was only to be expected that an increase in matrimonial alliances with families beyond Offa's Dyke, the movement among some gentry to centres of education at Oxford and Cambridge and to public schools, the impact of primogeniture on younger sons who were obliged to seek means of employment elsewhere, in addition to a gradual change in the attitudes of gentry generally to the traditional cultural scene would seriously affect the survival of native verse in strict metres. There are other reasons accounting for the decline in the bardic order and the use of the Welsh language but it is evident that this decline had set in well before the end of the sixteenth century. In 'the Storie of Lower Borowes of Merthyr Mawr' by Sir John Stradling (c. 1598-1601), there is a section relating to Meurig Dafydd's grateful visit to William Basset of Beaupre's residence to entertain him:

This bard resorting abroad to gentlemen's houses in the loitering time between Christmas and Candlemas to sing song and receive rewards, coming to Beaupre he presented the good old squire with a *cywydd, awdl or englyn* (I know not whither) containing partly the praises of the gentleman, and partly the pedigrees and matches of his ancestors. The gentleman, having perused the rhyme, prepared in his hand a noble for a reward and called the poet who came with a good will . . . Then replied the gentleman: hold, here is thy fee, and by my honesty, I swear if there be no copy of this extant, none shall there ever be, and therewith put it sure enough into the fire.

A tale it may well be, but it certainly hints at a sad truth, namely that the cultural interests of south Glamorgan gentry deteriorated at a more rapid pace perhaps than in any other parts of Wales. Although it is evident that the changing fortunes of the bardic order went hand in hand with the decline of the Welsh language in the households of an increasing number of gentry families, it is equally interesting to note that Meurig Dafydd did venture to compose an elegy on the death of the old squire and was probably paid for it!

This chapter has outlined some of the main developments in the history of the sixteenth-century gentry in east Glamorgan. When the broad general features of county life are considered it is evident that (i) they relied on possessing a good pedigree to maintain their status; (ii) their development needs to be examined within the context of the way in which they linked conventional attitudes with newer modes of conduct; (iii) their continued success was based primarily on their ownership of land and material resources; (iv) their public image depended on assuming an active role in regional government; and (v) their cultural interests increasingly spread far and wide and, where the bardic system still survived, gave them that marked sense of racial identity which enabled their successors in the early seventeenth century to consider themselves as 'Cambrians' or 'British' gentry under the Stuarts. In other words, the role of these landed proprietors in government and society in the first half of the seventeenth century had been well established in the sixteenth.

[For further reading see Glanmor Williams (ed.), *Glamorgan County History*, IV, *Early Modern Glamorgan* (Cardiff, 1974), contributions in volumes in the series *Glamorgan Historian* (vols. 19), ed. Stewart Williams, and *Morgannwg,* the transactions of the Glamorgan County History Society (1958-)].

REMINISCENCES OF DR. EMANUEL GROSS,
A PRISONER OF WAR IN SIBERIA, 1914-18.
Part Two Translated from the German

by

JOSEPH GROSS

Introduction.

Dr. Emanuel Gross was born on 13th October 1876 in Saaz, Bohemia, then a part of the Austrian Hungarian Empire. His father, Joseph was a dealer in hops, for which the region is famous. Joseph died young and left a widow, Adelaide and six children. Emanuel went to the local grammar school and then to Prague University, to study medicine. He specialised in gynaecology, and eventually set up in practice as a consultant in gynaecology in 1909. He married in that year and two children were born before the war, Joseph (now of Merthyr Tydfil) in 1910, Bettina in 1913. A second daughter, Maria, was born in 1921.

Dr. Emanuel Gross was called up to serve in the Austrian army in July 1914. He left a description of his life during the war years 1914-18, of which he spent the largest part as a prisoner of war in Siberia. He wrote these memoirs some seventeen years later. He died in Prague in 1938.

On joining the army Dr. E. Gross learned to ride and shoot and proceeded with his unit to Cracow, Russian Poland and the War Front. He was captured by the Cossacks at the end of August 1914 near Opole. We give here an excerpt from his Diary which he kept whilst a well-treated prisoner at TOBOLSK in Siberia.

Language studies.

I occupied myself by reading German books, which I borrowed from all possible acquaintances. The Library of the German rectory in particular had a number of classical books (and some trash), all of which I devoured. It was not until the summer of 1915 that I also began to read in Russian, learned it on the whole without a teacher, with the help of a dictionary. I was soon able to read newspapers and books and as a recreation I started to translate from the Russian into German. Besides this I kept a pretty detailed diary. Winter 1914. The events of the war did not seem to allow us to expect an early end. The defeat on the Marne became quickly known here and the military men, and particularly Nolte were sceptical about developments and we celebrated Christmas in subdued mood.

Christmas 1914.

Although we had Christmas Trees everywhere, even in the hospital and camp, although the Christmas fare was good and plentiful, yet the thought of home was worrying and did not allow a festive mood. In addition the frost had become unbearable. It was bearable at midday with brilliantly blue skies, but in the mornings it was hard to drive from Sever up the hill to the barracks in spite of being wrapped up in furcoat and shawl. All those who could manage it stayed at home. The schools were closed. The peasants in winter wear fur coats and fur hats, and just as the soldiers, practical three cornered shawls (bashliks) made of wool, which protect the neck and head, mittens and high white felt shoes (Valenski) often with colourful tops. When a Siberian shakes your hand in the street, he first takes his glove

30. Dr Joseph Gross. President M.T.H.S.

off, one prepares for this already from a distance, when one meets a friend. (Ladies do not do this). In winter it is only natural to shake the warm human hand, not the cold thick mitten. The peasants do not wear stockings, rarely rags to wrap round, and it is a comic sight in the hospital, when the men remove the white thick felt boot reaching to the knee, revealing the long trouser leg bound round with a band below the knee, then show the warm naked foot. During the summer the peasants wear Russian shirts (Rubaschka), leather belts, straw hats, shoes made from bark (Lapki). The more affluent population usually wear European clothes, but quite often a shirt blouse often embroidered (in the Slav manner), with leather belts and high leather boots. The children in winter wear furcoats, with the fur cap and gloves securely sewn on they look like small bears, as they are being pulled along on sleighs. They skate even on the roads where the frozen powdery snow gives a good surface or slide on primitive skis, fastened with thongs or twine. The grown ups love to travel in whole groups in a Treoika-sleigh for a picnic to a forest or a Tartar village. One takes provision and there is a samovar (tea urn).Well wrapped up one travels along with the speed of the wind, with red cheeks, the ladies shrieking, when one travels uphill or down. (Uchab is the name for a steep hollow, where the travellers are tumbled about while sitting on the floor on blankets). Arrived at the picnic place, one eats and drinks—vodka is taken along, student songs are sung, the balalaika is played with its sentimental sounds which are more sorrowful than gay. Here I remember the unusual name the Russians have for the piano, ROYAL, that probably goes back to the days of Catharine the Second.

East Yaks, nomad people.

In winter the East Yaks come to town, the nomad people, who live in the tundra to the north of the Gubernium. They have reindeer sleighs which are particularly fast and austere and gentle polar huskies. They wear furs of reindeer and bear, the former stitched with reindeer sinews edged with gaily embroidered material with fringes, they too have the fur gloves and caps securely sewn on. In the town they push their caps backwards and walk with long, black greasy hair, they have slit eyes, blunt, often depressed noses (syphilis). They behave like strangers in the town, are bringing berries and fish, but mainly furs: ermine, sable, marten, miniver (Siberian squirrel), snow and blue fox. Then whole linings for fur coats, already sewn and tanned (with wheat corn). The skins are of reindeer or sea lion (tjulen), silver white, of red fox and cross fox, which have a black cross on their back, are otherwise red brown. The East Yaks prepare very small pieces of skin, 3cm x 6cm, from the bellies and paws of the foxes. The women stitch them together with reindeer sinews and they give a light and warm fur material.

Astrakhan.

Elegant ladies wear sable, mink,and musk, persian lamb (Astrakhan). This latter however comes from the steppe to the south of the Omsk Gubernium. Here the Tartars breed black sheep, whose embryos furnish the fine black persian skins (Astrakhan). I later purchased a fur coat with Kangaroo lining which came from Australia and was softer and fluffier than opossum, with an Astrakhan collar for eighty roubles.

Tom Freuchen.

At Christmas 1914 there were several days of 40-42 degrees (frost) and just on the night of the second holiday there arrived our friend Tom Freuchen from Tjumen, to visit Rubritius and myself. He used the opportunity to accompany the wife of Consul Stieglitz, with whom he was acquainted. She came from Omsk, where she had brought her affairs in order, to follow her husband into exile. Freuchen told us, that the frost and storm had been so gruesome, that at some places the horses could not move forward, because the breath in their nostrils froze to ice and had to be removed with the whip handle. We spent a few pleasant days with Freuchen. He is the brother of the explorer of Greenland and surgeon Peter Freuchen, who later married an Eskimo wife and recently wrote an Eskimo novel. Tom Freuchen was representative of a Danish Butter Company, which exported Siberian butter to Denmark and there mixed it with Danish butter. Freuchen spoke good Russian, English, a droll German (ueber alles, an allusion to the German national anthem). He was a handsome, imposing man. He later sent me his picture in the fur coat of the East Yaks. He came from Nykjobing in Falster, his assistance facilitated my correspondence with home.

Mrs. Stieglitz.

The arrival of Mrs.Stieglitz increased and enriched the number of interesting houses of our acquaintance. He came from Moscow, where his father had emigrated, went to America as a young man, and finally settled in Omsk as representative of various commercial companies and became Swedish Honorary Consul. He there married the widow of a Russian merchant with two sons. She was older than he, and had good connections with the Russian authorities. He was not in the diplomatic service of Sweden and was therefore deported to Tobolsk at the outbreak of war. His fortune like that of all hostile foreigners was confiscated. Now his wife came to join him, after she had converted whatever was possible into money. She loved entertainment, so we were often invited to dinner. There was always wine, although Stieglitz only drank water, however in great quantities. His East German servant, a youngster from East Prussia, had constantly to pour out mineral water. The Consul often played the piano, he played charming little operetas.

Various pastimes.

Several exiles visited there, such as Groh, the piano teacher from Warsaw (his father came from Rumburg in Bohemia). He earned his living giving piano lessons. At the Consuls he played beautiful classical music. Groh also gave lessons to Rubritius, and later often played in our home. He married a Russian girl and went later to Rumburg with his wife and child. Nolte did not often visit at the Stieglitz'but he (Stieglitz) quite often went to greater parties at Nolte's. Poker was played regularly , which Stieglitz played with great skill, but which I avoided. I often played tarot in Sever, as well as Pika, without being a master of the game, but on the long winter nights there was nothing else to do. I also learned to play patience. At this time too we were invited to the Rendels, and got to know their acquaintances, the Chief Forestry Official, Grybanov and his chubby vivacious wife Anna, the surgeon Afonski, the oldest of the surgeons Pokrovski (he was called Ivan Ivanovitsch), characters that could have come from Gogol and Ostrovski. They all took pains to introduce us to Russian customs and food. Of these we found caviar and fish prepared in all sorts of ways particularly tasty.

Lent.

During Lent, milk, butter and meat are forbidden. There is only food cooked with vegetable oil (rape oil). On Lent Tuesday Blinni, large poured cakes made with buckwheat like

Livanzi (Czech for pan cakes), only larger, cooked in vegetable oil. They are being served by cook herself (with a red face and sweating), the Blinni wrapped in serviettes on plates. They are eaten with sour cream, caviar, marmalade, one drinks Vodka or tea, and eats and eats. We are invited to the Rendels, Gregorschevskis and Lindebergs, morning, noon and evening and have no hunger pains. Then we go again to Giganova, where Lydia Aleksejewna, particularly friendly with Rubritius, serves us with Pilmeni, small pieces of meat rolled in dough, cooked in broth, which taste heavenly. They are prepared for stock, and kept in small linen bags, hung up in the cold, and freeze like stones.

Winter transport.

Winter is the most beautiful time in Tobolsk. One can often walk in the noon sunshine without a fur coat. The snow is snow white, there is no soot or dust as only beech and birch wood is burned in the large stoves. The roofs are snow white, the smoke whirls gaily in the clear sky. The domestic animals too have winter fur,horses, cows, and the pigs grow long thick bristles. The dogs roll in the snow and eat it while running; the horses too have developed a thick fur. They stand for hours without cover in the open, or crop the spare grass on the snowbound steppe. The Siberian horse is small, has plump feet and a broad head, it is good natured and is well treated; the cows yield very high quantities of milk and the fat content of the milk is high. The only connection with the outside world is by sleighs, which travel even faster than the summer carriages. The roads in the steppe in summer are so wide from the traffic, that ten or more vehicles can drive side by side. In winter they are covered in deep snow, so that the coachman has to follow the old track. The sleighs are drawn by a single horse or three horses one behind the other. When passing another sleigh, the horses plunge into deep snow from which they can only extricate themselves with difficulty. Whole caravans of sleighs with goods for the North or bringing them to the town, go one behind the other, often with one driver only for six or eight sleighs. The patient beasts instinctively keep together in the track.

Hunting.

One often finds wolves and bears or shakals, thus the peasant coachmen are always armed. They hunt not only these wild animals but also elk, deer, snow and wood hens; particularly in the spring wild duck, wood cock, heath cock. The local inhabitants hunt the valuable animals for their fur on skis: marten, sable, ermine, snow and blue fox. They still hunt them with bow and arrow. They exchange them for flour, spirits, materials, primus burners, samovars. In order to avoid scurvy, they drink the blood of the killed reindeer and their milk and eat fresh fish, their entrails and also frozen fish. Certain kinds of frozen fish are also a delicacy for the towns people, as is fish dried in the sun and cut into cubes, reminiscent of bacon. Alcohol and syphylis are the ruin of these indigenous nomads, who are peaceloving and never offered armed resistance to the Russians, and besides the Christian faith, retained their old heathen beliefs with fetishes and shamens.

Alcohol prohibition.

I already mentioned the prohibition of alcohol which the Russian Government introduced at the outbreak of the war and carried out with remarkable energy. Hundreds of wagons and whole ship loads of cases with bottles of spirits (vodka) were brought to TOBOLSK from all parts of the Gubernium and stored in the enormous yard of our Vinny Sklad, all stacked one on top of the other to a height of two storeys. The yard was surrounded by a brick wall, the building too was constructed from red glazed bricks.

Two old watchmen prevented any attempt at theft. However it hardly ever came to that. Tobolsk was an ideal of honesty, the doors of the houses were never locked, there never was a case of theft or a break in. All taverns selling vodka were state owned and closed, the production of vodka was a monopoly and also stopped, we never saw any drunks, the usual sight in the streets before the war. Of course everybody had some stocks of spirits obtained before the prohibition, there was also some supply of cheap beer and one could still buy good and cheap supplies of wine from the state vinyards and cellars in the Caucasus.

In the cellars of the Vinny Sklad there were large iron containers and enormous covered pans with spirit. Mr.Groh, a German-speaking Russian and manager of the Vinny Sklad hospital, lived with his family in a house in the precincts of the Vinny Sklad. We kept good neighbourly relations with him. On holidays, he invited us to a Zakuska with a bottle of spirits, with a white or yellow seal. Vodka is seventy degrees or more proof. It is a fine distilled corn spirit, without any particular taste or smell and increases in value according to age. It is amusing how such a bottle is opened: after removing the seal, one strikes the bottle into the hollow of ones hand and the cork flies out. As a sign that one would like a drop of alcohol, one snaps two fingers on the collar. Alexander Alexandrowitsch Groh is a Russian of Polish descent, with a black moustache and pale features. He loves to joke and is no fanatic. He receives the so-called evaporation coefficient from the guarded treasure and we assist slowly with this evaporation!

The prohibition is intended to suppress all unrest in the case of a possible defeat and to ensure the sobriety of the army. However prohibition had serious drawbacks. As the war progressed peasants and smallholders began themselves to distil spirits from grain, Samosadka, Samogonka, and women and children were involved, who sucked through straws for testing and got senselessly drunk. Furthermore the distillation was often incomplete and people got poisoned with the fusel. Such Samosadka is traded illicitly for high prices, brought into the town, it smells and tastes terribly.

A celebration.

On the birthday of William the Second, in January 1915 we were invited to Nolte's home, about fifteen gentlemen, among them Dahn, Stieglitz, Schulz. The latter was a pharmacist from Omsk. An agent managed his pharmacy more or less faithfully for him, and from this agent Schulz received from time to time spirits diluted to vodka, (thus 40-45 degrees proof), in labelled bottles. For this holiday too Schulz had ordered some. With the cold zakuska we each received a small glass full, which we had to knock back in one swallow, after the toast to the Emperor : "salpom" (salve?). We all were petrified, for a short moment I felt a round hot hollow in my stomach. The spirit was 96 degrees! Otherwise one could obtain Spiritus (pure spirit) only at the chemists with a doctors prescription (to disinfect one's hands, for bandages etc). All the surgeons prescribed them to their acquaintances without fee, some to strangers for a fee.

Medical matters.

In February Mrs. Stieglitz was taken ill with a heavy illness of the gall bladder. I was her surgeon, for which I was taken to her large heart. Once in the night, Mr. Stieglitz had to fetch me. However because of his girth and shortness of breath, he could not walk so far. No hansom was available, so he climbed on top of the sleigh with the waterbarrel, which brought him to us. This winter was not too hard, although the men (the prisoners of war in Dr. Gross's care) suffered from nephritis, rheumatism, frostbites caused trouble now and then. However we were far from the railway, and only rarely received small transports of prisoners. Thus during the winter we were like a small peace time garrison, which we could well manage with four student medicos, as we only had to care for three to four thousand men. Now and then I was asked to a consultation by the Russian surgeons. In the beginning many local inhabitants came to us, but we eventually refused to treat them, as this went too far and was also frowned upon. Any money received from private practice, it was not a lot, was used to pay for our travelling to the POW camp or in the town to the civilian prisoners, and to the support of poor devils, which support was given often and gladly. I also received sufficient money from home, which I used to buy clothing and underwear, small improvements in the household and tobacco. I also bought some furs, and was able to send them home with Mrs. Arnet in 1916: a fur skin of a wolf was used as a carpet in front of the bed and gave my father in law much pleasure, and was held in awe by my son Seppl; white fox and ermine were worn by my small blonde princess Bettina instead of by my wife for whom they were intended. My Children! Their pictures stood on my table and were hanging over my bed. All my acquaintances learned to know them, saw them grow and had to admire their sayings! I knew them to be well protected at home in Kocvar, cared for by my wife and the loving grand parents. Often the longing was great, but I did not really have any worries, only the fear not to see them ever again.

The military cemetery.

In my leisure and longing I turned again to poetry, and as I review them now, nearly every poem deals with death. Our military cemetery in the forest was being faithfully guarded by Nolte and a committee, of which more later. It gradually grew and became one of the sights of Tobolsk with its orderly layout and wealth of flowers. In winter it was covered in snow and ice, with one or two dozen graves ready dug, during the winter one could not dig graves in the frozen ground. Many attending the funeral of a comrade thought: Is one of the open graves destined to be mine? But in summer everything was green and full of scent, grass grew richly on the graves, flowers bloomed, birches waved their long fan-like branches downwards and one's heart was filled with hope, which did not disappoint: there in the West, where the sun sinks in fiery red, like in the flames of the worldblaze, there are fields and a house where love and longing are waiting for me, a new life!

Siberian winter.

How beautiful was the sky in winter. The sun blazed in the blue sky like in Italy and at night the stars sparkled and the moon shone much brighter than with us. The Bear was in the zenith and the Polar star even nearer than at home. Before falls of snow, the moon had two or three glowing rings, and in rising she was enormous and blood red. When travelling into town one day and seeing it for the first time between the houses, I thought a building was on fire. A curious phenomenon occurred once when in snowy mist at sunset two smaller suns appeared on either side of the sun, each at a distance of the width of the sun. Coloured rings round the sun too were quite a novel occurrence for us.

I saw Northern Lights too, like sheet lightning. When the frost is most severe, wind rises and the skies become quite dark. Snow starts to fall relentlessly day and night. There is no light in the sky. Once it is over, the sky becomes shining clear and one can see the landscape for great distances. By February, the warmth of the sun at midday becomes so great that the snow melts on the roofs. About three o'clock, the frosts get severe again and then enormous icicles hang from the roofs and on trees.

Siberian spring.

In April the frost ceases. One has to clear the roofs to prevent great damage from masses of snow falling from them. That is a joyful preparation to receive the spring. For the first time since October, one can again see the red, green sheet metal roofs of the block houses, the grey slate roofs of the stone buildings. It does not take more than eight to fourteen days until spring is here. The snow melts in the streets, everywhere small brooks run downhill between the houses, that is a moving, joyful picture after the months of rigid silence on earth and always moved me to tears. As the snow melts under the poplars of the hospital, yellow and still green leaves appear. They are quickly collected for bedding in the stables. Leaves soon appear on the trees, the days are warm, light and windy, but almost without transition the blooms appear with the leaves in May, white poplar catkins, and birch catkins wave in the wind. There is only one flowering tree in Tobolsk, the jasmin, with its nasty smelling umbels. It grows in every yard, in many small gardens and is covered over and over with flowers. Swallows and song birds arrive in woods and town. Roses and fuchsias bloom in the small town gardens among lush greenery.

Siberian summer.

After barely four weeks of spring, summer is here which sets in in June, already with tropical heat. The temperature reaches seventy degrees in July and August with downpours of rain and thunderstorms, which arrive without warning with great speed and masses of clouds, with large amounts of rain, thunder and lightning, accompanied by myriads of flies, mosquitos and midges. They make it impossible to stay in the woods, during the heat of the day. Fortunately there are no malaria mosquitos in Tobolsk. In May the seed is sown, the earth turned over with a light plough only, no manure is used and there is a rich harvest at the end of August.

One feature of the landscape is the birch. The painter Bergtholt said later, that he could not paint another birch tree, so sated had he become seeing them. I am not so sensitive, and loved them in spite of seeing so many. They grow along the river banks, are dispersed among the conifers of the forest, and form whole groves in sandy soil. Mighty old trunks appear in winter white against white, with thin black rods like ghosts against the white sky, but in blue skies they glow beautifully in the sunlight like white satin. I always remember one small tree, a young pliant birchtree. It stood on a slope at the entrance to the ravine of the brewery, with its crown set against the sky, in autumn with yellowish glowing small leaves, standing out against the sunburnt brown grass floor, then in winter bare, tinged with red by the evening sun, in Spring with light green catkins, then overnight sprouting light green leaves and in Summer in the full panoply of leaves rustling proudly in the breeze. Thus I often think of the mighty cedars in the forest of Michalowsk-Skit, where I often travelled from Tobolsk (it was first a camp for soldiers, later for officers). The cedars had mighty ancient trunks, their crowns formed by wide-reaching branches, with long fine needles hanging down, a mighty network of roots at their base, which protruded far over to the road. Sheets of water formed there after rain and hundreds of butterflies and dragonflies were darting about. Wild flowers grew in abundance and birds flew about without fear. A Siberian proverb says: Here are flowers without scent, birds without song, women without love.

Prisoner of war movements.

The fall of Premysl (a large fortress in Poland) was a heavy blow for us. The Russians and Czechs celebrated it with military pomp and jubilation, and we were very pessimistic. Soon large new transports arrived from the fallen fortress, mainly of officers of the staffs of the fortress and of the artillery (Zimmerman, Zwiedinek). The opening of the river navigation brought generally large movements of prisoners of war, men and officers. It was intended to send the Slavs to southern garrisons, in separate camps, to prepare them slowly for defection. The activities of Dyrich and Masaryk in Russia led to a propaganda, which intensified in the year 1916. One felt little of this in Tobolsk, where mainly Germans and Hungarians were concentrated. Altogether there were some six thousand men and seven hundred officers, who were lodged in different quarters in the town, and in Michalowsk-Skit. They soon settled down with the help of their craftsmen. The Sever was left empty, Uxa and Heintze and the other gentlemen went away and Rubritius and I first moved into private quarters to the feldscher Klotschkov in the Upper Town, where we occupied a large airy room (all due to the favour of Lindeberg) and there we spent the marvellous summer of 1915 in idyllic quiet. We were quite free and drove into town, camp, barracks and officers quarters, visited Germans and Russians. The latter were on the whole less hostile towards Austrians than towards the Germanzi, who were considered the real warmongers.

The artist Bergthold.

In the meantime, Commander Pantuchin had been removed. Colonel Glas came, with whom I got into conflict. As Lindeberg was responsible for us, he took us into the precincts of the hospital. In the autumn of 1915 we occupied a large schoolroom of the medical school, with a huge white stove. Bergthold painted me beautifully in front of it, in a white coat, in full length, (Rubritius in uniform). I still see the sunburnt full face before me (my own that is to say), in yellowish/bluish tints against a white background. A good picture, the loss of which I regret. Rubritius hired a piano and Groh often came to visit us. Otherwise we lived a somewhat more secluded but peaceful life throughout the whole winter of 1915-16. I remember several of the officers. There was first of all Colonel Schroetter (he died 1935 in Komotau) a strong sixty year old, with white moustache. He took over the direction of the Support Committee, created by the Swedish Red Cross Mission in the late autumn of 1915. Of this later. He was a German from Bohemia, Chief of Staff of Artillery at Premysl, and a humane, just, man, who did much good. I did not meet him again, as he left Tobolsk in 1917 and went with the whole officers camp to Chabarovsk. From there they had an adventurous escape to Russia in 1918, in which Schroetter luckily escaped to Petersburg, where he arrived a week before me. Now he lives in retirement in Komotau as manager of the Museum, where I already visited him. He is well and hale, (i.e. about 1935).

Some captive officers.

The Chief of the General Staff of Premysl (a captured Polish fortress) was an arrogant elegant gentleman whose name I can not remember and the gentlemen of his staff formed a group of elegant almost exclusively gentile men. They studied a lot, mathematics, languages, they painted. There was Captain Zimmerman (whom I shall mention again), Captain Zwiedinek, the brother in law of Gustl Kohn in Salz, and other pleasant distinguished people. The group lodged in a former Hotel, mainly Hungarian gentlemen, there, too was much activity, there was much learning and playing, there was one group with Captain Erengi, Lord and Bittman (the latter became a pilot in Italy after his return and died there), a Hungarian Senior Lieutenant Technician, who collected literature about Rasputin, everywhere one subscribed to newspapers, translated, arranged courses for languages and all sorts of University subjects. Many a professional officer may well have there laid the foundation for a peace time civilian career.

These officers were strictly guarded, particularly in the summer, they were only allowed to go out under escort, however they were given the opportunity to go out, do shopping. They were only allowed to meet at divine service, which therefore was very popular. Attempts at escape were difficult, as Tobolsk was three hundred miles west from the railway. Only Captain Zimmerman with another gentleman arranged an escape disguised as peasants, helped by Tartars. They borrowed money everywhere for this purpose. However they only went as far as the centre of Russia, where they were caught and sent to a bad punishment camp in Inner Russia. As a result the discipline in Tobolsk was tightened so that only two or three gentlemen could go out shopping together and the rest were restricted to walk in the yard.

The officers group in Michalowsk-Skit were the best off, they were mainly Hungarians and Germans: among them Dub from Karlitz, two Hungarian colonels. They lived in an unfinished stone house which the Bishop of Tobolsk had had built in the precinct of a Monastery, in the middle of dense forests. They equipped it very beautifully, with doors, windows, partitions, furniture, they made everything themselves. Some even built pretty small block houses, which looked like retreats of monks, hermitages. One of the medicos, Pietrzak, who already lived among the men, provided the first care of the sick, otherwise Rubritius and I took it in turns to drive there; the sick of course went to the hospital.

We provided a room for officers, first in the old hospital, and later in the Vinny Sklad. Several of the gentlemen asked to be admitted to the hospital because they suffered from prisoner of war psychosis: they could not get on with their comrades, became irritable and quarrelsome.

In the mild atmosphere of the hospital they somewhat regained the facility to face again the monotony of the small officer camp which offered no physical recreation. We helped several of them to be transferred to Michalowsk-Skit, where there was more movement, freedom, even a large football field and where the forest air was beneficial. We lost one officer, a Hungarian, who suffered from melancholy psychosis. He was brought to the psychiatric department of the Gubernium Hospital and died of inanition. His funeral, which nearly all his comrades attended, took place in high summer under green birch trees, with flowers on all the other graves. It was a solemn ceremony, a catholic priest spoke a few words, I believe.

Another very beautiful Hungarian Senior Lieutenant Pognacz was, after the Revolution of 1917, seized by the delusion that ALL MEN ARE EQUAL and that he had to give up everything, he developed a regular paranoia and we had to exercise all our energy to get him transferred to the psychiatric clinic in Tomsk and from there hopefully transported home. It was heartrending to see mentally ill prisoners of war, many of whom did not even know their name, and whose language doctors and nurses did not understand. We visited them regularly and brought them tobacco or other presents.

The Swedes.

News came in the autumn of 1915 that a mission of the Red Cross was to visit the camp. The protection of the Austrians during the war had been taken over by the Danes, that of the citizens of the German Reich by the Swedes, but only the latter fulfilled this role with real love of humanity. The Danes were at heart more on the side of the Entente, as they wanted something from Germany, which they eventually obtained for their less than strictly observed neutrality. The river was already frozen over, it must have been well into November, and our soldiers suffered badly from the cold, when four Swedes arrived led by the Director, Krook (Crook), representatives of the Swedish Red Cross, accompanied by an officer from Petersburg, who had to supervise their dealings with the prisoners of war. The second Swede was an elegant Balt, named Yuenger, a merchant living in Siberia, who spoke perfect Russian, the third an engineer from Stockholm, the fourth a theologian from Upsala, all four splendid, if quite different types of this noble people.

These Swedes wore heavy, light coloured furs of bearskin, beneath them clothes made of leather. They brought one hundred and eighty three sleighs with comforts from Germany and Austria. Every three men received two boxes full of warm underwear, shawls, braces, sewing material, lovingly assembled by women in Austria and Germany, all of the same pattern yet with small variations. Each man received an overcoat (mainly Prussian dark brown cavalry coats), a half-furcoat (Attila), or a woollen Belgian blanket. They further distributed a quantity of pieces of uniforms, fur caps, mittens, guard fur coats and for the needy and sick there were gifts of money and loans. We surgeons helped in the distribution (another surgeon had joined us as camp surgeon: Dr. Talakerer, a solid broadshouldered Styrian). The Swedes arranged a festive meal in our honour, with wine and vodka and neighbourly talk. I was seated next to Junger, very knowledgeable about Russian literature. I mentioned Tchechov whose work I was then reading and translating, and he recommended Feth, then unknown in Germany, a friend of Tolstoy and lyrical philosopher. Afterwards Feth filled many of my leisure hours with work and enjoyment. Thanks to these warm things we actually had fewer cold related illnesses, however tuberculosis increased in the winter of 1915-16 and claimed many victims, particularly among people who had suffered severely from typhus and spotted typhus. The cramped living conditions made it inevitable that the less robust ones succumbed to the infectious tuberculosis. There was no isolation of new cases of spotted typhus, which constantly arrived from the country or by military transports from the garrison of Premysl or from the surrounding country, where this illness transferred by lice always occurred. In the Gubernium Hospital such isolation only occurred to that extent, that the patients were lodged in the infectious diseases barracks. In the Vinny Sklad we kept them in the former distillation room, which was equipped with stone tiles and was a light airy room, heated with steam. No infections occurred within the building, because Lindeberg arranged the installation of a large appliance to disinfect clothes and underwear in the Gubernium Hospital. There went all the clothes and underwear of new admissions and all vermin was safely killed.

No thought for the morrow.

I want to mention here, that when it got warm in the Spring of 1916, most of the soldiers sold their overcoats and blankets to Russians. They wanted to buy tobacco and did not think of the next winter, "we shall be home by then".

The Swedes also made the suggestion, accepted by the authorities, to form Aid committees for the prisoners of war. Colonel Schrotter became Chairman, we surgeons were members and the Russian Camp Commander was responsible for the management of the money. This was first Senior Lieutenant Nowoselow, a quite well read, pacifistic soldier, with whom we often had discussions about the causes of and responsibility for the war. We then already spoke enough Russian, to be able to debate with him. I recorded his arguments in my diaries in the form of a discussion. After him a young Ensign was appointed Commander of the camp, an irresponsible windbag, who absconded with the rest of the money left by the Swedes deposited in a bank account.

Matters administrative.

A reorganisation of the sanitary service occurred on the lst January 1916. The prisoner of war hospital was made independent of the hospital of the Gubernium. A surgeon with the rank of Major was appointed as Commander of the military hospital, Anatol Takowlewitch Warnakoff, with an Accounts Officer (Delouprawlajuschtschi) and an apothecary. Only the surgical and psychiatric cases remained in the Gubernium Hospital. Rubritius remained as subordinate of Lindeberg, whilst I, Talakerer and the medicos Subal (Viennese), Steich (from Aussig), Nowakowski (Pole) and Kutz (from Bosnia) cared for the hospital Vinny Sklad.

Dr. Ludwig Kirchmair (from Vienna), a surgeon of the Landsturm, became camp surgeon. He was a surgeon, an excellent doctor. However it was not possible for him to serve with Rubritius in the Gubernium Hospital, because these were not his orders. His activity in the camp was exemplary, he not only introduced lectures on hygiene for the men but introduced many practical measures in the camp. With the consent of the Russians, he like myself and Rubritius was taken into consultation by the other doctors. A white pointed beard made him look older, he spoke excellent Russian, as he had been in many camps, and was known as a professor. He had been Assistant (Registrar) of Bundiger and a well known surgeon in Vienna. He got on well with Lindeberg but relations with Warnakoff were tense from the beginning. Warnakoff came from the front, he had been the surgeon of a regiment of Cossacks, rumoured to have fallen from his horse and sent on leave because of a nervous complaint. Now he got this appointment in the interior, and was, as he said later himself, very unhappy to have to treat "enemies". Furthermore he was not up to the administrative and medical management of such a large hospital, he somewhat mistrusted us from the beginning, as we were on friendly terms with Lindeberg, with whom he did not get on well from the very beginning. Warnakoff decided that we surgeons of the Military Hospital should take our lodgings in Vinny Sklad (we rented a small house next to the Gubernium Hospital, which we furnished pleasantly), he gave us a military guard on orders from Omsk. We all had to go out under military escort (with the exception of Rubritius who remained permanently subordinate to Lindeberg). When the ladies saw me for the first time with a Russian soldier carrying a rifle, they cried. (Gribanova). In this enforced habitation, with strongly reduced social contacts (my escort accompanied me to Rendel, Giganova, and sat in the kitchen with tea) I concentrated still more on translating, the fairytale by Terschov

Konjek Gorbunok (the little Humphorse), Pushkin: The Prisoner in the Caucasus, innumerable tales by Tschechov, poems by Feth, Sologub, Sascha Tschernij, fairy tales and serious books, which I studied in Russian.

Doctors quarrel, patients died.

It was tragic, that because of the strained relationship between Lindeberg and Warnakoff, the former withdrew the permission to continue with the disinfection of the underwear and clothing of the patients in the Gubernium Hospital. The disinfector ordered by Warnakoff did not arrive from Omsk until late in the summer. The result was a house infection with spotted typhus! That was perhaps the most difficult time of the whole of my stay in Tobolsk. I soon recognised the house epidemic, as I knew the symptoms only too well and also knew by what means the disease spread: lice. When the first patients in the hospital, (suffering from simple rheumatism, eczema) and a few medical orderlies were taken ill and I entered the diagnosis: Typhus exanthematicus, Warnakoff crossed out the additional entry and reported in the monthly return to Omsk: Such and such a number of typhus cases. (Note: leaving out the word spotted. J.G.) When more and more were taken ill and I urged to obtain the disinfector, Warnakoff said on one occasion "perhaps that is only influenza with fever exanthem". My agitation grew, medicus Nowakowski, new sanitary personnel were taken ill, young men of an iron constitution died, who had been perfectly healthy until now. At this juncture the Brigade in Omsk, evidently alerted by the quickly spreading "typhus epidemic" sent us Dr. Sametz, chosen for his expert knowledge. Dr. Sametz came originally from Budweis and had worked several months in an epidemic hospital. I shall never forget the first visit of Warnakoff in the hospital. Sametz diagnosed spotted typhus in all cases so recognised by me, showed Warnakoff the lice in the beds of the sick, the lice in the rooms of the sanitary personnel, and Warnakoff had to admit the fact to Omsk. Sametz undertook the treatment of the infected patients, among them now came a particularly serious case: Dr. Talakerer.

Even before the arrival of Sametz, I agreed with Dr. Kirchmaier who saw the cases and interpreted them like me, to restrict the transfer of patients to the hospital and to send the most urgent cases only. Kirchmaier put the patients into the small sick room in the camp and said to Warnakoff, who noticed it: "Yes, you have a spotted typhus epidemic in the hospital". The greatest difficulty I encountered was to find replacements for the sanitary personnel taken ill with spotted typhus, as the whole thing soon became known in the camp. Within barely three weeks, Sametz himself, who lived in the hospital, was taken very seriously ill with spotted typhus. (At that time I still lived with Rubritius and could change in the hospital). In the meantime Talakerer, who suffered from erysipelas of the head in addition to his spotted typhus infection, had left his bed. Nowakowski recovered and I had to look after the hospital on my own again. Of those taken ill, a large percentage died, however well to be excused, because of the special circumstances: a diagnosis not admitted, no isolation, lack of trained personnel. Such an epidemic usually dies out with the coming of the warmer season. In the meantime there also arrived the disinfector from Omsk. The relationship with Warnakoff improved, helped by his gradual recognition of our worth, his better relations with Lindeberg, and particularly with Giganova, who informed him more accurately about us. His private practice too improved, and that also had a calming influence. His relations with Kirchmaier however remained permanently strained. The latter had a rigid, little yielding nature, different from me. I considered Warnakoff's type in the beginning as sick-pathological. Kirchmaier thought it perfidious and showed him his contempt openly.

Warnakoff used the first occasion, where Kirchmaier put himself in the wrong. We were not allowed to go out without escort, he enforced this strictly. It happened that Kirchmaier treated the ten year old child of a higher court official, as a consultant and with Warnakoff's permission. The child suffered from a lung infection. The child was improving, when Warnakoff, returning with me from an inspection of the camp, met Kirchmaier in a coach without escort. The next morning Kirchmaier had to report and Warnakoff, without saying a word, denounced him to the brigade at Omsk. As a result Dr. Kirchmaier was confined to barracks for thirty days. Kirchmaier then appealed to us surgeons to refuse any work as a sign of solidarity. I refused this, together with Talakerer, after talking it over with Rubritius, for the following reasons: the punishment meted out to Kirchmaier was formally justified, even if perhaps Warnakoff would not have made the denouncement to Omsk, if somebody else had been involved; that if we refused to work only the sick would suffer and that nothing else would be achieved, except that other surgeons would come. Kirchmaier was soon afterwards transferred from Tobolsk. One can see that we acted correctly, as our relations with Warnakoff improved, which meant more for our soldiers than the arrival of strange doctors, who would not have known the local conditions so well. We helped many a soldier, and many an officer, to be transferred to a neutral country or even to be exchanged because of illness. Warnakoff hardly ever re-examined their cases and relied on us completely. Rubritius left us suddenly in the summer of 1916. An order arrived from Omsk, that he had to go to Kaluga (in European Russia), where a surgeon was needed. We never learned whether Lindeberg was behind it (perhaps eventually becoming jealous of Rubritius's superior capacity as a surgeon).

Red Cross visit.

Thus I remained in the hospital with Talakerer and the four medicos (medical students). We lived there in a large room. The sick officers were in the former Lazarett (Marodenhaus), later we obtained the small house next to the Gubernium Hospital, mentioned previously, where we lived in 1916-17. After Christmas, Talakerer left us, because of petty conflicts, he was a quarrelsome man and, after his illness, very irritable and I remained alone with the students, while Talakerer lived in the former Maroden house and Dr. Sametz did duty in the camp. In the summer of 1916 we received a visit from the Red Cross Sister, Baroness Hussar. She visited all the camps, took notes, and distributed a lot of money. Dr. Sametz told her some very disparaging things about Warnakoff, which upset Warnakoff considerably. I told her the whole story of the epidemic truthfully, but said that the care of the sick now went on without any complaints. Lieutenant Junger accompanied her as supervising officer. We were invited to a meal.

Baroness Hussar described the war situation optimistically, we stood deep in Poland, the Russians seemed exhausted. When she asked me if I had some wish, I said that I would like to be exchanged as an invalid, or at least transferred to a neutral country, as I had been suffering from acute dysentery since the winter. This story grew to a heart complaint, from which I was supposed to be suffering, as she told my wife after a lecture at home. I actually applied to the Russians for an exchange, it was also endorsed by Warnakoff and sent on, but was never dealt with.

The combatants in the 1914-18 war.

This war was between the Central European Powers (Germany, Austria-Hungary, and allies) on one side and the Triple Entente (Britain and the British Empire, France, and Russia) and their allies, including the USA (which entered in 1917), on the other side.

LETTERS SENT TO MERTHYR TYDFIIL AND SWANSEA FROM THE GREAT WAR

On 3 July 1996 Dr Rosentyl Griffiths, Cardiff, presented to the Archive of the Museum of Welsh Life (formerly Welsh Folk Museum), St Fagans, eight letters sent home to Merthyr Tydfil and Swansea from soldiers serving in France during the Great War. (One of them in fact was addressed from the 'War Hospital' in Bradford.) Four of the letters were sent to the donor's father, the late Thomas Griffiths ('Brydan') who at the time resided at Maes-y-ffynnon, The Walk, Merthyr Tydfil. He was an employee of The Educational Publishing Co. Ltd., Cardiff, and was a highly respected member of and Sunday school teacher at Zoar Congregational Chapel, Merthyr. In fact, three of the four letters sent to him were by former members of his Sunday school class at Zoar. Another four were sent by Walter Vicarage (he was Mr Griffiths' nephew) to his immediate family in Swansea. These came later into Mr Griffiths' possession.

The eight letters were written in pencil by: David L. Davies, David Evans, Ben Lewis (all of Merthyr Tydfil) and Walter Vicarage (of Swansea). They are dated between 12 September 1915 and 29 May 1916. Collectively they form an important Welsh contemporary record of trench warfare and of the abominable conditions experienced at the front. How did the young recruits of 1915-16, we may ask, perceive the War? These letters written by four Glamorgan men in the battlefield provide some of the answers. In one letter home Walter Vicarage comments' . . . this is a war we cannot explain, you only know how it is going on when you are actually in it'. Despite the obvious hardship and deprivation, there was undoubtedly a feeling of adventure and comradeship throughout—'It is rather a funny game . . . many narrow escapes and excitement . . . There is plenty of sport attached to the game as well . . . Talk about fun . . . it has been a great experience . . . '. Ben Lewis, however, thought differently and expressed his feelings more profoundly—'The conditions under which we are fighting is really worse than the enemy itself. But I feel very proud to have been out to fight the enemy of civilization and rights . . . '.

The letters have been transcribed by Bethan Roberts, Cardiff, and edited by myself. They are published here in the hope that their contents will be of particular interest to historians of the period.

A. LLOYD HUGHES

Museum of Welsh Life, St Fagans

1 (3712/4)

Somewhere in France
Sunday 12th Sept. [19]15

My dear Parents Bro & Sisters

How sweet after a hard week marching from place to place to find ourself resting on a glorious Sabbath morn although not far from the firing line. I am pleased to say I am in the best of health and am enjoying the simple life. Of course only what I expected just now. We have had a fairly rough time feeding only on bully beef and biscuits and fruit that we picked and bought on the way as we were in a rather poor part of the country. But how we shift about. I am now in sight of the German trenches although I have not been in the trenches yet. Some of them have. Yes this is a war we cannot explain, you only know how it is going on when you are actually in it. I am at present writing this between two fine big guns who are booming away and shelling the enemy somewhere or other. Yet I am quite safe as they know not where they are. In fact some of our boys are actually playing football and I have enjoyed a nice swim. They are watching for you as well so you haven't to keep your head above water to[o] much. Some of the boys of another Reg. who are instructing us in our duties brought a sniper down from a tree last night. They saw a shot fire from the tree so they fired together and down something comes with a bump. It is rather a funny game but you can go on for years like this and never get hit if you are careful. I think we are only in for a couple of days but it will be quite enough as it is rather funny to see the boys busily engaged catching live stock. My word picking them by the dozen. What a game.

Well I am glad to say I am still well and as long as it keeps like it is now, have not much to fear.

I must again close with my very best love.

Y[ou]r boy Walt[er]

II (3712/5)

[Sept. 1915]

Dear Ma

Its a bit now and a bit again. We have come back from the trenches now so you see we are quite alright so far. We have seen many aeroplane[s] attacked. Our air men are good sports and the Germans attack them like fun but they are too smart for them. They brought one of the German aeroplanes down yesterday at the place we are now at.

I have not come across anybody I know yet since I have been here but some of the boys have met their brothers and today we met one of our boys who transfer[r]ed to the R.E. He has been twice or three times mentioned in despatches. He is a comical chap with his yarns. We have been most fortunate as regards weather and are at present in a very warm part and are in barns under cover or at least would have been had not the Germans shelled the roofs in. Its a sight to see some of the villages about here in ruin but nothing compared with other parts of the country as we are at present in what is regarded as a quiet part.

No doubt you will get my next letter from the trenches as we are expected to go in soon but by what I can hear you are quite as safe (where we are) there as in the billet we are at now. I should not be at all surprised to meet F. Bullock out here. You never know. I am glad to know you are all quite well [and] also [the family] at Brynamman.

I had a letter from Uncle Tom; he also told me Uncle David was there. I must write to him when I have time. I have only written to May once. I know she is in a stew about it, but I must try now and let you both have some news regular[ly] or at least as often as I can. Of course we have been so unsettled this week and I have had no possible chance to write you a decent line before.

I am glad you had my parcel but you need not keep my things [as] I do not require anything just now. We are getting bread, butter and everything now, also cigerettes [*sic*], but you can certainly send me a small parcel sometimes. It is too dark to write any more so I must close now with very best love to all.

Y[ou]r loving son Walt[er]

III (3712/6)

From the trenches
[Sept. 1915]

Well here we are at last and although we are in a part of the line where it is not to be compared with some others, it is quite enough.

Rather a creepy experience coming to the trenches in the dark stumbling over one thing and another, and falling down holes made by shells, and then at one point of the road where it was rather low we did not half have to duck. It was rather a game to see all our boys crouching on their hands and knees as the bullets were whistling over our heads and the Germans throwing those flares that light up the place for ever so far so you had to keep low; that was on our way to the trenches. Now we reach them and are going through passage after passage of trenches until we reach the fire trench where you keep low and have a pop at them now and again. Of course you cannot see any of them at night but you fire at places where you see them fire from. They, of course, have their snipers out and although we were shelled there were no casualties to our Reg. One boy got a smack with a bit of shrapnel but he was only bruised and scraped a little. I have had several letters from May and she is in a great fix about not hearing from me. She sent us a parcel but unfortunately it was all in a heap so if you do send one do send it in something strong. You can also send me a pot of Harrisons Nursery Pomade or some other High Explosive to kill the little creatures.

We were in the trenches for two nights and two days. My word what a game. I must now close as I am afraid my letter is too long now. Give my best love to all.

Best love Walt[er]

IV (3712/7)

Somewhere in France
Monday 27th Sept. [1915]

Dear Uncle [Tom]

I recieved [*sic*] your long letter and was glad to know you were well and enjoyed your holidays. We are also on our holidays (I dont think) sitting at present in my digs and the glare of the electric light has made my eyes sore, but our present apartments were more than acceptable after the nine days we have just done in the trenches and the march we had to do between the showers of rain before we reached it. But like all the old tumble down barns (as there are not many others in the parts we have been) they are a palace to the tired soldier.

This is our second time in the trenches and although we have not been out many weeks we have seen enough and have already learned that we are not out for a picnic as we have been very busy and had to get straight on with the business. Not like the majority having sometime at the base. We have been in billets resting not far from the firing line and have had to be on the move very often on account of it before we got shifted out by their big guns. We only shifted out in time from one place, as it was in ruin a little later, and every village we pass is in ruin. We have been most fortunate as regards casualties. I think only one killed and a few wounded, but many narrow escapes and excitement. We were resting in our dug-out the other day (I say resting as we dont get much sleep in the trenches, we do the business and watching in the night and rest in the day when we are not on duty) and a shell burst just in front of the parapet of our trench. Several pieces flew into the dug-out but apart from just striking one of the boys and bruising him a bit, it did no other damage. There is

129

plenty of sport attached to the game as well although things are all so uncertain. We have got some lads in our Platoon altogether English, Irish, Scotch & others and I can tell you some of them take beating with their ways, so you see it makes up for the little difficulties that naturally come in this game. I am pleased to say I feel fitter than ever and as long as you are in good health you feel good enough for anything.

We had a bit of excitement the other night. The Germans blew up a part of the trench on our left occupied by another Regiment of our Brigade and I can tell you it was rather excitement. Three of us just forty yards off their trench armed with bombs awaiting their attack with bullets and shells whiz[z]ing over your head, but their attack was a failure and a surprise for them to be met by our boys' rapid fire, and apart from about six being wounded by the trench being blown up, there was no other damage done on our side.

We have had three good days rest here and I expect we shall be going into the trenches again soon.

There are no books you can send me. In fact we have so many things to carry already but anything you think of sending you may. Some papers or something like that. In fact anything is acceptable now. But at present we have plenty of cigerettes [*sic*]. What would be better than anything else at present would be a battery for my lamp as they are very handy. Enclosed is a pattern.

Sorry I cannot write any more just now but I hope I shall have the pleasure of talking it over again although it is a bit soon to think of that.

Best love Walt[er]

V (3712/8)

Somewhere in France
Thursday 30th [Sept. 19]15

My dear Parents Bro & Sisters

I was more than pleased to receive your last letter and the day following your very useful and acceptable parcel. It was just a change and just what I wanted. Of course it all depends on where we are and the circumstances what parcels are most suitable. For instance our last time in the trenches we would have given anything for just a loaf of bread then again when we got back to our billets for rest where we could get some, all our parcels came but I can tell you they were very acceptable. In fact anything is very acceptable. A loaf of bread brown or a tin of salmon or anything when you feel like it. We dont require any cigerettes [*sic*] as we get plenty or as many as I require.

I heard from Jack this week and I see he is in a hospital at Rouen so he will be safe there for a while and I hope soon get better.

Well Ma I think my last letter was that I was again in the trenches but since, we have had a couple of really good restful days after marching miles after leaving the trenches. We went out Tuesday night trench digging and it was undoubtedly our worse experience as regards conditions. It rained pouring all the time and we had to trudge through mud over the tops of our boots through the trenches before we started our digging, so you can guess what we looked and felt like by the time we had finished. Talk about fun although we are not allowed to make any row night time we had many a good chuckle to see one boy after the other go ploughing into the mud as it was a task to stand, and then all of a sudden you would miss another as he had fallen down a six foot trench etc. Well that helped towards our merriment in such difficulties but I can tell you we were all jolly glad to reach our billet once more. The next day we had off to dry our clothes and rest and we were again ready to start off in the early morning for the place we are now at, and here am I at something about midnight, just after coming from the trenches after taking water up to the boys, writing this letter in my comfortable little house that was probably somebodys happy home. Here we are for this week although not actually in the trenches all together but just twenty minutes walk off the firing line in support of our other three Companies who are up there.

We are here for any emergencies and in the meanwhile take food and water and anything they require up. This is three different parts we have been now in the trenches so you see they have shifted us about a bit. You have no doubt read of our great advance along the line. Rather strange we were relieved that evening by another Regiment or we should have advanced as well, but they had the pleasure instead.

We have seen some destruction in the parts we have been lately and more than one tear. Poor old people having to clear off and leave their belongings behind. This place shows signs of great struggles and the wreckage of shell and bullets is to be seen everywhere. Rather strange I should have a letter from Mr Willoughby the day after I had enclosed his in my last one to you. I havent met any of the Tabernacle boys yet. I met a boy from Manselton, Rice from Waun Wen Rd., also Willie Burns [?] is an officer. Burns, the teachers son [from] Waun Wen Rd., and I just missed seeing Ernie Wheatley from Lamb Street. He was in the Regiment relieving us. Time is getting on so I must turn in and have an hour or so before I have to go on duty again. I am pleased to say I am in the best of health.

> Best love. Y[ou]r loving Son & Bro
Remember me to all   Walt[er]

VI (3712/9)

> Friday
> Dec. 17th [1915]

Dear Friend

I'm sending you a few lines as promised. We are now in France we've just come back from the trenches having been in for 3 days. I can tell you it has been a great experience, the bullets were whizzing over our heads, the big guns booming, the noise was terrible, there were quite a number injured and 1 killed, but not one from our own Battalion. Well dear Friend, I havent got much more to say only it was very cold for our feet in the trenches. When I'll come home I shall be able to give you a lot of news but we dare not write much as our letters are censored. My address is David Evans 17228 6 Platoon, B Coy 13 Batt RWF. This is the only way we're allowed to give our address in case it should come into the hands of the enemy. Dont put more on the envelope than the address I mentioned. Well Friend I must conclude with my kindest regards to Mrs Griffiths and the children; accept the same yourself From your old "Sunday School" pupil.

> David Evans

No. 2614
Ward E1
War Hospital
Bradford
Jan. 18 / 1916

Dear Mr Griffiths,

I beg to thank you very sincerely for your kind and much welcomed letter I received this morning. I was really very glad to hear from you and again I feel gratefull [*sic*] to you for your kind offer to help me in any form possible.

It gives me great encouragement to think that there are people at Zoar who are continually thinking of us young men who have joined up. I can honestly say that I spent the happiest time since leaving home when I was an active member at Zoar Sunday school and "Young peoples Society". And for myself personally, I feel proud to have been a member of your Sunday school class, although not for a very long time as I had to take a class of boys in the vestry. I was also very much taken to admire you by the way you used to visit all new young men members coming to Zoar and invite them to your Sunday school class, therefore leading them in the right path on their arrival in a new town, and before they had time to go astray on leaving their homes perhaps for the first time. May God bless you with health and strength to continue the good work which you have always done in his name and cause.

I am very pleased to inform you that I am regaining my strength wonderfully. Although not wounded very seriously, I have been suffering from trench fever, rheumatism and trench feet (which is a new complaint) unknown before the war. I was hurt in the left arm when I was partly buried by a shell from a "Jack Johnson" which blew up the trench and also its occupants. I was really lucky as some of my fellow comrades were killed and very seriously wounded. I am pleased to say that my arm is alright now again.

My feet were also very painfull [*sic*] for a very long time. This is really a new complaint to medical science and yet they dont really know the best way to cure them. They burn like fire all the time and must not have the bed clothes to touch them. It is caused by being in water for a long time.

The last time I was in the trenches for four days up to our waists in water and mud. That was on the Somme front and in front of Bapaume. I was in the Somme front all the time. The first time I spent a night in Camp at Mametz Wood before going to the trenches right along through Trones and Delville Woods.

There were no communication trenches and we had to walk across the open right to the front line trench, being shelled all the time and causing big casualties. The place is all shell holes and makes it difficult to go in and out of trenches in the dark. The conditions under which we are fighting is really worse than the enemy itself. But I feel very proud to have been out to fight the enemy of civilization and rights and I believe we shall see the end now in this spring or summer.

When I do visit Merthyr I shall certainly call to see you and Mrs Griffiths. Perhaps I shall be able to tell you my experiencies [*sic*] in France then better than on writing paper.

This is my first day up from bed the whole day, and I am feeling fairly strong and hope to be discharged in about a week or two again for convelacent [*sic*] Home. Well [*sic*], rhaid i mi derfynu nawr gyda Cofio[n] cyn[h]esaf attoch [*sic*] chwi a Mrs Griffiths. Gyda diolch yn gyn[n]es i chwi am eich llythur [*sic*] caredig.

Hope to be able to see you before very long.

      Yours very sincerely

      Ben Lewis

VIII (3712/11)

May 29th 1916
Somewhere in France

Dear Mr Griffiths

Am taking the greatest pleasure to write these few lines to you as promised, trusting that they will find you and your family in the very best of health, as they leave me at present.

The weather is lovely out here now. Wel[l] Mr Griffiths I havent been in the firing line yet, but we are not very far off all the same [*censored*] every day [*censored*]. Am sleeping in an old barn of a French farmhouse at present along with eight others, the hens, and the pigs are your [*sic*] daily visitors. They tramped all over us one night, they soon woke us up, but we are quite happy all the same; we dont expect to get everything here like when at home. Gr. David L. Davies 59911 99 Siege Battery R.G.A., Brittish [*sic*] E. Force, France. Wel[l] Mr Griffiths am glad to inform you that we get plenty to eat here, so we will manage allright [*sic*]. Wel[l] I must now draw to a close hoping that this will find you safe. Good bye.

      Kind regards

      [David] Davies

"LIFE IN THE LAMB"

by

ROSINA HUGHES

(NEE WALSH)

We moved into The Lamb in 1928 when I was one year old. I was born in Dadcu's house in Abercanaid for my father Bill Walsh was unemployed. Previously he had managed "The Mason's Arms" in Troedyrhiw for his aunt but when her daughter married she decided to take over the business. Father, mother and my sister Sheila had to move on.

My parents were delighted to have the tenure of The Lamb but they were disheartened at the state of the house when they arrived. There were some poor sticks of furniture and the whole house was dirty and smelly. Infected bedding had been left in one room so all the bedrooms had to be fumigated and the bedding burned.

My mother Ceinwen Elizabeth had been brought up in a caring Methodist home so hard work held no terror for her. She set to with a will and with a little help from a girl called Rosie she soon had the house shining like a pin.

My father was a good cellar-man and knew how to cosset the barrels of beer that were stacked on wooden stages in the cool below. Pipes led up to the porcelain beer pulls whence draught beer was served at the correct temperature after settling down, sometimes for days. Best beer stood in barrels on a wooden dais in the bar. This was seven pence a pint and draught beer was six pence. Rough cider was three pence a pint!

The Lamb was a poor place at first but father, in his quiet determined way, slowly changed it. At first it was difficult to sell the basic quota of beer and spirits he was obliged to take from the brewers. He told me once that his profit on a pint was one penny. He was always grateful to B. Harris Jones who kept the "Ladies Outfitters" next door. Bert brought a nucleus of good trade to the house. Soon word got around that here was good beer in a clean, convivial atmosphere.

"Patsy the Dray" brought beer every week. He called us "Sheila and Zena The Lamb" in retaliation. He had one or two pints of beer wherever he stopped and was like a toby jug with a mop of dark hair, blue eyes and a pink complexion. The beer was rolled down into the cellar from the front pavement where Patsy helped manoeuvre it into position. We always kept crusts and apples for the horse.

My first clear memory of The Lamb was lying in the big mahogany cot in one of the attics and wondering why I had been relegated to the cot while my younger cousin Barbara slept in my bed.

There were four attic rooms with dormer windows. One had been converted into a bath room with a huge concertina tank and a large bath on claw legs. I learned later that the Merthyr football team used to bathe here after a match. The fire in the big kitchen range roared like a lion on Saturdays to heat the water for so many people. Naturally the team trooped into the bar afterwards and drank numerous pints. Another attic room had a winch and a trap door. Pulleys dangled from the ceiling with tattered ropes attached. Beer had been brewed on the premises before the days of big breweries. There was a very large stone out-house in one of the yards where the beer had been fermented. We always assumed that the pub had been built in the early eighteen hundreds.

On the first floor was a comfortable sitting room which looked on to Castle Street. Here my sister and I spent most of our childhood in the care of a "maid". I think my mother gave Beryl McLoughlin five shillings a week to take care of us when she came home from school and at weekends. Beryl lived with her parents and sister Muriel in a tiny cottage opposite which was rented from the "Co-op". The latter stood on the corner of Castle and Glebeland Street. Taking the "Divvy" book we bought most of our groceries there.

Beside the sitting room there were four good bedrooms, the Long Room and a sizable toilet with brass fittings and a mahogany seat. Various clubs met here including the R.A.O.B. and M.O.O.S.E. A huge fire was lit in the winter and trays full of beer were carried upstairs. This all brought good regular trade to the house while my parents were young and healthy.

On the ground floor a stone passageway led from the front to the back of the house. Mary Davies scrubbed this floor every day for years. I do not know what my mother would have done without this large Irish woman who lived in the Quar. She brought up five girls on a small wage and did all our washing at the week end for which she received five shillings and a bar of soap.

The first room, as you entered, on the right, was called the "Smoke Room" but everybody smoked in those days. At the weekend the bar would be a haze of smoke but my parents never had any illnesses. My sister and I were kept well away from the business until we were much older. Next to the "Smoke Room" was the heart of the house, the kitchen. There was a "PRIVATE" sign on the door but this was where the women came to socialize and drink their Guinness or port and lemon.

The big steel range, a product of Cyfarthfa, always had a fire, otherwise there was no hot water. A vast oven on one side cooked very slowly and there was always a huge kettle simmering on the hob. On very cold days people would come in for a tot of whisky with hot water and brown sugar.

Picture a large table in the centre of the room, a couch and some comfortable old chairs and this was where the wives of the bar customers came mid week and Saturday to gossip, seek advice, swop recipes and "cure alls", which usually ended up with a sing song. I especially remember the two Mrs. Hills, Sal Richards, Mrs. Prosser and Mrs. Carey. Their meetings were a boon during the war when young husbands were away and their wives needed companionship and a bit of cheer. At the end of the evening all would go off cheerfully, a number up the British Tip. They all seemed large, generous and kind to me and at Christmas we had many presents.

The bar and lounge were on the left. The lounge was snug and private with sliding doors. There was a fire here too and small round mahogany tables, collectors items now. In the winter Betty, Mary's daughter, lit four fires every day. The house had thick stone walls and I never remember feeling cold as a child.

The lounge was where a number of teachers and other professionals met. Later this was the haunt of many of the council. I remember Havard Walters, Dan Jones, Bill Thomas, the saddler and Ron Baker who had a garage. They all had hilarious fun in this little room and formed a club which I believe was called the "30 club". They met in the Long Room one night a week to practice for a concert which never seemed to materialize. They would demand a "supper" two or three times a year. Mother had to do all the cooking which entailed two courses plus coffee and cheese which had to be carried up stairs. They enjoyed this immensely and a riotous evening would ensue.

My father was a good pianist and we had a long "Obermeyer" piano with a grand tone. Hayden Phillips conducted, father accompanied, Havard Walters sang in a light tenor, Ron Baker played cornet (in one key) and Bert (Harris) Jones played mandolin (after a fashion). The result was far from harmonious but all done with gusto and much laughter.

The bar was always a mixture of people. No woman would be seen here but at the side was a little snug with a screen at eye level where lone women came in to have a bottle filled and tucked under a shawl. These bottles always held more than a pint but they were always filled to the top.

There was a big tortoise stove in the centre of the bar and in the winter it glowed red hot. Some old cronies with clay pipes would come down from the lodging house in Castle Street and hug the stove for hours when it was frosty. Others would play cards at the corner table. "Little Billy", when he was well oiled with best beer, would get up on the table and do a clog dance. He was very small and wore laced-up boots. His friend, also brought up in an orphanage, was named the "Champion Scrubber". He claimed to have won all his medals for scrubbing floors in the orphanage. His chest was certainly covered with them but on closer inspection they proved to be Sunday School badges for good attendance.

Bill Thomas, who had the saddler's shop next door, came in two or three times a day for a "sup". He usually came from the serving side of the bar and vaulted the counter with ease. He could also shin up a smooth pillar in the bar. He challenged others to do this, many tried but no one succeeded.

The war started quietly enough but father, ever prepared, decided to strengthen the cellar with pit props. He'd been a coal miner and soon shored up the smaller area. We were ordered to run to the cellar immediately the siren howled its warning. I was asleep in bed the first time we heard "Moaning Minnie" and somebody came to wake me. I tore downstairs to find my beloved cat Ginger and with her howling a complaint ran down to huddle with gas mask and torch. There were a few tummy churning moments as we heard Jerry drone overhead then the steady "all clear" sounded.

Apart from a few incendiaries dropped on the mountain and dashes to the shelter, ours was a quiet war. We were very aware of the agonies of many of our customers and friends who had loved ones fighting on various fronts.

There was a huge map on the bar wall and after "D" Day all the various "pushes" were clearly marked with coloured string and pins. The war was won many times in that bar. Sometimes it would be full of Canadian soldiers from Senny Bridge. Fortunately they mixed in very well with the locals.

Beer was rationed during the war and first of all Dad tried to keep the quota for his (regular) customers. Of course the dray brought the barrels and within the hour news had spread—"beer in The Lamb". Once, when the back door was opened, there was a well behaved queue waiting which stretched almost to the Castle Cinema. In the end The Lamb opened three days a week, which meant for the first time in their lives Mother and Father could spend some days together.

Eventually they managed to get the lease of The Lamb. They had been tied to the Taff and Rhymney Breweries, who took the lion's share. Now Dad could buy as he wished. He introduced draft Bass and Guinness and was soon doing a roaring trade.

Sadly my mother died in 1958. Her genial disposition was greatly missed. Letters flooded in from many, many people. Neither my mother nor my father smoked or drank but they enjoyed the chat and the fun.

My father was landlord of The Lamb for over thirty years and I never remember his having any trouble with the police. Many of the police were our customers and if one was on duty outside on a cold or wet night he would wait until the sergeant had done his rounds then nip in at the back door for a hot toddy or a cup of tea while mother draped his damp cape over the guard in front of the fire.

"BILL", as everybody called him, was a taciturn man who looked rather severe. He was large with a shock of white hair. One old wag told him he looked "more like a broken-down preacher than the landlord of a pub". This made Dad chuckle for days.

Some years ago I stood on the site of the demolished Lamb and nostalgia flowed over me in great waves. I could recall so many sounds and feel the warmth of the place—the laughter, the singing, the many kindnesses, the behind the scenes hard toil to get everything right for the next day. This, so many people have told me, WAS A HOUSE WITH A HEART.

My father retired to Devon in 1961. I don't think he could bear the thought of Sunday opening. He divided his time between my sister and myself and truly delighted in his four grand-children. He died just before Christmas 1962. THE END OF AN ERA.

32. Bill Walsh, landlord, The Lamb Inn, Merthyr Tydfil.

33. Ladies outing from The Lamb. Mrs. Walsh, the landlord's wife, fourth from the left, back row.

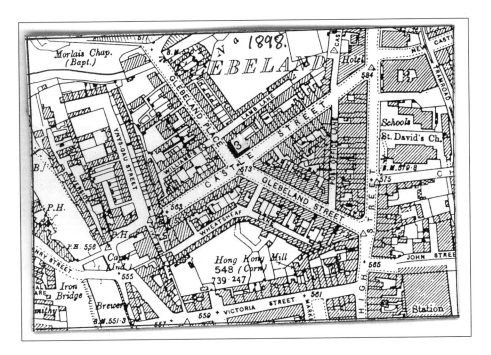

35. The Lamb Inn (3) and nearby streets, 1898.

143

36. A delivery to The Lamb Inn, Merthyr Tydfil.

37. Castle Street, Merthyr Tydfil. The Bee Hive Inn, landlord, Tom Donald, on left. Beer is being delivered by lorry to The Lamb, right.

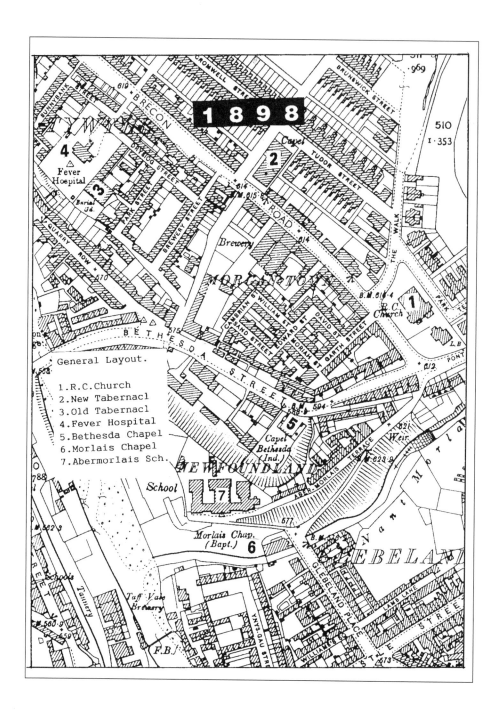

General Layout.

1. R.C.Church
2. New Tabernacl
3. Old Tabernacl
4. Fever Hospital
5. Bethesda Chapel
6. Morlais Chapel
7. Abermorlais Sch.

TABERNACL CHAPEL, BRYANT'S FIELD

by

T. F. HOLLEY

A congregation worshipped at the old Tabernacl Welsh Baptist church, Bryant's Field, Merthyr Tydfil, from 1836 to 1897.

In 1896 a movement arose to provide more central and comfortable accommodation for Tabernacl church.

I have conducted extensive research into the history of this Bryant's Field church, its pastors and prominent members, which I hope to publish in the future.

In this brief history will be found:

A. An account of the stone laying ceremony for the new Tabernacl, Brecon Road, which took place in 1896.

B. A report on the last sermon preached at old Tabernacl, Bryant's Field, in 1897. This latter contained a brief history of old Tabernacl.

C. A translation by Dr. William Linnard, from a book, IOAN EMLYN, with a portrait of Ioan Emlyn (Dr. J. Emlyn Jones).

D. A Merthyr Tydfil Art Union advertisement, 1866.

E. A map of the Bryant's Field area.

A.

"A movement was set in motion to provide more central and comfortable accommodation for Tabernacl Church. The idea was first mooted by Mrs. David Davies, wife of Alderman David Davies and when that lady died, Alderman Davies took up the movement with characteristic zeal. A strong Committee, with the pastor, Rev. David Price, as Chairman, and D. L. Jones and Evan Morgan as Secretaries, was formed. The self-sacrificing nature of the congregation, composed mainly of working men, was revealed when £1,000 was quickly raised.

The plans for the new chapel were entrusted to George Morgan of Carmarthen, who designed a building in the Norman style, containing, in addition to the main body of the structure, a spacious schoolroom. The main building comprised a handsome portico (porch with columns), a chapel capable of seating nine hundred, with gallery on three sides and an organ chamber and rostrum (pulpit) on the fourth side. There was also a minister's room, vestry and offices. The contract was given to John Jones, Glanynant, the cost when completed was expected to be £5,000.

The foundation stones were laid at a ceremony held in July 1896, the event was reported in the *Merthyr Express* for 11.7.1896. p.8. A large assembly gathered, composed of members of all Nonconformist denominations. Present were:

Rev. David Price, pastor of Tabernacl,

Mrs. Gwilym James, Miss Dora James,

Alderman David Davies and Miss Nellie Davies,

Alderman Thomas Williams, J.P.,

Colonel D. R. Lewis,

Mr. William Harris,

Rev. T. Salathiel,
Rev. J. G. James, B.A.,
Rev. Alfred Hall,
Rev. John Thomas, Zoar,
Rev. Mr. Griffiths, Cefn,
Rev. D. L. Jones,
Mr. John Jones, Glanynant,
Mr. Rees Abraham, precentor,
Councillors J. Lewis and W. Lewis,
Rev. Jason James, Penydarren,
Mr. Gilleland, Mr. T. J. Rice,
Professor Edwards, Cardiff.

In an address, Rev. David Price detailed the acquisition of the site from Mr. John Vaughan, solicitor. He wanted the new building to compare favourably with others in the district (perhaps St.Mary's?). Rev.Price stated that his congregation comprised four hundred members, plus three or four hundred other adherents, who were regular attendants. On Sunday evenings the congregation averaged seven hundred people.

Six foundation stones were laid in the front of the building, and one on the left side, they were laid in the following order:

By the pastor, for Mr. D. A. Thomas, M.P.,	Ten guineas
Colonel David Rees Lewis	Fifteen pounds
Miss Nellie Davies, dau. of Ald. Davies	One hundred pounds
Mr. William Harris	Ten guineas
Mrs. Gwilym C. James, for her husband	Twelve guineas
Mr. Thomas Williams, J.P.	Twelve guineas
Mr. David Davies	Four hundred pounds

Each "mason" was presented with a handsome silver trowel, suitably inscribed, and a boxwood mallet, and they all declared in the usual formula that "this stone is well and truly laid".

The amounts subscribed by those who laid the stones are shown. Mr. T. H. Thomas, Twyn, sent two guineas.

Letters of apology for inability to attend were read by Alderman David Davies. Mr. D. A. Thomas, M.P., telegraphed that he regretted he could not possibly attend, as he was engaged on the Railway Bills Committee. Mr. Gwilym James wrote to say that he could not attend, as he had to attend with the Urban Council at the Pentwyn and Neuadd Reservoirs. The High Constable, Mr. F. T. James, Mr. William Evans, Cyfarthfa, and Mr. W. L. Daniel also wrote, the latter being in London on behalf of the Chamber of Trade in support of the Bute-Rhymney Bill. Mr. John Vaughan also sent a letter of regret, enclosing a cheque for five pounds for the building fund.

Dr. Edwards, Cardiff, terminated the proceedings by proposing a vote of thanks to those who had assisted in the day's events.

In the evening there was a large congregation at the old Tabernacl chapel, when the Rev. C. Davies (Cardiff) and the Rev. G. Griffiths (Rhymney) preached Welsh sermons.

The collections were for the building fund."

B.

"On Sunday evening the worshippers at Tabernacl Welsh Baptist church held their last service in old Tabernacl, Bryant's Field, the new palatial building in Brecon-road will be used for the first time on Sunday next.

The pastor, the Rev. David Price, took advantage of the occasion to give a history of the life of the congregation, who are now so numerous. He explained that in the year 1834 some misunderstanding at Ebenezer church resulted in a split among the members, fifty four of whom left. Twelve of those joined Zion church, and the others went over to Penypound, Aberdare. The journey across the mountain, however, soon tired them, and they began to look round in Merthyr for a suitable place to hold their services in, and they procured a room not far from the old parish church. This they called Dan-y-pound. They worshipped in this room for about two years, but their membership increased so fast that they had to look around for more accommodation. It so happened that in 1830 the Armin Baptists had begun to build a chapel on Bryant's Field, the site of the building in which they were then worshipping, and they were too short of money to finish it, and they left it.

The Welsh Baptists bought the unfinished building for £25, and completed it at a cost of £350. It was then called the Tabernacl Bach. The treasurer of the building fund was Mr. William Williams, Abercanaid, father of the late Rev. Rufus Williams. The Tabernacl Bach was opened for public worship in August, 1836, and the preachers were the Revds. Dr. Jenkins, Hengoed; Saunders, Merthyr; Abel Jones, Merthyr; and William Lewis, Dowlais.

In March 1839, the first minister settled at the church. His name was Thomas Thomas, and he came from Erwood, in Breconshire. He died in 1840 and was buried in the graveyard close to the chapel. The Rev. D. R. Jones, of London, was then invited to take the pastorate. He did not accept the invitation.

In 1841 the late Rev. Benjamin Williams came from Maesyberllan, Breconshire. Mr. Williams was an exceedingly popular man. He was the father of the late Mr. Peter Williams, Editor of the Merthyr Telegraph, and grandfather of Mr. Williams, jeweller, High-street, Merthyr. His daughter is a publisher in Carmarthen town, and the denominational magazine, Seren Cymru, is printed there.

The membership of the chapel when Benjamin Williams settled in Merthyr was ninety five, but the building soon became too small. In 1842 the present (Bryant's Field) building was erected on the site of the old building, and at that time it was the largest chapel in Wales. It cost £2,200, and at the opening they were only able to pay off £100, so that the debt was £2,100 then. Just about this time a monster tea meeting was held in the chapel, and it proved to be about the largest tea ever given, 1714 teas were supplied.

The Rev. Benjamin Williams left in October, 1848, and went to London, and the debt when he left was £1,100. In December 1848, another minister took up the pastorate, the Rev. John Roberts, of Anglesey. He was, no doubt, one of the ablest preachers of his day. His success as a pastor may be estimated by the fact that in one month he baptised 143 people by immersion. He held the pastorate for about five years, and he was followed by the Rev. R. D. Roberts, who settled in Merthyr in 1854. Chapel membership was then 218, and possibly the chapel never enjoyed happier times than during Mr. Robert's ministry. When he left the debt was only £500.

The chapel then invited another Mr. Roberts, of Felinfoel, who accepted the invitation; but at that time his voice failed him, and he was unable to come. In 1864 the chapel was renovated at a cost of about £600, and in October 1864 Dr. J. Emlyn Jones, Cardiff, was appointed. In Dr. Jones's time AN ART UNION WAS STARTED, as the outcome of the idea of Mr. David Davies, who was then a young man; and, as a result of it, they raised £866, and the debt was paid off. In connection with paying off this, jubilee services were held, and the preachers were the Revds. R. D. Roberts, Llwynhendy; Williams, Hengoed; Jones, Abernant; and Lewis, Troedyrhiw.

Dr. Emlyn Jones remained at Tabernacl, Bryant's Field, about five years, and proved himself to be a hardworking man. He possessed many talents, and during his stay in Merthyr he published many valuable books. He was also a chaired bard.

In 1872 the Rev. O. Waldo James, from Hebron, Dowlais, accepted the call from Tabernacl. He left in 1877 for Aberavon. During his stay he received seventy three members into the chapel.

In September 1880, the pastorate was taken by the Rev. J. Ceulanydd Williams, who left for Maesteg in January, 1882, where he is at the present time (i.e. in 1897). He was quite a genius in many respects, and when the National Eisteddfod was held at Pontypridd, he was the chaired bard.

In August 1882 the Rev. Benjamin Thomas came from Haverfordwest College. He left in 1888 to succeed the Rev. Evan Thomas at Newport. After Mr. Thomas left the chapel was over five years without a settled pastor.

In August 1893, the present pastor, the Rev. David Price, settled in Merthyr Tydfil from Cwmtwrch, in the Swansea valley. During the present pastorate, 163 persons have been baptised into membership, that number being as many as had been baptised during the previous sixteen years. It was in the former years of Price's ministry that the need of a new building was felt, and in 1894 it was finally decided to take steps towards that end.

The new building, a most substantial and spacious one, is now complete, and the first services will be held in it on Sunday." (*Merthyr Express*. 4.12.1897).

In 1997 this Tabernacl chapel still stands on Brecon Road, Merthyr Tydfil, and is indeed a most impressive building.

Ministers, Tabernacl Chapel, Bryant's Field. Summary.

1839	Thomas Thomas, Erwood
1841	Benjamin Williams, Maesyberllan
1848	John Roberts, Anglesey
1854	R. D. Roberts
1864	Dr. J. Emlyn Jones
1872	O. Waldo James, Dowlais
1880	J. Ceulanydd Williams
1882	Benjamin Thomas, Haverfordwest
1888-93	No resident pastor available
1893	David Price, Cwmtwrch
1897	First services held in New Chapel, Brecon Road.

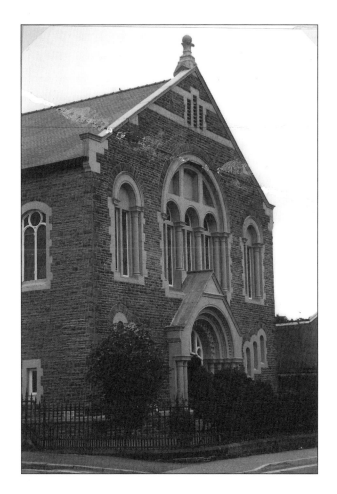

39. Tabernacl Chapel, Brecon Road, Merthyr Tydfil, 1994.

C

A translation by Dr. William Linnard, from a book IOAN EMLYN, by the Revd. D. Bowen, Ilston Press, Swansea, 1924. This gives a biographical account of Dr. J. Emlyn Jones, whilst at Tabernacl, Bryant's Field.

pp.33-35.

"The following account about Ioan Emlyn at Tabernacl, Merthyr, is by the Rev. W. R. Pelidros Jones, Caerau, Maesteg:

'Dr. J. Emlyn Jones was the minister in Tabernacl, Merthyr,in the period between the Rev. R. D. Roberts and the Rev. O. Waldo James. When the Rev. R. D. Roberts left in 1862 the church members numbered 222. I do not know what was the number when Dr. Emlyn Jones left. In the period between the departure of Rev. R. D. Roberts and the installation of Dr. J. Emlyn Jones, a call was made to Rev. Moses Roberts of Felinfoel, and though Mr.

Roberts accepted he was unable to carry out his intention because of ill-health, and he died of consumption at about that time.

'In 1864 several improvements were made at the chapel by painting and refurbishing it. It is said that the church at the time was extremely peaceful and loving, but was declining rapidly in numbers, for some reasons unknown to me. The session letters show there were over one hundred fewer members in 1864 than there were in 1861. But in October 1864 Dr. J. Emlyn Jones was installed as minister in the church. He came to Tabernacl from Cwmbach, Aberdare. Soon after he arrived the church enjoyed a great revival, and scores of members were added to its numbers. Dr. Jones worked hard not only to boost the numbers but also to reduce and clear the chapel's debt. In his time the annual Tabernacl eisteddfod was started, and this became an important event for a while in the town.

'The church was inspired to fight the debt, which was about £700 at that time. The late Abram Fardd gives an interesting description of the successful struggle with the debt in Dr. Emlyn Jones's time, in which the name of the late Alderman David Davies, the Glebeland, is prominent as a leading promoter of the movement. Here is an account of his description. The debt is pictured as Goliath, and Abram Fardd says 'A young man, a member of the church, Dafydd by name, rose up to announce war with the Goliath of the debt. He proposes a plan, namely the ART UNION, and assures the church (i.e. the congregation), if they cooperate, that they will get rid of the debt completely'

The minister accepted the plan with pleasure, but the plan aroused the anger of many of the older members of the church.

They told the young man he would be much wiser to stay in the shop to look after his uncle's goods than to bring new and unproved plans like this before the church. They asked him seriously if he really was so silly as to believe they could as a church with ART UNION and nothing else collect about £650 in one effort? But to no avail: on went Dafydd and his friends, and it was announced that the day of the effort would be 6th December 1866. And by the end of that day the sum of £886 had been raised. After paying off the whole debt of the chapel, £27 remained. On the day of celebration of the Jubilee, Abram Fardd got into the hwyl and sang:

> All debt was paid, the chapel is free;
> The church thanks God for the day;
> The time will come—O! dawn the day
> When all the chapels of the world are free!

'The Jubilee meetings were held on 17th and 18th February, 1867. The ministers serving in the meetings were the Revds. R. D. ROBERTS, LLWYNHENDY; Williams, Hengoed; Jones, Abernant; and Lewis, Troedyrhiw. And when the words of Abram Fardd were read out, it was an exciting sight to see Dr. J. Emlyn Jones casting all the (debt) notes into the fire. It is not certain how long Dr. Jones spent in Tabernacl. As far as we know, there is no record of the date of his departure; but it is understood he was there about four years.

Dr. J. Emlyn Jones (Ioan Emlyn) was one of the most able men that ever stood in a pulpit. He was a man of superior abilities and education. The Tabernacl church was privileged TO HAVE SOME OF THE BEST MINISTERS IN WALES, but according to one of them, the Revd. D. Price (at Bethesda, Swansea, 1924), Dr. Emlyn Jones was the most able of all the ministers that served Tabernacl, Merthyr.

p.58.

"For an appreciation of Ioan Emlyn as a writer and poet, see Dyfnallt in *Seren Gomer*, March 1920.

p.64.

He edited *Y Bedyddiwr,*
Seren Cymru,
Y Winllan.

p.65,66.

'He produced four books.
He composed six odes,
three cywyddau,
three poems in free metre, pryddestau.
He translated two works into Welsh.
He wrote a lot in the press.

p.67.

His thesis on *'The position of religion in Wales'* got him his M.A.
His essay on Hamilton got him his Ll.D. at Glasgow Univ.

p.70.

He was an eisteddfod adjudicator.

p.71.

'He won two of the main Chairs."
Ioan Emlyn's best-known work is "Bedd Y Dyn Tylaud", an English translation by Edmund O. Jones, Vicarage, Llanidloes, appeared in 1896.

The Pauper's Grave

Lo! a grassy mound, where lowers
Branching wide a sombre yew,
Rises as to catch the showers,
Jewelled showers, of heaven-sent dew.
Many a one with foot unheeding,
Tramples down its verdure brave,
Hurrying onward, careless treading—
It is but a paupers grave.

Workhouse hirelings from the Union
Bore him to his last, lone bed,
"Dust to dust", that sad communion
Woke no grief, no tear was shed.
Worn by woes and life's denials,
Only rest he now would crave:
Quiet haven from all trials
To the pauper is his grave.

E'en the rough-hewn stone is broken,
Where some rude, untutored hand
Carved two letters, as a token
Of their boyhood's scattered band,
And when bright Palm Sunday neareth,
When the dead remembrance crave,
Friend nor brother garland beareth
For the pauper's squalid grave.

Not for him the Muse which weepeth,
Carved in marble rich and rare;
Even now time's ploughshare creepeth
Through the grass which groweth there.
O'er the place where he is sleeping
Soon will roll oblivion's wave:
Still God's angel will be keeping
Ward above the pauper's grave.

(*Welsh Lyrics of the Nineteenth Century*. Selected and translated by Edmund O. Jones. First series. London and Bangor, 1896.)

Bedd Y Dyn Tylaud

Is yr ywen ddu, ganghennog,
Twmpath gwyrddlas gwyd ei ben,
Fel i dderbyn o goronnog
Addurniadau gwlith y nen:
Llawer troed yn anystyriol
Yn ei fathru'n fynych gawd,
Gan ysigo'i laswellt siriol—
Dyna fedd y dyn tylawd.

Swyddwyr cyflog gweithdy'r undeb
A'i hebryngodd ef i'w fedd;
Wrth droi'r briddell ar ei wyneb
Nid oedd deigryn ar un wedd:
'Nol hir frwydro â thrafferthion
Daeth i ben ei ingol rawd;
Noddfa dawel rhag anghenion
Ydyw bedd y dyn tylawd.

Mae'r garreg arw a'r ddwy lythyren
Dorrodd rhyw anghelfydd law
Gyd-chwaraeai ag e'n fachgen
Wedi hollti'n ddwy gerllaw:
A phan ddelo Sul y Blodau
Nid oes yno gâr na brawd

154

Yn rhoi gwyrdd-ddail na phwysïau
Ar lwm fedd y dyn tylawd.

Ar sedd fynor nid yw'r awen
Yn galaru uwch ei lwch,
A chyn hir drwy'r las dywarchen
Aradr amser dynn ei swch:
Un a'r llawr fydd ei orffwysfa,
Angof drosto dynn ei hawd;
Ond er hynny, angel wylia
Ddaear bedd y dyn tylawd.

("Y Bedyddiwr", Mehefin, 1854.)

D.

THE MERTHYR TYDFIL ART UNION

PRIZE DRAWING,

IN AID OF THE BUILDING FUND OF THE TABERNACL.

THE DRAWING will take place at the TEMPERANCE HALL, on THURSDAY, December 6th, 1866, in the presence of,—J. Shapton, Esq., High Constable; John Giles, Esq.; William Harris, Esq.; T. Stephens, Esq.; B. Kirkhouse, Esq., Llwyncelyn; T. Curnew, Esq., Plymouth Works; W. Gould, Esq., and other gentlemen.

FIRST PRIZE:—ANY ARTICLE OR ARTICLES CHOSEN AND PURCHASED BY THE SUCCESSFUL DRAWER, OF THE VALUE OF

£50

PRIZE	VALUE £ s.
2nd—A Brilliant-toned Pianoforte in Walnut	25 0
3rd—A Superb Gold Lever Watch	12 12
4th—A Handsome Pony	10 10
5th—A very beautiful Eight-day Clock	8 8
6th—An Elegant Mahogany Chest of Drawers	6 6
7th—A rich Paisley Shawl	4 4
8th—A superfine Black Suit of Gentlennen's Clothes	4 4
9th—A Beautiful Mahogany Couch	3 3
10th—A highly chased Electro Teapot, with Coffee Pot to match	2 2

PRIZE	VALUE £ s.
11th—A pair of Woollen Blankets	1 12
12th—A beautiful Welsh Flannel Gown Piece	1 10
13th—A Travelling Portmanteau	1 5
14th—A Rosewood Writing Desk with brass caps	1 1
15th—A Lady's Rosewood Writing Desk	1 1
16th—A Set of Trays	1 1
17th—An Elegant Swing Looking Glass	1 1
18th—A neat Chimney Time Piece	1 1
19th—A Fine-toned Concertina	1 1
20th—A Leather Dressing Case	1 1

PRIZE	VALUE £ s.
21st—A Lady's Dressing Case	1 1
22nd—A Handsome Cruet Stand complete	1 1
23rd—A Silk Umbrella	1 1
24th—"The Slave Market," a Beautiful Engraving	1 1
25th—"The Highland Bride," a Beautiful Engraving	1 1
26th—A pair of Gentleman's elegant Walking Boots	1 1
27th—A Whitney Overcoat	1 1
28th—A fine Waterproof Overcoat	1 1
29th—A Rich-toned Concert Flute	1 1
30th—A Beautiful Table Cover	1 1

In addition to the above Prizes, there will be above TWO HUNDRED other valuable ones, comprising Timepieces, Engravings, Woollen Shawls, Flannel Aprons, Flannel Shirts, Turnovers, &c, Prime Welsh Hams, Caerphilly Cheese, together with other articles, edible, useful or ornamental.

TREASURER: T. J. Evans, Esq., Brecon Old Bank. AUDITORS: W. Jones, Esq., Cyfarthfa Works; and J. W. Russell, Esq. HONORARY SECRETARIES: T. Phillips, Esq.; and W. Hopkins, Esq. CORRESPONDING SECRETARY: Mr. D. Davies, junior, 3, Glebeland, Merthyr.

The Drawing will be on the principle of the Art Union, and the successful numbers will be published in the MERTHYR TELEGRAPH, Merthyr Express, and the Cambria Daily Leader, of December 14th, 1866.

TICKETS SIXPENCE EACH; or a Book containing 12 Tickets for Five Shillings.

[5743]

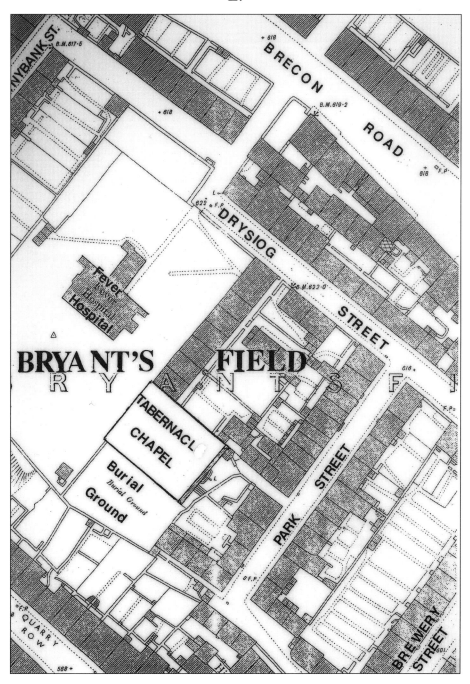

42. A Map of the Bryant's Field area.

43. Members and Guests. Merthyr Soroptimists. Twenty fifth Anniversary Dinner.

SOROPTIMIST INTERNATIONAL
OF
MERTHYR TYDFIL
THE FIRST FORTY YEARS

by

SYDNEY JONES

What is Soroptimism?

Soroptimism means the best of sisters. It is a world-wide organisation of service clubs for professional women. It's purpose is to promote the aims and objects of Soroptimism and to promote international understanding and goodwill.

How did Soroptimism begin?

The first Soroptimist club was formed in 1921 in Oakland, California. A similar organisation was founded in 1920 called the Bristol Venture Club, the two organisations later merged.

The first Soroptimist club in Europe—The Greater London Club was founded in 1923.

The link between the American and European Federations was formed in 1928 creating Soroptimist International. A third federation evolved in 1934, The Federation of Great Britain and Ireland, to which the Merthyr Tydfil Club belongs.

By 1978 the number of countries with Soroptimist clubs had grown to fifty five, giving a wide range of cultural and economic backgrounds, with a fourth federation inaugurated, The South West Pacific.

Membership.

There were over sixty thousand members in two thousand clubs in fifty five countries in 1978.

Membership of a Soroptimist club is by invitation only, each member being a representative of her business or profession, chosen for her individual qualities. Members can attend meetings of any Soroptimist club anywhere in the world and they meet once every four years in an International Convention in different parts of the world. Soroptimist International is represented at the United Nations and co-operates with U.N.E.S.C.O. and U.N.I.C.E.F. and supports projects promoted by F.A.O., W.H.O. and U.N.E.P.

The aims and objects of Soroptimism.

1. To maintain high ethical standards in business, the professions and other aspects of life.
2. To strive for human rights for all people and in particular to advance the status of women.
3. To develop a spirit of friendship and unity among Soroptimists of all countries.
4. To quicken the spirit of service and human understanding and universal friendship.

These aims and objects are read out by the President before each business meeting of each club.

How did Soroptimism begin in Merthyr Tydfil?

A meeting to begin a club in Merthyr Tydfil was held at the home of Margaret Stewart Taylor on June 18th 1957.

Miss Stewart Taylor read Anglo-Saxon and English Literature at St. Hilda's College, Oxford. She became Chief Librarian and Museum Curator at High Wycombe before becoming a full time lecturer in cataloguing and classification at University College, London. After the war, Miss Stewart Taylor became the Chief Librarian and Museum Curator at Merthyr Tydfil.

After her retirement she wrote many books including the novels *Another Door Opened; The Link Was Strong; Marian's Daughter.*

She also wrote, *The Crawshays of Cyfarthfa*, a travel book on St. Helena, *Focus on the Falkland Islands*, and a historical romance, *Napoleon's Captor.*

Margaret Stewart Taylor was a true ambassador for Soroptimism.

Miss Stewart Taylor was a member of the Brecon Club and the initiative to form a club in Merthyr Tydfil was taken by the Cardiff Club.

At this inaugural meeting, sixteen ladies representing the professions, business and industry were present as well as the President of the Divisional Union and three members of the Cardiff Club.

The founder members of the Merthyr Club were:

Miss C. Bevan	Miss B. Renfrey
Dr. C. Clark	Mrs. B. Roberts
Miss M. Davies	Miss S. L. Romet
Mrs. T. C. Dey	Miss M. S. Taylor
Mrs. D. Evans	Miss P. M. Taylor
Miss A. Jennings	Miss G. Thomas
Miss E. Jennings	Mrs. M. Thomas
Miss M. Owen	Miss V. Wood
Miss S. Chapple	Miss R. O. Knight.

Sadly our fortieth year saw the death of Mrs. B. Roberts, our last surviving founder member, still a member of the Merthyr Tydfil Club.

Friendship links between Merthyr and Crescent City, U.S.A., and Rennes, France, were set up and a Presidential badge was purchased at a cost of £34. The Charter Dinner was held on the 28th March 1958 at the Hoover Restaurant, at which the Charter was presented.

After the presentation of the Charter the club began to raise money to support local charities and began service to the community which continues today.

The Aberfan Disaster in 1966 prompted the Merthyr Club to start a fund in memory of one of our founder members, Miss Anne Jennings, who died in the disaster. Miss Jennings was Head Mistress of the school.

The money raised (£1,000) was donated to the Kidney Research Unit for Wales and was used to help purchase a kidney grafting machine.

In 1990 on the death of Miss Margaret Stewart Taylor, who had been made an Honorary Member in 1974, funds were raised and a room was dedicated for prayer and meditation in St. Tydfils Hospital. A stained glass window was commissioned for this room which was dedicated to Soroptimism. The dedication was by the Reverend Nanette Lewis-Head.

Soroptimists give freely to community projects by donations of time, equipment or financial help. The Merthyr Club uses various activities to raise money, for example, autumn

44. Cutting The Cake, 25th Anniversary Dinner.
L to R: Mrs. Babs Roberts, Miss Margaret S. Taylor, Dr. Catherine Clark, three FOUNDER MEMBERS, and President Mrs. Bette Cunnington. 1983.

fayres, jumble sales, nearly new shops, raffles and coffee mornings. Among some of our memorable events, Christmas at Cyfarthfa Castle was held thanks to the generosity of Afon Taf High School Senior Choir and Orchestra under the baton of Mr. Jonathon Gulliford. The venue being the splendour of the newly renovated rooms at Cyfarthfa Castle Museum and Art Gallery.

In contrast a very successful Study Evening was held at St. Tydfil's Hospital to raise awareness of OSTEOPOROSIS, a bone condition which affects women and men.

Soroptimist International Merthyr Tydfil bases its programmes and fundraising on the Soroptimist International Programme, which is divided into six programme areas.

45. Presentation. 25th Anniversary Dinner. L to R:
Mrs. Olwen Leebrook, Divisional President; Miss Thelma De Louw, International President, GUEST SPEAKER; President Mrs. Bette Cunnington. 1983.

1. Economic and Social Development.

Equal opportunities.
Economic literacy.
Economic and social integration.
Women as entrepreneurs.

2. Education.

Literacy.
Parenting.
Training for women and girls.

3. Environment.
Quality of air, water, soil.

Wastes.

Biological diversity, sustainable development.

4. Health.
Promotion of wellness, prevention of illness.

Support systems.

AIDS.

5. Human rights, status of women.
Women and violence.

Rights of the child.

Human rights.

6. International goodwill and understanding.
Refugees.

Sharing projects.

Foster knowledge of different cultures, economic systems and lifestyles.

Our Harvest Supper is held in October and we enjoy meeting the public and visitors from other clubs.

We have an annual 'AT HOME' where we entertain other clubs.

There is an Annual Dinner to celebrate our Charter.

In March we have our Welsh Tea, we invite members of local charities to join us and we distribute our charity monies. Our Welsh Tea of apple tart and cream, bara brith, Welsh cakes and lashings of tea is held in high regard by all who attend.

Some projects undertaken by the club.

1962	Looking further, young people at leisure.
1966	Looking further home and society.
1967	Looking further, towards understanding the welfare of the Senior Citizen.
1972	Environment, shared with Rhondda, Pontypridd, Aberdare clubs.
1980	International goodwill and understanding.
1990	Literacy Project.
1993	Osteoporosis awareness.
1997on	A study of local environmental problems.

The club meets twice a month at Pentrebach House on the first and third Wednesday of each month. The club would like to thank the manager and his staff for their generosity and unfailing good humour which has been greatly appreciated.

One meeting is a business meeting, the other is usually a speaker meeting which helps with our projects. At our Annual Dinners, the President invites a Speaker to talk to our guests. The topics ranging from "Medicine is a woman's job in Russia" given by Dr. Mary Esslemont, C.B.E., J.P.., LL.D.,M.A., B.Sc. to "Punishment should fit the crime" says "Fabian of the Yard".

Members are also energetic in their participation in Federation. Miss M. S. Taylor and Mrs. Maisie Davies were both Divisional Union Presidents. Mrs. Maisie Davies was made an Honorary Member of the Merthyr Club in 1987 and is still an active member and an inspiration to our members. She has given many years of devoted service to the club and continues to support its efforts.

46. Presentation of cheque to Managing Director of Company at Dursley, Glos., for supply of water-pumping equipment for Mozambique, 1983. L to R. M.D., Bette Cunnington, President, Mrs. Maisie Davies.

47. Margaret Stewart Taylor Chapel, St. Tydfils Hospital, 1990.

Membership of S.I. Merthyr Tydfil, 1997-98.

President	Mrs. Sue Medd	Secretary, Afon Taf School.
Secretary	Mrs. Sydney Jones	Head of Year Two, Afon Taf.
Treasurer	Mrs. M. Barlow	Tax Adviser.
Past President	Mrs. D. Kertesz	Gynaecologist.
President Elect	Mrs. H. Aylward	Dispensing Optician.

Members.

Mrs. Jan Caswell
Mrs. Bette Cunnington
Mrs. Suzanne Doolan
Mrs. Angela Tyler
Mrs. Claire Jones
Mrs. Margaret Rees
Mrs. Brenda Roberts
Mrs. June Pullman
Mrs. Maria Thomas (our newest member)

Senior

Mrs. Necia Jennings
Mrs. Ceridwen Adams-Morgan
Mrs. Joan Bennett
Mrs. Mary Bevan
Mrs. Maisie Davies
Mrs. Margaret Davies
Miss Vera Gammon
Mrs. Mair Jones
Miss Marjorie Griffiths
Mrs. Dorothy Harverson

Past Presidents of Soroptimist International Merthyr Tydfil.

1957-59	Miss M. S.Taylor, M.A., F.L.A.
1959-60	Mrs. E. M. Dey, R.I.A.M.
1960-61	Dr. C. Clark, M.B., Ch.B. D.P.H
1961-62	Mrs. B. Roberts
1962-63	Miss D. K. Wood, B.A., Dip.Ed., Psych.
1963-64	Miss A. Jennings
1964-65	Miss Margaret Wills
1965-66	Mrs. G. Williams, D.N.(Lond)
1966-67	Miss M. S. Taylor, M.A., F.L.A.
1967-68	Mrs. Olivia Francis
1968-69	Miss Phyllis Bevan, B.A.
1969-70	Miss Marjorie Griffiths
1970-71	Mrs. Necia Jennings
1971-72	Mrs. Margaret Davies
1972-73	Mrs. Non Francis-Williams
1973-1974	Mrs G. M. White, S.R.N.
1974-75	Mrs. Maisie Davies
1975-76	Miss Ira Lewis
1976-78	Mrs. Mair Jones, S.R.N.
1978-79	Mrs. Joan Bennett, B.Sc., Dip.Ed.
1979-80	Miss Vera Gammon, M.B., B.S., F.R.C.S., D.L.O.
1980-81	Miss Marjorie Griffiths.
1981-82	Miss Margot Lewis
1982-83	Mrs. Dorothy Kertesz, F.R.C.O.G.
1983-84	Mrs. B. Cunnington
1984-85	Miss Janet Oates
1985-87	Mrs. Peggy Barlow
1987-88	Mrs. Jan Caswell, B.Sc., Dip.Ed..
1988-89	Mrs. Helen Aylward, B.Sc., F.B.C.O.
1989-90	Mrs. Dorothy Kertesz, F.R.C.O.G.
1990-91	Mrs. Bette Cunnington
1991-92	Mrs. Peggy Barlow
1992-93	Mrs. Margaret Rees

48. Fortieth Anniversary. 1997-98 Dinner
   L to R: Mrs. B. Roberts; Mrs. Sue Medd, President; Mrs. Maisie Davies, Honorary
   Member; Mrs. Necia Jennings.

49. L to R. Mrs. Jan Caswell, Mrs. Peggy Barlow.

1993-94	Mrs. Claire Jones, M.I.E.H.
1994-95	Mrs. Sydney Jones, B.Sc.
1995-96	Mrs. Suzanne Doolan
1996-97	Mrs. Dorothy Kertesz, F.R.C.O.G.
1997-98	Mrs. Sue Medd

NEW MEMBERS WELCOME!

Whilst membership is by invitation, any professional business lady who is interested in becoming a member, should contact any of our members for details. We are keen to increase the number of new members.

CLUB NEWS.

Our recent friendship link with Brighton, Australia, was cemented by Mrs. D. Kertesz, an inveterate traveller who has visited many clubs abroad.

Mrs. Marjorle Griffiths has attended meetings of the Barbados Club.

Mrs. Maisie Davies has attended meetings of the Kuala Lumpur Club and two clubs in Bangkok.

Mrs. Necia Jennings and Mrs. Maisie Davies have attended meetings in Colombo and Sri Lanka.

Our water pump which we presented to Mozambique in 1983 is still in use.

We continue to support several organisations and charities abroad.

At home in 1997-98 we have supported The Cancer Research Campaign (Cymru), The Groundwork Trust, Tarian, The Samaritans.

We have also sent a donation to S. I. Harare in Zimbabwe to help set up an organisation similar to Childline.

Many of our members also give freely of their time to support local charities and initiatives.

The author thanks all club members for their help in compiling this History, special thanks to Mrs. Jan Caswell and Mrs. Maisie Davies.

Welcome to

Soroptimist
International

For more information call   0161 480 7686

ABERCANAID, SOME REMEMBERED YESTERDAYS, PART FIVE

by

EDWARD RHYS-PRICE

Some further episodes in the life of Abercanaid-born Edward Rhys-Price, a rolling stone who "gathered some moss" and died a rich man.

Australia.

Eventually I decided to go back to the USA. I packed my bag and went down to Southampton in an attempt to earn some money and work my passage to America.

I was not allowed to choose which ship I worked on. I was sent on to one which was going to Australia, with the promise that afterwards I could work on one which was going to the States. The voyage took several weeks and I remember that one of the crew members drew an advance of wages at each port we went to so all he had to take home to his wife was a few pounds.

I had never been to Australia before. We were warned that parts of Sydney were very rough and that we would be mugged if we were not careful where we went. The food was very good but drinking places had to close at six otherwise no work would be done next day. We went to Western Australia as well and at each port girls would call out in joking fashion "Here come another crowd of Pommies".

Food was plentiful after the shortages in war-time Britain, and I spent fifteen pounds on food to take back to my sister in Abercanaid. There were plenty of sweets too and many of the men took a lot back home with them.

America.

When I got back to Southampton I was lucky enough to get a job almost straight away, this was because I was prepared to do anything, even washing dishes, to enable me to get some money together. I used to keep my suitcase packed and I watched the newspapers for details of ships' sailing times and destinations. Then I would wait at the foot of the gang-plank of any bound for America until someone called out for a steward. Even so, I could not find work in America as easily as that because I needed to find a friend who would stand guarantor for me. Each time the ship docked in New York I went in search of someone and at last I found my friend Teddy Boldt. He agreed to stand guarantor for me and in the brief time I was in New York he got me admitted to the night club where he was working as a bar tender and in this way I heard several well-known singers, one of whom was W. C. Handy, composer of St. Louis Blues.

As soon as I had enough money I applied in England for a visa and had to go up to London for a medical examination. This way I could enter the States to look for work with no trouble, because of being given a clean bill of health in England. Teddy Boldt found me a temporary job as a part-time waiter at the Lamb's Club. This was in a Victorian building with the kitchen in the basement. It was exclusively for actors, and I never saw a woman there. One day I found myself waiting on Edward G. Robinson. In spite of the fact that many of his film parts were of gangsters, I found him a very courteous, quietly spoken man. If any agent wanted to find a particular actor they always looked for him first at the Lamb's Club and out of work actors knew this. We always knew if an actor was out of work as they ordered scrambled eggs. The management insisted that staff must be treated with civility but pay was low.

Thomas Cook, Fifth Avenue.

One day on the spur of the moment I went into the building which houses the St. George's Society, which is run by English people. I asked if they could help me find a job. They had one vacancy in the offices of Thomas Cook, the Travel Agents on Fifth Avenue. I explained that I had never done any office work but they said I would find it plain sailing, as it was in the travellers' cheques department. I found the work easy to learn, the pay was low but I was tired of looking for work and I stayed there for two years. In my department the numbers on used travellers' cheques had to be entered in ledgers and every so often two of us had to go to the main post office in New York to collect them. I have never forgotten the inscription engraved around the top of this huge building. "Neither rain nor snow nor sleet nor gloom of night stays these couriers from the swift completion of their appointed rounds". I think these words are by Cardinal Richelieu. There were always guards on duty, usually coloured men with pistols in the holsters at their sides and we had to show our identification passes before being allowed in to the necessary department. There always had to be two of us. We travelled there on the subway, but once we had the cheques in their sealed parcels we had to return by taxi, at the Company's expense.

Many parcels came to the office from abroad. The stamps from these were carefully removed and every so often they were sent around the office in a box, and we were allowed to take a certain number. I was not interested in stamp collecting myself, but I used to give them away to friends.

New York Institute of Dietetics.

I was in my early fifties at this time and one day saw a newspaper advertisement for the New York Institute of Dietetics on Fifth Avenue, some way from the office. I was tired of working for low pay, but without a trade it was all I could do. For a long time I had entertained the idea of opening a Health Food Shop in London. I can't remember where I first got this idea, it had been with me even before I had managed my brother's restaurant in Chiswick. But I knew I would need training and the capital. The Institute seemed to me to be the answer to both problems because it would give me a training to enable me to get a better job, and so be able to save money. I went along to the Institute and asked about the course. The fee was several hundred dollars, which I hadn't got, but I was told I could pay in installments. Classes could be attended in the daytime or at night, so I enrolled for the night classes and kept my job at Thomas Cook during the day. Sometimes it was so hot in the building in the Summer evenings that I would doze off. But I graduated on the twentieth day of August, 1954, and was given a handsome certificate.

A trainee with H. L. Green, New York.

One Saturday I dropped in to the snack bar attached to a large department store, for a cup of coffee and a piece of cake and got talking to the manager of the food section. I asked if they ever took on part-time staff as I was bored on Saturdays, having nothing to do, as I was still working at Thomas Cook's. He said they did and I arranged to start in the snack bar on the following Saturday. When I mentioned that I would soon be graduating from the Institute, the manager said that he had graduated from there himself, and then added "Have you thought of coming to work for our Company?" This was the H. L. Green Company, with stores all over the eastern states, so I asked what the pay would be. I would get twice as much as I was getting at Thomas Cook's after graduation, and would receive full wages while I was training. In addition if I could get the snack bar to show a profit I would get a bonus.

My first job as a trainee was downstairs, washing dishes for both the restaurant and the snack bar for a week. The idea was that I should try my hand in each of the different departments. Another one of my jobs in the six to eight weeks of my training was to keep a check on the amount of stock we carried. Coca-Cola syrup was used to make the drinks, and this came in gallon jars. It was then mixed in the dispenser with soda water and the drinks would be drawn off as required. Of course it would have been unheard of for a customer to go into a snack-bar for a Coca-Cola and be told we had sold out, so we did everything we could to make sure this never happened. Sometimes I would go to another H. L. Green store to borrow anything we were short of and employees from other H. L. Green stores knew they could come to us in the same way.

In the snack-bar we sold Coca-Cola, ice-cream, banana splits, coffee and cake, and in the restaurant meals were served. The turkey dinner there was very cheap and consisted of one slice of turkey with lots of potatoes, stuffing and gravy. Vegetarian dishes were also served and other meals usually found in restaurants. The turkey dinner being so cheap acted as a "come on" or loss leader, as we would call it today, to attract people in. I helped to write menus but didn't have anything to do with the preparation of the food. Sometimes the manager would walk around with me and point out things which might be improved and sometimes the girls working there would ask me questions for which I then had to produce the right reply. In short my job was to see that everything was running smoothly and try to anticipate any problems before they arose.

H. L. Green, Detroit.

The first place I was sent to after my training was a H. L. Green store in Detroit. Here the hamburger section was losing money and they wanted me to find out why. I was in the kitchen one day watching the coloured cook making the hamburgers when I picked up one and decided to weigh it. The meat weighed three and a half ounces, instead of the two ounces it should have been. The cook was immediately up in arms protesting and said that she had been making the hamburgers that way for years. She made so much fuss that the manager in charge of the whole store came in to ask what was going on. I explained that I had been sent from New York to ensure that the lunch counter started making a profit, but that would be impossible as long as the meat weighed three and a half ounces instead of two. He told the woman she must weigh the meat before putting it in the machine, which stamped out the rissoles, instead of putting in simply what she thought fit. After two months of this the hamburger section started showing a profit. A salesman who came to the kitchen told me how easily something like that can happen. He had won the contract to supply the steaks for a large Dinner and to make sure of getting it had cut the price down as low as he could, but he still lost money because the scales he weighed the meat on showed an ounce less than the actual weight.

Near the lunch counter was the ladies' hat department. I had unbounded admiration for the woman in charge. She had only one arm, whether it was due to illness or accident I never knew, but she had overcome this disability admirably and even drove a car.

Quite soon after I got to Detroit I was in the kitchen one day when the Italian we bought our vegetables from came in. I looked at what he had brought and refused to have it. It looked as though he had brought the poorest of all his produce to us. He made a fuss, saying he had been supplying the kitchen for years without complaint.

Once more the store manager came to intervene on hearing the noise, and on seeing the vegetables told him to go and not come back.

There was no trouble in getting alternative supplies as people were always coming offering vegetables, so we could choose the best.

The trouble with the lunch counter in Detroit before I went there was that there was no-one to oversee what food was bought and how it was used. I stayed there nine months, working from nine in the mornings until nine at night, except on Mondays when we closed at five. These sort of hours do not give much scope for going out and spending money. In fact the Christmas I was in Detroit all I had for lunch on Christmas Day was a sandwich, because everywhere was closed.

Home to London.

As soon as I felt I had enough money saved up, I handed in my notice. The manager was furious about it but I stood my ground. I changed my money into travellers' cheques and took the first boat home. I didn't want to wait about for one which didn't have a full crew, so instead of working my passage I went as a paying passenger.

If I could have my life over again I would stay at school as long as I could and learn a trade. I have lost count of the number of times I have stood in line in New York and other places trying to get work. As soon as I admitted I had no skills I was turned away. I found it a sickening and degrading experience.

As far as getting an education goes, I consider that America is one of the finest countries in the world, if not the finest. It does not matter who you are, or who your father was, if you want an education you can get one, by day or night. You have to pay for it yourself but perhaps THAT MAKES YOU VALUE IT MORE. As far as jobs go, if you have got the skill to do a job it is yours, with or without references.

My own business.

When I got to London I put my money in a bank and looked for a room. I found one in Bedford Park, Chiswick, for ten shillings a week and was lucky enough to get a job as a porter on the London Underground while I looked around for a suitable empty shop. One day I had a stroke of luck. My niece, Marion, was working for an estate agent and she told me there was a shop becoming vacant at 35, Turnham Green Terrace, a former opticians. As soon as she told me I went down to the office and asked if I could buy the lease. It cost me

£350 of the £500 I had saved, and legal fees, timber, carpenters' and electricians' wages brought it to £456. Here is a list of the costs I wrote down at the time:

	£	s	d
The lease	350	00	00
Legal fees	9	15	00
Fittings	14	00	00
Printed Letterheads	1	00	00
Rates to September 1956	18	11	4
Hardware		13	00
Hardboard	1	3	6
Removing rubbish left by previous owner		5	00
Paints	1	3	00
Carpenter's wages	9	16	00
Electrician's wages and materials	5	12	00
Living expenses/incidentals/white coat	45	00	00
Total	£456	18s	10d

So there I was with an empty shop and £50 to put up shelves and buy stock. I found a carpenter who agreed to work for me in the evenings when I was there to help him and we were able to buy all the planks we needed from the shop just across the road from us. We put up shelves on just one wall to start with, and I bought second hand scales. When I heard a chemist's shop was closing in Shepherd's Bush, I went and bought a counter from there, then I placed an order with Mapletons of Liverpool, wholesalers and manufacturers of health foods. But the salesman said he could not accept my order unless I paid for the goods in advance. When I had finished paying for everything I had just four pounds left.

A tough time.

When my goods arrived I arranged them on the shelves and opened for business on Friday, 21st July 1956. I called my shop "Chiswick Health Stores". Plenty of people came in out of curiosity, asking me "What's this?" and "What's that?" but my total takings for the day were between three and four pounds. I called myself all kinds of a fool and began thinking that I would go bankrupt and have to get a job again.

This went on for several months and I did everything I could to get trade. People at the B.B.C. at Broadcasting House would come in and ask if I would be open at 6.30 when they finished work. Normally I closed at six but I always said "Yes". Even if they only bought one or two things it was all money coming in. Some people asked if I could deliver and I would take their goods around after work. One woman sympathised with me having to do this after a day's work and I told her "Perhaps things will look up before long and I will be able to employ someone". This is what I eventually did but for a long time I had to struggle on my own.

I was desperately worried about my lack of customers and my depression was not helped when my nephew Thomas came up from Aberdare and told me his meat stall made a profit of fifty pounds per week. I never closed for lunch and ate a few biscuits and drank a cup of tea. On Thursday afternoons when the shop was closed I would go to the wholesaler to buy fresh stocks of dried fruit. He always insisted that as mine was a health food shop I must take the kind without preservatives in it. Then I would go back and weigh it up in bags and do the same with the sugar. If necessary I would do this on Sunday as well. My only relaxation was reading, THANK GOD FOR PUBLIC LIBRARIES! I had no money to go anywhere.

Tombstone inscriptions, Chiswick Cemetery.

But I did get in the habit of taking a walk to Chiswick Cemetery and reading the verses on the gravestones.

One of my favourites was :

> Warm Summer sun smile kindly here,
> Warm Southern wind blow softly here;
> Green sod above, lie light, lie light;
> Goodnight dear heart, goodnight, goodnight.

Another was similar but ended :

> Dream on, dear heart, in blissful sleep,
> Enfolding me still in your love so deep.

And here are two from another cemetery

> To live in hearts we leave behind is not to die.

And:

> A good wife and good health are man's best wealth.

Into hospital to die.

Of course this neglect of myself could not go on without my health beginning to suffer. One day I felt so poorly I forced myself to go to Dr. Morgan Evans. He called his partner in to look at me and they agreed I must go into hospital straight away. I protested, but he was adamant so I sent a telegram to my sister, Olwen, and she came up the next day to take care of the shop. I spent two weeks in hospital and then a week in a convalescent home in Brighton before being allowed home again. When I went in to see Dr. Morgan Evans so that he could sign me off he told me "I did not expect to see you walk in here again. I sent you into hospital to die". The good food and the enforced rest did me a world of good and I took up my work again with increased vigour.

The business succeeds.

At last came the turning point for which I had been hoping. It happened on a wet Tuesday when I didn't really expect to have any customers. A man came in and began asking questions about the goods on display. I thought he was simply sheltering from the rain but I answered politely and then began to re-arrange things on one of the shelves, leaving him to browse. When I turned around again the counter was full of goods. "Excuse me, sir", I said, "but which of these things do you want to take?" "All of them", he told me.

I felt as though someone had thrown a bucket of cold water over me. "All of them?" I repeated, trying to keep the shock out of my voice. I dashed down to the cellar for a box and packed all the goods into it before he could change his mind. Then I wrote out the bill and held my breath. He paid at once, although I didn't breathe freely until he left the shop. From then on things began to look up. I do not mean that every day was a bounty day, but things certainly did begin to go more smoothly from then onwards.

To save money I was living in a small room where I hardly had space to turn around. This cost me ten shillings a week. There was another shopkeeper lodging in the same house and one day he told me about the wonderful eggs he sold which were delivered straight from the country. The next Thursday, after I had shut my shop, I went along to his delicatessen about half a mile away and bought a tray of eggs, two and a half dozen. I sold them all next day and gradually bought more from him until I decided to ask the wholesaler to deliver to me direct. First I had half a case but soon I was selling six cases a week.

Local characters.

This shopkeeper looked and spoke like a character out of Dickens. He had suitcases in his room which must have been over a hundred years old. He had a motorcycle, and spent more time taking it apart than riding it. One evening I asked him to go to the cinema with me. I cannot remember what film I wanted to see but he took half an hour to think about it and then said "No". Another man who lived in the house was kept by his sister, who sent him money from America every month. He drank it all away and was broke by the end of three weeks. He kept asking me to give him a job but I felt he was the last person I wanted working for me.

Our landlady, Mrs. Morgan, had a spaniel of which she was very fond. When she said "Walkies" it would fetch its collar and lead. When it died she was so upset she took to her bed for three days.

As my business improved I put up more shelves until three of the walls were covered with them. Soon salesmen began calling, trying to persuade me to buy a cash register, a new counter, new scales and all kinds of other things. "No need to pay any deposit ——" they would say but I simply told them I had no money to spare and I never succumbed. I kept my money in one of the small drawers I had bought when the chemist shop closed, although in time I did buy a second-hand cash register.

I also took on two part-time helpers in my shop for the afternoons. One, Mrs. Edith O'Keefe, had been born in Wales but lived in London for many years. She had worked for my brother Glyn in his restaurant in Chiswick and when Glyn no longer needed her he asked me to give her a job. I could leave her in charge and if any goods were delivered which were not of best quality she refused to sign for them. My brother had paid her two shillings and sixpence an hour (12½p) but I paid her three shillings (15p) an hour as she was worth her weight in gold to me.

Another girl who worked for me would have nothing to do with men. She kept all her love for her fifteen cats. One day I went to the house which she shared with her aunt and had cats climbing all over me. I vowed I wouldn't go there again. Her name was Mary Webb and she was an excellent worker.

Daphne Day, Chiswick artist.

As things improved I moved into a different area to lodge, at 20, The Avenue, Chiswick, which is on the way to Acton. I had rooms in the house of an artist called Daphne Day. She lived in the middle flat where she had her studio. Another artist lived on the ground floor and I lived at the top of the house.

When Daphne was commissioned to paint a portrait of one of the nobility she asked me to wear his robes while she painted them. He told us one day he was so depressed he felt like committing suicide, but when Daphne said she had a cold he started away from her in horror and told her to keep away from him.

I liked Daphne's work so much that when my niece, Cheryl, came up to London I commissioned Daphne to make a natural portrait of her for me, which she did. Later she also did a portrait of me in pastels. Before I left London I bought a self-portrait of Daphne and I have the three pictures to this day. While I was still living in the house she did a portrait of Sir Winston Churchill from a photograph and it was an excellent likeness. Daphne was a Sagittarian and liked lots of friends around her, but although she was so good-looking she never married.

Daphne Day's father, who was a widower, lived in the house with her. He was a taxi-driver. One day he was taken ill and I went with him in the ambulance to the Middlesex Hospital. Next morning Daphne came to tell me he had died. Later in the morning a lady who was a famous spiritualist came into the shop. I had recently been able to help her by recommending a course of vitamins. While we were talking she fell silent and said "Who is this man in a grey suit who is standing beside me? He seems to be telling me he has just died of chest trouble". "It sounds like Daphne Day's father", I told her. "He has a message for you" the woman went on, "He says you will soon be leaving here".

There was a strange sequel to this. Some months later I was watching "The Fugitive" on television in my room. This was a serial about a doctor on the run. Halfway through, at about fifteen minutes to eight, I felt someone tug at my jacket. I shifted on the sofa and felt a tug on the other side of my jacket so strong that it almost pulled me to the floor. I got up, switched off the television, and saw Daphne's father standing in the room with his arm around a woman. He gave me his familiar, cheerful V sign, the same as Winston Churchill had always used during the War when having his photograph taken, and said to me, "I am happy now". I went down at once and told Daphne what I had seen. She made me describe the woman's clothes and knew at once that it had been her mother with him.

Some interesting customers.

For most of the nine years I had the shop I was fortunate in having a very good working relationship with the Mapleton's representative. As soon as he saw I was staying for more than six months he gave me all the credit I needed. He would bring things such as walnuts or dried fruit when the West End shops were overstocked and I was able to buy these at substantial saving. He always reminded me when to order certain goods to get them at the right time, for example, walnuts had to be ordered in the Summer to arrive in the Winter because they came from India. They were ready shelled and I sold them for three shillings (15p) a pound. A restaurant owner from Kensington used to come for a box of them from time to time as he used a lot in his cooking so I would cut the price for him a bit.

My customers were an interesting lot. They used to come to me with their problems so that I felt like a father-confessor at times. One of them was a retired missionary who suffered from gall-stones but he refused to have an operation to get rid of them. Where he got the idea from I don't know, but he cured himself by drinking the juice of freshly-squeezed orange, first thing every morning for two weeks. He told me that he urinated into a glass container and could actually see the stones being passed as broken fragments. I told him he ought to write an article about his cure for one of the health magazines, but whether he ever did or not I don't know.

One very strong minded woman, a vegetarian, was diagnosed as having appendicitis. She was due to go into hospital for an operation but she beat the doctors to it. She put alternate hot and cold compresses on the site of the pain and it got better on its own. Her parents-in-law were a devoted couple who always went about together. The mother-in-law got gangrene in her leg and died and the father-in-law who appeared perfectly healthy, died shortly afterwards.

One of my regular customers was so crippled by rheumatism that she could only walk with the aid of two sticks. After some years her doctor decided to treat her with gold injections but it turned out she was allergic to these. It was decided to commit her to a home for incurables but before she went, her daughter took her for a holiday to Jersey. There she met a lady from Lancashire who had been crippled with rheumatism for years but had cured herself with cider vinegar and kelp tablets. My customer followed her advice and was cured.

One Monday morning I was taking stock of the items in the shop when I was seized by a pain around my waist. I knew it was not indigestion. It was so bad that I locked the shop door and dragged myself into the little back-yard to get some fresh air. As soon as I was able to I went to the telephone and asked a friend to come and take me home. I went to bed and after a few hours of intense pain I fell asleep. The following morning I received a letter from Olwen informing me that my eldest sister, Jemima, who had looked after me as a child, had suffered a stroke the previous morning. It was about the time that I had felt the pain.

Annual visits to Abercanaid.

Business went well until I had owned the shop for about seven years. Then Mapletons were taken over by another firm dealing in iron goods and after that everything seemed to go wrong. Goods failed to arrive on time and it was a nightmare trying to keep the shelves filled. At about the same time my bread supplies went haywire. I had always bought my bread from a gold medal baker at Ealing named Harries and he delivered it warm to my shop first thing every morning. The smell of that Allinson's nutty wholemeal bread had almost been enough on its own to draw the customers in. But once the business was taken over by Ranks I never knew when the bread would arrive.

I had my shop for nine years altogether and each Christmas I went back to Wales to spend a few days with the family in Abercanaid. I closed the shop at six and dashed up to Paddington to catch a late train. As soon as the train emerged from the Severn Tunnel and I saw the lights on the hills of Monmouthshire, my worries about the shop would drop away and I would feel a new man. I always went to the house of my sister Olwen. She was the youngest of the family and had kept on my mother's house, as my mother was by this time dead. Olwen had married a man from the West Country who had come to Wales as a boy. This was Ivan Warry and he was an electrician and skilled mechanic. If Olwen was not in, her daughter Cheryl used to lay the table and make a cup of tea for me. It is Cheryl's son, my nephew, who now owns the gold watch and chain I bought soon after going to New York.

Naturally, going back to the family home revived memories of my mother. I had been living at Llanvaches when she had passed away. Maud and I had gone to the funeral service which was a very solemn affair and was conducted in the house. She was buried at Cefn Coed cemetery, in my father's grave. This woman, who I am sure under different circumstances would have been a doctor because of her healing hands, was greatly missed by the village. When her name and age were recorded on the tombstone her age was given as seventy six but while researching my family's origins at Somerset House I found she had been seventy eight when she died.

I had a wonderful few days at Christmas visiting old friends and the scenes of my childhood. If I went back to Abercanaid at Easter I would take my favourite walk across the mountains to Aberdare if the weather was fine, with only the sheep grazing around me and the skylarks singing high above for company. Then I would buy tea in a cafe in Aberdare and catch the bus back to Merthyr before walking the one and a half miles back to Abercanaid.

My first visit to France.

In all my travels I had never been to France. One of my customers was a retired military attache who had spent a great deal of time there. He whetted my appetite by telling me what a beautiful city Paris was and he also lent me books about the country. "Perhaps I shall see it one day", I said to him and this came about in a quite unexpected way. A French au-pair girl came into the shop one day with a Chinese boy. She could speak fluent English. We got talking and she invited me to visit her and her parents if I ever went to Paris. Her name was Marie-Rose.

So one Bank Holiday, armed with a phrase book and a guide to the places of interest, I went there. I booked into a small hotel and asked someone to ring the telephone number Marie-Rose had given me. Next day she and her father arrived by car and took me to their home, about thirteen kilometres from Paris. They gave me a splendid lunch and then drove me around the area where they lived, showing me the sights. Her father was a locksmith and could speak no English. Neither could her mother, but Marie-Rose translated for us. As we passed a church where a wedding was in progress her father pointed to the bridegroom and said "Le victim!" I remember one of the church officials was wearing old-fashioned knee breeches.

Next day I explored Paris on my own. I wanted to see the burial place of James the Second but repairs were being carried out there and the place was closed. Another disappointment was being unable to go into the house where Alexandre Dumas had lived as this was also being repaired. I wanted to see the Bastille but that had been razed to the ground.

One place which did not disappoint me was Versailles. I went there on a coach-trip and walking through the beautiful rooms and gardens, I was amazed at the money which must have been spent on it by Louis the Fourteenth, the Sun King. At the same time I felt what a terrible waste it had been when people had been starving in the streets.

While in Paris I went on the Metro. I liked the fact that when the train came in the gates onto the platform were closed so that only those on the platform could board the train. This prevented all the pushing and jostling I remembered from the time when I worked as a porter on the London Underground. With one ticket it was possible to travel anywhere on the Metro and one could even buy a book of tickets to save buying one each day. However I did not realise there are classes on the Metro and when a woman ticket-inspector started shouting at me I had to ask someone else what I had done wrong. He explained to me that I was in the wrong class so I asked him to tell the inspector I would get into the correct one at the next station.

Another mistake I made was when paying a taxi-driver for a short journey. He came at me like an old cockerel and I had to ask a passer-by what was wrong. I was told I had not given enough tip so I asked the man how much I should give.

Of the five days I spent in Paris on this occasion, one was wet, but by chance I picked up a discarded newspaper and saw that the film "How Green Was My Valley" was showing at a cinema in the city. I copied down the location and stopped passers-by until I found one who could tell me how to get there. First I would speak in English and if that didn't work I would try my French, "Quel direction pour la?". In this way I eventually got to the cinema and it seemed very odd to be sitting in a French cinema listening to Welsh voices (with French sub-titles), and seeing Welsh scenery on the screen.

Other visits to France.

When Marie-Rose married Jacques Combrettes, a farmer, I sent them a wedding present of matching china and I sent some of the same to her sister. On one occasion when I went to stay with them at their farm house Marie-Rose asked her sister to take me out. The sister took me to a place where a large cave was open to the public. A stream ran through it, with guard rails at the side, and electric lights in the roof. On the far side of the stream were the bodies of five women. They were preserved in some way, possibly by the lime in the water which dripped from the roof of the cave. The guide could speak no English and Marie-Rose's sister could speak very little so I had no way of finding out about them but I can remember that one body seemed to be in perfect condition. I still keep in touch with Marie-Rose and her husband.

On another visit to France I was in an open square where soft drinks were being sold. I bought a bottle of lemonade direct from a stall and had drunk half of it when a man rushed up to me and began talking very excitedly and pointing at the bottle. When I could get someone to translate for me I understood that this was the man whose job it was to serve the lemonade to the people at the tables. In getting it for myself I had done him out of a tip, so to pacify him and show that I had acted out of ignorance I gave him a few coins.

I climbed up to Montmartre one day to see the beautiful church of Sacre Coeur. I thought it the most beautiful church I had ever seen. In America I had visited the memorial to George Washington and thought that Washington was the loveliest city I had ever seen but after seeing Paris I revised my opinion. I went to the top of the Arc de Triomphe and saw the eight boulevards which converge there, a magnificent sight.

In Montmartre I found a shop selling pancakes, the lightest and crispest I have ever tasted. There was a row of bottles of liqueur so that one could pour the flavour of one's choice over the pancakes, or have them plain.

On another visit to France I went to see the tomb of Napoleon at Les Invalides and was shown around by an old soldier. I had read somewhere that when the Germans overran Austria, Hitler had given instructions that the body of Napoleon's eighteen year old son was to be disinterred and taken for burial next to his father at Les Invalides.

(To be concluded).

51. Some members, Treharris Male Voice Choir, 1997.

TWENTY FIVE YEARS OF PLEASURE

by

A. A. JAMES

A BRIEF HISTORY OF THE TREHARRIS MALE VOICE CHOIR.

Choir formed, first performance given.

On Monday 11th October 1961, a meeting was convened at the Treharris Workman's Library with the sole purpose of forming a Male Voice Choir. The meeting was called by Alderman Sam Edwards following many requests from interested men of the locality. The meeting was well attended and the seeds of the choir were sown, i.e. The Treharris and District Male Voice Choir.

The appointed Musical Director was Mr. Ted Hilbourne, and David Edward Rees was appointed accompanist to the Choir. Practices commenced at Bethel Vestry the following Monday with between sixty and seventy choristers present. Practices were regular and the only reason for reduced practice numbers was shift work of members.

The first performance in public was at Brynhyfryd Chapel; a capacity audience was present. This was on 4th March 1962. On 29th April 1962 the Choir presented a Celebrity Concert at the Palace Cinema with Kenneth Bowen (tenor) and Anita Sargeant (soprano); this concert was sold out three weeks before the night.

More concerts and a radio broadcast.

Concerts came in quick succession at Merthyr, Dowlais and Nelson. Treharris, at this time, was the only Choir in the County Borough. Another major concert was arranged at The Palace with Richard Rees and Gerald Davies, two of the most popular artists at this time.

The Choir was becoming well-known and concerts were held at Brecon, Abergavenny and Maesteg. An invitation was received by the Choir to broadcast on the then famous radio programme "All Together", which was relayed on Saturday evenings. The programme was recorded at Quakers Yard Grammar School with Stuart Burrows and John Morgan, the compere being Alun Williams.

Weston visit, 1965, and television appearance.

At last, on 30th October 1965, the Choir crossed Offa's Dyke to sing for the first time out of Wales, at Weston-super-Mare Town Hall. Concerts followed at regular intervals and the Choir was asked to make a film with Aber Valley Male Voice Choir, based on the tragic Senghenydd Colliery explosion. Following many rehearsals and trips to Senghenydd, the film was completed. It appeared on television on several occasions and was called the "Master Singers". Robert Vas, the producer, took this film to America and won a major award in an International Film Festival.

Aberfan Disaster, 1966.

In 1966 a Gala Concert was arranged at The Palace Cinema, when the Choir appeared in concert with the Max Jaffa Trio and Betti Jones, the charming Cefn Coed soprano.

In October, the valley was plunged into sorrow by the Aberfan Disaster. Members of the Choir were involved and also many friends of members. The Choir's Annual Dinner, due to take place that week at Brecon, was cancelled and immediate plans were made for a concert for the Aberfan Disaster Fund. Stuart Burrows and Elizabeth Rust (two artists who had previously sung with the Choir) gave their services free. Other concerts were arranged for the Fund and one was even arranged at Clevedon by Lilian Jenkins, a Councillor at Clevedon, who was originally a Treharris girl.

New accompanist, Mass performed.

David Edward Rees retired as our accompanist and was succeeded by Mrs. Mary Lewis-Davies. Concerts were arranged frequently, sometimes eight a month, and the Choir was well served by two local artists, Ethel Clee and Towyn Evans.

The Choir had learned the Cheribini Requiem Mass in D Minor and on one occasion it took the bull by the horns and performed this Mass on a Sunday afternoon at Glasbury's St. Peter's Church, and then travelled on to Abergavenny and performed the same work at St. Mary's on the same night. This Mass was in Latin and the Choir was possibly the only choir performing the full Mass in Wales at this time, performances being made at many churches in the area.

Concert bookings were now getting near to London, with concerts at Reading, Burnham, Caversham, Wexham and Rickmansworth. The Choir was also in demand in the Midlands at Bedworth, Malvern and many other places.

First Royal Albert Hall concert.

The Choir rehearsed some twelve months for the first 1,000 Male Voice Concert at the Royal Albert Hall. This was truly a wonderful concert where 10,000 Welsh Exiles were present to enjoy a feast of music.

One of the aims of the Choir was to encourage young talent and two young artists who sang with the Choir at the time were Annette Merriman, a very talented contralto from Cwmaman, and Treharris born Lynda Adams, soprano.

Among the many nights to remember in the early days was one at the Pavilion, Weymouth, when the audience rose to give a standing ovation.

Retirement of Dr. E. Foster.

In May of 1970, the Choir was asked to entertain the public at Tabernacle Chapel, Treharris, at a Presentation Night to Dr. Elton Foster, who had served the community for forty years and was retiring.

More nights to remember at The Palace Cinema featured the Foden's Motor Works Band and artists of the opera world, such as Margaret Price, Elizabeth Rust, Marion Studholme and William McAlpine, to name but a few.

An American Choir entertained.

The ill-health of our brilliant accompanist, Mary Lewis-Davies, forced her to retire and Mary was followed by capable accompanists such as W. Lloyd, J. Ward, Judith Smallwood and Martin Edwards.

Combined concerts with local choirs were frequently arranged, but a combined concert at Reading with Reading Male Voice Choir was a new step and proved a very successful venture.

Treharris Choir was invited to appear at Cheltenham Town Hall with Rhymney and Dowlais Male Voice Choirs, which finished up by candlelight due to a power failure. The visit to Wales of Fenton High School Choir of the U.S.A. was a wonderful opportunity for Treharris Choir to host this choir following their visit to Llangollen. A wonderful musical evening took place and another bond was made.

A visit to Cornwall.
A visit of the Treviscoe Choir was arranged and the Choir spent a very pleasant weekend at Treharris. Memories of this fine Cornish choir are still vivid in our minds. The Treharris Choir was invited to St. Austell, the home of the Treviscoe Male Choir, and a wonderful weekend with a feast of music took place. Many members of the Treharris Choir still have visits to St. Austell, and Treviscoe Choir members visit Treharris.

A bond with Bolton.
When a Choir member left the area to live in Bolton, the bond was made with Reg Parry, a fantastic worker at Bolton for all charities. He was, and still is, a member of Victoria Methodist Hall at Bolton. It would be impossible for anyone who has been to the great Victoria Hall (the home of the Methodists at Bolton) to say anything in any way to fault this auditorium we had the pleasure of singing in. Our visits to Bolton developed into friendly, regular affairs and many friends were made.

Rickmansworth, Worcester, Southam and Watford visited.
Other venues where the Choir gave repeat visits were Rickmansworth, Worcester, Southam and last, but not least, Watford, where the Leggetts School Association was formed to assist their school in activities and in the provision of a mini bus for the school. Members of the Leggetts Association are great friends of the Treharris Male Choir, forming their own "Fan Club" to travel to the Royal Albert Hall when the Choir appeared there, to Bolton and even to Treharris for concerts. In September 1975, the Choir was asked to provide entertainment for the opening of the new Community Centre at Nelson, at the invitation of the local council.

The Choir at this particular time was fortunate in having the services of Ann Beynon (soprano). Ann is a Treharris girl with a wealth of talent and had received her training under Valetta Jacopi, a former Principal of Sadlers Wells and Covent Garden. Ann was always in great demand and never failed to please.

Visits to the West Country were now getting more regular with concerts at Salisbury, Thornbury and Trowbridge.

Benefit concert for New Zealand rugby star.
With preparations for the Royal Albert Hall concerts, the Choir was frequently learning new music and one piece that will always be remembered is Stead's '100 Psalm' which was most demanding. The Choir first performed this piece at Aylesbury, when the Welsh Appeal Concert Committee invited Treharris Choir to sing in aid of the Tony Taylor Appeal. Tony was a New Zealander who was badly injured playing rugby for Aylesbury Rugby Club and

was a patient at Stoke Mandeville. The famous Sir Ludwig Guttman, the founder of the hospital spinal unit was present together with Tony's mother, who was flown from New Zealand to be present at this concert. Sir Ludwig was delighted with the '100 Psalm' and congratulated the Choir for their handling of the mechanics of this demanding piece so well.

Elaine Hadley, new accompanist.

1977 proved to be a very busy period for the Choir. This was indicated by the areas covered—Rickmansworth, Oakhampton, Henley-on-Thames, Liverpool, Manchester, Derby, Bury St. Edmonds and Bolton.

Due to ill health, J. Ward resigned as Choir Accompanist, but the Choir were delighted to gain the services of Elaine Hadley, an Associate of the Royal Victoria College of Music, who was virtually thrown in at the "deep end" at Bury St. Edmonds, but emerged with flying colours.

A tragic fire occurred at Treharris where two children lost their lives. A concert for the fund was arranged immediately to assist the Arnold family.

Our Rickmansworth contact, Mrs. Glenys Fenton, had taken up residence in Taunton and was soon involved in organising a concert in an area starved of choral singing.

At a concert in Rickmansworth Elaine's daughter, Rhian, was invited to give some pianoforte solos. It was immediately apparent that Rhian was destined for greater things for she had already won a scholarship to attend the Welsh College of Music and Drama at Cardiff, this being the first step in carving out a musical career for herself.

Dr. Parry and Joe Erskine.

The TV film "Off to Philadelphia in the Morning" was to be made at Merthyr, based upon the life of Dr. Joseph Parry. Treharris was invited to take part and the film was shown on television as a three-part serial.

The Choir was next invited to sing at the London Palladium where a benefit concert was arranged for the ex-heavyweight boxer, Joe Erskine; due to a TV mix-up the concert was held at the Rainbow Theatre. The concert was a memorable occasion, this due to the wealth of talent on the programme and the sporting personalities present.

1500 Year Festival, Merthyr.

1980 was again a busy period for the Choir; concerts at Watford, Rickmansworth and Battersea. The Merthyr Tydfil 1500 Year Festival was discussed and it was agreed that a massed male choir concert would be held at Rhydycar Leisure Centre with Stuart Burrows and Betti Jones. Six days following this concert the Choir was at The Royal Albert Hall where one thousand male voices were under the baton of Noel Davies.

Bolton, 1981.

Back to Bolton in 1981 for the sixth visit, when it was announced that the concerts given by the Choir at Bolton had raised £5,000 for Bolton charities. This year the Choir visited Watford for the fourth time, although delayed by storms and roadworks on the motorway.

A concert with a top Guards band was always the Choir's ambition; this materialised in 1982 when the Choir was in concert with the band of the Welsh Guards at Rhydycar.

A visit to Germany.

Following a concert at Kidderminster with the Carol Hopkins Singers, the Choir reached their ambition to sing in Europe. As a result of a letter published in the Western Mail, the Choir wrote to Germany to the St. Josefstal Male Choir at Saarbrucken and this letter was the start of this visit to attend this fine Choir's 70th Anniversary concert. The Choir travelled to Germany by coach and arrived to a wonderful welcome by the German Burgomaster with exchange of gifts. On the Saturday night a Gala Concert with the famous German Choir and other artistes took place, this was a night never to be forgotten; this four day visit to Germany must be one of the highlights of the Choir's history: many friends were made and a return visit was imminent. The Choir were fortunate to have Alex Robertson, a local man who had a good knowledge of German and was able to make our visit to Germany a greater pleasure.

Following our return from Germany the Choir were soon travelling again with concerts at Fishguard, Bristol and Southam, these venues all within a month. On June 19th.1982, the Choir presented its 21st Anniversary concert when Ted Hilbourne conducted the Choir for the last time. Maryetta and Vernon Midgley, and William Davies (organist) were the artists and seven hundred people were thrilled with a feast of music.

New musical director. Visit by German choir.

Under its new Musical Director, Gwilym Morris, the Choir continued with great success, appearing in concert with Coleford Silver Band and fund raising concerts at Watford and Bolton.

In 1983 we were delighted to have the St. Josefstal Choir to visit us and to appear in concert with us. Preparations were made to make this visit highly successful. This was achieved by the efforts of all members of the Choir, the Supporters Society and many friends of the Choir. The concert which also involved The Carol Hopkin Singers was of such great quality it was the topic of conversation for many weeks. A social gathering followed at the Empress Ballroom, Abercynon, where three hundred people were entertained to a Buffet and a fantastic social evening, which passed into the next day so easily. The German friends departed on Sunday morning when a wonderful farewell was arranged with Choir members, wives, hosts and many newly made friends present to see their coach depart from Treharris bus station.

Festival of Castles.

Once again Treharris Male Voice Choir was ready to take part in the Festival of Castles arranged by Merthyr Borough with Cefn Coed, Dowlais and Ynysowen Male Voice Choirs and local artistes Phillip Joll, Helen Willis and Gareth Jones. Concerts at Melksham, Southam and Croydon were attended and an invitation to entertain the "All Blacks" Rugby Union side touring the country was readily accepted.

The Rotary Club at Huyton requested the Choir to appear in concert at the Huyton Suite, Liverpool and Ann Lawrence, soprano, appeared with the Choir for the first time. This was an excellent concert with many encores being requested.

The ninth Albert Hall Festival.

The ninth festival of one thousand Welsh Male Voices arrived and the Musical Director on this occasion was the Musical Director of Pontardulais Male Voice Choir. Another memorable occasion.

A new Community Centre was made available at Treharris and the Choir was invited to appear during a week of festivities, with Betti Jones. At this time, the Choir Treasurer had to retire from office due to ill health. Haulfryn Rees had been a devoted Choir Officer for over twenty years.

Another concert at Bolton with Ann Lawrence was a great success. It would be unfair not to mention and thank Madam Edith Norcross for the professional way she accompanied artistes who have performed with the Treharris Choir at Victoria Hall, Bolton. Ann Beynon, Cyril Cotton, Betti Jones, Ann Lawrence. What a grand lady (Madam Norcross) in the Autumn of what must be a wonderful musical life.

A new accompanist and musical director.

Due to the illness of Mrs. Elaine Hadley and the college commitments of Rhian, who were joint accompanists for the Choir, we were again fortunate in having the services of Ann Marie Ives who served the Choir for several concerts. To add to our problems, Gwilym Morris resigned due to personal reasons and Ted Hilbourne came out of retirement to help out but requested that we apply for a new Musical Director.

We were fortunate in gaining the services of Brian McGrath, who had a good musical background, having wonderful military band experience at Sandhurst.

Elaine and Rhian Hadley returned, there were concerts at Southam, Nelson, Treharris and Bristol, and a massed Male Voice concert at St. David's Hall, Cardiff.

Bishop Desmond Tutu.

The famous Bishop Desmond Tutu was given the Freedom of the Borough of Merthyr Tydfil and the Choir was invited to take part in this ceremony at Rhydycar Leisure Centre.

In June 1986, a very sad occasion took place when a memorial service took place at Brynhyfryd Chapel to the late Lemuel Hughes, a founder member of the Choir.

To complete the twenty five years of pleasure, concerts were arranged at Watford and the return visit of Treviscoe Male Voice Choir.

The period 1987-97.

During the years 1987-97 the number of choristers unfortunately declined. The Choir, however, broadened its horizons and in addition to regular local concerts has travelled to the U.S.A., Germany, France and Ireland. The musical director is now Miss Llinos Everett of Penderyn and the accompanist is Miss Anna Smith of Treharris. Practice nights are Monday and Thursday in the Navigation Hotel, Treharris. New members are always welcome.

52. Seventy nine members, Treharris Male Voice Choir, 1965.

189

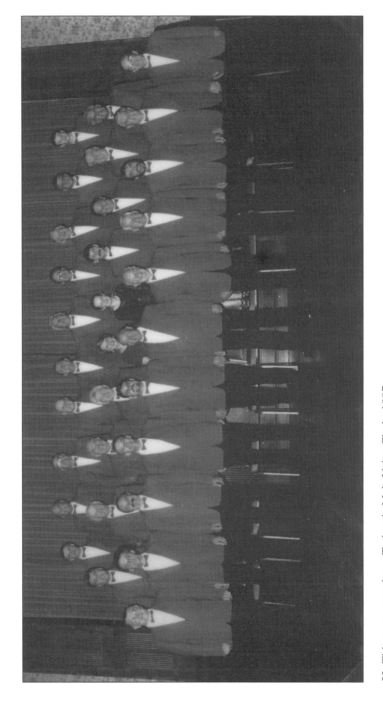

53. Thirty one members, Treharris Male Voice Choir, 1997.

190

A VISIT TO JOSEPH EDWARDS' STUDIO, 1854

TRANSCRIBED

"incisa notis marmora publicis,
Per quae spiritus et vita redit bonis,
Post mortem ducibus."

(The names of public citizens, good leaders, engraved on marble slabs
which restore life and breath to them after death.)

"A few weeks ago, we were called upon, in the exercise of our editorial duties, to notice the erection of a Monument in St. Botolph's Church, Colchester, to the memory of one, who by honourable industry and strict integrity, had well entitled him to the *"incisa notis marmora publicis"*, and the sons of William Hawkins, Esq., by that act of filial affection, were at the same time performing an act of public duty, for after all *"the stored urn, the animated bust"* are long abiding, though silent, monitors, plastic moulds, fashioning, it may be, the "minds and manners of youth" into like shape, and giving them impressions which afterwards remain through life. Nor is this all: art is fostered, for monumental sculpture has contributed some of the most divine creations to the lengthened catalogue of the Sculptor's work, a catalogue containing the names of the most distinguished Sculptors of all ages.

"While Mr. Joseph Edwards, the talented artist of Mr. Hawkins' monument, was in Colchester superintending the erection of his work in St. Botolph's, he did us the favour to invite us to visit his Studio; an invitation we took an early opportunity to accept. And our visit to his *atelier* in Robert-street, Hampstead-road, afforded us many further satisfactory proofs that Mr. Joseph Edwards is a distinguished disciple of high art, whose rising popularity will speedily bring him more prominently before the world. Wales will be honoured by his genius: Merthyr Tydfil will gladly inscribe in honourable terms the name of one who is destined to be ranked as one of her most eminent sons. But to the contents of Mr. Edwards' studio.

"Besides the models of the monument to William Hawkins, Esq., and family, at St. Botolph's Church, and that beautiful one to Mrs. White, at Berechurch, we observed another to the late Right Hon. Sir Bernard Bosanquet, one of Her Majesty's Justices of the Common Pleas, which has an abstract group in alto-relievo of 'Religion consoling Justice in her grief'. It was exhibited in the marble at the Royal Academy last year, and, among other favourable accounts of it, was noticed in the *Art Journal* as being 'profoundly expressive, and carried out with an exquisite feeling for the beautiful'.

"There is also a model, recently commenced, for a mural monument to the late Duke of Beaufort, which is chiefly architectural in design, and contains, among other decorations, some of the military accoutrements of the Duke, who was most devotedly attached to the military profession.

Joseph Edwards.
(From a photograph by R. Crawshay.)

"And there is another just begun for the Rev. R. W. Bosanquet, to commemorate his father, CHARLES BOSANQUET, Esq., of Rock, near Alnwick, containing a medallion likeness of the deceased.

"Among the busts modelled by Joseph Edwards, are those of the late Sir G. H. Smyth, Bart., of Berechurch Hall; Sir Ivor Bertie Guest, Bart., when about nine years old; Dr. Snow Beck, F.R.S.; the Rev. John Guthrie, M.A., Vicar of Calne; S. R. Bosanquet, Esq., of Dingestow Court, author of a 'New System of Logic', together with a few busts and medallions of ladies.

"We were much pleased with a beautiful ideal head from the episode in Thomson's *Seasons,* of LAVINIA, illustrative of these lines:

'The modest virtues mingled in her eyes,
Still on the ground dejected, darting all
Their humid beams.'

And a model of A CHILD ASLEEP, intended to be suggestive of the following charming sonnet by Hood:

'Oh 'tis a touching thing to make one weep,
A tender infant with its curtain'd eye,
Breathing as it would neither live-nor die,
With that unchanging countenance of sleep.
As if its silent dream, serene and deep,
Had lined its slumber with a still blue sky,
So that the passive cheeks unconscious lie
With no more life than roses, just to keep
The blushes warm, and the mild odorous breath.
O blossom babe! So calm in thy repose,
So sweet a compromise of life and death,
'Tis pity these fair buds should e'er unclose
For memory to stain their inward leaf,
Tinging thy dreams with unacquainted grief.'

"There is also an *alto-rilievo* of the SPIRIT ASCENDING, surrounded by the text, "The spirit shall return unto God who gave it; and sorrow and sighing shall flee away'.

"Among numerous admirable sketches are three in bas-relief, for which a medal was awarded at the Cardiff Eisteddfod, in 1851.

"The first and largest of these three *bassi-rilievi* is a delineation of THE DAUGHTER OF THE DAWN, as Homer names the 'bright rosy-fingered Aurora', in a quotation from the Odyssey, on account of the rilievo itself. The aim "was to represent her as if floating calmly along with no more seen than the face and hands in an orb of light, the hands being gently folded on her breast, while the face looks devoutly upwards, as if breathing some divine song of praise, intermingled, it may be imagined, with inspired words of supplication for the speedy increase of all things pure and holy among the various nations of the earth. This view of the subject was suggested by the following lines in the Merchant of Venice:

'Look how the floor of heaven
Is thick inlaid with patines of bright gold!
There is not the smallest orb,that thou behold'st,
But in his motion *like an angel sings,*
Still quiring to the young-eyed cherubim:

54. Portion of Joseph Edward's monument to William Hawkins, Colchester.

"KNOW THYSELF."

55. Joseph Edward's bas-relief,, "Know Thyself".

Such harmony is in immortal souls;
But while this muddy vesture of decay
Doth grossly close it in, we cannot hear it.'

"The second bas-relief is intended as a design commemorative of the Great Exhibition. It represents BRITANNIA, IN THE PRESENCE OF MINERVA, REWARDING THE GENIUS AND INDUSTRY OF THE WORLD, WHILE THE SPIRIT OF PEACE ATTENDS THE CROWN'.

"The third of these sketches is that of 'A Philosopher directing the attention of a youth to the Delphic precept—in Greek—KNOW THYSELF inscribed over a niche containing a bust of THALES, author of the precept'; 'than which', as Dr. Johnson observes in the *Rambler,* 'there is none more famous among the masters of ancient wisdom'; 'being indeed' as he further remarks, 'a dictate which, in the whole extent of its meaning, may be said to comprise all the speculation necessary for a moral agent; and can be applied to the light and gay, as well as to the grave and solemn parts of life. For, not only the Philosopher may forfeit his pretences to real learning, but the wit and the beauty may miscarry in their schemes by the want (lack) of this universal requisite, the knowledge of themselves.'

"Another very beautiful sketch THE WEARY RE-ASSURED being, in the words of Milton, 'A solemn Vision, telling of things which no gross ear can hear'; in which, it may be fancied, the Weary in a dream is urged, by the Visionary Being floating in supernatural light near him, to be of good cheer, and to remember ever, that 'they that be wise, shall shine as the brightness of the firmament; and they that turn many to righteousness, as the stars for ever and ever'.

"In concluding this notice of our visit, we must not omit to mention another (sketch) for a grand statue, which Mr. Joseph Edwards designates, THE FUTURE HIGH POET-PRIEST OF SCIENCE, pointing to, and, it may be imagined, explaining the full meaning of the modern precept 'STUDY NATURE' seen on the tablet held in his hand. It is intended to foreshadaw the hoped for greatest of great men on this revolving globe of ours, who may at some future time appear, when all the main sciences will have been far more perfected than they are at present; and who, with a true giant's might, will wield them all for the well-being of man upon earth, and clearly point out the happiest holiest, and most glorious way to heaven." SUSSEX GAZETTE.

(It may be remembered that Mr. Edwards was recently at Badminton, modelling a bust of the present Duke of Beaufort; and has since, we believe, been commissioned by LADY CHARLOTTE GUEST to make a bust in marble of the late Sir John Guest. Ed. C. & M. Guardian.)

(Cardiff and Merthyr Guardian. 29.12.1854. p.1. col.6.)

The assistance of Mrs. V. Saunders, Tutor and Lecturer in Classics and Ancient History, Gorseinon College, Swansea, is gratefully acknowledged.

VISIT OF A MAORI PRINCESS
TO MERTHYR TYDFIL, 1903

by

T. F. HOLLEY

In 1903 a representative New Zealand band, the HINEMOA BAND, toured Great Britain, giving more than seventy concerts, over a period of six months.

Twenty six versatile musicians were selected by the conductor, Lieut. Thomas Herd, from New Zealand's leading bands. Each bandsman subscribed ten pounds towards the cost of the tour. Bandsmen wore blue-black uniforms with silver fern cap badges. The author has not located a picture of the Hinemoa Band.

The band was accompanied on tour by two accomplished Maori vocalists, Chief Ranginia (tenor) and Princess Te Rangi Pai (contralto).

The object of the tour was to raise funds for the UNION JACK CLUB, London, to enable the Club to erect a building to provide accommodation for soldiers and sailors when on leave in London.

The arrangements for the tour were badly handled and the Band played indoors during the English summer, when people were either at the seaside or in the park, so financially the tour was something of a flop.

Highlights of the tour were performances at a Massed Bands Concert with twelve of the leading British Brass Bands of the day in the Crystal Palace, London; and a Grand Concert in the Royal Albert Hall in conjunction with the four Guards Bands, the Queen's Hall Orchestra (HENRY J. WOOD, conductor), the Leeds Choral Society and soloists including CLARA BUTT, MARIE HALL, ANDREW BLACK, BEN DAVIES (Swansea) and MADAME ALBANI. On the latter occasion (25th June 1903) King Edward VII and Queen Alexandra were present in the Royal Box.

Included in the Hinemoa Band's British tour were visits to Welsh towns including Brynmawr, Cardiff, MERTHYR, Mountain Ash, Newport and Swansea.

The Band had a poor reception at Swansea on 5th June 1903, in spite of considerable advance advertising. One paragraph published before the Hinemoa Band's arrival read:

"The visit to Swansea of the New Zealand HINEMOA BAND should prove an attractive novelty in again introducing us to representatives of Maoriland, who last visited us ten years ago in a very different guise, that of footballers.

The Maoris, as is well known, have attained a standard of civilisation and a respect from their white neighbours, the depth and sincerity of which are best perhaps attested by the fact that inter-marriages are common and popular, and have led to the happiest results. Such mixed alliances with the aboriginal population are, as a rule, elsewhere regarded with detestation, but Maoriland is perhaps the one indubitable and genuine triumph over barbarism which civilisation has yet recorded—and possibly will ever record". (The Cambrian. 29th May 1903).

Two accounts relating to the visit of the Hinemoa Brass Band to Merthyr Tydfil now follow.

"The famous Hinemoa New Zealand Band, under the conductorship of Lieutenant Herd, will give two concerts at the Drill Hall, Merthyr, on Whit Tuesday, 2nd June 1903.

56. Princess Te Rangi Pai, 1906.
Photo courtesy of Alexander Turnbull Library, Wellington, N.Z.. Ref. No. F-58373-1/2.

This Band recently appeared before the Prince and Princess of Wales at Marlborough House.

In addition to this excellent combination of colonial instrumentalists, the following singers will appear:

The Princess Te Rangi Pai, a beautiful Maori Princess (her mother Herewaka, head of one of the leading tribes, married Colonel Porter). The Princess possesses a rich contralto voice, and will sing Maori songs and English ballads. This lady has an extensive repertoire, and sings in ENGLISH, FRENCH, ITALIAN, GERMAN and MAORI; the famous Maori chieftain, Ranginia, a magnificent tenor; and Mr. Bantock Pierpoint, the well-known English bass, who sings a grand new song entitled "The Union Jack in town".

The proceeds of these concerts are in support of the UNION JACK CLUB, about to be formed in London for the use of soldiers and sailors when passing through the Metropolis. The site of the proposed Club is near Waterloo Station, and one of its special features will be the large number of bedrooms available at a low cost.

For each successful provincial concert given an additional bedroom will be added to the Club premises, and the brass plate placed in it will identify the room with the town in which a sum of not less than £100 is raised. The movement has the sympathy and support of such well-known men as Earl Roberts, Sir Frederick Treves, SIR A. CONAN DOYLE, while Mr. J. Henry Iles, whose name is so closely associated with Band Festivals and Competitions, is responsible for the management of the present tour, whereby he hopes to raise a sum of at least £20,000 for the furtherance of the laudable objects of the UNION JACK CLUB".

(*Merthyr Express.* 23.5.1903. p.4. col.6.)

"The Merthyr visit of the celebrated New Zealand Band did not excite the amount of interest it deserved, but the audience made up in enthusiasm what they lacked in numbers.

The Band is on tour in Wales, towns to be visited including Merthyr, Newport, Mountain Ash, Brynmawr, Swansea and Cardiff, for the purpose of assisting the proposed Union Jack Club, particulars of which have previously been published.

The Band is accompanied by the Maori Chieftain Ranginia, whose action songs in native costume were a picturesque and thoroughly interesting feature; the PRINCESS TE RANGI PAI, whose fine stage presence and splendidly cultivated voice won for her hearty encores; and Mr. Bantock Pierpoint, the eminent basso, whose magnificent singing made him a great favourite, and he was deservedly encored.

The Princess possesses a charming and natural manner, being a lady of culture, and her fine contralto voice, which was of great compass, displayed pure enunciation and full rich tone.

The Band, under Lieut. Herd, played with great skill and precision, and the variety of styles in the programme showed the extensive character of their repertoire; their tone was pleasingly free from harshness, and the varied styles of compositions were interpreted with musicianly taste.

One of the items was a dramatic scene "A Maori patriotic greeting", introducing the scena performed before the Prince and Princess of Wales during their visit to New Zealand; all the Band members took part in this amusing and curious exhibition.

A different programme was given in the evening, when there was a VERY LARGE ATTENDANCE, and Dr. Biddle, the High Constable, explained the objects of the concerts. He thought that MERTHYR OUGHT TO RAISE £100 in order to be entitled to give one

57. A concert party in Rotorua, 1906.
1. Gertrude Hunt, accompanist & mother of Mrs. Annette Tootell. 2. Princess Te Rangi Pai. 3. May Moon. 4. Makereti Papakura (Maggie Papakura), 1873-1930.
Photo courtesy of Alexander Turnbull Library, Wellington, N.Z.. Ref. No. F-58374-1/2.

bed the name of the town, and suggested that a subscription list should be opened later on to realise that object. He would be pleased to receive and forward to the proper quarter any subscriptions sent to him.

The tour in England is being managed by Mr. G. W. Wilton, who came over with the Band from the Southern Seas".

(Merthyr Express. 6.6.1903. p.4. col.8.)

Mrs. Annette Tootell spent over ten years researching the life of Fanny Rose Porter, Princess Te Rangi Pai and published authoritative items on the subject in 1970 and 1981. Mrs. Tootell was the daughter of Gertrude Hunt, accompanist to Princess Te Rangi Pai.

The Princess was the eldest of eight children, four girls, four boys, born to Colonel T. W. Porter, a veteran of the Maori wars, and Herewaka, only daughter of a paramount chief who signed the Treaty of Waitangi on behalf of east coast tribes.

Originally called Fanny Rose Porter, she was, through her mother, a Princess in her own right, and it was for this reason she adopted the name Te Rangi Pai, which, translated from the Maori, has been rendered "The Supreme Heaven" or "The Beautiful Sky"

The Porter family lived in GISBORNE, then moved to WELLINGTON where the girls were educated at Brougham House, an establishment for young ladies run by a Mrs. Sheppard, whose daughter Florence later married Colonel Porter after the death of his first wife.

The Porter family moved back to Gisborne where Col. Porter was Mayor four or five times. They lived at Heatherlea beside the Kaiti River and in the days of Pollard's Opera Company, touring members were often guests.

Fanny Rose Porter married John Howie, civil servant, on 15th October 1891, he later became Collector of Customs at Gisborne.

A Mr. R. S. Smythe encouraged and persuaded Fanny to go to AUSTRALIA to study singing. In 1898 she and her husband sailed there in the RUNIC.

In 1900 she arrived in LONDON and studied under three celebrated teachers, Charles Santley, baritone, Dr. Sibley, oratorio and Mr. W. Carter, ballad.

Te Rangi Pai's reputation was greatly enhanced by appearances at the Royal Albert Hall and the Queen's Hall. Two notable engagements at the Royal Albert Hall in 1902 involved performances at the Saint Patrick's Day Grand Irish Festival and at the St. Andrew's Eve Grand Scotch Festival. However, singing in oratorios in cathedrals gave her the greatest satisfaction. Her voice was acclaimed as the most beautiful that New Zealand had ever produced. She had an unusual range for a contralto and her tall, commanding figure and impulsive nature won ovations wherever she appeared.

Perhaps this commanding presence was the reason for her success in an IRISH ENCOUNTER AT KILKENNY where the programme ended with the (ENGLISH) National Anthem.

"All the concert party came on stage and we were received with applause, as we had had a good many encores", she said.

"I started to sing the solo of the National Anthem when a perfect storm of hisses and yells greeted me. For a moment I was at a loss, MY LOYALTY HAD NEVER HAD SUCH A SHOCK BEFORE. But I was equal to the occasion and, disregarding the storm of hisses and noise, I sang at the top of my voice. The stage manager said "COME OFF" but I was

not to be beaten. MY MAORI SPIRIT WAS UP and I just stood still and sang for all I was worth. I finished my solo and we sang the chorus too, despite the noise".

Te Rangi Pai was invited to attend Buckingham Palace to see her father Colonel Porter (a Boer War veteran) receive his citation from Queen Victoria. Colonel Porter led the VICTORY PARADE, riding his horse MAJOR, claimed to be the only horse out of eight thousand to return to New Zealand from the Transvaal. In August 1902 Colonel Porter led the New Zealand contingent in the Coronation Royal Review in London. He was made a C.B. (Companion of the Bath) for his services as a commander in the South African War.

The deaths of her mother Herewaka and youngest brother Robert late in 1904 and her own ill health led Te Rangi Pai to return to New Zealand in 1905.

She made several popular tours through New Zealand in 1906 and 1907, further health problems and disputes with her father, who had sold her mother's extensive Maori land interests, sapped her strength and she was forced to retire.

In the latter part of her life she taught singing and composed songs, her most famous composition is "Hine e Hine". She painted her favourite flowers—roses, pansies and violets—into the kowhaiwhai patterns on the rafters of the Te Whanau-a-Kaiaio meeting house at Te Kaha.

Fanny Howie, Princess Te Rangi Pai, died at Opotiki on 20th May 1916 and was buried at Maungaroa, under a pohutukawa tree. She was survived by an adopted son and her husband, who was later buried at her side. The solitary roadside grave is marked by a headstone and plaque.

APPENDIX

A Grand Matinee Concert was held at the LYCEUM, Newport, on Wednesday, 3rd June 1903 (the day following the Merthyr Concerts), under the Patronage and in the Presence of:
His Worship the Mayor and Mayoress of Newport, Right Hon. Lord Tredegar,
Hon. Col. Ivor Herbert,
Col. Wallis,
Col. Fothergill Evans,
Col. J. A. Bradney,
Col. A. G. Goss,
Major C. O. Smeaton,
Major W. C. Staveley,
J. Mitchell Innes, Esq.
The following account appeared:

"It has been decided to establish in London, near Waterloo Station, a club for Sailors, Soldiers and Marines, to be known as the Union Jack Club, as a memorial to those who fought and died in South Africa and China. The proposal is to acquire the site, build and equip the institution, and then to hand it over to the Services for their use. For the purpose of providing money for this work, concerts are being held all over England, and Mr. Sydney Cooper, lessee of the Lyceum, Newport, undertook the organisation for South Wales.

Two concerts were held at Merthyr on Tuesday; on Wednesday afternoon a matinee was given at the Lyceum, Newport. The New Zealand Band, the chief band of Australasia (under Lieut.Herd), were engaged, and the vocalists were the Princess Te Rangi Pai, the Chieftain Ranginia, members of the Maori race, and Mr. Bantock Pierpoint. The New Zealand Band numbered twenty four performers. There was not a single reed instrument, but the brass was

60. Headstone on the grave of Princess Te Rangi Pai.
Photo courtesy of Alexander Turnbull Library, Wellington, N.Z. Ref. No. F-58376-1/2.

so beautifully modulated and balanced, that there was no sense of incongruity in an indoor performance. The players produced a beautiful tone, their light and shade was of that right kind which genuinely expresses feeling, and their performances were entirely enjoyable

Led by the Chieftain they gave "A Maori Patriotic Greeting", an interesting illustration of a native custom. Mr. Bantock Pierpoint has a baritone voice of beautiful quality, and he sang "Since I have loved thee" and "To Anthea" with splendid expression, one with the depth of lover-like devotion, the other with all the vigour of passionate protestation; while he proved himself an ideal ballad singer in "Nelson's gone a-sailing", and the encore, a song with the refrain "Oh, this love, this love".

The Princess Te Rangi Pai sang with excellent expression, and was encored for "The only Days".

The Chieftain Ranginia, whose picturesque dress made his appearances doubly attractive, sang with rare sincerity, and won a recall for "Home, sweet home", while as an encore to "Annie Laurie" he gave a native action song, with chorus by the band".

(South Wales Weekly Argus. 6.6.1903).

BIBLIOGRAPHY
HINEMOA NEW ZEALAND BAND, 1903.

Merthyr.
  Merthyr Express. 23.5.1903. p.4. col.6.
  Merthyr Express. 6.6.1903. p.4. col.8.

Newport, Gwent.
  South Wales Weekly Argus. 3.6.1903. Advertisment.
  South Wales Weekly Argus. 6.6.1903. Lyceum Concert.

Swansea.
  The Cambrian. 29.5.1903.
  The Cambrian. 5.6.1903. Large advertisment.
  The Cambrian. 5.6.1903.
  The Cambrian.12.6.1903.
  South Wales Daily Post. 23.5.1903. Advertisment.
                           27.5.1903. Large advert.
                           3.6.1903.
                           5.6.1903. Advert.
  The New Zealand Mouthpiece. November 1961. pp.14-15.
  "The First New Zealand Representative Band. The Hinemoa Band. U.K. Tour, 1903." S. P. Newcomb.

PRINCESS TE RANGI PAI.
The Gisborne Times. 22.5.1916. p.5. Obituary.
New Zealand Biographies. 1970. Volume Three. pp.25-26. A. Tootell.
New Zealand Biographies. 1981. Volume Three. pp.189-90. A. Tootell.
The Dictionary of N.Z.Biography.Volume Three. 1901-1920. (Auckland University Press, 1996). Tony Chadwick.

ACKNOWLEDGEMENTS

Photographs and photocopies were supplied by The Alexander Turnbull Library, National Library of New Zealand, Te Puna Mátauranga o Aotearoa. Thanks to R. Flury, H. Mathie, Janet Horncy.

Permission to publish the photos was granted by the Alexander Turnbull Library, PO Box 12349, Wellington 6001, N.Z. Telephone 64-4-4743000.

Photocopies were received from The Cambrian Indexing Project, Swansea Central Library, Alexandra Road, Swansea, SA1 5DX. Thanks are due to County Librarian M. J. Allen and R. Brighton.

Photocopies were obtained from Merthyr Central Library courtesy of Reference Librarian Mrs. Carolyn Jacob.

Photocopies were obtained from Newport County Borough Library, John Frost Square, Newport, courtesy of Ms. Susan Pugh, Reference Library.

THE WAY WE WERE
1929-39

by

ROSINA HUGHES
(BORN WALSH)

Most mornings I woke to the sound of Binner clanging on his anvil. I would lie there and try to fit words into the changing rhythms. The smithy was behind our house and Binner whose real name was EVAN OWENS was the gentle quiet man who worked there. On wet, no-school days, he allowed us to work the bellows of the huge forge or try to lift the biggest hammers. There were usually two or three wags sucking their pipes and commenting on the various horses to be shod. These varied from small Welsh cobs to great cart horses. The smell of singed horse hair wafted down the lane. Binner made most of us a miniature copper horse shoe, I still have mine.

Lamb Lane, behind our house, The Lamb Inn, ran up to Castle Yard, which was a wonderful place to play. At one time the Castle Inn had stood there but now all that remained was a litter of stones and a derelict shed. We children played houses and shops among the rubble and held concerts in the shed. One large rectangular stone was in great demand as a shop counter. We used dock (sorrel) leaves for kippers, the seeds for sugar and patted mud-butter into shape with two pieces of slate. We girls were learning to be wives and mothers while the boys played more robust games of cowboys or soldiers by the river or up in the small plantation above the British tip. The latter was a marvellous place to hide during the pea shooting season when the stems of the Bog Bean were ripe for picking. Many people were taken unaware by a sharp sting at the back of the head as they went about their business.

Some of the older girls decided to hold a concert in the old shed and charged "A PIN TO COME IN". A solid plank of wood had been placed across two large laundry baskets to make a stage. One pretty girl with sausage curls did an Irish jig and strayed too near the end of the plank. There was a loud crack and she disappeared into the basket. I'll never forget her tear-stained face as she hauled herself out. The few boys present laughed without mercy.

There were about six small cottages in Lamb Lane, two up and two down, as they say. Each had a toilet at the end of the row and each had one tap behind the door. I went to the first house many times and there was always clean sand on the flagged floor, a daily coal fire and an oil lamp on the table. Most of the cottages housed several children. One woman had only the upper half of her left arm. It was fascinating to watch her cope with the family wash in a tub out of doors in fine weather. How she scrubbed and wrung out those clothes was a work of art.

The Lamb stood on a cross road. "Our patch" consisted of the Glebeland from the British Tip to High-street and Castle-street from the Castle Cinema down to the Iron Bridge. We played with many children here and front doors were always open to us. If I ran into a friend's house at meal times I was always asked to pull up a chair, or if I had already eaten, there was usually a comfortable chair by the fire with a pile of comics under the cushion. We played out of doors unless the weather made it impossible.

61. Miss Nash's dancing class. The author's sister SHEILA, back row, far right. The photographer was J. Leslie Francis, Merthyr.

Towards the river on the right was a row of terraced houses above street level. Two Jewish families lived here, next door to each other, the SIMONS and the SILVERMANS. Lorraine Simons' father was a tailor and sat cross-legged on a low table in the front room, always sewing while he sang Yiddish songs. Mrs. Simons was a plump, pleasant woman who scrubbed the wooden floors until they gleamed white. There were other children, Davina, Abie and more. When it was Passover and fasting time they gave us large perforated sheets of unleavened bread to take home.

Another Jewish family called Jaffy had the end terrace house near the Castle Cinema. Mr. Jaffy repaired clocks and watches and Mrs. Jaffy had a sweet shop in her front room. She did a very brisk trade here because her goodies were cheaper than those at the Cinema which were pre-wrapped. Mrs. Jaffy broke up the toffee with a little hammer and weighed it on a brass scales. All the sweets came out of jars. We went to a few riotous parties at this house and found the Jaffys a kind loving family. The younger daughter Anita was our special friend.

A few doors down from the Jaffys was the Chinese Laundry. Their family name was SUEY and we soon made a friend of their daughter who adopted the name of Jean. Behind the shop they lived in traditional Chinese style wearing long robes and eating great bowls of rice, chopped meat and cabbage. Figs, dates, lychees and Turkish delight were always on offer. Their son Billy's betrothed wife arrived from China and they had a family of healthy boys. Old Mrs. Suey never integrated into the community and was eventually admitted into a mental home. Jean, who was always one of the brightest girls in the class, left for China just before the 1939-45 War, to become a nurse. We had only one letter from her.

Opposite The Lamb, on a corner site, was the CO.OP. You would always find women waiting to be served here. Chairs were provided for them and it was quite interesting to listen to the gossip. Each order, especially on pay day, took-a long time, FOR EVERYTHING HAD TO BE INDIVIDUALLY WEIGHED AND WRAPPED. Bacon and ham went under the hand slicer, cheese was sliced with a piece of wire, butter was patted into shape and sugar and tea hand-packed into pink or blue bags. A ham bone cost four pence and with pot vegetables and lentils made a hearty meal for four people. Biscuits were displayed in tilted glass-topped tins and one could buy as little as a quarter pound. Later pre-packed biscuits came on the market but they didn't taste as good and you couldn't buy the broken ones for a penny a bag.

The CO.OP. owned the tiny houses either side of the shop. The McLoughlins lived in the first on the Glebeland side and must have paid a peppercorn rent. This house consisted of one small room plus scullery and one and a half bed-rooms. At the rear was the usual cobbled yard plus toilets. BIG LOSSIN as I called him, was a miner and he and LITTLE LOSSIN brought up two daughters to be lively, clean, well-mannered girls. Beryl married Bazil Waite, whose parents owned the printing shop beneath Southeys the Stationers.

Further down the Glebeland was the Echo Office where my friend Myrtle Taylor lived. The newspapers arrived by train from Cardiff and were dumped outside the shop and then doled out to the paper boys. Most of these boys were under age but eager to earn extra money. Some were bare footed and had no coats or sweaters even in the bitterest weather. They stood outside public houses and cinemas or waited for trains and trams to unload. They whistled and sang and shouted "Echo Yere" in raucous voices. Most of these boys came from "under the arches" where we were forbidden to go. This quarter was entered under a big stone archway and had an open gutter running through the cobbles.

Mr. and Mrs. Nicholas kept the fish and chip shop below the Echo shop. Mr. Nicholas's real name was Nicholas Altmeyer and he came from France between the wars. The chip potatoes were cleaned in a shed in Lamb Lane then trundled in a barrow by a young boy, down to the shop. On the menu was hake, skate or haddock plus chips for three pence. Upstairs tea, bread and butter accompanied the menu at sixpence. Dandelion and Burdock plus a vicious green looking limeade sold at tuppence a bottle, with a marble in the bottle top.

Mrs. James kept the little general shop opposite "Nick the Fish". Like Mrs. Addis and Ike Davies at the other end of the Glebeland she sold everything from pickles to paraffin. Eggs were thirteen for a shilling and mother always tested them in water to see if any were bad. If there were I had to promptly take them back. I remember buying tiny celluloid dolls, liquorice pipes, sweet cigarettes, tobacco coconut, two sorts of sweets all for a penny. The smell of paraffin pervaded the shop but never tainted the food.

Mr. and Mrs. Elleman kept the newsagents' shop next to The Wheatsheaf Inn, which was diagonally opposite our house. This was our favourite shop and comics were a penny plain and twopenny coloured. CHIPS and BUTTERFLY were full of entertainment but RAIN-BOW and CHICKS OWN were for smaller children and quite beautiful. When I was seven years old my sister and I went down with scarlet fever so were isolated in a bedroom at the far end of the house. The Ellemans sent us each a beautiful book with coloured illustrations. All our books were removed and burned in case of infection. Oh! how I moaned over the loss of those books.

The area from the Lamb up to the British Tip was a safe place for young children to play. There were very few cars and never more than one bus standing on the corner. Evan Owen senior who had also been a blacksmith, took it upon himself to stand at the cross road and direct any traffic. If there was any bullying in our street games we would run to Mr. Owen or to Carney who lived in the lodging house. Carney, who had lost a leg and with a crutch and shoulder length hair looked like Long John Silver, also paraded the streets and sorted out our squabbles. Mr. Owen however was much more in demand because he was a horse doctor as well as a frustrated policeman. Once, when my cat Ginger was bitten by a rat, Mr. Owen came in every day to pop a pill into her mouth and put a home made salve on her paw. The wound healed quickly and Evan Owen consumed a number of free pints.

According to the season our games varied between skipping, whip and top, hop scotch and ball games. Victoreen Nicholas had a proper sledge so she had many friends when the first snow came. I remember having a ride on the slope down to the river and I remember even more the stinging pain of a snowball or rather ice ball thrown by Leonard Addis. I had a lump on my head for days.

One game we played was very dangerous but nobody stopped us playing it. It was called "Skinny Lighto" and I suppose it was a type of bondage or slave game. Three or four boys would chase a few girls and tie them in a line with a long piece of orange rope. The boys would grasp the other end of the rope and run shouting "Skinny Lighto". It was a great feat of balance to remain upright especially spinning round a corner. If one fell everybody fell in a heap laughing. Vaseline was the cure-all for cuts and grazes when we went home.

Josie kept a green grocers shop next to B. Harris Jones, the outfitter. She kindly gave us the plaited rope that came round the orange boxes. Once I was sent to the lodging house next to her shop to deliver a message. I entered a large room with a stove and a number of old men sitting around the walls. I was taken aback by the smell and left quickly.

62. Abermorlais Infants School. Class 1G. 1929.
1. Rosina or Zena Walsh, aged two.
2. Lorraine Simons.
3. Sheila Walsh, sister of Zena.

Poor Josie was given a rough time on Guy Fawkes night. She was very plump and very pretty with dark curly hair and rosy cheeks. She was kindly too and gave poor children any bruised fruit. The boys repaid her by creeping into her shop and throwing "jacky jumpers" under her skirts. How I longed to be grown up so that I could wear these long skirts that our mothers wore. When I reached my teens the dresses were short!

I cried so frequently to go to school that mother asked Mrs. Barry who was in charge of the "babies class" if I could possibly attend. Mrs. Barry was an uncertificated teacher who spent all her teaching life in reception class. She said I could not have my name in ink but she would write my name in pencil at the bottom of the page and I could have a mark. At the end of the year I had the best attendance and I was still only three.

We sat on small chairs behind small tables for hours. Somehow we learned phonetics by copying our letters onto blackboards. We counted beads on a large abacus and learned the rudiments of addition and subtraction. For recreation we were offered blocks or clay. We sang nursery rhymes and little Welsh folk songs, while a large glass-fronted cupboard full of toys stared at us daily. It was never opened.

When Mrs.Barry wanted absolute silence she had a very clever ploy. She told us to fold our arms and look up at the filigreed circle where the gas pipe entered the ceiling. If we were very, very quiet we would see the fairies dancing within the circle. Several children shouted "I can see 'em" but try as I may I could only see blackness and filigreed shadows.

Once when we streamed out of school at four o'clock, a rope had been tied across the road and beyond it a T FORD CAR. Two men had fixed an oval frame to the door of the open topped car and without ceremony we were picked up one at a time and photographed in the frame. Some children screamed and fought thinking they were being kidnapped but most of us sat placidly within the frame and bought the photographs which arrived at school the next week.

There were many deprived children in our area, some without shoes or adequate clothing. We took all our cast off shoes and clothes to school where they were doled out by GOV-ERNESS (Miss Richards) in her room. Undernourished children were given a daily helping of cod liver oil or Scott's Emulsion. Ring worm was painted with Gentian Violet after hair had been shaved off. We all had regular medical examinations in Governess's room where there was a gas fire. Tuberculosis swept through families and twice I saw a small white coffin come through a door in Glebeland Street. Coffins were often carried on the shoulders of six men all the way to Cefn cemetery, followed by many mourners in black. Men would doff their caps and lower their heads until the procession had passed.

A wealthy benefactor named John Morgan gave poor children a party once a year. He had white hair, a full white beard, his usual attire was plus fours and a Norfolk jacket. These parties were held in a shed at the end of a lane on the left of Glebeland Street. Each child was given an entry ticket and all came out whooping with jollity and sporting paper caps and balloons. Afterwards each child was given a ticket for a free ride to Cefn Coed on a tram and once Beryl Loughlin wangled a ticket for me.

I had been to Cefn on a tram many times, it only cost a penny, but this was different. For a start I shouldn't have been there so it was a bit like forbidden fruit.

Everybody sang "Pack up your troubles", "One man went to mow", and "Daisy, Daisy", I'd never heard the latter, so when I arrived home I asked mother "what's an anssadoo?" I thought it must be something desirable since everybody wanted Daisy's. My mother rolled about laughing and much to my chagrin told all her friends.

212

63. Rosina's husband, Allen, photographed in the model T Ford car.

Saturday was the best day of the week for us. No school, dancing class in the morning and "pictures" at five o'clock. Mother had only to threaten to ban the cinema trip and we were immediately compliant. Dancing we could take or leave.

Miss Nash held dancing classes in a large room in her house in Gwaelod-y-garth. I must have been very young when I wore a blue and yellow dress, a white wig and danced a min-uet with Dr. Thomas's son Ronnie. My sister was a daffodil and lost her trumpet shaped hat in the first minute. I enjoyed the classes but after a while Beryl didn't take us any more. Perhaps mother could not afford the one shilling and six pence per lesson.

Betty and Muriel the daughters of our cleaning woman usually escorted us to the cinema but before we set off there was much discussion upon whether we would go in the sixpenny seats at the back or opt for the fourpenny seats and have twopence to spend. We normally decided on the latter because once the main film started we could sneak back to the better seats.

There were five cinemas in Merthyr at that time. Lowest on the list was the Electric which funnily enough had only gas jets on the walls and such poor ventilation that the walls ran with condensation when there was a full house. This was the last resort and showed only third rate films. We usually managed to get into the five o'clock performance of the Castle Cinema. The first six rows were full of jostling, teasing, sometimes fighting children. Hair was pulled, pea nuts and sweet-papers thrown until the programme started. Usherettes in braided uniform flashed torches and sometimes hauled noisy children out. There were babies in shawls and people eating fish and chips or pies. As soon as the feature film started there was "hush" and we were transported to another world. These were our idols, larger than life. We danced with Fred (Astaire) and Ginger (Rogers), rode the plains with Roy Rogers and Gene Autrey and rolled in the aisles with Charlie Chaplin and Laurel and Hardy.

At half time Gene Lyn whirled up on the Wurlitzer (organ), turned and smiled at the audi-ence, settled his full evening tails and burst into a medley of popular songs. The organ flashed all colours of the rainbow and accompanied by drums, trumpets and cymbals we shouted our heads off as the words flashed on the screen. What a way to get rid of our "agro" as it is called today.

The following week many teenage girls adopted the hair styles of Jean Harlowe, Greta Garbo etc.. Eye brows were plucked and the length of clothes varied. Everybody wore berets after a film with Ida Lupino. My father commented that he had seen a girl "not so much wearing a beret but walking at the side of it".

We felt safe on our patch. There was a strong sense of community and fair play. Grown ups were always within running distance and bullying was frowned upon as being a show of weakness rather than strength. One big boy was boycotted for a few weeks because he kept spoiling our games.

Communities of long standing were decimated with the arrival of large housing estates and with it went that sense of belonging we all had. Often generations had lived in the same house.

I was lucky to have a colourful, safe and secure childhood with the freedom to run on our patch. When my mother could not find us at tea time my father would say, "leave them alone they'll come home when they're hungry " and we always did.

64. Bust of Dr. Mary Davies sculpted by her father MYNORYDD. Cyfarthfa Castle Museum and Art Gallery, Merthyr.

64A. Dr. Mary Davies, wife of Cadwaladr Davies.

DR. MARY DAVIES, SWEET SINGER, GREAT LADY

TRANSCRIBED

Mynorydd.

In the early years of the nineteenth century, there was born, at Merthyr, a boy who gave early promise of genius, for music and sculpture. A member of his father's chapel choir and a good flautist, young William Davies, taking his courage in both hands, yielded to the lure of London, and journeyed thither to seek his fortune. He became a sculptor by profession, yet he never lost his early love for music. He was for many years precentor at the famous Charing Cross (Calvinistic Methodist) Chapel, and conductor of the London Welsh Musical Society; and he remained, to the end, a devoted Eisteddfodwr, receiving the Gorsedd hall-mark "Mynorydd".

To him, in 1855, was sent Heaven's gift of a baby girl, whose name adorns this page, and whose fame became world-wide.

Early triumphs.

To the delight of her fond father, little *Mair* soon gave ample proof of her rich endow-ment. Lovingly and carefully he supervised her early training. Her *debut,* in her teens, was in a charmingly appropriate setting. Mynorydd had executed in marble a bust of Edith Wynne, the *doyenne* of Welsh singers. This was presented to this great *artiste* at a gathering of London Welshmen; among them Brinley Richards, and my old Bridgend fellow-towns-man John Thomas (Pencerdd Gwalia), the Queen's harpist. The sculptor's little daughter captivated them all by her sweet singing.

There and then was *Mair's* musical career launched. Edith Wynne and Brinley Richards took her in hand. She promptly won the Welsh choral scholarship to the Royal Academy of Music. There, she studied hard under Randegger and Sterndale-Bennett; while there she was awarded the "Rosa" Gold Medal and the "Nilsson" prize, open to all comers.

Ballad singer.

Mary's debut as a professional singer was at one of the Brinley Richards concerts, in London in the late 1870s. In 1880, she undertook the *role* of Marguerite in "Faust" at Manchester, Hallé conducting, at the first performance of Berlioz's opera in English. Almost at a bound, Mary Davies found herself in the first rank in her profession. She was in constant request at the great musical festivals the "Three Choirs", Chester, Norwich, and Huddersfield.

Speedily she became one of the leading artistes at the London Ballad Concerts at St. James's Hall, where her ballad singing created a *furore.* It is not too much to say that Mary Davies gave to the ballad a new lease of life.

The 1880s were the days of "royalty" songs. A professional singer received a fee for each rendering of a new song put on the market. Much rubbish was thus foisted on an unsuspect-ing public by enterprising publishers and greedy *artistes.* Mary Davies set her little face like a flint against all such chicanery. None but the best was good enough for her *repertoire.* As a result, the magic words "Sung by Mary Davies" on the cover of a song was a veritable hall-mark and ensured its sale, by thousands.

Her fine soprano voice had not a high range; it was almost mezzo, but her middle register was superb. Her phrasing and intonation were perfect. She was always "in the middle of the note". Her voice production was remarkably fine. Hers were pure chest notes, effortless.

At the Eisteddfod.

She never forgot the rock from which she was hewn. All her life long, she loved the Eisteddfod and all things Welsh. She sang at the "National" at Mold in 1873. Thereafter her name was prominent at nearly every one of our National festivals. In later years, she was a frequent adjudicator, particularly of folk-song competitions.

A garland.

I want to pay a tribute, long overdue, to the warm-hearted welcome and wholehearted encouragement always given by Mary Davies and her devoted father Mynorydd to hosts of struggling young Welsh musical students in London.

Dear old Mynorydd used regularly to visit the Royal Academy of Music and the Royal College of Music, ferreting out lonely and home-sick Celts. At the weekly "At Homes", at Sheffield Terrace, all were welcome. Each, in turn, was called on to contribute to the informal programme. Before departing, Mynorydd would usually conduct one of Gwilym Gwent's Welsh glees. Woe! . . . to whoever failed to satisfy him in the art of sight-reading, of which he was a consummate master.

Mary Davies's talents were ever at the command of sweet charity. Numberless good causes and charitable institutions, again and again, benefited by her freely proffered services. Her name on the bill of a charity concert always proved a certain draw and ensured a crowded house.

Marriage.

In 1890, Mary Davies bade farewell to the concert stage the scene of so many triumphs, two years after her marriage to Mr. Cadwaladr Davies, the Registrar of the North Wales University College, Bangor. Here she resided for a year or two, until her husband's breakdown in health necessitated his resignation, when they returned to London, always her spiritual home. Meanwhile, she had been elected a Fellow of the Royal Academy of Music, and had been for some time an examiner for the Royal Academy, and the Royal College of Music.

Honours.

Mary Davies's beloved Nation was not slow to honour its gifted daughter. That was a great "Degree" day at Aberystwyth when she received her cap and gown, as Doctor of Music. Alongside her, receiving their Doctorates, stood two other old friends of mine, O. M. Edwards and Timothy Richard.

Welsh folk-songs.

Space fails me to tell all the great story of Mary Davies's pioneer work in the collection and collation of Welsh folk-songs.

So far back as 1837, Miss Maria Jane Williams, of Aberpergwm, had won a prize at the Abergavenny Eisteddfod for a modest collection, published a few years later.

During Mary Davies's sojourn at Bangor, Dr. Lloyd Williams had inoculated her with the germ of his own enthusiasm for Welsh folk-songs. Her imagination was captured and speedily she set to work.

Lloyd Williams had established among his Bangor students a society, "Y Cantorion" (The Songsters), and had set them hunting North Wales for old-time melodies, sung by pedlars and by travelling tailors, as they plied their trade from town to town and farm to farm; and for others, vaguely remembered by old folk from childhood days.

From these modest beginnings sprang the "Welsh Folk-song Society", established at the Caernarvon "National" in 1906, and which has ever since gone from strength to strength. Mary Davies gathered round her a band of willing workers; among them Lady (Herbert) Lewis, Miss Morfydd Owen, and Mrs. Jane Williams (an octogenarian!).

Gems unearthed.

These ladies, with other enthusiasts, scoured Wales in search of old Welsh tunes. The wise-acres warned them there were none to be found, that they were on a wild goose chase. Undeterred and undismayed, they carried on. One by one, gems were unearthed; in the workshop, in the farm, in the train; others were collected from the Welsh colonies in U.S.A., a few from far Patagonia!

Later, Sir Alfred T. Davies gave timely encouragement from Whitehall, by inaugurating the celebration of Gwyl Dewi Sant, by the singing of Welsh folk-songs in the schools. Dr. Lloyd Williams remained at his post as musical editor. Harry Evans threw himself wholeheartedly into the work. Llew Tegid rendered yeoman service in the translation and setting of words for the music.

Mary Davies, from the outset, undertook the secretaryship of the Society, later becoming its President. The very titles of many of our folk-songs are delightfully quaint. Here are a few, picked at random:

"Gee, Ceffyl Bach",
"Robin Goch",
"Y Blotyn Du",
"Hub i'r Galon"
"Y Gog Lwydlas"
"Yr Hen Wr Mwyn",
"Dacw Mam yn Dwad".

And the lilt of the old-time tunes is captivating.

A cameo.

Dare I attempt a cameo of Mary Davies as I last saw her? Dainty, short in stature, but with so much of dignity and with bearing so erect as to make her seem half a head taller than her actual inches. A wide, generous brow, a beautiful little acquiline nose, tiny ears like pink shells, beautiful blue eyes, and, although nigh on four score years, with the complexion of a girl; her regal little head with its aureole, not of gold, but of snow-white hair, fine as spun silk.

Mary Davies's triumphs left her absolutely unspoiled. To the end, she remained the same charming unaffected winsome personality as in early years.

Truly—A VERY GREAT LADY!

(From *GREAT WELSHMEN of MODERN DAYS*. Sir Thomas Hughes, 1931.

ANECDOTES OF SOME LOCAL ARTISTS

by

T. F. HOLLEY

Some account has been given, in previous volumes of the Merthyr Historian series, of five well-known artists associated in one way or another with Merthyr Tydfil.

William Edward Jones, painter of portraits, was featured in Volumes Six and Nine. Penry Williams featured in two essays in Volume Seven, Joseph Edwards, sculptor, is to be found in Volumes Four and Seven, William Jones, a sculptor who emigrated to Australia, is also the subject of an essay in Volume Seven and Sir Thomas Brock features largely in Merthyr Historian, Volume Nine.

The present essay brings together what I know of nine nineteenth century Merthyr artists, some more famous than others. Can a Merthyr family archive provide further information on any of these people, all well-rooted in the local community ?

The following artists are discussed:

1. Harry Dyke Pearce, artist and patron of fellow-artists.
2. Tom Prytherch.
3. J. O'Neill, junior, and his pupil David Jones. Jones had previously worked with David Price, monumental mason.
4. Miss Jessie Harrison, later Mrs. Godman.
5. David Davies, Dewi Ddu, illustrator.
6. William Thomas, shoemaker-artist.
7. David Price, sculptor-monumental mason, once a pupil of Joseph Edwards.
8. The Rev. J. G. James, Market-square Church, art critic.

HARRY DYKE PEARCE

1A. "Harry Dyke Pearce was born in Church-street, Merthyr, in 1848, and was the only son of T. J. Pearce, one of the founders and proprietors of the Pontycapel Brewery Company. Harry's mother was a daughter of Thomas Davies, sometime proprietor of the Bush Hotel, and a sister of Mrs. McEachern, and of Mrs. Shapton, of Somerset-place.

"Having received locally a good rudimentary education, Harry developed a taste for farming, and for two years studied agriculture at Cirencester College. Upon leaving college he tried his 'prentice hand at a small farm which his father bought for him near Pontycapel, Cefn Coed, but he speedily relinquished this bucolic pastime for one more congenial to his tastes.

"Harry Pearce had, at an early age, conceived a passion for the fine arts, and had given evidence by his efforts of no ordinary ability. He therefore went to London to study under a Royal Academician, who now occupies a distinguished position in the world of art. Under his tuition Pearce acquired a fair insight into the mysteries of painting, and developed a love for his favourite occupation, which increased in intensity as years went by.

"In this domain Harry Dyke Pearce was not so much an idealist as a REALIST. Ruskin tells us that 'the power, whether of painter or poet, to describe rightly what he calls an ideal thing, depends upon it being to him not an ideal, but a real thing'. These words apply with especial force to Harry Dyke Pearce. He always held that the more true the picture was to nature, the greater was the art which it contained. Pearce had bought several Academy pictures which now adorn his house, and are of great value. One of his chief delights was the internal ornamentation of his home, and Penybryn bears ample evidence of his wonderful taste in home decoration.

"H. D. Pearce was a sincere friend to many a struggling artist and HAD MATERIALLY ASSISTED MR. TOM PRYTHERCH AND MR. RAPHAEL JONES (son of William Edward Jones, painter of portraits). One of Pearce's latest acts was to obtain for Raphael Jones a valuable connection with several London illustrated papers. It was not alone, however, in the realm of painting that H. D. Pearce's peculiar gifts manifested themselves. Pearce was a WOOD-CARVER OF EXCEPTIONAL ABILITY, and was a very successful modeller from the clay.

"He had also devoted himself to electrical engineering, and had fitted up a workshop where he installed a dynamo run by an Otto gas engine. Horticulture was also a favourite hobby, and his hot houses contained some beautiful specimens of rare plants and exotics.

"Pearce married his cousin, the daughter of Mr. Thomas Davies, manager of the West of England Bank, Aberdare, and was therefore brother-in-law to Mr. Gilbert Davies, manager of the Metropolitan Bank, and his only sister is the wife of Dr. Webster, Merthyr.

"H. D. Pearce was a most devoted husband and father and his sudden and almost tragic death will be a severe blow to Mrs. Pearce and the three children. The two sons are at Cheltenham College, the little daughter is taught at home."

(*Merthyr Express*. Saturday. 2.11.1895. p.8. col.l.)

1B. "Harry Dyke Pearce's paintings were admirable, those of 'The Cefn Soup Kitchen Boy', which obtained a prize at Cardiff some years ago and old 'MAGWS', life size, in the habiliments of her work-a-day duties, are exquisite specimens of what a true artist can produce."

(Obituary. *Merthyr Times*. 7.11.1895. p.8. col.3.)

The MAGWS painting is today (1997) housed in the Cyfarthfa Castle Museum and Art Gallery, Merthyr Tydfil.

1C "We have once or twice had the pleasure of noticing the oil paintings of Mr. H. D. PEARCE, son of our former and much respected fellow townsman, T. J. Pearce, of Cefn, and pointed out the high class of artistic merit to which those pictures bore testimony. Passing the window of Mr. Meredith's shop in High-street, on Tuesday, where we generally find some pictorial gems exhibited, we were attracted by the portrait in oil of a young lady well-known in Merthyr, and which bore H. D. Pearce's signature. This picture struck us in a moment, from its life-like character. The portrait is a graceful profile in which the lineaments are faithfully copied and thrown out with a distinctiveness which is most effective without being too prominent; the lights and shadows are introduced harmoniously; the flesh colouring in every part, and particularly the face, throat and bosom, is the perfection of what combines to produce a warmth of tint and heightened effect in the due gradations of light and shade.

"The natural happy expression of the face has been reproduced with a completeness which leaves nothing to be desired, and the placing of a beautifully painted rose and maiden fern, at the bosom, is an appropriate detail which adds a grace and charm to the picture. The work itself is also of that exceedingly fine character which will bear close inspection, and this in our opinion is one of the brightest merits of any oil painter. We congratulate the painter upon his production, of which as a work of art of high merit he may well feel proud.

(*Merthyr Express*. 16.1.1875. p.8. col.l.)

TOM PRYTHERCH

2A. "Mr. Tom Prytherch, who brought fame to Dowlais as a gifted painter, died at Fronheulog, Cefn Coed, the residence of Colonel J. J. Jones, on Sunday last. The famous artist had been touring the South of England with Col. Jones and his family during the last month, and subsequently accompanied them on a visit to Somerset, where he was taken ill. Prytherch was conveyed to Fronheulog by Col. Jones, but, despite the best medical attention and skillful nursing he passed away from bronchial pneumonia and heart failure, at the age of sixty one.

"Forty years ago Prytherch was a very popular figure among the young people of Dowlais, of which place he was a native. A clever draughtsman, he was employed in the drawing office of the old Dowlais Iron Company. Showing exceptional talent as a painter in water colours and black and white sketches, he came under the notice of the late Mr. W. Pritchard Morgan, formerly M.P. for Merthyr Boroughs during that exciting and memorable contest in 1888, when W. P. Morgan contested and defeated Mr. Ffoulkes Griffiths, the nominee of the Liberal Association.

"Tom Prytherch drew a series of cartoons and caricatures of W. P. Morgan which caught the attention of John Vaughan, solicitor, the election agent. So pleased was the future Member with the clever work of young Prytherch that arrangements were made for Prytherch to further his studies at Slade's famous Art School. There Prytherch had a brilliant career and afterwards became an artist of repute in water colour and oils and was a frequent exhibitor at the Royal Academy. Prytherch delighted in landscape painting, and one of his pictures of a Pontsarn scene was considered a masterpiece of its type.

"A bachelor, after completing his studies he lived with an aunt, Miss Everall, at Wroxeter, near Shrewsbury, and the interment took place there on Wednesday last at Prytherch's expressed wish. His brother, John Prytherch, to whom Tom was much attached, died at Bronheulog, Penydarren, about two months ago, and his death had an effect upon Tom Prytherch's health. Tom's numerous contemporaries in Dowlais and elsewhere genuinely mourn the loss of one of the most gifted sons of Ironopolis."

(*Merthyr Express*. 17.4.1926. p.12.)

2B. "From 1892 Prytherch was based in Wroxeter working on commissions for Lord Barnard of Raby Castle, and exhibiting a Wroxeter Church interior at the Royal Academy in 1901. Prytherch contributed illustrations to several books of Welsh folk lore and history, and to a series of photogravure portraits of Welsh Princes. He died at Wroxeter on 11th April 1926, and was buried in the municipal churchyard.

"Further biographical information can be seen in the Revd. Mardy Rees': *Welsh Painters, Engravers and Sculptors* (1911) and in obituaries of Prytherch in the *Western Mail* for 13th April 1926 and the *Merthyr Express* for 17th April 1926.

The National Museum of Wales owns a 1910 watercolour of *Cader Idris* (Drgs 4264) and an undated watercolour of the Great Hall of *Stokesay Castle* (Drgs 4267), both deriving from the 1975 bequest of ISAAC AND ANNIE WILLIAMS. A photogravure portrait of Bishop William Morgan, purchased in 1903, is also held.

(Tim Egan. Dept. of Art. National Museum of Wales.

2C. "From time to time there appear in the shop windows of Merthyr, works of art that would form the nucleus of an art gallery. Messrs. Hepworth are at present displaying a very fine study in still life from the brush of G. F. HARRIS and in the window of Messrs. R. T. Jones and Co. are also very fine oil paintings by Tom Prytherch. One of these represents 'A Gypsy Encampment' and the other 'A Pool on the Taff', which bears a very striking resemblance to Pontsarn. The figure of a maiden seated on a mossy bank impart to the scene an air of romance."

(Merthyr Times. 16.7.1897. p.6. col.l.)

2D. "Our readers will next week have an opportunity of viewing the latest production from the brush of Tom Prytherch, the accomplished Dowlais artist, whose efforts from time to time have afforded us great Pleasure to notice.

"This beautiful oil painting is seventy two inches by fifty two inches, and the subject is the Charlton Hills, Shropshire. Competent art critics have pronounced the picture to be a MASTER PRODUCTION and by far the most ambitious of Tom Prytherch's efforts. It will be on exhibition at Mr. W. M. Davies's clothing establishment in High-street next week.

"THE PICTURE WILL BE DRAWN FOR ON THE ART UNION PRINCIPLE."

(Merthyr Express. 7.7.1894. p.4. col.7.)

PRYTHERCH'S "CHARLTON HILLS" CAN BE VIEWED IN CYFARTHFA CASTLE MUSEUM AND ART GALLERY.

2E. "The forthcoming concert for the benefit of Tom Prytherch will take place on 9th May, 1892, and may be anticipated with interest since Miss Maggie Davies, A.R.C.M., Miss Kate Morgan, Dr. Cromwell Jones and Mr. Tom Lewis have been engaged. It is hoped also to have a string quartet in evidence, of Merthyr friends.

(Merthyr Express. 23.4.1892. p.8. col.4.)

An extremely long account of the concert appeared, see M.E. 14.5.1892. p.8. col.5. Miss Maggie Davies, later Mrs. Hutchenson, was accorded a chapter in David Morgans's book "Music and Musicians of Merthyr and District", 1922.

2F. "A letter from the secretary of the benefit fund raised on behalf of Tom Prytherch expressed his gratitude to all who in any way patronised the recent Christy entertainment.

"Tom Prytherch still remains at Llandrindod and there his brush is not idle, but he will, it is presumed, shortly resume his studies either in London or Antwerp.

"The Christy Minstrels propose visiting Rhymney shortly and will perform at Merthyr on 15th January, 1891."

(Merthyr Express. 29.11.1890. p.5. col.6.)

A long account of the very successful Christy Minstrel Entertainment appeared in the *Merthyr Express* on Saturday 22.11.1890. p.5. col.7. Mr. W. Pritchard Morgan attended.

2G. "Much life is being infused by promoters into the arrangements for securing by means of a minstrel entertainment the wherewithal to meet the expenses of a year's study at

Antwerp on the part of Tom Prytherch, whose praises as a promising artist have so often been proclaimed. Tom was fortunate in gaining the patronage of Mr. W. Pritchard-Morgan, M.P., who maintained the young man at London and enabled him to spend about fifteen months at the Kensington School of Art, at the end of which time Pritchard Morgan intimated his intention of withholding further support.

"Prytherch's reason for choosing Antwerp is that his year's course and maintenance would cost about forty pounds only in that town, whereas in London it would be more than double that amount. The proceeds of the minstrel entertainment to take place on the thirteenth prox. will be supplemented by a subscription list. The success of the entertainment is assured by the fact that Mr. W. Hughes,A.C., will act as musical conductor of a male-voice party of minstrels from whom very good singing may be expected, and Mr. W. Knox will be the interlocutor (Master of ceremonies) and Mr. M. L. Walters, stage manager; total number taking part, forty."

(M.E. 20.9.1890. p.5. col.5).

JOHN O'NEILL, JUNIOR

3A. "In another column may be seen an advertisement referring to the studio opened by Mr. J. O'Neill, junior, at the rear of "Alma Cottage", Dowlais, that young artist having commenced business on his own account as a portrait painter.

"A visit to the studio shows that the paintings are drawn from life, and differ materially from the common photograph paintings whose length of life is so very uncertain. Mr. O'Neill has already executed several paintings, and we commend the portrait of his mother, which is on view in the shop window of Mr. Austin.

It is significant that most of the leading tradesmen of the town have already joined the kit-kat club formed, and a peep into the studio reveals a number of well-known faces. We wish the young artist well deserved success, and would again repeat that the studio is well worthy of a visit."

(M.E. 18.10.1890. p.5. col.8.)

3B. "There is at present exhibited in the shop window of Messrs. Masters & Co., High-street, an admirable portrait of Mrs. Mansfield, executed by Mr. J. O'Neill. It has been drawn and painted from life and we congratulate the young artist on the faithfulness of the likeness."

(M.E. 15.11.1890. p.5. col.l.)

3C. "A novel picture painted by John O'Neill, junior, entitled 'THE CUBA MILLS STEAM HAMMER' attracts attention to the window of Mr. Mansel's shop in Church-road. John O'Neill has studied and painted the subject on the spot, much care being displayed in the technical part of the work. We should like to see more of the same class of work, dealing, as it does, with a portion of the mechanism which has helped to make Dowlais what it is.

"We learn that John O'Neill has nearly completed an equestrian portrait of Mr. R. P. Rees, of the mounted infantry, to be on view shortly.

"It should be added that in the same window is to be seen a good photograph of the Rev. Father Jeremiah McCarthy, whose ordination took place a few months since, and of whose enthusiastic welcome we gave a report at the time. The photo is by Mr. E. B. O'NEILL.

(Merthyr Express. 25.7.1891. p.8. col.3.)

3D. "Mr. John O'Neill, Alma Cottage, has this week exhibited two of his latest pictures. The first is a portrait of MORGAN L. WALTERS, of the West End Stores, which is exhibited in one of the windows of J. S. Davies's outfitting establishment in High Street, Dowlais.

"Mr. Walters appears mounted on his PNEUMATIC TYRED SAFETY BICYCLE, and looking for all the world as if he thoroughly enjoyed his elevated position. The portrait was, it is scarcely necessary to state, taken from life. The background is a lovely bit of scenery, sketched at Pangbourne and brought down to do duty for this picture. The likeness is an admirable one. Several capable judges pronounce it to be the best thing John O'Neill has turned out from his studio.

"The second picture is a portrait group of the late Mr. Wilson (of Miriam Buildings, High Street, Dowlais) and his family. It was painted from photographs, and is exhibited in one of the windows of Messrs. Austin and Sons establishment."

(Merthyr and Dowlais Times. 18.3.1892. p.3. col.5.
See also: M.E. 19.3.1892. p.8. col.4. Dowlais notes.)

3E. "Mr. John O'Neill, junior, late of Alma-cottage and now on a brief visit to Dowlais, has within the last couple of weeks received a scholarship at the Municipal School of Art, Manchester. The scholarship is of the value of £60, and is tenable for two years. Altogether there were four examinations in drawing, painting, etc. and more than a dozen candidates for scholarship came forward. The victory of John O'Neill is all the more creditable inasmuch as it was gained at a time when he was very ill. It need only be added that O'Neill left Dowlais about six months ago and took up his residence in Manchester. The Manchester School of Art has over five hundred students, and is the principal school of its kind in the city."

(Merthyr Times. Friday. 28.7.1893. p.5. col.3+4.)

3F. "News has reached Dowlais of another brilliant success gained by one of its sons. MR. DAVID JONES, who at one time worked with DAVID PRICE, monumental mason, went to Manchester and studied drawing and painting under JOHN O'NEILL, junior, whose own success we chronicled recently.

"At the recent Science and Art Examination in London, David Jones sent in the following works in order, if possible, to gain the Art Master's Certificate, viz.,

shading from models,

shading from cast,

outline of cast,

sheet of perspective problems,

sheet of geometrical problems, and a sheet of architectural drawings.

"David Jones and his friends had the satisfaction of finding that the whole of the six works were accepted, this being a more complete success than was gained by any one else in the district. David Jones, who lives with John O'Neill, is thus possessed of some of the highest certificates in the district."

(Merthyr Times. 25.8.1893. p.8. col.3.)

3G. "We notice in the shop window of Mr. Austin, decorator, Union-street, Dowlais, a fine picture by our fellow townsman, Mr. John O'Neill, junior, (now at the Manchester Municipal School of Art).

"The picture, the subject of which is a Greek bath, was painted in competition for the LANGTON PRIZE of the value of £15, open to all students of the above School of Art, our Dowlais boy being the successful competitor, beating all comers. Walter Crane, the celebrated artist, was the principal adjudicator and has expressed his opinion of Mr. O'Neill in the following words

'From the opportunities I have had of seeing Mr. John O'Neill's work at the Manchester School of Art, I am of the opinion that John O'Neill shows considerable promise in painting and designing, also in sketching in black and white; and indeed, I feel certain that whatever branch of art he undertakes to master, he will be a credit to the School.'

O'Neill has also a small study from the life, which gained him a five pound prize, again beating all his competitors in the School of Art. We are glad to see Dowlais (good old Dowlais) to the fore in art, and beating the Sassenach on his own ground. If any of our local Rothschilds want to secure good work, now is the time, as John O'Neill returns to Manchester in a few days. We add our congratulations to those of Mr. Walter Crane."

(Merthyr Times. 3.1.1895. p.6. col.2.)

JESSIE HARRISON, MRS.GODMAN

4A. "At a Council meeting of the Royal Society of Painters and Etchers, held last week, the election of four associates took place. Of the fortunate candidates, one was a gentleman named Schröeler, and the others were ladies named respectively Crawford, Williams and Harrison. The last named is Miss Jessie Harrison, Dowlais, a young lady who has scored repeated successes in the artistic world, and has thus been famous, not only in the eyes of her friends in Dowlais, but all over the country. Jessie is the daughter of the late Robert Harrison, chemist, and niece of M. Harrison, chief cashier to the Dowlais Iron Company. Both Jessie's father and mother were devotedly attached to painting and drawing, although they never publicly exhibited their work.

"A brother of Jessie's father, John Harrison, gained considerable distinction as an artist before his talented niece was born, and many people in the southern part of the country are today the proud possessors of some of his pictures. (J. Harrison is mentioned in T. E. Clarke's book "A Guide to Merthyr Tydfil". Published in 1848, reprinted by Cardiff Academic Press in 1996, it may be purchased from Mrs. Jacob, Merthyr Central Library.) John Harrison's forte was, like Landseer's and Rosa Bonheur's, animal painting.

"Almost from the day she began to walk, Jessie Harrison displayed a marked affection for painting and drawing and her father did all he could to encourage her in the development of her talent. He imparted to her all the knowledge of art he himself possessed, and then sent her to the Swansea School of Art, where her studies were carried on under the supervision of MR. HOSFORD. Miss Harrison paid unremitting attention to her work, and her perseverance was rewarded about three years ago by her winning a famous triumph, in the shape of a scholarship, which entitled her to two years tuition at the South Kensington School of Art.

"But brilliant as this success was, it was completely dwarfed by what followed. Under the tuition of MR. F. SHORT, the young lady continued to make marvellous progress, and soon displayed an innate creative genius, which at once told heavily in her favour when competitions for prizes and scholarships were being decided. Jessie first won what was called the National Training Scholarship, and thus was enabled to attend all the classes and lectures free of charge. In the middle of last year (1892) Jessie won the National Art

Training Students Scholarship, of which only four are established, and are open to all the country. Only one of these scholarships can be allotted at a time, so that to secure it as Jessie Harrison did, was the highest possible tribute to her brilliant talents.

"Latterly, Jessie Harrison has shown a decided preference for etching and has done a great deal of work for the authorities of the South Kensington Museum. It is customary to include in the Museum catalogues, etchings of all the notable things, and the work of executing them has been entrusted to "the little Dowlais girl" whose work has received the highest praise from the authorities.

"Naturally enough Jessie Harrison had the honourable ambition of becoming an associate of the Royal Society of Painters and Etchers, and like many others who coveted the honour, she submitted specimens of her work to the Council; as stated above, she was successful.

"Unfortunately the people of Dowlais have not an opportunity of seeing any of their talented townswoman's work for Jessie Harrison has never publicly exhibited her pictures. Her relatives and a few friends in Dowlais have some of her pictures. In Merthyr Mr. Frank James, Mr. C. Russell James, and one or two others have been similarly favoured. We hear that the people of this district will have the pleasure of seeing specimens of Jessie Harrison's work at the forthcoming Church bazaar. Etc . . . We congratulate Miss Harrison, who has thus done credit to her native town by securing an honour that no other inhabitant of Dowlais has ever won.

(Merthyr Times. 10.2.1893. p.3. col.6+7.)

4B. "It is with a considerable degree of pleasure that we chronicle the unique success of a Dowlais young lady, Miss Jessie Harrison, eldest daughter of Mrs. Harrison, Brynonen. The Harrison family have for many years past been identified with the Dowlais Works, the late Mr. M. Harrison having occupied the position of chief cashier, whilst his brother, the late Mr. R. Harrison, chemist, father of this Jessie Harrison, died several years ago.

Two of the sons occupy good positions in the works, and the eldest daughter has been prosecuting her studies in painting in London for several years past with conspicuous success.

"In one sense she has, therefore, been lost to Dowlais for a while, but ever since her departure for London, and from the time that she won a scholarship at the South Kensington Art Schools, her townspeople have been reminded in a forcible and pleasing manner of her existence by the public announcements of fresh honours won by her from time to time. The late Mr. Harrison was very fond of painting as an amateur, and that to some extent may account for the talent possessed by his daughter, who was last week one of the three lady artists elected associates by the Royal Society of Painters.

"In the *Ladies Pictorial* for last week a splendid engraving of Miss Harrison appeared, and there can be no doubt in the minds of those who have watched her career that the distinction so recently won will be eclipsed in the future by yet higher honours. Her talents reflect credit upon her native place and Dowlais people will doubtless be proud of her achievements.

(M.E. 11.2.1893. p.8. col.4)

4C. "A friend has very kindly sent me a copy of the *Pall Mall Magazine* for July, containing as the picture of the month a beautiful etching entitled 'Street Scene, Rouen', from the stylus of that clever artist, Miss Jessie Harrison, daughter of the late Mr. Harrison, Dowlais.

"Its beauty has been pointed out to me before in the reading room of the Merthyr Tydfil Library, where a copy of the magazine may be seen, but neither the artist who drew my attention to it nor myself knew at the time that it was the production of one of our fellow townswomen.

"My correspondent humorously remarks that Dowlais can produce something else besides steel rails, and there can be no doubt that in Miss Harrison the Ironopolis of the hills has turned out an artist who is destined to be the maker of many valuable contributions to the world of art. Her success in South Kensington prognosticated (forecast) a brilliant future for her, and it says much for her position in London art circles that her services have been requisitioned by the leading magazine of England."

(*Merthyr Express.* 1.8.1896. p.5. col.7.)

4D. Jessie Harrison Godman painted portraits, landscapes, and miniatures, produced etchings and taught. She exhibited her work in the period 1893-1936.

She was to be found at London, 1893; Dowlais, 1897; School of Art, Warrington, 1898; London, 1899 and 1907; Banstead, Surrey, 1904.

(*Ex. The Dictionary of British Artists*, 1880-1940, compiled by J. Johnson and A. Greutzner.)

Plate Section

Etchings by
JESSIE HARRISON
DOWLAIS

Plate 1: Street Scene. Rouen. Etching by Jessie Harrison.
By permission of The British Library.
Shelfmark/Manuscript Number PP6004gln

Plate 2: Bridge and Fir Trees. Etching by Jessie Harrison.
Photo courtesy of Victoria and Albert Museum.
RCAL.271-1916

Plate 3: Italian 15th Century Medal. Etching by Jessie Harrison.
Photo courtesy of Victoria and Albert Museum.
RCAL.272-1916

237

Plate 4: Portable Altar, German, 12th Century. Etching by Jessie Harrison.
Photo courtesy of Victoria and Albert Museum.
E.159-1900

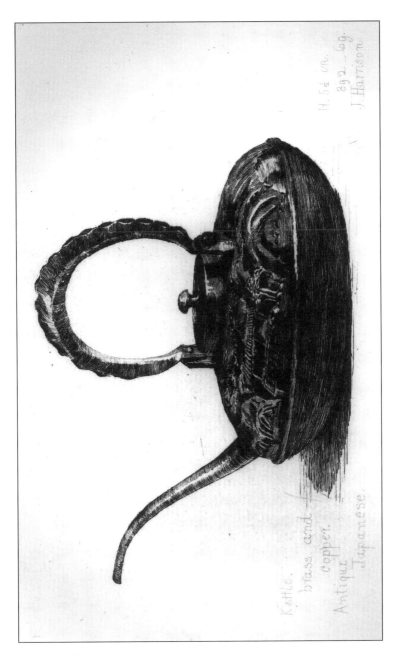

Plate 5: Kettle, Brass and Copper, Antique Japanese.
Etching by Jessie Harrison.
Photo courtesy of Victoria and Albert Museum.
E..158-1900

241

Plate 6: Coffer, Spanish, ca.1600, Silver. Etching by Jessie Harrison.
Photo courtesy of Victoria and Albert Museum.
E.160-1900

243

Etchings by Jessie Harrison, Dowlais.

Street Scene. Rouen.	British Library Reproductions.	9870582
Bridge and Fir Trees.	V & A Picture Library.	RCAL.271-1916
Italian 15th Century Medal	V & A Picture Library.	RCAL.272-1916
Portable Altar, German, 12th Century.	V & A Picture Library.	E.159-1900
Kettle, Brass & Copper, Antique Japanese.	V & A Picture Library.	E158-1900
Coffer, Spanish, ca.1600, Silver.	V & A Picture Library.	E.160-1900

Please note that the last four items are sketches from Victoria and Albert Museum objects. The museum numbers of these objects are 205-1866, 11-1873, 892-1869 and 275-1879. This information enables comparison of the sketches with the original objects.

DAVID DAVIES, DEWI DDU
ILLUSTRATOR

5A. "Work of art. In the shop window of Messrs. Masters & Co., clothiers, Market Square Buildings, Merthyr, is the beautifully illuminated Address, which was a short time ago presented to Mr. Philip J. Phillips, superintendent of the Prudential Assurance Company, by the agents in Merthyr, Dowlais, Penydarren, Treharris and District, as a mark of the esteem in which he is held by them.

"The Address was executed in a masterly manner by Mr. David Davies, DEWI DDU, of Merthyr."

(Merthyr Times. Thursday. 31.5.1894. p.5. col.l.)

5B. "On Monday evening a meeting was held at Pontmorlais Chapel, to make a presentation to Mr. D. J. Rosser, High-street, on his departure for Swansea. The Chair was taken by Mr. Edward Matthews. The following gentlemen addressed the meeting, all testifying to the good work Mr. Rosser has done during his stay at Merthyr, and greatly regretting his departure:—Messrs.

Joseph Harrison, secretary,

Francis Knoyle,

J. Davies, Brecon Road,

J. Rees,

T. Rees, *Merthyryn,* who read verses appropriate to the occasion,

Revd. D. G. Evans,

Mr. Gilliland,

Mr. Morgan Morgans and others.

"Then Mr. John James presented an Address to Mr. Rosser, with a suitable speech. The Address was composed by the Revd. D. G. Evans, and artistically executed by DEWI DDU, David Davies.

Llyfr Trydydd Jubili y Cyfundeb was also presented to Mr. Rosser. Miss Lizzie Jones, Thomas Street, presented him with a splendid motto executed by herself." Etc . . .

(The *Merthyr Times.* 2.8.1894. p.5. col.l.)

5C. "In the shop window of Messrs. Phillips & Co., High-street, is the framed Address which was presented to Major W. Bell, Merthyr Vale, on his elevation to the commission of the peace for the County of Glamorgan.The work was executed in a very artistic manner by David Davies, DEWI DDU, Brecon Road."

(The *Merthyr Times.* 16.8.1894. p.5. col.1.
and M.T. 4.10.1894. p.7. col.2.)

5D. "A movement is on foot for making a presentation of an illuminated Address and purse of gold to Mr. William Morgan, late conductor of singing at Zoar Chapel. The Address, which has been beautifully executed by David Davies, DEWI DDU, is now on view in Messrs. Hepworth's High-street shop window. Mr. Morgan's departure for Pontypridd is much regretted."

(Merthyr Times. 16.4.1896. p.6. col.2.
and M.T. 7.5.1896. p.8. col.3.)

WILLIAM THOMAS
SHOEMAKER-ARTIST

6. "At Merthyr Police Court on Tuesday, before MR. R. A. Griffith, Stipendiary, and other Justices, William Thomas, a shoemaker, of Quaker's Yard, and who is also a clever amateur artist, was charged under the DEFENCE OF THE REALM ACT with making sketches of the Taff Vale Viaduct at Quaker's Yard on Sunday last.

"Chief Constable Wilson said the defendant was seen by a Taff Vale railway signalman making a sketch of the bridge. The structure was guarded by the military. Sidney Blake, the signalman, said he saw the man sitting on a stile on the old tramway. He was about twenty yards away from the bridge, and he noticed that accused was sketching. Another signalman came on the scene and the accused hurriedly put something in his pocket. That aroused witness's suspicions and he went to him. He met Colour Sergeant Jones, who assisted to arrest the man. Defendant admitted he had been sketching and said he wanted to make an oil painting. William Thomas said it was necessary for him to go to the bridge to get a proper perspective. He had been an artist for four years; it was a hobby of his. He had no intention whatever of going there to do any harm or mischief against the King and country. Thomas added: I have paintings here to show I am an artist.

"Colour Sergeant Evan Jones, of the third Supernumerary Company, on duty at the bridge in question, said he saw the defendant put a book in his pocket when witness and the signalman approached him. Thomas said he had been sketching for an oil painting. The Stipendiary Magistrate called for the sketch. Chief Constable Wilson said he sent the sketch to the authorities and it had not been returned. The Stipendiary: It ought to be in court.

"P. C. Prosser said he had known William Thomas for two years, he had a good character.

"In answer to the charge Thomas said 'What I did I did quite innocently'.

"The Stipendiary administered a caution and dismissed the case, remarking that the bridge was not a naval or military work."

(Merthyr Express. 9.6.1915. p.3. col.3.)

DAVID PRICE
SCULPTOR

7. "David Price, sculptor, Pant-road, died on Tuesday of last week. Price, who was in his sixty ninth year, was one of the best known men in the district, and was highly popular with all sections of the community. He was born in 1851, his parents being David and Sarah Price, who came to Dowlais from Trecastle, Breconshire, and kept the Ivor Castle Hotel on Pant-road.

"When a youth, David Price was very artistic in temperament, and went to London to study sculpture under the great sculptor, JOSEPH EDWARDS. Filial affection, however, a noble trait, proved too strong, and David Price returned home and followed the employment of a monumental mason, and many of the tombstones in Pant Cemetery bear testimony to his artistic workmanship.

"For years David Price and his sister Miss Mary Price, carried on the business at the Ivor Castle, but with her death a few years ago he retired from the hostelry.

"David Price was elected a member of the old BOARD OF HEALTH in the early seventies, and later captured a seat on the BOARD OF GUARDIANS, but he resigned both bodies owing to his inability to perform his duties conscientiously through pressure of work. David Price was an ardent Oddfellow, and had been treasurer of the Loyal Prospect of

Hope Lodge since 1877. He was also one of the trustees of the Dowlais District of Oddfellows until it was recently merged into the Merthyr district. Price had filled all the Chairs including the P.P.G.M., and was the Dowlais representative to the annual conference of the Oddfellows for years.

"Fond of study and a great reader, David Price was a man of rare intellectual attainments, and being an excellent conversationalist, with a fund of good humour, his company was eagerly sought for.

"For the last thirteen years Price had suffered from DIABETES but exhibiting marvellous self-control in regard to his diet, he had combated this fell disease. About the latter part of last year (1918) Price had a seizure, but manfully kept at his work until his *protégé*, Mr. Harry Watts, was demobilised from the Army last February, and Watts was to carry on the business.

"David Price's youngest sister, Mrs. D. W. Huggins, Clarence Hotel, and another sister, Mrs. Probert, widow of Mr. J. Probert, Stationmaster, Brecon and Merthyr Railway, are left to mourn." Etc.

(*Merthyr Express*. 20.9.1919. p.11. col.l.)

REVD. J. G. JAMES
ART CRITIC

8A. "The sermon preached at Market-square Church, by the pastor, the Revd. J. G. James, on 'Pictures', on Sunday last, was largely illustrated by references to the Royal Academy pictures of the year. The text chosen was 'Whatsoever things are true, whatsoever things are pure, whatsoever things are lovely, think on these things'.

"The preacher showed that such a collection of pictures representing as they do the best English art, could not be estimated merely at their artistic value, but formed a tolerably accurate estimate of the value of the social and religious ideals of the people. The best pictures of the nation always indicated in some measure the best thoughts and feelings of the nation. Pictures are a language, as music and literature are, language in which to embody what St. Paul told us to think upon, whatsoever things are true, pure and beautiful.

"The Revd. James then described some of the more striking pictures of the year; Sir Frederick Leighton's 'Spirit of the Summit', 'Sanctuary', 'Calumny', 'Piloting us Home', 'Gold', etc. and indicated the lessons of each, and the general teaching of the whole. In conclusion the preacher insisted upon the close connection between Christianity and the fine arts, that a painter could not be successful without the 'soul' and that a man with a 'sacred soul' must be the better for it in every department of his activity and even his art production. Herein the preacher found the justification for introducing such subjects into the pulpit, because Christ claimed all the best men, and only the best in all men." (M.E. 14.7.1894. p.5. col.6.)

8B. "The Revd. J. G. James, B.A., during his recent visit to London, devoted a considerable time to the annual exhibitions of pictures, and on Sunday evening next he will preach at Market-square Church on 'Lessons from the pictures of the year'.

"The sermon will no doubt be of great interest, as Mr. James is an art *connoisseur* as well as a powerful preacher.

"He also WIELDS THE BRUSH with great dexterity and has painted a large number of very pretty landscapes."

(*Merthyr Times*. 18.7.1895. p.3. col.l.)

8C. " 'The Pictures of the Year' was the subject of a sermon delivered by the Revd. J. G. James at Market-square Church on Sunday night last to a large congregation. The picture he made reference to was ALMA TADEMA'S 'Spring'.

"Then he dealt with the increased interest taken in the romantic element in the Academy, especially the pictures of chivalry.

"Mr. James described the war series, and dealt with the impressionist school of Newlyn, showing how that school represented the very commonest institutions in daily life in a realistic fashion, and did their work by idealising the simple, the poor and the working classes.

"Revd. James also dealt with the famous landscapes of Macwhirter and the new spiritualistic element which had been introduced by Dicksee and others in 'Speak, speak' and 'The Reverie'.

"Mr. James expressed himself very much in favour of not separating religion from art, for art really represented the best views of religion as an indication of the faith and aspirations of the people but on the other hand the preacher was greatly opposed to the idea of art for art's sake, as exemplified in the history of Oscar Wilde".

(*Merthyr Times*. 25.7.1895. p.3. col.2.)

71A James Keir Hardie (1856-1915)

KEIR HARDIE ESTATE, MERTHYR TYDFIL

by

BARRIE JONES

Introduction

The year 1998 marks the fiftieth anniversary of the construction of the Borough's largest concentration of post war prefabricated buildings. At the time of its construction Keir Hardie Estate was the largest council housing site within the Borough with 276 properties. The Estate is unique not only for being named after arguably the most well known socialist, but also all its streets are named after prominent Labour politicians.

Ysgubornewydd

Built on a greenfield site, part of Ysgubornewydd farm, the estate is separated from Twynyrodyn to the north by the remnants of the Dowlais Railway or Incline. It was linked to Twynyrodyn by the road bridge crossing the incline adjacent to Ysgubornewydd farm-house and below Twynyrodyn school. This carried the parish road from the Plymouth Ironworks and the farm to Twynyrodyn. Already in a dilapidated state of repair the bridge was only used as a footbridge. Shortly after the completion of the Estate the railway cutting was filled in and a permanent access road was laid in its place. I can recall when a small boy seeing the incline with it railway and trucks still in place.

The Council acquired 43.9 acres of freehold land at Ysgubornewydd at a cost of £3,100 plus fees. Part of the Mardy Estate, at the time of its purchase it was tenanted by W Price of Glyndyrus Farm. The tithe map and schedule of 1850 show the farm covering a larger area, a total of 54 acres of meadow, pasture and wood. At that time the greater portion of the farm was tenanted by Aaron Lloyd, (39 acres), the farm was later reduced in size by the construction of the Dowlais Railway through Cae Lewis Thomas, Cae Jenkin Hopkin, Cae Main, Cae Sgubor and Cae Cant Llaeth.

Thus the Dowlais Railway cut off a sizeable portion of the original farm from the farm-house, making the later development of the Twynyrodyn side more practicable. By the time the Council started its housing development the area between the Incline and Gilfach Cynon was already a fully established community of houses, shops, chapel and school.

Map Ref.	Description	Cultivation	Acres	Roods	Perches
	Ysgubornewydd Farm:				
1389	Cae Jenkin Hopkin	Meadow	3	1	24
1390	Cae Lewis Thomas	Meadow	1	3	16
1391	Cae Pen Twyn	Meadow	3		18
1392	Waste	–	2		
1393	Rubbish and Waste	–	3	3	8
1394	Y Waun	Pasture	2	2	4
1395	Cae Main	Pasture	2	2	23
1396	Cae Pwdwr	Meadow	2	2	4
1397	Road and Waste	–	2	1	12
1400	Cae Sgubor	Meadow	2	2	20
1401	Cae Dan y Ty	Meadow	1	2	7
1402	Homestead	–		1	8

1403	Coed Sgubor Newydd	Pasture & Wood	1	2	
1404	Part of Coed Sgubor Newydd	Pasture & Wood	2		
1404a	Cae Pant	Meadow	4	3	18
1405	Cae Ishaf Y Cwm	Pasture	3	3	22
1406	Part of Cae Ishaf Y Cwm	Pasture	5		24
1398	Cae Thomas Rosser	Meadow	6	3	10
1399	Cae Cant Llaeth	Meadow	2	3	4
	Total Measurement		**54**	**0**	**22**

Source: 1850 Tithe Schedule

After the construction of the estate part of the field structure could still be seen. The open space between Jowett Avenue and Wheatley Place displayed the remnants of hedge rows and fence lines enclosing a small oak wood or copse, the remnant of Coed Sgubor Newydd. The 'green' was dominated by a very large oak tree situated half way along and near to Jowett Avenue. Two other large oaks were on either end of the 'green'. Except for the one oak tree opposite number 12 Jowett Avenue, all the trees were cut down when Greenwood Close, the Council's first Old Aged Pensioners (OAP) sheltered scheme, was constructed on this open site.

The New Estate

It was intended that the estate would have ten shops, a community centre and nursery school. Although under construction from the winter of 1946/47 it was not until the following January 1948, (5th January 1948, minute 865), that the Housing Committee decided on the name of the estate and its first five roads. The record of the committee debate gave no reason for the choice of names but it clearly indicates the Committee's pride in the Labour Party and the role of prominent socialists in the provision of social housing. Alderman T. Edmund Rees stated: "There are good names among those chosen, but I would like to see one road called Winston Churchill in recognition of the great war-time leader". The Mayor (Mr Claude Stanfield) said "they only become great when they pass on".

Keir Hardie Estate—*James Keir Hardie*, 1856-1915, Founder member of the Independent Labour Party, (I.L.P.), First Labour Member of Parliament for Merthyr Tydfil from 1900-1915, sharing the constituency with D. A. Thomas, Liberal, (Viscount Rhondda).

Aneurin Crescent—*Aneurin Bevan* 1897-1960, Member of Parliament for Ebbw Vale, 1929-1960. Minister for Health and Housing, 1944. Responsible for the National Health Service Act of 1946 and the National Assistance Act of 1948. In housing promoted the urgent repair of war damaged housing, prefabricated housing and subsidies to local authorities to provide low housing rents. For a brief spell in 1951 he was the Minister of Labour.

Glasier Road—*John Bruce Glasier*, 1859-?, Alone of the 'Big Four', including Keir Hardie, Ramsey MacDonald and Philip Snowden who were prominent in the Independent Labour Party, never became an MP preferring rhetorical performances at street corners to parliamentary manoeuvres. An art nouveau craftsman, poet and together with his wife, Katherine Conway, joint editor of one of the ILP's journals.

Jowett Avenue—The Housing Committee agreed an alternative spelling of the road as Jowitt Avenue. *William Allen Jowitt*, later Baron Jowitt of Stevenage, 1885-1957, was Lord Chancellor in the 1945 Labour Government and was partly responsible for the introduction of the Town and Country Planning Act 1947. It is likely that the road was named after him and not Jowett, however the road name continues to be spelled with an 'e' not an 'i'.

Frederick William Jowett, 1864-1944, First commissioner of works in the 1924 Labour Government, twice President of the Independent Labour Party. Member of Parliament for West Bradford, 1906-1918, East Bradford, 1922-1924 and 1929-1931.

Wallhead Road—*Richard Collingham Wallhead*, 1869-1934, Independent Labour Party, (I.L.P.), Member of Parliament for Merthyr Tydfil from 1922-1934, Chairman of I.L.P. 1920-1923.

Wheatley Place—*John Wheatley,* 1869-1930, Minister of Health in the 1924 Labour Government, responsible for the Housing (Financial Provisions) Act 1924, known as the "Wheatley Act" which introduced a 15 year programme to build 2.5 million homes at affordable rents, providing nearly 100,000 houses a year.

The planned shops and community centre never materialised, a new nursery and infants school was built near the Incline on the opposite side of Gilfach Cynon on the field known as Gwaun Y Mardy, part of the Mardy farm. Only one shop was built on the estate, on Glasier Road opposite the entrance to the estate from Twynyrodyn, this was later converted into a Laundromat. Further housing was provided on the remaining 'greens' and the political emphasis on road names continued with these later developments.

Dalton Close—*Hugh Dalton*, (Baron Dalton) 1887-1962, Economist and Chancellor of the Exchequer from 1947 in the post war Labour Government, Minister for Town and Country Planning, 1950-1951, Minister for Local Government and Planning, 1951.

Greenwood Close—*Arthur Greenwood*, 1880-1954, Minister of Health 1929-1931, he was responsible for the 1930 Housing Act which instituted slum clearance. Thanks to him more houses were cleared in five years leading up to the second World war than in the preceding fifty years, but this was only half of Greenwood's target. He later held ministerial appointments in the wartime and post war Labour Governments.

A total of 280 properties were planned for the first phase of the estate, 100 concrete houses, called Wimpy No Fines, and 180 British Iron and Steel Federation houses, (B.I.S.F.), prefabricated steel houses. In fact only 96 concrete houses were built, in the autumn of 1947 the contractors reported that they had struck a piece of bad ground and that eight houses could not be erected. The Borough Engineer advised that these eight should be added to the Galon Uchaf scheme where 150 B.I.S.F houses and 26 Apprenticeship Scheme houses were being built. In fact only four fewer were built, not the eight as reported. It is possible that the piece of 'bad' ground was at the lower end of Glasier Road where the odd numbered houses start slightly higher up the hill than the even numbered houses.

With later additions to the estate the total number of dwellings increased to 319 summarised as follows:

Street	Number of houses					
	BISF	No. Fines	OAP	Flats	Other	Total
Glasier Road	24	61	0	0	1	86
Aneurin Crescent	98	1	0	0	1	100
Wheatley Place	19	3	0	0	0	22
Jowett Avenue	19	0	0	0	0	19
Wallhead Road	20	31	0	0	0	51
Greenwood Close	0	0	27	1	0	28
Dalton Close	0	0	0	10	3	13
Total	**180**	**96**	**27**	**11**	**5**	**319**

To serve this large number of houses a small maintenance depot was built on the spare piece of land near the Twynyrodyn entrance to the estate, the remnant of the farmhouse plot. From this site a small number of Council tradesmen kept the estate in good repair, being so close to their work they were at the beck and call of tenants.

At the time Keir Hardie Estate was the largest council housing site within the Borough and in keeping with its showcase image of social housing the Council invited the Minister of Health and Housing, Aneurin Bevan, to officially open the estate. The Minister's private secretary wrote to the Council on the 7th January 1948 regretting that the Minister would be unable to accept the invitation and the estate was opened by Mr William Thomas of the Welsh Board of Health.

The opening ceremony took place on 29 January when after opening the door, Mr Thomas gave the keys to number 1 Aneurin Crescent to Mr David Leslie Jones. Mr Jones, the first tenant on the estate, moved in from Church Terrace, Pentrebach with his wife and two small children. Presiding at the opening ceremony, the Mayor, Mr Claude Stanfield said that when the site was finished it would be the finest in the Borough.

Post War Housing

Built during a time of industrial relocation and growth new housing was essential for key workers as well as new families and it was the Council's policy to ensure suitable housing for such workers. In May 1947 the Housing Committee re-emphasised its intention that one in ten new council properties would be allocated to key workers. On the Keir Hardie Estate this ratio was not achieved with only 18 first lettings from a total of 272 houses, employees of firms catered for were:

Firm	No.
Hoover Ltd.	5.
Bondor Ltd.	5.
O. P. Chocolates Ltd.	2.
Welsh Products.	2.
Thorns Electrical Industries.	1.
Lines Bros.	2.
Sewerage Scheme.	1.

This estate in keeping with others within the Borough was built at a time of extreme shortages of manpower and materials following the war. Problems were encountered very early on in 1947 with a shortage of experienced gas jointers causing delays in the supply of gas to the first phase and consequently electric cookers were supplied to some houses as an alternative. Later in the same year the provision of electric services was also giving concern as houses were nearing completion. This was because of a shortage of armoured electric cable and the problem persisted into the new year. In June 1948 the contractor Gee Walker and Slater Ltd. regarded the position of no lighting or cooking facilities as serious and the Council's officers were in urgent correspondence with the Government's Materials Priority Officer to expedite the supply of cables required.

The Council was in the embarrassing position of having 12 B.I.S.F. houses completed weekly without electrical services connected and the Borough Engineer recommended the provision of temporary metal hobs. The hobs made in the Council's workshops and fitted to the grate of the coal fire would give room for a kettle and a pan and provide temporary cooking facilities. The Council agreed to let properties to those tenants agreeable to the temporary use of the hobs and without lighting subject to a rebate on the rent. At this time B.I.S.F. properties were also being offered to applicants where only gas cooking was available but with no electricity for lighting.

The majority of families allocated new housing during this post war re-housing programme were from poor or over crowded housing and the Council encountered problems with infestation. In May 1947 the Housing Manager sought the Committee's approval to introduce a fumigation programme of prospective tenants furniture and effects to prevent infestation of the new properties. This required the training of key council officers in the techniques of fumigation and the temporary use of houses on the new estates as fumigation centres. It is not known if Key Workers had to go through this process but in some cases with local families fumigation proved ineffectual. Failure to install gas and electricity services on time led to delays in letting the completed houses, this resulted in some empty houses being infested during the summer months. Thus families who had seen their furniture and possessions go through the fumigation process had to request further fumigation of both home and furniture.

Delays in letting and inadequate heating, combined with severe weather in early 1948 were to give both contractor and Council further problems. Severe frost on the nights of the 20th and 21st of February resulted in the fracture of the joints of service pipes to the kitchens of 38 houses. A total of 57 radiators cracked, 2 copper cylinders collapsed and 4 back boilers burst. Problems with winter freezes were to plague many a householder for some years to come; experience with heating large open houses and adequate precautions against frost took some time to master.

For the first time the Council encountered problems associated with large scale housing provision. In January 1948 the Housing Manager referred to the confusion over identifying individual houses on large sites without house numbers. Consequently at the following meeting the Committee approved the fixing of metal numbers to the front doors on all houses on the Estate. Following comments by the contractor, Gee Walker and Slater, Ltd., that new tenants were using down pipes as makeshift line posts for washing lines the Council made it policy that all houses should be supplied with metal washing line posts.

British Iron and Steel Federation (B.I.S.F) Steel Framed Houses

The estate's 180 prefabricated houses, known by the locals as the 'pre-fabs' were mistakenly thought by many people to be for temporary use only. In addition to Ysgubornewydd, the Council embarked on a programme of construction of prefabricated properties on a large scale at Galon Uchaf (l50 houses). Other smaller groups were constructed such sites as; Canonbie (24), Brickfield Crescent (16), Cae Mari Dwn (26), Jones Terrace (16), Taff Glen View (22) and Queens Road (4). Prior to the construction of B.I.S.F. units the Council had constructed numerous Arcon prefabricated bungalows at Ynysfach, Rhydfach and Merthyr Vale.

In 1944 various non-traditional house construction systems were assessed by the Interdepartmental Committee on Housing (Burt Committee) to identify the most promising for immediate development. The B.I.S.F. steel framed house was one of those selected and two prototype houses 'A' and 'B' were erected at Northolt, Middlesex. Only 'A' and 'B' appears to have gone into production and a programme was planned for the construction of over 30,000 three bedroom semi-detached houses in England and Wales, while over 4,000 were planned for Scotland. The programme was later extended to include 1,048 terraced properties, these merely being extensions of a pair of dwellings.

The type 'A' frame was fabricated from rolled steel sections with roof trusses of rolled steel or tubular sections. Of the claddings available, render on mesh for the ground floor and profiled steel sheet on the upper storey appears to have been adopted almost universally. The vertical ribs of the original cladding to the upper storey are a prominent feature that identifies B.I.S.F. houses. The roof was clad with profiled asbestos cement sheeting.

B.I.S.F. dwellings were usually built as two-storey semi-detached houses and the internal lining is of 3/8 inch plasterboard fixed to 2 x 1 inch timber framing secured to the steel framework. A glass fibre quilt 1 inch thick is sandwiched between the steel framework and timber framing.

A typical 'pre-fab' in Wheatley Place had the following facilities:

Hall with doors leading to the front room and kitchen, under the stairs near to the kitchen door was a wide cupboard housing the gas and electricity meters. Under the stairs there was space large enough for my mother to keep her Singer sewing machine with its metal treadle.

The kitchen was supplied with a gas cooker and fitted units, alongside the wall separated by the hall door were two pairs of full length metal storage cupboards. Between the cooker space in the corner of the kitchen and the wash basin was a narrow cupboard in front of the boxed in soil pipe from the upstairs bathroom. This cupboard was used by my mother to store dusters, shoe polishes etc. Under the wash basin was a gas tap which could be connected to a gas heated water boiler, the boiler was a galvanised cylindrical tub which was wheeled out on washdays from its place under the kitchen wash basin.

Leading from the kitchen was the dining room with a large window looking out into the rear garden.

From the dining room double doors lead into the front room which was dominated by a large almost full length window, all the windows in the house were metal framed with metal fittings. This room was heated by a coal fire which backed on to the wall separating the dining room from the front room. The fire place was dominated by a large mantle piece that extended around the chimney flue and was made of pre-cast concrete. The fire could be lit with a gas jet fitted into the front grate instead of the traditional gas poker. This greatly assisted the work of lighting the fire but to save gas, most people still relied on wood and paper and the trusty blower. Lighting the fire had its dangers, on one occasion when lighting the gas, I ended minus eyebrows and eyelashes. The fire served as the only heating but with the aid of a small back boiler it heated the household hot water tank and three small radiators. These were narrow versions of the traditional heavy cast-iron radiators, one in the dining room and one each in the two main bedrooms.

Upstairs leading from the landing were the three bedrooms and bathroom. The bathroom situated at the rear and over the kitchen had the W.C., washstand and traditional white cast-iron bath. The large front bedroom housed the airing cupboard with hot water tank, situated alongside the chimney flue. It would not take much hot water use before this went cold and re-heating the water would take ages, most people eventually had electric immersion heaters fitted to boost the heating. The front and back bedrooms were separated from each other by fitted wardrobes, a double in the front and a single in the back. These filled the space between the airing cupboard and the party wall. The smallest bedroom, the box room, was in the front over the hallway, to maximise space a fitted dressing table with two small drawers was built over the slope created by the rise of the stairs.

The side entrance into the house, known as the "back door", lead into the kitchen through a porch. The porch was formed by the space made in a single story side extension of the house between an external W.C. and the storage shed. Part of this shed was a sectioned-off coal bunker, coal could be gathered from the porch by means of a small hatch at floor level. Unless the bunker was full, which would be very rare, collecting coal from the hatch was difficult and this hatch was rarely used and therefore the coal bucket was filled by trips into the dark shed. Over the years this large bunker would fill up with small coal and hunting for suitable coal lumps could take some time.

B.I.S.F. houses were innovative also in the provision of electricity, the Housing Manager reported to the Housing Committee in January 1948 that new patent electric wall sockets were fitted to the houses. These required plugs which had an additional third leg, a safety device in the form of a fuse, which was screwed into the plug. New tenants were not prepared for this innovation and the Housing Manager obtained permission to purchase one gross of the fuses and 500 plugs for sale to incoming tenants.

Conclusion

In the August of 1948 one of the last properties to be tenanted was number 37 Wheatley Place, my parents with their two young children had the home they had waited for at long last. In October of that year I was born in the front bedroom of that house. I do not know if I was the first of the new 'Sgubor' generation but both the estate and I celebrate our 50th birthday this year. Much has changed over the years, some of the houses have been refurbished and many have been sold to the tenants under the 'Right to Buy' legislation. The estate has lost some of that uniformity of character typical of the old council estates and can no longer boast of being the largest Council housing estate in the Borough. However it still remains the largest concentration of prefabricated houses in Merthyr Tydfil and a testament to post war social housing, I look forward to celebrating its 75th Birthday in the year 2023.

SOURCES AND SELECT BIBLIOGRAPHY

Printed Books and Articles
Davies W. L. *Bridges of Merthyr Tydfil.*
Dictionary of National Biography
Building Research Establishment Report. *The British Iron & Steel Federation steel framed house.*
Who Was Who, Vol. iii & iv.

Manuscripts & Maps
Merthyr Tydfil County Borough Council Minutes 3rd February 1947 to 6th September 1948.
Merthyr Tydfil Tithe Map and Schedule 1850

Newspapers
Merthyr Express 10th & 31st January 1948

WILLIAM EVANS, IRONMASTER,
BORN IN IRON, CRADLED IN STEEL

by

J. BRYNMOR JONES AND T. F. HOLLEY

Introduction.

In 1856 the General Manager of the Dowlais Iron Works, John Evans, retired, and was succeeded by William Menelaus (1818-1882). Some account of the life and achievements of Menelaus appeared in an essay by us in *Merthyr Historian* , Volume Seven, 1994. Edward P. Martin (1844-1910) returned to the Dowlais Works in 1881 to serve as deputy general manager under William Menelaus. E. P. Martin was appointed General Manager in 1882 on the death of Menelaus. Our essay in *Merthyr Historian*, Volume Six, gave an account of the achievements of George Martin and his three sons, Edward P. Martin, H. W. Martin and A. H. Martin.

At the turn of the century, following the amalgamation of the Dowlais and Cyfarthfa Works, and the formation of Guest, Keen and Nettlefolds Ltd., Edward P. Martin retired and William Evans was appointed General Manager of the Dowlais, Dowlais-Cardiff, and Cyfarthfa Steel Works and Collieries belonging to Messrs. Guest, Keen and Nettlefolds, Ltd..

This essay gives an account of the life and achievements of William Evans, whose home at the time of his death in 1915 was BRYNTEG, Merthyr Tydfil.

William Evans's family.

William Evans married Elizabeth Evans, daughter of John Evans, Beaufort. This union was blessed with three sons and four daughters:—

John Evans, eldest son,

Rees Tudor Evans, later Captain, 1/5 the Welch Regiment, Richard Stanley Evans, later Lieutenant, 5th. Battalion, W.R.,

Margaret Amy Evans, eldest daughter; Edith Mary Evans, who married William John Dan Rees; Elizabeth Evans; Eunice Martha Evans.

All these children were alive in 1915, when their father passed away, except John, the eldest son, who tragically died in 1914, aged thirty seven years. However, both Capt. R. T. Evans and Lieut. R. S. Evans made the supreme sacrifice in the 1914-18 War.

John Evans.

This John Evans was born at Rhymney on 23rd January 1877. He was educated at Shrewsbury School, and on leaving school entered the pattern workshops at Cyfarthfa Works. He passed through all the fitting shops with the greatest credit and then went to the Barrow Hematite Iron Works to be taught the management of blast furnaces. John Evans completed his term there, returned to Cyfarthfa and was appointed blast furnace manager. He held this post till Cyfarthfa Works was acquired by G.K.N. Ltd..

His father then became general manager of all G.K.N. Ltd. South Wales Works, and John Evans was transferred to Dowlais as Works Manager, in succession to Mr. Carlyle. In this position John Evans proved successful in every respect. His early death was due to over-work and self-neglect, he did not spare himself.

John Evans married Mabel Hannah Davies, second daughter of Rhys Davies, Courtland Terrace, Merthyr, there were three children, Rhys William, John Russell, and Gertrude Elizabeth. The family lived at Gwernllwyn Uchaf, Dowlais.

Amongst other interests, John Evans was President of the Dowlais Male Voice Choir, conducted by Mr. W. J. Watkins, F.R.C.O., L.R.A.M., and no one was better pleased at the success of the choir than was John Evans, who was delighted when they scored the victory at London National Eisteddfod. John Evans afterwards presided at the supper given the choir at the Royal Exchange Hotel, Brecon Street, when a very happy evening was enjoyed.

William Evans's collection of portraits.

In his will William Evans allocated his portraits as follows.

To his son John Evans, portraits of:—

Robert Thompson Crawshay,

Edward Williams, Ironmaster,

William Menelaus,

E. Windsor Richards, Ironmaster,

Mrs. William Evans,

William Evans.

To his daughter, Edith Mary Rees, he bequeathed a portrait of herself.

William Evans, technical achievements.

William Evans was born at Abergwesyn in Breconshire, came to Dowlais with his parents, and was educated at Dowlais Schools under the famous schoolmaster, MATTHEW HIRST. From school Evans went into the Dowlais Works, first as an accountant at the blast furnaces, from which position he was gradually promoted until at the early age of twenty five years he was manager of one of the blast furnace departments. William Evans had early training under that prince of managers, William Menelaus.

The Dowlais Company were pioneers in Bessemer steel-making, the production of suitable pig-iron for this process was early introduced, and William Evans experienced the initiation and development of this essential branch of the business. During his term as manager the good old palmy days of furnacemen passed away. Their favourite native ore, the much esteemed Welsh mine, had to be abandoned on account of the high price of getting. Ores from Spain and other foreign countries were imported upon a large scale. With such a large number of furnaces, producing nearly every variety of pig-iron, from ores at that time of unknown qualities, contending with analytical chemists of distinction and with agents at other departments, of great practical knowledge and skill, and under the keen scrutiny of one of the shrewdest of general managers (W. Menelaus), it is not surprising that William Evans got to understand thoroughly the mysteries of pig-iron making.

Also the Dowlais Company directed their attention to the manufacture of *SPIEGELEISEN,* (a manganese iron alloy used in the making of Bessemer steel), all that was used at that time was imported from Germany. With commendable application and assiduous care William Evans followed up the new process until every obstacle had been overcome, and the routine of production well-established. When it is known that only one other firm had succeeded in producing this material in this country, it was not without cause that Mr.Menelaus was pleased, and, to shew his appreciation of the services rendered by William Evans, he handsomely remunerated Evans.

Aged twenty seven William Evans left Dowlais to take charge of the blast furnaces of the Rhymney Iron Co., Richard Laybourne was general manager there. W. Evans helped superintend the change from iron manufacture to steel making at Rhymney.

When William Evans had set steel manufacture at Rhymney going in proper order, he directed his attention to producing the requirements of a Bessemer establishment, such as pipes, stoppers, tuyeres, loam and gannister, all of which he had turned out at Dowlais but which had to be purchased at Rhymney. Evans's practical knowledge of details led him to select the most suitable fire clay and to have proper machines and other appliances erected, and in a very short time pipes and tuyeres were produced, quickly and economically.

The limestone and sand quarries were under Evans's control, this enabled him to select the best sandstone for gannister making, a quarry was opened and a plentiful and cheap supply of excellent stone obtained, this gannister was soon made also at a very considerable reduction in cost as compared with that purchased from Sheffield and elsewhere. These items effected a great saving upon the year's work. The Board of Directors forwarded a cheque for £100 to William Evans, in appreciation, with a complimentary letter.

Two versions of William Evans's next career move exist. One version has him returning to Dowlais for a period, then proceeding to Stockton-on-Tees. The other version has him going directly from Rhymney Works to Erimus Works, Stockton.

Many South Wales trained managers were persuaded to move to the ironworks in the north of England in the second half of the nineteenth century. These included Edward Williams (son of Taliesin, grandson of Iolo), William Jenkins, David Evans (originally from Llwydcoed), Richard Evans, all were drawn to the north. About 1880 William Evans followed them, appointed manager of the Erimus Works at Stockton-on-Tees. William Evans was engaged at Stockton while the Cyfarthfa Works were being rebuilt for steel manufacture under the direction of the aforesaid Edward Williams, consulting engineer.

The Erimus Works were originally laid out for working Dank's patent puddling process, but were closed when the iron rail trade collapsed. The owner, who was also a broker on a large scale in the pig iron trade of the North, decided upon erecting a Bessemer pit and entering the steel trade. Having to buy all materials, including pig iron, *spiegel,* coke, as well as others of less importance, and with small machinery adapted for iron rolling, which necessarily was of insufficient strength, the conditions were heavily handicapped. But, as stated in several trade journals, Mr. Muller's difficulties were principally from want of capital, and his suspension was chiefly due to transactions in pig iron. Here, William Evans had to experience for the second time the difficulties of starting new works and the selection and training of suitable hands was a matter of some importance. In consequence of engineering defects most of Evans's attention had to be given to the mills, and his practice with machinery as well as with rolling mill work generally provided invaluable experience. His untiring industry, close application, and enthusiastic devotion to duty left nothing undone his experience could suggest, and, with the means at hand, accomplish. These characteristics did not escape the attention, but received the decided approbation of the owner. William Evans's training was most thorough, his experience in all branches connected with steel-making extensive, and his advantages in erecting and starting new Works singularly exceptional.

William Evans was next appointed Works Manager of Cyfarthfa and these works flourished. A paragraph in the *Merthyr Express* stated: "Evans appointment to the management of the new Works at Cyfarthfa, therefore, seems to be an apt example of the right man being put into the right place. We heartily congratulate Messrs. Crawshay upon their selection, and especially upon the fact of his being A DOWLAIS BOY, DOWLAIS TRAINED, and sincerely trust, for their sakes, as well as for the prosperity of the town and district generally, that a prosperous career in steel making is before them. They are almost alone in their representation of our old ironmasters. The DARBIES have become extinct, the FOTHERGILLS beaten out of the field, the GUESTS—greater in the trade than ever in one sense—still have become transformed into landlords by union with the territorial aristocracy, but the CRAWSHAYS still remain, and have the means and determination, we hope, of proving worthy of their illustrious forefathers and of upholding the traditional renown of the great Iron King. We also have pleasure in congratulating our old neighbour and brother Mason upon his return to his native parish, and trust that having seen the foundations well and truly laid he will be spared to complete satisfactorily, to start successfully, and to conduct profitably the new Cyfarthfa Steel Works".

William Evans proved abundantly before he had been long at Cyfarthfa that the choice was a good one, no better could possibly have been made. Under his vigorous and skillful administration Cyfarthfa flourished and expanded, and was brought into and kept in the front rank of steel works. There were FOUR blast furnaces of the new model to begin with, but William Evans was not long before he had sufficient inflow of orders to require the erection of a FIFTH with corresponding extensions of mill plant and other accommodation in the yards.

Concurrently there was a very important development of the collieries and augmented output. So matters went on until the then Lord Wimborne sold the whole of his Steel Works and Collieries at Dowlais, Cardiff and Abercynon and the new firm of Guest, Keen and Co., Ltd., came into existence in 1900.

For a couple of years Dowlais proceeded under the new regime, with Mr. Edward Martin as managing director, and Cyfarthfa as a vigorous rival and competitor in the steel and coal trade.

Then came about another great change, the new proprietors of Dowlais acquired by purchase the whole of the interests of Messrs. Crawshay Brothers, Cyfarthfa, Ltd., in the Cyfarthfa Works and Collieries and there were important consequences at both places. Mr. Edward Martin retired from the position of managing director at Dowlais.

William Evans was then appointed General Manager of the Dowlais, Dowlais-Cardiff and Cyfarthfa Steel Works and Collieries belonging to Messrs. G.K.N. Ltd. His was a position of enormous responsibility. He proved his competence for the exceptional trust. A strong man, with a strong mind and a clear vision of purpose and means to ends was required and was found in W. Evans.

He continued in the arduous post with unfailing assiduous personal attendance, and few and brief breaks for holiday relaxation and regeneration of energy and health, down to the day of his death.

William Evans was one of the great captains of industry, whose names will be imperishably associated with the rise and progress of the metal and coal trades of South Wales. He was from first to last a self-made man, owing all his advancement to his own merits and self-cultured abilities. Evans carried on a tradition almost peculiar to South Wales, but to Dowlais and Cyfarthfa especially, of having locally bred and trained men in the occupation of the highest positions. Though William Menelaus was a Scotchman, hailing from Edinburgh, he was a South Wales trained iron-master, having made his beginning at the Abernant Works and progressed to Dowlais. Before Menelaus they were all Dowlais men at

Dowlais, and Dowlais men continued there down to the end of William Evans's tenure of the management.

William Evans was a man of strong will and determination, and somewhat hasty in temper, but when his wrath had blown off, all was serene, and those who took the trouble to study his ways and methods and to adapt themselves to his requirements, found it an easy matter to work harmoniously and pleasantly with him. Evans always maintained the best and most pleasant relations with his workmen. He had a high sense of duty and never spared himself in its discharge, and he expected those who served under him, and upon whose faithfulness and devotion to duty he depended for the general success and welfare of the enterprise, to be not less self-denying in the performance of duty.

Official appointments.

William Evans spared time from his many industrial responsibilities to serve as a Justice of the Peace for the Counties of Glamorgan, Monmouth and Brecon. He served as Chairman of the Monmouthshire and South Wales Coalowners' Association, and was a member of the Council of the Iron and Steel Institute, and also a Member of the Institute of Civil Engineers.

Politically William Evans was a Conservative, being an Imperialist, a Tariff Reformer and an opponent of Home Rule. He was a member of the Constitutional Club, London, and the County Club, Cardiff.

A highlight of William Evans' career was a visit by King George the Fifth and Queen Mary to the Dowlais Works in 1912.

Bibliography.

William Evans, J.P., M.Inst.C.E.

South Wales Leaders: Social and Political. Ernest Gaskell. *Illustrated History of the Loyal Cambrian Lodge of Freemasons*, Merthyr Tydfil, 1810-1914.

A visit to Rhymney Works. Western Mail. 7.11.1879. p.3. col.4. W. Evans appointed to Cyfarthfa Works. *Merthyr Express.* 12.8.1882. p.5. col.1.

John Evans and Hope Presbyterian Church, Merthyr. Western Mail. 3.9.1902. p.6. col.7.

William Evans received H.M. King George the Fifth and Queen Mary at Dowlais Works. M.E. 29.6.1912. p.10. col.3-6.

Workmen's letter of thanks to W. Evans for access to Royal visitors. *Merthyr Express.* 6.7.1912. p.5. col.4.

Death of John, William Evans' eldest son.

Merthyr Express. 14.2.1914. p.10. col.6 and 21.2.1914. p.3. col.5.

John Evans died intestate, Letters of Administration were granted to his widow Mabel Hannah Evans on 23.3.1914. John Evans' estate was valued at about £8,000.

Obituary, William Evans. *Merthyr Express.* 20.2.1915. p.5. col.2+3.; p.9. col.5.; Cardiff Times. 20.2.1915.

William Evans' Will, probate granted 11.5.1915. See also *Merthyr Express.* 22.5.1915. p.6. col.6. He left estate valued about £40,000.

To avoid confusion, it should be realised that ANOTHER WILLIAM EVANS was also a pupil of William Menelaus and served as the Mechanical Engineer at Dowlais Works. His home was Bryniau House, Pant, his Obituary appeared in the *Merthyr Express*, 20.1.1912. p.9. col.4.

DAVID JONES, SENIOR, WATCHMAKER, OF MERTHYR TYDFIL, 1861

TRANSCRIBED

"DAVID JONES, SENIOR, watchmaker, of Merthyr Tydfil, was born in the farm-house of Blaencennan, at Gwnydda, near Llangadock, in the year 1766.

Had he possessed no inborn talent, the chances are that by growing up according to the examples around him, he would have simply vegetated at Blaencennan, as a plain, drudging farmer. If a little adventurous, and inclined to see the world, he might in the course of years have visited Merthyr in the character of a pig-seller or butter-vendor; have domiciled at the "Crown", paying the lawful pence before being allowed to sleep, wandered perhaps into some of our celestial quarters, and figured in the witness-box of the Police Court, as Shirgaers and Cardis are wont to do, when they lose sundry pounds sterling by the nimble fingers of the fair and frail.

But David's mind was above pigs and turnips, and though he carried on the business of a farmer after his parents, he also cultivated with rare perseverance the talents bestowed upon him. Early in youth he felt a great liking for watchmaking, and about as early showed his neighbours that he had a wonderful ear and taste for harmony. These were marketable gifts, and so he set up a little shop in the town of Llangadock, and with the proceeds of this, and his farm, was content.

Strange to state, David Jones's knowledge of watchmaking was gleaned without the aid of any instructor. He was never in any shop as assistant or apprentice, but gained his learning by dint of untiring perseverance. Jones's great musical attainments were also gained in the same manner, and were early put to a practical purpose in the erecting of a large organ for Llangadock Church. This was a clever performance, well proved, when an organist from London was appointed to play the organ regularly, AND FOUND THE INSTRUMENT IN TONE AND SOLIDITY WORTHY OF A FIRST-CLASS MAKER.

In Llangadock, as Jones grew in years he grew in favour; from one step of worth and respectability he mounted with sure firm strides. He became a member of the OLD BARON COURT, the stray bit of feudalism left high and dry by the stream of time, and also assisted in the establishment of an excellent school, was a Volunteer in the old days when the fear of French invasion was paramount, and most people expected some fine morning to discover perfide Albion covered with men in peg top trousers, baggy withal, and the inevitable sacre on their lips, and that they would then and there act, like the locusts which covered the land of Egypt.

David Jones's knowledge of music, and superior practical skill, also introduced him to Lord Dynevor, who made him a master of his Band, and gave him a free entrance to the Castle. Jones was a frequent visitor to Dynevor Castle, and always treated by the old Lord on terms of the greatest friendship.

Many anecdotes are current at Llangadock of Jones's proficiency in music; he would leave a room instanter at the sound of one false note, for the discord pained him as if he had been wounded. To mark the appreciation of his skill one of the finest violins in the country was presented to him before he left for Merthyr, by a gentleman of the neighbourhood, who, with a great many others, were not slow in expressing their unfeigned regret that the genius of the place should leave the scene of his infancy and early successes for a distant town.

But David found trade very dull at Llangadock, and tidings were coming to him unceasingly of that California of Wales, MERTHYR TYDFIL, of the great number of its inhabitants, the fabulous wages paid, and general prosperity of everybody, statements coloured by imaginative countrymen, which prompted him to leave.

And so he left, and in the year 1816, with little capital beyond his skill, opened a shop opposite the field whereon now (1861) stands the Market House. Here he speedily gained an excellent business, and won the friendship of men who once held the highest positions in the town. Christopher James, and others of the James family, Henry Jones, and a great number of the principal inhabitants, ranked him as their friend. While at this shop Jones exhibited a fine illuminated clock, the second or third in the country, THE INVENTION OF HIMSELF AND HIS SON, which attracted crowds to the High-street. At a certain hour the mechanism was so arranged as to put the light out, and to this day (1861) grey haired men, who were then young, relate of the unpleasant sensation felt in running home to find David Jones's clock DARK.

His ingenuity was not confined to clocks. Long before dentistry had risen into a science he constructed a tooth for Mr. Christopher James, which, I believe, that gentleman still possesses The Church organ, too, came in for its share of the worthy tradesman's ingenuity, but one of his crowning feats was in the repair of a celebrated clock in the house of Williams, of Perthygleison, said to have been a masterpiece, with its chimes and bells, but of most intricate construction.

From some cause or other this clock became disordered, and a great many craftsmen were employed from time to time in repairing it, but to little good. At length Jones was sent for, and having undertaken the job, the clock was exhibited in his window to the great delight of the inhabitants. For a long time it was the curiosity of the town, and when it was taken away, thenceforth to be a model time-keeper, one of the finest "lions of the village" was lost to sight-seers.

These were the days when Cobbett flourished, when the doughty old Radical lashed the TIMES, and the TIMES lashed him, with strength and fury, the days when instead of the MILD, SENTIMENTAL, SEMI-RELIGIOUS, POETICAL, NOVEL PAPERS that are retailed and devoured everywhere, the "Gridiron", with its fine roasting properties, and satiric powers, existed in its prime, and scattered the broadest truths, as well as the fiercest Radicalism, over the land. The "Gridiron", as the "Political Register" of Cobbett was called, from its bearing a resemblance to one on the first page, found many subscribers here in Merthyr, one, in particular, now an aged gentleman, whose eye may glance kindly over this memento, and recollect as he does, the many times when, with the "Register" in his hand, he has marched down to Jones's shop, and there discussed Cobbett's views with interest and ability. He was one of Jones's warmest friends, and will, I doubt not, agree in ascribing to the old man great inventive powers, strong memory, keen observation and a fund of vigorous and original thought, which certainly he possessed, though hidden to the majority under a calm childlike simplicity of character.

David Jones was one of those living illustrations of the truth, that the lover of music is generally a man without guile, for the man who loves harmony will not fail to dislike and avoid all that is discordant or antagonistic to harmony, shunning vice, (for what is vice but the human being inharmonious, with the mind ill-strung, and the passions, like the bass, out of keeping with the higher and softer notes), and in all the relations of life studiously seeking those associates most congenial, those duties and pursuits most in unison, with his own cultivated taste.

At the Eisteddfod held in the Lamb Inn David Jones was a conspicuous member, and so respected by all, that when it was removed to the White Horse Inn, by one consent he was elected the president of the Cymmrodorion. While in this capacity Jones invented the celebrated clock watch, which, in addition to the usual properties of the repeater, spontaneously struck the hours without touching the pendant or anything whatever. Striking watches have a greater antiquity than Jones's time.

Two varieties of striking watch were produced before James the Second and Council, and warmly approved of, but the invention of our old townsman was not only different, but in many respects superior to those of QUARE and BARLOW. And while they and others of a similar and later date were fashioned by the aid of the best instruments, Jones's instruments, tools, and all materials of the clock were made by himself.

When exhibited the clock caused the strongest admiration, and aroused so much attention, that the Cymmrodorion Society at the White Horse Inn gave a prize of one pound for six englynion to "Y Gloch Oriawr". Many competed, but the prize was awarded to our townsman, Cawr Cynon. This was in 1837, eleven years after the Cymmrodorion had been established at the White Horse Inn, and when it was in the full zenith of its usefulness.

Throughout his career David Jones was a zealous member of the Cymmrodorion Society, and with his venerable appearance, and pleasant affable character, won the cognomen of "Yr Hen Llwyd" and retained it until his death.

After he had lived many years in the High-street, he removed to the corner of the Glebeland, next door to The Lamb Inn and but a short time before his decease, to the house next to the "Temperance Hotel", where a memento of the old man remains in the form of a clock face over the door.

David Jones died in 1842 at the ripe age of 82, and was buried in the old churchyard. There, amidst a host of the villagers, many of whom may yet receive a tardy tribute to their virtue and their worth, the old man sleeps, one who preferred the path of knowledge to the furrow of cornfields, the tilling of the mind to the cultivation of pastures, and instead of passing through life a serf, became in the broadest and truest sense of the word a gentleman." (*Merthyr Telegraph*. 9.2.1861. p.4. col.1+2.)

Robert Burns.

MERTHYR TYDFIL AND ITS SCOTTISH CONNECTIONS

by

HUW WILLIAMS

For much of the 19th century Merthyr Tydfil was the most cosmopolitan town in Wales. The town's international instincts lasted well into the present century and in many ways until this day. The availability of work and well paid at that, relative to the times and sur-rounding places, attracted thousands of able-bodied migrants to the area and induced a pattern of population movement and absolute growth that continued for most years of the 19th century during the town's most dramatic expansion and prosperity. Inward migration remained largely unabated until the advent of the First World War. Merthyr Tydfil was the archetypal "melting-pot" on an American scale for these formative years, unprecedented in its headlong population increase and in its ethnic and inter-racial mixture of peoples at each census date from 1841 until 1921. Connections of religion, of family ties through marriage and by friendship, of news, gossip and curiosity for a place as Merthyr Tydfil lured others here; the twin catastrophes of famine and persecution propelled several thousands more in the course of the second half of the 19th century and in the years leading to the Great War to seek a safe haven in the relatively tolerant industrialised society that Merthyr Tydfil offered. A hundred fold unique, individual, personal reasons motivated many to consider Merthyr, the best known, largest town of the South Wales coalfield, as an alternative dwelling place from that of the poorly endowed Welsh countryside, Ireland or central and eastern Europe. The quest for the good life, to put it no higher than that, surely inspired many to come here: shops and markets, music halls and later on, the cinema, concerts, sporting and recreational facilities, places of worship, schooling for children—these were some of the features that made up a body of inter-locking communities which as an entity came to be Merthyr Tydfil at the eve of the 20th century.

COSMOPOLITAN MERTHYR TYDFIL

By 1914 the Welsh language as the predominant lingua franca in the town was on the decline in absolute numbers of population, a consequence but only in part of the cosmopoli-tan influx to the town after the 1850s of non-Welsh speaking immigrants. In 1891 some 68% of the inhabitants of Merthyr Tydfil were counted as Welsh speakers; this had fallen to a half of the total population by 1911 and down to 40% by 1931. Prior to the second half of the 19th century, the pattern of migration Merthyr-wards had been largely of Welsh speak-ers, rural in origin and principally from the three south west counties of Carmarthenshire, Cardiganshire and to a lesser extent from Pembrokeshire. This constant transfusion of a Welsh culture, its customs, habits, music and verse from an innate Welsh thinking and Welsh speaking population, irrevocably shaped Merthyr Tydfil in its crucially formative decades of the 19th century. There is evidence of non-Welsh speakers learning the rudi-ments of the Welsh language for purposes of the workplace, in chapel worship and in the increasingly sophisticated inter-connectedness of civilisation and street life in the town cen-tre and in the very Welsh-inclined satellites of Dowlais, Heolgerrig and Cefn Coed.

The single most noticeable group of migrants which stood out by virtue of numbers and significant settlement patterns within the town during the 19th century was, of course, the

Irish. Opportunities of work, life chances, a network of ministering Roman Catholic priests—all provided a powerful magnet for the stricken Irish to be pulled towards this town and especially in the years of the late 1840s and 1850s after the infamous potato famine of 1846-47 which pushed thousands of helpless Irish land dwellers to the mainland of the United Kingdom. The Welsh ports of Swansea and Cardiff were obvious points of reception along the Bristol Channel and adjacent to the Irish Sea and thence the Irish crowds moved inland to the best known Irish centre—Merthyr Tydfil. Numbers of Irish by the 1920s comprised about an eighth of the total population of the town, some 10,000 in total, of whom over 5,000 were concentrated in Dowlais and some 4,000 or more in the Merthyr Tydfil area (Williams). A not insignificant Jewish population had established itself in the town by the 1920s, originating from several lands which had made up the old Austrian-Hungarian Empire of central Europe, from the burgeoning Russian Empire, from the countryside and towns of Poland and from the several Baltic satellite states suffering under the Russian yoke. The simple capitalist connection of making profitable steel brought a handful of Spanish workers to Dowlais in the last years of the 19th century, The mighty Dowlais Iron Company, seeking new supplies of iron ore for its continued steel manufacturing prowess, had bought a controlling interest in the Orconera Company of Bilbao in northern Spain where iron ore deposits were readily available. Alphonso Street in Penywern was one delightful tell-tale symbol of the resettlement of Spanish workers and their families from the Basque province of Spain to Dowlais. Their colourful rituals of fiesta, Roman Catholicism and language sat fairly comfortably alongside the numerous Irish taverns, St. Patrick's Day parades, Roman Catholic churches, a Jewish synagogue and the professional activities pursued by several prominent Jews of the town. A few Italian families had also ventured to Merthyr Tydfil by the onset of the First World War and in the years after it as part of a different cultural and social association with the South Wales valleys. Ice cream manufacturing and vending, usually out of distinctive town centre cafes, became the hallmarks of the Italian immigrant to a town such as Merthyr Tydfil and, like the Irish and Spanish migrants, there was readily available the apparatus of Roman Catholicism to see to the spiritual needs of these non-Welsh peoples.

Merthyr Tydfil's Celtic connections were invariably Welsh in origin and Welsh speaking in daily life. (1. My maternal ancestry is of rural mid Wales stock, from Llandinam in Montgomeryshire, who came south initially to the Rhondda Valleys with David Davies, coal entrepreneur, and thence gravitated to Merthyr Tydfil.) The Irish were easily the most numerous migrant group arriving from the Celtic fringes of the British Isles. Some Cornishmen had ventured into South Wales in the course of the 19th century, some very short term in the nature of their stay as strike breakers in the early 1870s during the coal stoppages of that time. As traditional hard rock miners, these Cornishmen were terrified by the all too obvious dangers of the fiery, deep Welsh coalmines. Sea-faring and railway connections took some workers from Somerset, Devon and Cornwall to the expanding opportunities for industrial work in the towns of South Wales, notably Cardiff where several Cornish families thrived in business connected with the ever increasing port and rose to local prominence within Cardiff affairs. (2. My paternal ancestry hails from Falmouth, of sea-faring stock who came to Merthyr Tydfil to take up the opportunities of work on the valleys' local railways.) But what of any Scottish links and traditions in and of a town such as Merthyr Tydfil?

THE SCOTTISH CONNECTION

There were hardly droves of Scots on an Irish scale entering the town in the 19th century, in the hey-day of Merthyr Tydfil as the most important Celtic centre in Wales and comparable with the capital centres of Edinburgh, Glasgow and Dublin. The constraints of geography and the tedious journey from north to south for the prospective migrant were undoubtedly factors conspiring against a ready flow of Scots and Welsh interchanges. A buoyant Scottish Lowland economy centred on the great cities of Edinburgh and Glasgow provided ample work for the indigenous Scottish population. The Roebuck family at its Carron Works at Falkirk near the Firth of Forth was an ironmaking concern which was almost exactly contemporaneous and on a similar breathtaking scale in its early years as those enterprises which were being created around Cyfarthfa and Dowlais in the last quarter of the 18th century. The infamous Highland Clearances of the mid 19th century in their well publicised and savage impact on the native Scottish population propelled thousands of upland crofters and fishers abroad, to the colonies of the Victorian Empire such as Canada and Australia, but hardly to old South Wales, despite the positive economic prospects of Merthyr Tydfil, Cardiff and the Rhondda Valleys in the second half of that century. Several prominent Scottish names did make their deserved impact on the age of iron, steam and later coal and appear in the pages of the history of Merthyr Tydfil. One such example was William Menelaus (1818-1882), chief engineer and later, general manager of the vast Dowlais enterprise at the demise of its greatest figurehead, Sir John Guest in 1852. Menelaus it was who almost single handed at Guest's death took the Works from the increasingly archaic practices of iron smelting into the modern, Victorian age of steel and ensured the prosperity and longevity of Dowlais long after all its rivals (including the Carron Works) had been effectively eclipsed. The contentious Dowlais lease, the renewal of which in 1848 in effect almost hastened Guest's end a few years later, was also in the hands of a distinctive Scottish connection, that of the Bute family on whose lands the original Dowlais enterprise had been located. By the 19th century they had control of the rapidly expanding port and industrial town of Cardiff, into which they poured vast amounts of money in opening new docks, renovating fantasy castles and providing Cardiff with a unique civic architecture and master plan to enable it to claim its status as the de facto capital of Wales. The Scottish connection became poignantly connected in 1900 with the election of James Keir Hardie as Member of Parliament for Merthyr Tydfil. Not lost on one historian was the irony of Hardie as a Socialist, radical spokesman for the inhabitants of the town, originating from humble coalmining stock out of the Lanarkshire and Ayrshire coalfields of Scotland, more than wagging a finger at his landlords, the same Bute family, and all that they stood for in the heady Edwardian years immediately prior to the First World War.

It was noted that the early iron masters in South Wales who were themselves in the first few generations migrants to a town such as Merthyr Tydfil sought help and advice from selected skilled workers, managers, agents and personal friends who hailed from the same places as these owners. Men from Shropshire, from the north east of England, from Yorkshire, from Cumberland and from Scotland gravitated to the South Wales iron settlements not long after the first ores had been smelted. They came essentially in a trained, supervisory, professional capacity. With a handful of trusted, skilled workers they became the first representation of a rather elite industrial workforce, to emerge by the 19th century as what has been termed a labour aristocracy. It was the Irish as navvies, occupied in the intensively laborious work of canal cutting that typified this ethnic group within the South Wales labour force of the early canal age; it was rather the Scots who took up the skilled tasks of railway locomotive driving and supervision during the next great era of modern transport, the railway age of the 1840s onwards. Some Scots found themselves in coal mining or as land agents; some entered a local trade in the rapidly expanding town of Merthyr Tydfil as publicans and shop keepers; others were employed as ministers of religion, as doctors and school teachers. On the face of it their combined influence and identity could hardly have amounted to any substantial impact on town life, given such few numbers and the rather disparate nature of their early employment and settlement in Merthyr Tydfil during the late 18th and early 19th centuries. As late as the census of 1871 only some two hundred persons classified as Scots born were enumerated in Merthyr Tydfil at that date and the figure remained constant down to 1911 with men easily outnumbering women in a ratio of 2:1 as a commonly found emigrant pattern of settlement. (Scottish figures at any date from mid 19th century were always less than a tenth of the equivalent Irish numbers resident in the town at each census.)

Contemporary opinion, however, occasionally saw differently and detected, for example, a concerted monopoly emerging by the Scots in certain lucrative trades in the town by the 1850s and a tendency towards a pattern of residence in the more desirable quarters of the Thomas Town part of Merthyr Tydfil by that same mid century period. It is this unique feature of Scottish migration into and residence within the town from the early 1830s onwards that is considered worthy of comment and analysis here. It has as its terms of reference the peculiar concentration of Scotsmen in the town's local credit drapery trade and a consideration and analysis of the place and importance of the Merthyr Caledonian Society as a social and cultural focal point for such Scotsmen who resided in and near Merthyr Tydfil during the 19th century.

THE CREDIT DRAPERY TRADE

J. Ronald Williams, local historian of Dowlais and Merthyr Tydfil, in an article published in the *Sociological Review* for 1926 examining the influence of foreign nationalities on the life of the people of Merthyr Tydfil, almost as an after-thought in his penultimate paragraph, remembered that there were Scots living in the town. He dismissively summed up their presence in two sentences, as their having established there the travelling drapery business, known locally as "packies" or packmen. A bane of 19th century everyday life in the larger towns and cities of England and Wales was the travelling packman, likened to a vagrant, hawker or pedlar of the commonest sort and seen by contemporary, respectable tradesmen as a most undesirable and unwarranted burden on the public and especially on the innocent housewife. Such was the prevailing view held in Merthyr Tydfil among a section of the business community, to judge from a series of correspondence contained in one of the town's local newspapers. There had been speculation for some time and not just confined to a thriving trading and business centre like Merthyr Tydfil either, that legislation was sorely needed to curb the worst excesses of the itinerant trader. By definition he moved from town to town or within areas of a given town at will, paid no taxes and was accountable to no higher authority. These were the predominant motives for a series of anonymous and highly acrimonious exchanges by letter published in the pages of the *Merthyr Telegraph* for the months of May to July 1857.

The inaugural salvo of mid May from "A Merthyr Tradesman" had as its context the subject of the establishment of a Trade Protection Society in the town as a necessary institution to protect honest tradespeople from being victimised "by itinerant imposters"—hawkers of various goods—despite the best endeavours of the local police force to license these practices through the existing powers of the law. The local book trade, the writer pointed out, had suffered because of this practice of street selling from a dealer who had entered the town. The letter closed with the promise of further details to add to those already expressed, "and 'show up' the doings of the itinerant Scotch pedlars". The author called for a meeting to be held at The Temperance Hall and for a Trade Protection Society to be set up, similar to one formed two years previously to counteract railway abuses (*Merthyr Telegraph*, 16 May 1857).The message was clear: such travelling traders were Scottish in origin who had found their way to Merthyr Tydfil and district and were a menace to legitimate, native businesses; and they had to be stopped forthwith. The same anonymous author returned to the same subject but with more venom at the end of the month (*Merthyr Telegraph*, 30 May 1857); and in a more detailed letter he confidently outlined his case amid closely worded accusation and recrimination directed at the town's Scottish drapery trade. Twenty years ago, he alleged, there had been some half a dozen travelling Scotsmen in the Merthyr area "who hired and plodded on with their packs comparatively unknown and unheeded; now their name is legion". He estimated their number at a hundred and fifty. It was this travelling practice rather than their personal character with which, admitted this "Tradesman", he took issue. He went on: "It is with their traffic I have to do; which, besides being highly injurious to the legitimate trader, is, I believe, demoralising the population in a great, if not greater, degree than the beershop". A system such as this prevailed throughout the land, he argued, but owing to Trade Protection Societies being established elsewhere, it was on the decrease. Alas, not so in Merthyr Tydfil and its immediate neighbourhood where "it is increasing daily". The drapery trade, he asserted, was entirely in Scottish hands and there were only twelve to fourteen drapers of local origin in existence in Merthyr Tydfil and Dowlais. The letter writer continued by quoting from Henry Mayhew's contemporary account of the capital city's poor in his celebrated London Labour (1852) to seek further definitions of the pedlar tallyman as a hawker. "The great majority of the tally-packmen are Scotchmen," continued the anonymous "Tradesman". "These men live in private houses, which they term their warehouses". The actual sale to a customer on the doorstep was likened to outright bullying where the voice "is often spoken with a broad Scotch accent, the speaker trying to make it sound as much like English as possible". Exorbitant charges were then entered into. For example, cloth selling at ten shillings per yard at its usual price was charged by the packmen at nearly eighteen shillings; a dress-piece sold for double the normal price; calico was ten pence rather than the shop price of sixpence. Almost inevitably the buyer would default on an instalment of the purchase deal, explained the writer; "then follow brutal quarrels and frequently assaults". A county court order was usually enacted as a further consequence and the pawn broker was an unavoidable part of this miserable descent towards indebtedness. "That this system is a highly profitable one to the pedlar, is proved by the fact, that most of them who, but (only) four or five years ago were living in the back streets in obscurity, are now living in the best houses in Thomas-town; riding their horses, and enjoying all other luxuries, which the respectable tradesman, with his heavy rent, and settled character, cannot indulge in."

In conclusion, argued the author of this correspondence, strict regulation of these practices was an absolute necessity, preferably through the creation of a Protection Society; a licensing system whereby packs were clearly marked was needed. "In addition, a good talented Welsh lecturer should be engaged to address the working-classes; and forcibly point out to them, in our own expressive language, their folly and improvidence in encouraging a system so ruinous to themselves". (*Merthyr Telegraph*, 30 May 1857).

This detailed second letter together with the first provoked in turn a lengthy reply, again anonymous, in the same pages of the *Merthyr Telegraph* (6 June 1857). Its main theme was to take to task the general tenor of this "Merthyr Tradesman" and answered on each substantive count the allegations made therein against the town's itinerant Scottish draper. The writer at the outset disputed the contentious definitions of a pedlar by the previous author and asserted, for instance, that customers in the Merthyr area were generally supplied from shops in the evenings out of convenience; he had never heard the term "ware house" as used by the earlier writer in that way. As to the number of Scottish "pedlars", the figures, he asserted, were incorrect (six to a hundred and fifty) and he denied that the local drapery trade was entirely in Scottish hands. An interesting passing reference contained in this third letter dated the first Scotsman settling in Merthyr Tydfil at about 1819 but provided no evidence for this early date. The "Merthyr Tradesman" replied in the issue of 13 June. "There is not a drunken or improvident woman all over the hills that is not in debt to the Scotchman or pawn broker". Some twelve to fifteen years previously, he continued, there was but one pawnbroker in the Merthyr Tydfil and Dowlais areas but at present there were over a dozen. The cause was clear: "The Scotch system has called them into existence". Furthermore, children, the writer maintained, often got their first lesson in lying by the Scotch system! (Merthyr Telegraph, 13 June 1857). Adopting this time the pseudonym of "A Scotsman", the same author replied again and challenged the first correspondent on several points of detail in another copious letter (Merthyr Telegraph, 20 June 1857). He came to the rather virtuous conclusion regarding the local tradesman that "his ribaldry shall be to me as harmless as the falling autumnal leaves, and shall be as little noticed". The final broadside in this particular series of exchanges, of 4 July 1857, again came from the Merthyr man and contained a largely anecdotal reiteration of the charges against the Scots in general and their trade practices in the town.

Aside from this brief altercation through these letters to the local press, the reality of the Scottish-based drapery trade in Merthyr Tydfil does reveal some measure of truth in the arguments put forward by both these contentious correspondents. The town's local trade directories for key years of the 19th century cite "Tea Dealers and Drapers" in their pages with the extra proviso of "Travelling" against certain names there. Local born men of the town in the main were counted as resident traders; several distinctive Scottish names appear with regularity in the listings as itinerant drapers. Furthermore, several volumes over the late 19th century decades portray an enclave of these Scots drapers being concentrated in the Thomastown area of Merthyr Tydfil congregated around Thomas Street, Union Street, Newcastle Street and Church Street.

There is no substantive evidence that a Trades Protection Society as called for so stridently in 1857 was actually established in Merthyr Tydfil in the course of the 19th century. Local government regulations through by-laws, stricter licensing of street trade and market activities, institutions such as the local Chamber of Commerce and several professional business and trade associations guarded against the feared worst excesses of "the Scottish trade". The Scots for their own part had for several years by the time of this correspondence in the *Merthyr Telegraph* looked after and protected their own kind. One of the arguments put forward by the anonymous "Merthyr Tradesman" for setting up a local Trade Protection Society in the town was to counteract the already well-established existence of a Scottish mutual organisation, the Merthyr Tydfil Caledonian Society.

THE MERTHYR TYDFIL CALEDONIAN SOCIETY

"The Scotch drapers of Merthyr have a society, the objects of which are to facilitate the collection of debts, and for general mutual protection in their trading pursuits". This was one detail from a local newspaper account of the twentieth anniversary dinner of the Merthyr Caledonian Society held at the Bush Hotel in January 1860, where "thirty gentlemen including the principal Scotch drapers of the district and several commercial and other invited friends sat down". (*Cardiff and Merthyr Guardian*, 28 January 1860). A Caledonian Society had probably been first set up in the town in the late 1820s. The Jubilee Banquet of that same Society in 1897 alluded to this early date, although there are no exact accounts and references to a founding meeting (*Merthyr Express*, 30 January 1897). Meetings of about twenty to thirty or so traders moved between the Star Inn, the Angel, the Bush Hotel on High Street and the Wheatsheaf Hotel on Glebeland Street from about 1850 onwards, the latter two well appointed venues being the principal meeting places in the last quarter of the century as the Society's gatherings increased in popularity and in numbers in attendance to judge from local newspaper accounts of the time. Certainly Merthyr Tydfil's was the first such Society established in Wales; hitherto Bristol had been the nearest location and guests from the major towns in Wales and from further afield, occasionally from Scotland itself, attended these large meetings in the remaining two decades of the 19th century and in the 1900s. The Society's aims were not just for the protection of Scottish trade but were wider and embraced a range of social benefits afforded to members. Its motto, quoted by more than one speaker at the annual gatherings, spoke of "Mutual Protection from foes without and mutual protection to friends within". The late January date each year became a well noted focal point in the new year's social calendar and provided the Society's annual dinner with all the vestiges of that great ritual for all Scottish inhabitants in a town like Merthyr Tydfil—a Burns' Night celebration on or about the poet's birthday of 25 January each year. Typical Scottish fare featuring haggis, whiskies and Caledonian pudding and latterly in the populous dinners of the late 1890s and 1900s, guest pipers and tartan trimmings, were much in evidence.

An explanation of the Society's main functions was provided during the speeches at the dinner of January 1868. Prior to its foundation those engaged in the local drapery trade had necessarily incurred great losses through the removal of customers out of towns and away from their creditors. It was therefore thought desirable to form a mutual society to enable debts to be collected from these wayward customers on an organised basis (*Merthyr Telegraph*, 1 February 1868). The Society's dinners increased in scale and in popularity and centred for some fifteen years at the Assembly Rooms of the Bush Hotel in the town. Here met the most prominent Scottish traders of Merthyr Tydfil and Aberdare, Cardiff, Newport and from elsewhere to partake of a lavish menu, listen to speeches, join in toasts and enjoy hearty song and verse. Membership was not, however, confined to Scotsmen alone. It was pointed out in the local press report of the January 1889 banquet at the Wheatsheaf Hotel that some Welshmen were also on the membership roll (*Merthyr Express*, 19 January 1889). Increasingly the town's Members of Parliament found themselves in attendance, usually proposing one of the major toasts for the evenings celebrations and the guest lists which came to be printed in the later accounts of the press reportage of these dinners by the late 1890s included most of Merthyr's prominent Scotsmen together with representatives of the town council, the clergy and the town's several newspapers. Several Scottish personalities stand out within these detailed accounts of the Society's meetings each New Year as representative of the drapery trade in the town and as active members in the Scottish life of Merthyr Tydfil and as mainstays of late 19th century local society in general. Two men claim attention here out of several who can rightly be considered as having a major influence on the well-being of this town in the years leading up to the Great War: (1) John Forrester (2) Angus Mackintosh.

(1) John Forrester (1816-1896)

Replying to the toast "The Merthyr Caledonian Society" given by H. W. Southey at the 1896 banquet, Forrester revealed in an eloquent address some of his family's origins and connections with the town of Merthyr Tydfil. His father had started business there in 1839 and had joined the nearest Caledonian Society of the time, then located in Bristol. A Merthyr Caledonian Society, he stated to the audience, was formed in 1841, an organisation with which he had himself been "intimately connected" for a quarter century, sometime as its Honorary Secretary. A "John Forrester" appears in the pages of *Hunt's Directory* for 1848 under the columns of "Tea Dealers & Drapers". Forrester was one of several Scots in the latter category, with his address listed as Cross Street. The family drapery business had moved to Union Street by the following decade, then to Victoria Street (where one Quintin Forrester had been located in the 1848 directory). By 1859 John Forrester, father and son and of the same name, were established in Thomas Street; the exact addresses were number 21 and number 50 respectively, as cited in *Webster's Directory* of 1865. Each was listed as a "travelling draper". By the 1871 publication of *Kelly's Directory* John Forrester had moved to 15 Newcastle Street on the edge of Thomastown, surrounded now by several Scotsmen pursuing the same drapery trade and concentrated in the Thomas Street and Union Street parts of the town. Upwardly mobile within the town's social circles as well as prosperous in business, Forrester was cited in the 1878 directory as an "auctioneer & valuer & surveyor", to be found at 98 High Street; by the 1880s he had obtained a private residence at number 3 Glebeland as auctioneer, accountant, surveyor & valuer, stock and share broker. Forrester died at the end of July 1896. He "belonged to that group of Scotchmen who may be said to have established the foundation of the wonderful business which has been built up in the district by the credit drapers" (*Merthyr Express*, 1 August 1896). He had served the town well, although not born in it and was a pivotal member of that Scottish community in exile in Merthyr Tydfil for the greatest span of the 19th century. He, along with several fellow Scots and their families, became a mainstay of the town's Market Square Congregational Church, commonly known as the English Speaking Independent Church, formed in 1838 and which proved attractive to a wide range of Welsh, English and Scottish worshippers in the town. It had connections with the Loyal Cambrian Lodge and was the influential Berry family's place of worship as well as that of the Forresters. Two ministers who served the Market Square Chapel from 1866 to 1887 hailed from Scotland (the Rev. Johnstone from Forfar and the Rev. Simcock from Paisley.) The Rev. S. R. Jenkins, on his induction to the Chapel in 1898 remembered that he "had come to Merthyr as a Welshman to preach English in a Scotch Church". Market Square was known locally as the "Scottish Kirk": its central location at the heart of Merthyr Tydfil gave its influential congregations a sense of importance and social status in the town's business circles, in its local politics and in the civic life of the place out of proportion to the size of this religious establishment.

John Forrerster, son of the deceased, continued with the family business at 133 High Street, to quote the 1906 edition of *Kelly's Directory*.

(2) Angus Mackintosh (1852-1914)

Here was another Scottish incomer to the town, to make a substantial impact on Merthyr Tydfil life in the second half of the 19th century up to the First World War. He arrived in Merthyr about 1873, again in typical Scot's fashion as a credit draper and rose to prominence in town affairs to such an extent that he represented the Town Ward on the old Urban District Council for several years in the 1890s. He was an influential member at the time when Merthyr was putting the final touches in its civic edifice of a town hall, when further expansive works of water supply and drainage were being implemented—all towards the long hoped-for granting of borough status to the town. Mackintosh chaired several meetings of the Caledonian Society and also served as President. At the Jubilee celebrations in 1897 he was President of the Bristol, West of England and South Wales Credit Drapers' Association and brought this body's meeting to Merthyr Tydfil. He was a member of the Loyal Cambrian Lodge and acted as its Worshipful Master in 1898. He retired from the town in 1905, back to his native Scotland where he had purchased for some £12,000 the expansive Holme Estate near Inverness and where he settled into rural pursuits and local affairs until his death in 1914. His connections through kinship with the Mackintosh of Mackintosh more than well served the town's Caledonian Society in its annual New Year celebrations.

As an aside to these brief biographies of Scotsmen in Merthyr Tydfil, another prominent travelling draper from Scotland who made his mark in the town was Thomas Nibloe. Local directories locate him in 1901 living at Clyde House on Union Terrace and five years later at Tydfil House on Courtland Terrace, another of the Scottish exiles in residence in the relatively well-to-do Thomas Town quarter of Merthyr Tydfil. He was another active member of the Caledonian Society, took an influential role in local affairs, was involved in the Credit Drapers' Association and was a highly successful businessman in the town. He was, for example, Chairman of Directors of the Merthyr Central Laundry, newly opened at Penydarren on the site of the old brewery in May 1911. Nibloe was indeed a prime mover within the powerful Buckland (Berry family) circle within town affairs and politics during the latter years of the 19th century and the Edwardian era of the present century. A fuller treatment of this particular Scotsman and citizen of the town is awaited in a future volume of the Merthyr Historian.

Several meetings of the Caledonian Society in the late 1880s and early 1890s were held at the Wheatsheaf Hotel on the Glebeland, if only for the reason that the owner was none other than a fellow countrymen to the Scots members of the Society—Lodowick Mackintosh (McIntosh). Together with his wife, Henrietta, this establishment provided splendid fare for meetings of the Society. At his death in 1894 the Society reverted to the Bush Hotel, a former favourite venue, where the Jubilee Banquet was held in January 1897. A Thursday evening was preferred to Friday, it was stated, for the convenience of a better late train service out of the town (*Merthyr Express*, 30 January 1897). With Angus Mackintosh presiding, some hundred and twenty members and guests were in attendance.

Duncan MacDonald, piper to the Mackintosh of Mackintosh, and piper Laughlan MacBean of Pontypridd accompanied the evening's proceedings. It was a regular gathering of the clans, stated the *Merthyr Express*, and considered that probably at no other time had so many Scotsmen been gathered in Merthyr Tydfil for one occasion. The annual conference of the Bristol, West of England and South Wales Credit Drapers' Association was also being hosted in the town, Angus Mackintosh as its President that year, and shared venue certainly accounted for the large numbers at the Caledonian Society banquet. Here Thomas Nibloe proposed the customary toast, "The Memory of Burns". The Credit Drapers' Association had met a few days earlier at the same Bush Hotel and afterwards had toured the Cyfarthfa Works where members were "greatly impressed with the operations carried on there " (*Merthyr Express*, 30 January 1897) Merthyr's delegate at this Association's conference was Thomas Nibloe with Angus Mackintosh chairing the proceedings. The agenda inevitably returned to the vexed issues of pedlars and hawkers and to the licensing of these person's trade. Many members thought it lamentable that the Association should be branded with the common characters who hawked boot laces and tinware (*Merthyr Express*, 30 January 1897),

The middle and late 1890s saw the activities of the Caledonian Society probably at its zenith in terms of popularity and local influence. Prominent citizens of the town addressed the annual meetings and provided detailed commentary and opinions on the issues of the day: on the Boer War and the undoubted fighting spirit of the Scots and Welsh in that and indeed in all wars; on civic matters where the town was heavily involved in erecting a new town hall, new drainage systems and water supply "the best water supply was undoubtedly that of the City of Glasgow but next to that came Merthyr" was a sentence from one speech to the 1898 banquet, reported in the *Merthyr Express*, 29 January 1898 ; a general hospital; recreation grounds and the protracted Incorporation Inquiry. By the turn of the century the Society's aims were in essence unchanged from its earliest days. J. E. Williams of the town's Lloyds Bank in his toast to "the Merthyr Caledonian Society" repeated in outline at the 1902 meeting that the Draper's Club had been formed to bring Scotsmen together and in particular any new arrivals in the town and to assist those who might be in temporary want. In this way, through mutual self help, he believed, many a lame dog had been helped over a stile (*Merthyr Express*, 25 January 1902). The following year a Grand Scotch Ball, arranged by the newly established Burns' Club in the town to celebrate the poet's birthday, was held at the Drill Hall. The Caledonian Society had assiduously kept note of this auspicious Scottish date for decades without advertising this national celebration as such. Now "a Merthyr Burns Club formed from the younger generation" had taken on the mantle. Many kilts were displayed and the undress uniform of various Scottish regiments were present, quoted the *Merthyr Express*'s account of 7 February 1903 of that first meeting. It went on: "Not only in decorations and costumes was the affair stamped with 'Scautch', but in little catches of conversation its origin was revealed." The backcloth to the proceedings was a large scene of Burns's humble cottage with overhead, above the stage, the motto "Welcome to our first Scottish Ball." A noteworthy departure from those occasions that had gone before under the guise of the Caledonian Society was the ban on alcohol for sale at this new event, perhaps a gesture towards Merthyr's most famous adherent to the temperance cause and its preeminent Scotsman by now, James Keir Hardie, Member of Parliament. The town's two M.P.s were present at this inaugural meeting, Hardie and D. A. Thomas. Hardie gave the Burns grace before the meal and provided after dinner a detailed and eloquent toast to Burns. A splendid programme of music, given by Gwilym Lewis and his band, followed the speeches; some fifty eight dances were given in total. "So great was the success," concluded the *Merthyr Express*, "that the word 'annual' may now be taken for granted". (7 February 1903).

SOME REFLECTIONS ON A COMMON CELTIC TRADITION

On the face of it South Wales and a town such as Merthyr Tydfil within it on the edge of the coalfield possessed little in common with Wales's Celtic cousins from Scotland. Separate traditions, distinctive and very different cultural influences at work on an evolving history of each nation from an early date, a definitive geographical separateness, linguistic divergences from a one-time common Celtic tongue—all made for a Welsh and Scottish experience as two nationalistic entities to set alongside Ireland and England in making up what Hugh Kearney has called, "The Britannic melting pot". The sum effect by the 19th century, of Queen Victoria's reign, was a United Kingdom of the British Isles and of an Empire overseas created in the perceived dominant image of England and Anglo-Saxon traditions. Historians, argues Kearney, have become accustomed to thinking of the British Isles in terms of four national histories, each of which could be dealt with separately in its own terms: English, Welsh, Scottish and Irish. This, he maintains, is a very simplistic view of the 18th and 19th centuries: "The history of the British Isles during this period resembles that of the United States more than is commonly realised." And in this sense the history of a town like Merthyr Tydfil in this modern period, as one of the nearest embodiments in Wales of an "American" experience of multi-ethnic population growth, could be rightfully considered as a crucial experience. The multi-ethnic character of modern Britain, Kearney concludes, is a continuation of 19th century trends. Merthyr Tydfil was certainly a part of that process. The rapid industrialisation of this town had thrown up some unlikely affinities with other areas of the British Isles: the Irish connection has been well documented in South Wales and appears with regularity in the 19th century press, notably in the Cardiff and Merthyr Guardian, for example. Cornish links were less populous but nonetheless important. Relationships with Scotland were being created on a number of different levels: a link through common business with the Scottish Lowlands has already been noted in this essay with reference to the Carron Iron Works. A century later Glasgow and the surrounding townships on and about the Clyde were demonstrating a new radicalism in class politics, expressed in the twin creeds of Socialism and Syndicalism, and which found rich connections within radical South Wales on the eve of the First World War and especially in the Merthyr of Keir Hardie. In that sense, the new forces of coal rather than iron in South Wales which were now seeking to change the old order of 19th century Victoriana, made the presence of Keir Hardie (1856-1915), M.P. for Merthyr Tydfil for the years 1900 to 1915, the most important and dynamic symbol of a shared Welsh-Scottish working class destiny. His innate attraction to the potentially winnable parliamentary seat of Merthyr Tydfil for the newly-formed Labour Party at the so-called "Khaki" General Election of 1900, was in part based on his Scottish-based sentimental attachment for Welshmen, (Morgan) and which never left him during his illustrious political career in the town. Keir Hardie, the man and his politics, steeped in his native Scots' reverence for the work of Robert Burns, appealed to a very broad spectrum of the diverse Merthyr electorate at the beginning of the 20th century; he gained his fiercest support, for example, from the Irish franchise within the town who looked to him for nothing more than his anti-English and anti-Establishment views. His was the reasoned voice of Socialism, acceptable to an increasingly articulate constituency which the Merthyr Boroughs had become by 1900. Hardie's code of ethics, according to his finest modern biographer, Professor K. O. Morgan, derived from Burns and from the Old Testament. As Hardie repeatedly claimed, it was the folk poetry of Burns to which he often turned with its simple message of human comradeship and equality, readily adaptable to the age he knew. (Morgan) For these years down to 1915 Hardie was Scotland personified in South Wales. His was the single most important influence on the fledgling Labour Party in its formative years of the 1890s and 1900s, to be succeeded by another Scotsman, Ramsay MacDonald as the first Labour Prime Minister. These Merthyr years were very much the age of Keir Hardie, to quote Morgan again.

Outside the world of politics a Scottish-based cultural pedigree, inevitably focused on Robert Burns (1759-1796) as the central figurehead in Scottish life and in the shaping of a modern Scottish identity after his death, bears comparison with a similar Welsh flowering through rural-based hymn writers, music and literary traditions. These cultural forces were to become increasingly urbanised as part of the processes of an Industrial Revolution in South Wales in the late 18th and early 19th centuries. By 1850 the capital of this Welsh Renaissance was, of course, Merthyr Tydfil. Thomas Stephens, one of the town's literary giants of the 19th century, understood very well these links with Burns and spoke on the subject of the connections between Celtic Wales and Scotland at a Burns' centenary Dinner, held at the Bush Hotel in the town in January 1859. Two men with Scottish connections also took part, with H. A. Bruce, M.P. for the town, presiding and William Menelaus of the Dowlais Works speaking on "the Poets of Scotland" (*Cardiff and Merthyr Guardian*, 29 January 1859).

The concept of industrialisation, seen as a series of fundamental processes on a human level with social, economic, political, scientific and religious consequences, was essentially an "English" experience as far as the Celtic lands of the United Kingdom were concerned. Scotland like Wales to a large extent suffered an Anglicised invasion of entrepreneurial capital and ideas through the presence of an upper strata of inventors, ironmasters, bankers and tradesmen, to set in motion the Industrial Revolution of the 18th and 19th centuries. According to one eminent social historian, industrialism (his word) had all the makings of a semi-colonial economy (Perkin). Wales and Scotland, on the eve of differing degrees of devolved Assembly powers, are still painfully working out this shared common legacy of a dominant Anglo-Saxon hegemony.

This review has attempted a broader consideration of the Scottish influence on Merthyr Tydfil in the town's crucial years of the 19th century. It goes beyond the well documented observations of "Scotch Cattle", that urban/rural guerilla campaign along the line of the heads of the valleys to the east of the town, where allegedly some of the despised targets were small-scale Scots ironmasters and pit owners with their small bands of native workers who were highly resented by the indigenous majority Welsh workforce. Or was the campaign directed at the supposed Scottish blackleg labourers as resentment at the presence of troops of the Scots Greys and Highland regiments patrolling the area after the Merthyr Rising of June 1831? That event, after all, had as its catalyst the presence in the town of the 93rd Foot of the Argyll and Sutherland Highlanders, the alleged assault on one of its number, Private Donald Black, making a working class martyr out of Richard Lewis (Dic Penderyn) in those early days of June. Modern Welsh and Scottish histories represent shared as much as divergent strands in their respective fabrics which have, in turn, contributed richly to the making of a modern British state. Professor Keith Robbins in his elegant Ford Lectures at Oxford, published as *Nineteenth-Century Britain* (1989), makes note of the curious triangular relationship between England, Scotland and Wales on the one hand, and the internal dynamics within these regions on the other. An understanding of Merthyr Tydfil's history, as a pivotal element within this broad, national framework, and an appreciation of the Welsh and non-Welsh elements which have contributed to the fabric of this town, make these conflicting trends of integration and regional diversity that much better understood.

REFERENCES

Scant attention has been paid to the subject of the Scots in Merthyr Tydfil in the town's standard histories and recourse has therefore been made to other sources, notably the files of the local press and in particular the pages of the *Merthyr Telegraph* and the *Merthyr Express* and to local trade directories. Precise references are contained within this essay. The content and style of this article has been, to a large extent, governed by a remarkably detailed compilation containing miscellaneous newspaper accounts of the Merthyr Tydfil Caledonian Society for the years 1841 to 1910, subsequently printed and published in a limited edition by Dr. T. F. Holley under the title of *The Merthyr Tydfil Caledonian Society* (1997).

J. R. Williams' article "The Influence of Foreign Nationalities On The Life of The People Of Merthyr Tydfil" is to be found in *The Sociological Review*, vol. XVIII (1926), pp. 148-152. Specific local references used in this essay include the two histories on *Market Square Chapel: Market Square Congregational Church 1838-1938*: *A Brief History* (1938) and *Market Square United Reform Church*, 1838-1988 (1988).

On the place of Keir Hardie in the town, see K. O. Morgan's earlier essay, "The Merthyr of Keir Hardie" in Merthyr Politics: *The Making Of A Working-Class Tradition*, ed. Glanmor Williams (1966), pp. 58-81, and which is still the best single collection of essays as an introduction to the town's modern history. See also the same author's later and more detailed biography, *Keir Hardie: Radical and Socialist* (1975).

On Menelaus see T. F. Holley and J. Brynmor Jones in their essay "William Menelaus of Dowlais" in *Merthyr Historian*, volume 7 (1994), pp. 153-171. On the Scottish dimensions within the phenomenon of the Scotch Cattle and the Merthyr Rising, see the two pre-eminent masters on these events: the late Professor David Jones's, *Before Rebecca* (1973) and the late Professor Gwyn A. Williams's, *The Merthyr Rising* (1978). On the precise Scottish connection of the Carron ironworks, see R. H. Campbell's *Carron Company* (1961).

Some of the main texts which I have found particularly useful in outlining the several themes and arguments contained in the last section of this essay are: Hugh Kearney, *The British Isles: A History Of Four Nations* (1989); Harold Perkin, *The Origins Of Modern English Society* 1780-1880 (1969) and Keith Robbins, *Nineteenth-Century Britain: England, Scotland and Wales. The Making Of A Nation* (1989).

Carolyn Jacob at Merthyr Tydfil Central Library helped me to juggle various figures on the Scots population for several census dates and immediately supplied on request miscellaneous reference texts with her usual cheerful efficiency and commentary. Once more my modest and tardy contribution to a volume of the Merthyr Historian owes a principal debt to Fred and Vida Holley, for their hospitality, friendship and patience in Celtic abundance and in providing me with such a wealth of material and references on "Scottish Merthyr Tydfil" and on the Caledonian Society in particular, from which this essay is largely derived.

71B. Mr. Thomas F. Harvey
(Photo courtesy of Mrs. Carolyn Jacob and Mr. David Thomas)

DEVELOPMENTS I HAVE OBSERVED IN THE COUNTY BOROUGH OF MERTHYR TYDFIL, 1870-1925

by

T. F. HARVEY

A talk delivered at Merthyr Tydfil Town Hall to Merthyr Chamber of Trade, Councillor H. M. Lloyd, President, in the Chair. Mr. T. F. Harvey, C.E., was for many years surveyor to Merthyr Council and in 1925 was one of the consulting engineers to the Taf Fechan Water Board.

"I must go back many years for early reminiscences, but hope you will not find me very tedious. It was in 1870 that I first came from Abergavenny to Merthyr. I had been engaged as resident engineer for the construction of railway extensions to THE LONDON AND NORTH-WESTERN South Wales system, and in 1870 had to carry out the construction of the railway from Rhymney Bridge, through Dowlais Top to the Dowlais Station of the Brecon and Merthyr Railway. This section was opened early in 1873.

It was not my intention to remain in the Merthyr district, but, to my great surprise, an appointment was offered me by the Dowlais Company. I had not realised that I was in favour with the heads of the Dowlais Works until the offer came, just as the railway was being completed. Previous negotiations on business matters had sometimes led to differences of opinion. However, I accepted the unsought offer, and in May 1873, became Civil Engineer to the Company, and in the same year was elected an Associate of the Institution of Civil Engineers. It is over half a century ago. I was then only a young man; I was only thirty.

A picture of Merthyr as I first knew it is not easily visualised. An outstanding figure was John Griffith, the sturdy Rector of Merthyr. The wicked war of 1870 between Prussia and France was raging. My sympathies were entirely with France but I am afraid a majority of our population wished success to the Prussian Army. The Rector would occasionally inveigh against Prussia in his sermons. He once called the King of Prussia, who was soon afterwards crowned Emperor of Germany, 'that Royal Prussian butcher' . There is no Emperor of Germany today (1925).

The old Post Office Corner and the small shops forming High-street and Glebeland-street were more useful than imposing. They have given way to the more modern requirements. My old friend, CHARLES WILKINS, postmaster and local historian, has long passed away from amongst us. The Castle Hotel, now, alas, a ruin, was a fine hostelry where the best of material comforts could be had. Its proprietor, Mr. Roach, was a most worthy man. He even had the hardihood to introduce a hansom cab into Merthyr. He loved horses, and was a long time making up his mind whether or not the Welsh hills would throw too much strain on the horse, with the driver perched up so high behind. Like many other things, the once-beloved hansom has gone.

About once a month my revered chief, JOHN GARDNER, would come down from Westminster to view the work in progress on the railway we were constructing, and he always invited me to dine with him at 'The Castle', where he was an old and honoured guest. These old days were happy days for me. I loved my work and put my whole heart and

283

soul into it. As the old adage has it everybody 'should work while he works, and play while he plays'.

It is singular, but true, that in the days of my boyhood many people disparaged the present and talked about the good old times, the days before the railroad. We boys used to hear about the wonderful doings of the past, about the Duke of Wellington and 'Bonyparte', about the Battle of Waterloo, about the climate being better in the good old days, the crops heavier, the families larger, and the beer stronger. People grumbled then, especially the farmers. The pessimist will always be amongst us. The pessimist neglects to think of the continual changes always occurring on this planet of ours. These are Nature's secrets of humanity's slow, evolutionary progress towards perfection.

WHAT CHANGES HAVE TAKEN PLACE.

Looking back I recollect how difficult it was for me to make up my mind to become a member of the Dowlais staff. I had for three years been strenuously engaged in the construction of the railway, and had little inclination to go near the steelworks and furnaces. I had only been through the Works two or three times. One of the occasions was with old Professor Blackie, of Edinburgh. It was my wife's desire to settle down that influenced my decision. What changes have taken place since then! How many of the prominent men of that time have gone! How different Merthyr of today (1925) to Merthyr of 1870. Merthyr then held its head high as one of the chief iron manufacturing centres of the country, aye, of the world.

When I commenced my duties at Dowlais the Company had lost the services of two first class men, I refer to Edward Williams, who went to Middlesborough to manage the BOLCKOW VAUGHAN WORKS, and to William Jenkins, who was manager for the CONSETT COMPANY. A prolonged struggle between the Dowlais Company, and their colliers, led by THOMAS HALLIDAY, had just ended.

It became transparent at once that the antiquated methods in vogue for dealing with the transit of the ores from Spain to the furnaces must be improved upon, and I had the privilege of making great alterations to the Works railways and sidings and erecting gauntrees for the reduction of costs.

The Bedlinog Pits were being sunk, to which I laid out the connecting lines of rail. Alas! they are closed today. But the outstanding feature of the period was the introduction of the Bessemer process of steel making, necessitating the importation of hematite ores from Spain and the giving up of the use of the Welsh argillaceous ores. The Dowlais management had courageously seen the far-reaching consequences of this simple and revolutionary method of producing steel by the Bessemer converter, and before I joined the staff, had brought the process into operation.

It should be borne in mind that at the head of the Dowlais management were two men of great capacity. I, of course, refer to GEORGE THOMAS CLARK and WILLIAM MENELAUS, the latter being the actual and practical manager of the great Works. My duties brought me into much more intimate contact with Menelaus than with Mr. G. T. Clark. In common with the several agents for the different departments, we took instructions from Mr. Menelaus. He had a shrewd knowledge of character and ability, and was an indefatigable worker. It was not difficult to discuss questions relating to the work going on with him, as, besides being a good engineer and a very acute and able man of business, he was a man of wide knowledge. He hardly interfered at all with the management of the collieries, which were in the most capable hands of MR. MATTHEW TRURAN, a most successful manager.

ORIGIN OF GREAT INDUSTRIAL CONCERNS.

It is interesting to think for a moment about the origin of great industrial centres. All the ironworks in South Wales were, as a matter of course, originally established close to the northern outcrop of the South Wales coalfield, where the native ores are found in the coal measures, and the mountain limestone is abundant, and where all the minerals could be worked without great cost. Looking back to the time when the railways of this country were in their infancy, and travelling east to west, you would find ironworks at Nantyglo, Ebbw Vale, Sirhowy, Tredegar, Rhymney, Dowlais, Penydarren, Plymouth, Cyfarthfa, Aberaman and Hirwaun, all flourishing concerns in the early days of railroads, and sending iron rails to all parts of the world, the United States of America being large customers. The railway system throughout the world is, as every one knows, due to the genius of the sons of Britain. Men of courage and quick intuition, which is a quality of genius, seize opportunities, and lay down the foundation for material prosperity. They march along the path of evolution, always ready to do away with outworn methods, and make practical the results of newer scientific research. Thus when the old laborious method of iron making gave way to the modern method of steel making, there was an assured future before Dowlais. Mr. Menelaus should be regarded, and I have no doubt is regarded, as an early pioneer. He thoroughly believed in the gospel of work. There is no truer gospel, believe me, for the working out of our material salvation.

I have spoken of Mr. G. T. Clark and Mr. Menelaus. They seemed to remind one of the great fly-wheels of the old-fashioned steam engines, keeping everything in steady movement and motion. Mr. Clark was a very distinguished man, eminent in many directions. He took great interest in the old and famous Dowlais Schools, which the people were justly proud of.

There were several interesting men amongst the principal agents, devoted to their duties and to the interest of the Company, their main object being to keep the wheels turning and the Works going. MR. GEORGE MARTIN, with whom I was principally associated, was a very old agent of the Company. He was a prominent man, highly esteemed by all who knew him, and was Chairman of the Merthyr Local Board of Health. To look at him you would be reminded of the old song 'The Fine Old English Gentleman' He rode a fine grey mare, and had the seat of a good horseman. I cannot speak too highly of George Martin.

Of course, I had frequent contact with the assistant Works managers, the mechanical engineer, the blast furnace managers, one of whom, WILLIAM EVANS, ultimately became general manager, the steel works and mill managers, who were all tried and experienced men.

Nor can the office staff be left out in this hasty reference to the men who were concerned in making the Works prosperous. It was a funny old-fashioned office right in the heart of the grime and smoke of the Works. DAVID JAMES, the secretary, was a model of discretion. THOMAS JONES, the cashier, a native of the locality, and father of the present general manager, knew his work well, which included other responsibilities than that pertaining to his principal department. In fact, the main wheels, as well as the smaller ones, of the whole machine, fitted well together, and Dowlais in the old days was a pattern to be followed.

While I was at Dowlais I could not help being practically interested in the various metal-lurgical processes. Eventually I took out a patent for hot blast stoves, which I believed would cheapen production, but the patent was not put to the test, and did not bring me any reward. I had a scheme for bringing the molten metal from No. 19 blast furnace in the Ivor Works down to the steelworks by a line of rails but it involved tunnelling under the main road and under Dowlais House. Mr. Menelaus arranged an interview for me at Dowlais House, but I was forewarned that the scheme was not likely to be approved. It was a pretty interview, Mr. Clark thought it very bold of me to suggest a tunnel for a railway line under Dowlais House. He supposed I knew that it was the home of the Guests. That clinched it.

KING OF THE WORKS.

I cannot close these remarks upon Dowlais as I knew it without one more reference to Menelaus, the veritable 'King of the Works'. He was not often away on business. He left his home punctually at nine in the morning, and walked up through the Upper Works, where some of the agents would meet him before he went down to the General Office. He wore a top hat, which in those days, was the usual and proper thing to do. We noticed that if the hat was tilted a little backwards we might have a stormy interview, while if the tilt was a for-ward one it was pleasant to meet him. Some months after I entered the Dowlais Works, my old chief wanted me back, and offered me an appointment which I was anxious to secure. But I knew I was bound to the Dowlais Company under a three months' notice. I tried to get away but Menelaus was inexorable. He would insist on my staying every day of the full three months but he raised my salary.

Menelaus did not live to a ripe age. He left a very valuable bequest of oil paintings to the City of Cardiff. Merthyr was then without a Museum or Art Gallery. When Menelaus passed away I felt I had lost a friend, a man whom I sincerely respected, and could always rely on—almost a great man.

Mr. Menelaus was followed in the general management of the Works by Mr. E. P. Martin, who built a new steel plant at Dowlais and the great Cardiff Works on the East Moors.

Time will not permit of my entering into any account of the last couple of years I served the Dowlais Company, and I must hasten to the next chapter of the developments I have observed in Merthyr Tydfil.

It was in 1885 that I was appointed engineer and surveyor to the Merthyr Sanitary Authority in succession to the late Samuel Harpur, who for many years had been the able engineer of the Merthyr Local Board of Health. Mr. Harpur had a high reputation and was well known as an authority on sewage disposal. He won golden opinions in connection with the Merthyr sewage scheme, and the farms he laid out at Troedyrhiw and Abercynon. Samuel Harpur was a man whom Merthyr was proud of, and whom I was proud to follow".

(*Merthyr Express*. 25.7.1925. p.7. col.1+2+3.)

Mr. T. F. Harvey, engineer to the Taff Fechan Water Supply Board, continued his reminis-cences in another address to Merthyr Chamber of Trade, delivered in September 1925. Councillor H. M. Lloyd, J.P., President, was in the Chair.

CONCLUSION OF MR. T. F. HARVEY'S REVIEW.

"I am glad of this opportunity of speaking again in a supplemental way on the subject of the 'Developments observed in the Merthyr County Borough during the last fifty-five years', because on looking over what I had to say at your last meeting, I find that there is a lack of completeness in my remarks. They want amplification. The reason is obvious. The subject is too large to be dealt with in the course of half an hours talk, and I had, therefore, to leave out much of interest, which otherwise would have been included.

I began my address by referring to the construction of the London and North-Western Railway extension from Rhymney Bridge to Dowlais, commenced in 1870, under my direction as resident engineer on behalf of the Company, but I did not say that the work was let by contract to Messrs. Brassey and Field; nor did I say that from 1866 to 1868 I had been engaged by this eminent firm on other railway work as executive engineer, their agent being the well-known JOHN MACKAY, who afterwards became a notable contractor on his own account, and whom it was a pleasure to be associated with.

Backwards from that period for very many years, Thomas Brassey, father of the present Earl Brassey, was a world renowned railway and public works contractor, THOMAS BRASSEY! His name was a name to conjure with.

His 'Life and Labours', written by Sir Arthur Helps in 1872, and dedicated by permission to Queen Victoria, reveals a wonderful man, a man whose merits and high character, as well as great gifts, were freely acknowledged, a man beloved by his workmen and adored by his several agents who carried out his contracts both in the Eastern and Western hemispheres. A man who won a high reputation for trustful large heartedness, and for skill and integrity. His main ambition seems to have been to provide employment for his fellow countrymen.

There were no such things as Limited Liability Companies in the early days of Brasseys' career, but that does not mean that giant enterprises were not well carried out. Our railways were not built by Limited Liability Companies, nor, to go much further back, were our noble abbeys and cathedrals.

Brassey took an interest in his men and knew them. He was a born leader of men. Brassey, after finding out the necessary qualities in a man, would admit him as partner for the carrying out of an individual contract. There were more than twenty such partnerships, besides the partnership of Brassey and Field.

Between 1834 and 1870 Mr. Brassey and his partners constructed over 6,500 miles of railway in Europe, India, Australia, South America and Canada, besides great docks and other public works.

It is related that in the early days, about 1843, a railway contract in France was being carried out involving a viaduct 100ft. high and one third of a mile in length, WHICH FELL. This was a staggering blow which Brassey and his partner met manfully. It was a hard lesson. The first thing to do is to build it up again, they said, and this huge structure was rebuilt within six months. There was no hesitation, but an instantaneous realisation of their responsibility to fulfil the contract they had entered into.

It seems to me interesting to recall instances of integrity, hard work, perseverance, courage and insight, without which mere ability counts for little. It seems to me that human nature, speaking generally, is tractable and amenable to that divine command, 'Do unto others as you would they should do unto you'. And that, notwithstanding the turmoil and strife of these latter days, there is in every human being a spark of the divine, either a tiny, latent spark, or in the more evolved individual, an effulgent ray, and that the main business of our life should be to act in such a fashion as to draw out the good in ourselves and in others.

I find I made an error in referring to the visit of the Edinburgh Greek Professor to the Dowlais Works to a date previous to my engagement there. It occurred in 1877. PROFESSOR BLACKIE had been visiting his very old friend, JOHN MACKAY, who brought him to Dowlais, and they went through the Works with me. Blackie was greatly interested in the various operations going on in the several parts of the Works, the smelting of the ores in the Blast Furnaces, the Bessemer process of converting cast iron into steel, the Siemen's Furnaces, the various rolling mills, and so forth, which were at that time in full swing. Blackie afterwards wrote some lines when at Oban in September 1877 as a memento of his visit.

PROFESSOR BLACKIE ON A VISIT TO DOWLAIS STEELWORKS.

When visiting the Iron Works at Dowlais in the month of May last, I was struck with the breadth of chest and grandeur of brawn displayed by one of the workmen wielding a gigantic hammer. The following lines are a humble attempt to fix down the impression made on me at that time by the Works and workmen:—

By heaven! an arm that might belong to Jove,
Launching red thunders from the starry field.
Or that celestial smith who forged the shield
For hot Achilles, which his mother's love
Bore proudly down to Troy; while mine, poor mine,
Against that swelling majesty of brawn
Shews like a pole stuck in a gardened lawn,
To prop sweet peas and slim stalked jemmamine.
How brave he works, with stroke on stroke, to free
The glowing ingot from the encasing mould.
Or guides the mountain's molten bowels rolled
In wreathed fire, with sparks of bickering glee!
What makes our England great? A triple charm,
Iron and coal, and this man's brawny arm.

John Stuart Blackie. Oban, September 15th 1877.

I spoke of the famous Dowlais Schools and of that eminent man, MR. G. T. CLARK, who took such great interest in them, but had no time to refer to the schoolmasters of the period. MATTHEW HIRST was a splendid type of the practical headmaster. He grounded his boys well in elementary education, many of whom have had successful careers. MISS OLIVER, the headmistress, was again exactly the kind of woman for training her girls. The number of boys and girls, including the juvenile departments, was about one thousand.

I cannot leave out the mention of dear old white-headed GEORGE HOULSON, who was headmaster of the great Infants' Department. Why, the children were so fond of him they would almost cling about his legs if he were walking down the street. I recollect walking with him one morning on his way to school and he spoke of TYNDALE. I thought he meant PROFESSOR TYNDALL, and began to eulogise this prominent scientific man. He stood and looked at me with such rebuking eyes. 'I don't mean that man of science', he said, 'I mean a far greater man, WILLIAM TYNDALE, the early translator of the Bible'.

George Houlson was assisted in the management of his department of the huge school by his son, MR. ABRAM HOULSON, and his daughter, MISS EMMA HOULSON, who, like their father, were beloved by their scholars.

By the system of a small percentage or poundage, which never varied, kept by the Company out of the wages earned, every workman was entitled to send his children to the school, and also to have medical attendance for himself and family by the staff of doctors

72. G.T. Clark, Dowlais Works.
    The centenary of his death in 1898 was marked by Glamorgan History Society, a multi-author book on many facets of scholarly life was produced. This book was edited by Brian Ll. James, M.A., 8, Grove Court, Birchgrove, Cardiff. CF4 4QS.

the Company employed. The workmen, therefore, by this method of contribution, paid for the priceless boon of education and for doctor's attention and medicines, and most of them thought themselves fortunate in having to pay so little.

I have spoken of the Dowlais Schools but not of the architect. They were designed by the famous SIR CHARLES BARRY, and the spacious building as originally built was a very fine specimen of school architecture. The school has of necessity been added to in recent years (i.e. ca. 1925) for greater accommodation, but the architectural features have been utterly destroyed.

A stranger coming for the first time down the high road from Dowlais Top would be sure to pause when he came near the 'GUEST MEMORIAL'. This fine and unique example of classical architecture was also designed by Sir Charles Barry. The first floor made a magnificent ballroom, and many a dance has been enjoyed on it. I always think when I pass the place that the considerable area of ground around this noble building should be turfed and planted with hardy trees and shrubs and flowers, and lovingly cared for. The building is a monumental one and must not be forgotten.

The main purpose of this address is to deal with the developments which have been carried out during the quite recent years at the great Dowlais Works of Messrs. Guest, Keen, and Nettlefolds, Limited, but before dealing with this vastly important matter I want to fill a gap or two in my previous address.

CYFARTHFA WORKS.

One does not feel inclined to dwell too much upon the now almost dismantled Cyfarthfa Works, but it seems fitting to give them a place in this review. The famous ironmasters, the Crawshays, had for generations carried them on with successful activity, but in 1874 the old ironworks closed down, the forges and furnaces became silent, the lights went out, and a sad gloom was cast over the town.

The stoppage of the Cyfarthfa Works in 1874 took place, according to MR. EVAN LOUGHER, of Merthyr, under the following circumstances.

A MR. KANE, from the North of England, came down to South Wales in his capacity as secretary to the Iron Works Union, and prevailed upon the iron workers of Cyfarthfa, Dowlais and Plymouth to send in their notices to cease work under the then conditions. Mr. Robert Crawshay had taken a contract for iron rails which was not quite completed. He received a deputation of his workmen and asked them to continue for another three weeks to complete the contract and to trust to his honour afterwards.

The spokesman for the men said that they must see Mr. Kane first and must get his consent. Mr. Crawshay had in previous times of depression in the trade kept his Works going and stocked puddle bar to the extent of thousands of tons for future use. He frequently paid wages for a long period to his workmen at what was known as the 'Castle Mill' when there was no work to do. They formed part of the deputation, and one of these same men was the spokesman.

The uncompleted order for rails was finished at the Dowlais Iron Works, which was kept going.

Thus ended the iron-making era in Cyfarthfa. Sometime after the interview of Mr. Crawshay with his men and their refusal to work, he confided to one of his trusty workmen his decision, and said 'William, the tie is broken, I shall not start Cyfarthfa Works again. If the men had listened to me I would have kept the Works going, even if I had to stock the iron in Cyfarthfa Park'.

Some years passed away before the gloom was dispersed. But in the early 1880s the hammer again sounded on the anvil, and Cyfarthfa once more became a hive of industry.

A new firm, Crawshay Brothers Limited, had been formed, and the reconstruction of the Works on the most modern lines was undertaken. MR. EDWARD WILLIAMS, of Middlesborough fame, was entrusted with the construction of new Blast Furnaces, new Steel Works and Mills. My friend, MR. EDMUND HAMBLY, was engaged as engineer to the firm. The work was energetically carried on, and after a while the lights again appeared, the furnaces flamed, the Bessemer converters threw out their sparks of fire and an army of men were again earning their daily bread. The song of work was again bravely sung—there should be no song so dear to the human heart as the song of work. To find work, or to endeavour to find work, and to do it with all our might should be the watchword of every human being under the sun. There should be no joy like the joy of work. There can be no bodily health without work, and certainly no health of the soul without it.

And so for several years under the able management of the well known WILLIAM EVANS, of Dowlais, who was trained under the eye of WILLIAM MENELAUS, this compact and modernly equipped Steel Works at Cyfarthfa was kept prosperously going until the later evil days came upon us.

Soon even the traces of its existence will almost disappear, for the work of demolition is proceeding apace. How easy it is to pull down and destroy, a fool can destroy, how difficult it is to build up and construct. But surely there must come a recovery of industrial health; surely a way will be found out of the 'slough of despond'.

I expect you can recollect Mr.Holchouse's horse buses plying between Merthyr and Dowlais, sixpence up, fourpence down. I remember when even this very limited accommodation did not exist, and when the people had to walk. The doctors say that walking is the most healthful of exercises, as it brings more muscles of the body into play than any other form of exercise. Anyhow, I had plenty of it in my younger days. People nowadays (1925) will not walk half a mile if they can ride. Today the motor bus, the charabanc, the motor car, the motor cycle, are seen here, there and everywhere, all triumphs of mechanical ingenuity, laughing at hills and disdaining gradients, often to the danger of the public, rushing along as if life must be all hurry, thoughtlessness and excitement, and not as it should be, A CALM, SELF-POSSESSED ENJOYMENT OF LIVING AND LEARNING. How glorious to get out of the town and into this beautiful country of ours in the summer-time, and be driven slowly, not more than twenty miles an hour, so that the eye has a chance of seeing, and the soul of drinking in a little of the elixir of Nature's marvellous panorama.

These remarkable latter day inventions are formidable competitors with the railways and the trams. When the idea of a 3 feet 6 inch gauge electric tramway here in Merthyr was first mooted it met with opposition in influential quarters who would not be convinced, when I urged that an electric car was really a safer vehicle than an omnibus of the same width as it would always run in exactly the same position on the road. In those days the Sanitary Authority would not take the initiative of construction, and it was left to private enterprise.

OUR TRAMWAYS.

The Merthyr electric tramways were laid down in 1900 and opened in 1901. The same year also saw the inauguration of a supply of electricity in the town by the Merthyr Electric

Traction and Lighting Company. I think it worth noting that the Company's power station stands on a part of the site of the old Penydarren Iron Works, where that remarkable mechanical genius, Richard Trevethick, the real inventor of the high pressure locomotive engine, was working out his problems more than a century ago. ALL HONOUR TO HIS NAME.

On 17th September 1910 the Mayoress of Merthyr, Mrs. Frank Treharne James, opened the new Cefn Bridge and drove a tramcar over it. Subsequently the tramways were extended through Cefn Coed to the 'Morning Sun' Inn, and that section was opened in July 1914.

The Company in 1911 extended their mains so as to be able to supply electricity to Troedyrhiw, Merthyr Vale, Aberfan and Treharris, which involved the erection of a transmission line at extra high pressure to which transformer stations have been connected.

In 1914 the Merthyr and Treforest generating stations (the latter belonging to the South Wales Power Company) were interconnected.

In 1915 the Thomas-Merthyr Colliery Company commenced taking a supply of power from the M.E.T. & L. Company's mains and in 1920 they erected a high pressure branch line and transformer station of their own, to relieve the other mains.

Let us hope that with regard to electrical supply for most purposes further progress will continue to be made, and further developments take place in the near future.

I might have mentioned, when I spoke before, but time was limited, the building of small branch FREE LIBRARIES under the CARNEGIE BEQUEST, which was done in various parts of the Borough, also the mistake of the Corporation in not purchasing SHILOH CHAPEL in Church-street, which I urged should be done, FOR A CENTRAL LIBRARY. This Central Library is not yet built (i.e. in 1925). The Shiloh Chapel is now the Miners' Hall, and is a splendid example of how the celebrated railway engineer, BRUNEL, used to do his work. The VALE OF NEATH RAILWAY COMPANY (broad gauge) had to acquire the then existing small Welsh Wesleyan Shiloh Chapel which stood on the Merthyr Station site, and had the present new structure erected in substitution for the old one.

The Mardy Isolation Hospital of the Merthyr Corporation was opened in 1907 by the late Mr. Keir Hardie, M.P. This institution was very sorely needed. I naturally made a careful study of the problem and took the greatest pains in designing the buildings to provide in the most modern fashion for the various requirements which were outlined by the Medical Officer of Health, Dr. David J. Thomas, and at the same time to plan the buildings in such a way as to leave space for large future extensions and additions which have since been provided under the guidance of Dr. Duncan, the Medical Officer of the Corporation.

In giving a short description of the Merthyr Waterworks, I ought to have recorded that in 1908 some negotiations took place between the Merthyr Corporation and Cardiff as to the desirability of promoting a scheme to construct the Taf Fechan Reservoir as a joint enterprise. Negotiations extending over a considerable time with Newport for the taking of the additional supply they required from the Taf Fechan Reservoir also, unfortunately, failed to materialise.

"And now we must get back to the Dowlais Works and try to realise what developments have taken place there since I relinquished my appointment under the Company in 1885. In my former observations I only just touched upon the period when the late Mr. E. P. Martin was the general manager of the great concern. I stated that 'he built a new steel plant at Dowlais and the great Cardiff Works on the East Moors'. The Bessemer steel plant Martin laid down at Dowlais consists of two twenty ton converters and one twenty ton crane; three cupolas for re-melting the recarburising materials; one hydraulic ingot stripper, drying stoves, and a ganister mill.

The mills Martin laid down in connection with this plant, the cogging, roughing and finishing mills do not need to be fully described here. They were well designed for the terribly heavy work they have to do.

AN AMAZING TRANSFORMATION.

By the courtesy of the present (1925) general manager, Mr. Howell R. Jones, I have been able to go over the Works and see for myself what has been done during the last two or three years to bring the Works up to date, and to enable the Company to have a chance of successfully competing for a share of the world's orders. The Works are crying out for orders, which, let us hope, will soon become more plentiful.

Within the last couple of years an amazing transformation has been effected. A mint of money has been expended. That modern word 'Electrification' gives the clue to what we shall have to endeavour to describe. I am not easily astonished. Astounding things are always happening on this planet of ours, and one learns to view them calmly. I must say however, that as one gets older one feels more glad to be an infinitesimal living part of this beautiful small living planet, swiftly spinning and revolving with its sisters in exact harmony and rhythm around their little sun, our little solar system itself having a still vaster movement amidst far greater suns and systems. ORDER, HARMONY, RHYTHM are plainly written in Nature's book everywhere around us and above us, but, as in the past, so in the present, feeble, unevolved man taking a mean advantage of his priceless boon of free will, given to him without stint, so that he can do what he chooses, does, in his little, silly, thoughtless way, foster and stir up discord and restlessness and strife and war, and seems bent on trying to stop the upward march of the evolution of the human race towards greater perfection and happiness. I am led to this little digression because of the harmony and rhythm to be seen in the mechanical movements of gigantic machinery under the spell of 'electrification'. You move a small lever or a switch and great ponderous masses of complicated machinery become animated with motion and obey your command as if you were a god.

DOWLAIS IS A WONDERFUL PLACE.

It was here that the first Bessemer ingot was ever rolled into a bar of steel. Henry Bessemer sent the steel ingot down from the Midlands to the Dowlais Works. When you walk up through the upper portion of the Works, called the Ivor Works, you see the same buildings on your left as of old, fitting shops, smiths shops, and other necessary buildings for the carrying on of the Works, but the eye does not dwell upon them, for, to your right the whole of the area of the Works is very modern. Great new structures occupy the space where formerly stood the blast furnaces and mills. The first thing that strikes the eye is a tall and imposing ferroconcrete structure, 130 feet high, with chimney 20 feet higher. We are looking at the new coking plant, consisting of a battery of 30 Otto regenerative by product ovens, 38 feet long, 10 feet 2 inches high and 21 inches wide, producing 2,000 tons of coke per week. Electrically driven machinery lifts the huge doors of the ovens when the coking process is complete. The coal is washed in the Coppee washery at the Old Works, and brought in trucks to the new drainage bunkers, twelve of them each 20 feet in diameter, and made of reinforced concrete. Their total capacity is 3,000 tons. From these drainage bunkers the coal is conveyed by belts, elevators and conveyors to the service bunker for the coke ovens, which has a capacity of 2,500 tons.

The by product part of the plant is laid out to deal with the important by products from the coal, and can, if necessary, be duplicated. It consists of a sulphate of ammonia plant, crude benzol plant, and a tar dehydrating plant. The sulphate of ammonia is sent away in sacks of two hundredweight (2 cwt.).

At the Ivor Works a fine new foundry has been erected for producing the castings required in the Works. What a contrast to the old foundry I recollect. The building is 150 feet long and ninety feet wide, divided into two spans of 45 feet each, and equipped with three cranes, the largest one being a 30 ton crane and all electrically driven. The conception of an electric generating station for supplying power on a large scale would, only a few years ago, have been considered a rash Utopian idea, but today, one sees that fabulous amounts of capital have been found and trustfully expended in harnessing electricity and making it subservient to man for all sorts of uses and purposes, and one is struck with wonder at the skill shown in the design and construction of the various examples of modern machinery, both large and small, to be met with nowadays everywhere.

WHAT DOES IT ALL MEAN ?

The bees make honey like they did 30,000 years ago. They industriously go from flower to flower, and come home laden with honey, as they did when the Great Pyramid of Egypt was being built. But the man-made hives we provide for taking our share of their honey are not the same as the hives of the ancients. I think we can see that man, in his long process of evolution from small beginnings must, to get his daily bread, work his way upwards through all sorts and diversities of experience, and that the various phases he passes through from age to age while on the earth are Nature's way of teaching him and fitting him for higher planes of existence. The laws of Nature are inexorable. The secrets of Nature are always being deciphered by patient study and hard work and every discovery increases our knowledge.

The new power station at the Ivor Works is a very large and lofty building constructed of steel with brick panels. It contains the most modern machinery, which would take too long to describe. At this station electricity is generated at 6,600 volts, and distributed by means of an electrically operated control switchboard. In close proximity to the power house is the large new boiler house built entirely of steel, and containing four water-tube boilers fitted with chain grate stokers and super-heaters, and capable of evaporating 30,000 lbs. of water per hour at a pressure of 200lbs. per square inch. Power is supplied through an overhead transmission line 7 1/2 miles in length to the collieries at a working pressure of 6,000 to 6,600 volts. Power is supplied to the steelworks by means of underground cables, at a pressure of 6,600 volts to the various sub-stations, and is then transformed to give an alternating current of 400-400 volts to the many small motors, whereas the large motors are coupled direct to the 6,600 volts main. The Old Works power station below the Goat Mill is now (1925) a converting station.

Going from the Ivor Works to the Old Works we come to the blast furnace plant, which comprises four furnaces, two of which are charged mechanically by an inclined electric hoist. Three of the furnaces are 80 feet high; the other 70 feet. The blast temperature is 1,000 to 1,400 degrees Fah. There are sixteen Cowper hot blast stoves, ten of them 80 feet high.

Two of the American type of large blast furnaces and their blowing engines were erected about 1907, during the time of the general managership of the late MR.WILLIAM EVANS, who was a personal friend from 1873 until his death. The engines are housed in a fine building 174 feet long, 50 feet wide and 53 feet 6 inches high. There are three blowing engines of the vertical compound condensing quarter crank type with Corliss valve gear. They admirably perform their work, as would naturally be expected, the modern engine having a vastly higher efficiency than the old-fashioned heavy ponderous beam engine, which we used to so admire.

THE METAL MIXERS.

And now we come to the modern metal mixers, of which there are two of 120 tons capacity each and one having a capacity of 750 tons. I shall only deal with the large one. This huge leviathan of a machine will hold 750 tons of molten metal, which is poured into it from ladles holding 30 tons brought down by rail from the furnaces. It is fired by gas from three large gas producers. It is turned on its trunions by an overhead electrical 50 ton crane, which process seems almost as easy to accomplish as the winding of a watch. The molten metal from it is conveyed in ladles to the Bessemer plant by locomotive engines.

In connection with the electrification of the finishing mill, a large balancing room has been built, 95 feet by 70 feet by 24 feet 6 inches high, which contains machinery of the most interesting kind, including a forged steel fly-wheel weighing 30 tons, running at a speed of 600 revolutions per minute. It would take too long to describe the machinery and the meaning of this rapidly revolving fly-wheel and the motor-generator sets. The fly wheel will give up some of its stored energy as and when required for the economical running of this modern plant.

DOWLAIS LEAPS TO THE FRONT.

I must mention the railway steel sleeper plant, electrically driven, which will turn out 200 sleepers per hour. Long ago someone was inspired with the idea of the steel sleeper, as in tropical countries the white ant attacks and destroys timber sleepers. The design is now brought to a high state of perfection. Clever men have invented the shearing, pressing and hydraulic punching plant by which they can be economically made. This machinery worked by electrical power seems to run as smoothly and easily as the domestic process of making an apple dumpling.

As in the days of the invention of the Bessemer (process), so in these days of electrification, Dowlais leaps to the front.

The men who are responsible to the shareholders of the Company have, heaven knows, no easy task, but it seems to me that, beyond a shadow of doubt, they have adopted the wise and prudent course in modernising their Works. Otherwise, if they had lagged behind, the Works would have fallen into disrepute. A decrepit old age would have come upon them, and orders would flow to other modernised Works. It is our hope that they may reap their just reward and find ever increasing employment for the army of workmen.

THE SPIRIT OF CO-OPERATION.

We live in difficult times (1925) and, as I think, in times that can only be made less difficult by the adoption of a wholehearted and willing spirit of co-operation. We are all dependent on each other. 'One and all' the motto of the Cornishman, is a good one, for the whole of humanity is really a vast brotherhood. Nowadays we see many things which are very distressing, especially to those of us who believe that we are on the earth for the main purpose of doing 'Work while it is yet day'. 'What-soever thy hand findeth to do, do it with all thy might'. The tendency seems to be to obey the commandments of men more readily than the Commandments of God. 'Thou shalt not work too many hours or work too hard', on the face of it, is a command that could not possibly have been given by a god, or even by a hero. What is left to a man worth possessing if he thus deprives himself of his free will? 'Love thy neighbour as thyself' is in direct contradiction to the practice, and yet our hearts tell us the ideal is god-like.

Is the time coming, I wonder, when of necessity another Moses must arise to lead the people to other lovely distant lands, where untold riches cry out to be unearthed, and wild wastes cry out to be tilled and made use of to supply the needs of man, whose duty it is to courageously grapple with his problems of life, often so hard, in the spirit that should animate the inheritor of an immortal soul. Life is real; life is earnest. Let us do our best to make it joyful.

The President expressed the hope that when the general public read the able address, the workers would be re-inspired and take to heart the words of one so experienced as Mr. Harvey. He felt sure that the address would have great weight, not only with business men, but with the workers.

Councillor Isaac Edwards, in moving a vote of thanks to Mr. Harvey, expressed the belief that the address would be most valuable in years to come because of its interesting record. He complimented Mr. Harvey upon his ability, and mentioned the fact that many years ago Mr. Harvey was awarded a gold medal for a paper he read to the Institution of Civil Engineers.

Mr. A. Parfitt seconded, and Dr. W. W. Jones, in supporting, said huge changes had taken place in Dowlais with the desire to benefit the locality, and they all hoped that the Dowlais Company would meet with their due reward, and that the inhabitants would benefit thereby.

The proposition was carried unanimously, and Mr. Harvey, in returning thanks, referred to the Thomas Gilchrist basic process, in the experimental stage fostered by the late Mr. William Menelaus".

(*Merthyr Express*. 19.9.1925. p.14. col.3+4.)

CREDITS

Cyfarthfa Castle Museum and Art Gallery for permission to photograph Joseph Edwards' bust of George Thomas Clark.

BACHEN BACH O ABERFAN, ERIOED, ERIOED
A personal view of the history of Aberfan

by

RAYMOND JONES

"I am going to pack . . . and I am going from the Valley."

I freely admit that I have never been able to read beyond these words which begin and end the first paragraph of Richard Llewellyn's 'How Green Was My Valley.' The memory of my own departure many years ago, the pain of nostalgia and the 'hiraeth' that the words engender have always proved too powerful—and I cannot read on.

I don't know how common this feeling is, but I suspect that there must be many who have identified with Huw as he finally leaves his Welsh home. Certainly that famous musical son of Merthyr, Joseph Parry, who went 'Off to Philadelphia' always retained a very special place in his heart for his birthplace. Significantly, the nom-de-plume he chose for his winning entry in the 1863 National Eisteddfod in Swansea was 'Bachgen Bach o Ferthyr, Erioed, Erioed.' Though thousands of miles away in Pennsylvania, he remained a Merthyr Boy—for ever.

This is rather a tortuous way of justifying my choice of title. More simply I could have re-iterated James Baldwin's view that 'you can take the child out of the country, but you cannot take the country out of the child.' So, my starting point has to be this: no matter how long I've been away, and however far my journey has taken me . . . I am, and shall remain, always an 'Aberfan Boy.'

I was born and brought up in Aberfan during the 1930s and 40s. After leaving the village and in the intervening years I returned to visit friends and family frequently, subsequently with my Treharris-born wife and two sons. My younger son, Alistair, chose to study Aberfan for his 'O' level History project, and it was his research which led me to consider incorporating his account of the early beginnings of the village with some personal reminiscences of my life there in the mid Twentieth Century.

Beginnings

The earliest reference to the Aberfan area is said to exist in a Latin manuscript—the *'Cognatio de Brychan'* the earliest copy of which is to be found in a British Museum tract called *De Situ Brecheniauc* (Folio X). This has been dated at about 1200AD, and incorporates much earlier stories of Brychan and his family. The tract is in the famous Cotton Collection, and the Brychan material occurs in *Vespasion A xiv*—the original having been written in Brecon Priory.

From the *Cognatio* we learn that Brychan was born near Brecon, spending his early youth in military activities before succeeding his father as ruler of Garth Madryn (re-named Brycheiniog) around 400AD. Brychan may have had four wives and up to fifty children—estimates vary—but nearly all of his family became wandering holy men and women—'Saints'—living within religious communities.

The generally accepted, traditional story, and one which links Brychan with the Aberfan area, tells of Brychan, in old age, journeying from his court in Talgarth sometime around

ANNO TRICESIMO

Georgii III. Regis.

* *

C A P. LXXXII.

An Act for making and maintaining a Navigable Canal from *Merthyr Tidvile*, to and through a Place called *The Bank*, near the Town of *Cardiff*, in the County of *Glamorgan*.

WHEREAS the making and maintaining a Canal for the Navigation of Boats and other Veſſels from a Place called Merthyr Tidvile, in the County of Glamorgan, to and through a Place called The Bank, near to the Town of Cardiff, in the ſaid County, will open Communications with ſeveral extenſive Iron Works and Collieries, and be of publick Utility: And whereas ſeveral Perſons herein-after named are deſirous, at their own Expence, to make and maintain the ſaid Canal; but cannot effect the ſame without the Aid of Parliament: May it therefore pleaſe Your Majeſty that it may be enacted; and be it enacted by the King's moſt Excellent Majeſty, by and with the Advice and Conſent of the Lords Spiritual and Temporal, and Commons, in this preſent Parliament aſſembled, and by the Autho-

4 19 N 2 rity

73. Preamble of the Act making the Merthyr to Cardiff Canal.

450 to 480 AD to visit his third daughter, Tangwystl, at her summer residence, Hafod Tanglwys, in the environs of the present village of Aberfan. Having lingered a while, Brychan eventually left Tangwystl (on August 23) together with his twenty-third daughter Tudful and a few retainers, to be followed a little later by his sons, Rhawn and Rhun. Marauding Picts attacked the two sons, killing them both, but not before Rhun gallantly defended a small bridge over the River Taff. The bridge in Troedyrhiw bears his name—Pontyrhun—to this day. The barbarians devastated the farm at Hafod Tanglwys and then caught up with Brychan's small band, putting them to the sword. It is not certain where Tudful died, but there is a legend that she knelt and prayed devoutly, surrounded by her captors, before being brutally cut down. The popular belief that she was martyred is enshrined in the name Merthyr Tydfil—the resting-place of the martyr Tudful.

So, how reliable is the evidence which links Brychan with Aberfan and Tudful with Merthyr?

As previously stated 'the generally accepted, traditional story' links Brychan's daughter, Tangwystl, with the farm, which still exists in Aberfan, called Hafod Tanglwys, and this, if it's true, establishes the farm's date at around 450-480 AD. If it's true . . . !

Though most people, professional writers and lay, accept the traditional story, there has been doubt expressed by at least one academic.

In the 1980s my son contacted Dr Oliver Padel, currently at the University of Cambridge, but at that time the Place-Names Research Fellow of the University of Exeter's Institute of Cornish Studies, to check on the reliability of the story. The reply was surprising. Apparently the tract Cognatio de Brychan contains no reference to the Hafod Tanglwys story at all.

In fact it does not give Tanglwyst or Tangwystl, or anything like that as the name of a daughter of Brychan.

In P.C. Bartrum's "Early Welsh Genealogical Tracts" (pub: 1966) the name Taghwystyl is given as the name of one of Brychan's daughters, though *Padel* considers this to be a mistake *"since all other sources give that daughter's name as Tudwystl"* (*Padel* pers. com.). The source of the traditional story seems to be "The Lives of the British Saints" by S. Baring Gould and J. Fisher, published in four volumes, 1907-13. *Padel* considers this to be *"a very unreliable book."* In Volume 4, P.208 of that book the connection is made between Brychan's daughter, mistakenly named as Tangwystl, and the farm Hafod Tanglwys. Thus, from the apparent similarity of the daughter's name (Tangwystl) with the place name (Hafod Tanglwys), there grew a story which connected the two.

So is this compelling story an invention? a myth? or is it factually true? Scholars will, no doubt, continue to debate the issue. I'm inclined to follow the great traveller George Borrow's advice when confronted with a keen advocate of the "truth" of the story of another Welsh prince, Madoc. Borrow clearly regarded the Madoc story as a myth, but to those who fervently believed it to be true he said "the idea is a pretty one . . . therefore cherish it".

(Whatever view is taken of the Tangwystl connection with Aberfan, there is no dispute over Tudful's connection with Merthyr Tydfil.).

In my youth the farm at Hafod Tanglwys was one of at least three active farms in Aberfan. During the war years my mother and I visited the farm, from time to time. I recall the 'old fashioned' air of the place and the warm good nature of the farmer, Mr Fleming, and his wife. Some villagers suspected that the hard-working Mr Fleming, because of his 'foreign' accent, might be a German—and therefore, a spy! However, we all happily bought milk from him whenever he and his horse and cart visited our streets. Our jugs were filled from his ladle which dispensed creamy white milk from a large churn, with a little extra added at the end, for good measure. It turned out that Mr Fleming was, in fact, a Belgian and therefore an ally!!

Another farm, at Ynysygored, was an even more atmospheric place with its courtyard, large barns and lime kiln. Milk was delivered door to door from this farm, too. A third farm may have had a name—possibly Aberfan Farm or Perthygleision Farm—but in my youth it was always known as 'Hughes's Farm.' Mr Hughes and his sons were also familiar sights in the village delivering milk in their horse-drawn carts.

My son and I revisited these farms in 1982. At Hafod Tanglwys we met the owner, Mr Oliver, and his daughter. Repairs were being carried out to the low-slung buildings and we noted that the roof tiles were not of slate but, seemingly, of thick squares of local stone, millstone grit. It is tempting to speculate that this feature indicates a good age for the farm, but quite how old is not at all certain.

Ynysygored retained its highly individual air with its courtyard and windowless barns, long narrow slits being a feature shared by Hughes's farm, though the latter, like Hafod Tanglwys, retained thick millstone grit tiles on at least one building.

In 1982 Mr and Mrs Llywelyn Davies continued the family ownership of Ynysygored Farm, but at Perthygleision Farm, I was told, Mr Peter Hughes remained a 'tenant grazer' only.

So, how old are the farms of Aberfan?

Even if Hafod Tanglwys dates from 450-480 AD then there seems no further reference to it in Saxon or Norrnan times, nor in the Middle Ages. Perhaps John Leland, the king's widely-travelled antiquary, during a visit to Glamorgan in the 1530s, might have seen some cultivation in the Aberfan area when he wrote:

" . . . many hills and woods good plenty, but few villages or corn except in a few small villages about the river sides."

During the reign of Elizabeth I, from 1588, Protestant worship was conducted at local churches. Statutes were issued compelling attendance at the services. It appears that one small, roughly built church existed at Capel Y Fan at this time, overlooking Aberfan, and this might well have numbered among its worshippers farmers from Aberfan farms.

In later years (1877) a Baptist Chapel was established in Aberfan, but the first Baptist cause seems to be associated with Berthlwyd Farm some 3 or 4 miles from Aberfan, in the mid 17th Century. By the close of the 17th Century, according to Charles Wilkins, the celebrated Merthyr Tydfil historian, there were 93 farms in existence in the Merthyr area, with Hafod Tanglwys, Perthygleision and Ynysygored included in the list. There is also mention of an Aberfan Farm, and also of 'Jenkins of Aberfan, a Yeoman.'

Through old parish records Wilkins followed the progress of these farms after the rise of the iron and coal industries. There was clearly a substantial increase in the value of these farms—as judged by their rateable values—which may be a reflection of the existence of coal beneath the land. Wilkins compares the rateable values at three dates, as follows:

Farm	1769	1866	1905
Ynysygored	£8.0	£53.0	£47.7s
Pantglas	£1.0	£75.0	£42.10

Ynysowen	£9.0	£50.10	£50.10
Aberfan Fach & Fawr	£6.0	£90.0	£105.5s
Hafod Tanglwys Uchaf	£36.0	£74.0	£21.0s
Hafod Tanglwys Isaf			

The 1866 values form the high point, and by 1905, in the main, values had fallen, possibly due to some worked-out coal seams, or a drop in the value of coal. Wilkins lists five farms in Aberfan during this period with two of them, at some stage, subdivided into 'small' and 'large' (Fach and Fawr) or 'upper' and 'lower' (Isaf and Uchaf). My childhood memory is only of one Hafod Tanglwys farm, and this is the one that survived the disaster in 1966 and appears on maps as H.T. Isaf (the upper) which I last visited in 1982.

The first habitation destroyed in the disaster was Hafod Tanglwys Uchaf which I had always regarded as a smallholding rather than a farm. It was known locally as 'The Ranch' and its well-known resident was always affectionately known as 'Maggie the Ranch.' I think the owner was Mr Morgan Thomas.

Wilkins' researches suggest that if there was an Aberfan community in the early 18th Century it probably consisted of a few scattered farms only. However, in the second half of the 18th Century many changes were in store for Aberfan: Canals, Railways, Coal mines and an Iron Industry all exerted a formative influence in the growth of Aberfan.

The Industrial Revolution was in full swing in Merthyr from the mid-1800s onwards, with the great Iron works of Dowlais, Cyfarthfa, Plymouth and Penydarren in production on a grand scale. However, much more modest furnaces were, it seems, in operation over 200 years earlier—and very close to Aberfan.

There is good evidence of a works at nearby Pontyrhun (owned by a Mr Thomas Erbury) in 1625, and it is possible that a furnace existed a few miles in the other direction at Pontygwaith. The name implies that a "works" (gwaith) was there at some time, though there is some confusion over its location.

The coming of the Great Ironmasters to Merthyr from 1867 onwards created prodigious enterprises which were to have a direct influence on the growth of Aberfan. Initially this effect was concerned with transport and communications and took the form of a Canal that was to pass directly through Aberfan at the side of Ynysygored Farm and a short distance below Hafod Tanglwys Farm.

The production of iron in Merthyr required a means of transportation to the coast, and at first this was by way of pack animals over the mountains to Gelligaer and Caerphilly and then on to Cardiff. When a road was built on the Valley floor in 1776 this enabled wagons to be used. These were drawn by four horses, attended by a man and a boy, and carried only two tons of finished iron.

This was a slow and costly means of transport, probably reducing the Ironmasters' profits by as much as £14,000 a year.

New techniques for smelting were developed around 1787 and this led to a rapid increase in output and the need for greatly improved transport. The growth of the population, too, meant that feeding, clothing and supplying essential goods and materials posed an increasing problem. The solution was sought in the construction of a Canal, and the initiative for this bold venture may well have come from Francis Homphrey who was familiar with the Staffordshire and Worcestershire Canal in the 1870s.

301

After an initial survey, "An Act for making and maintaining a Navigable Canal from Merthyr Tidvale to . . . Cardiff" (Pic. 73) received Royal approval on 9th June 1790. The Canal was opened in 1794 and was 25.5 miles long, with 51 locks rising 543 feet, a short tunnel and a *"stupendous and inspiring aqueduct"* over the Taff at Abercynon. One of the locks at Aberfan, at 14' 6" tall, was said to be the highest in the country. In February 1794 it was reported that *"The Canal . . . is completed and a fleet of Canal boats have arrived at Cardiff . . . to the great joy of the whole town. The Canal . . . passes along the sides of stupendous mountains."*

This proved to be one of the most profitable of the Welsh Valley Canals, and between the years 1817 and 1840 over 1,734,316 tons of iron were carried on the Canal as it passed through Aberfan. Compared with the old road transport of iron, the Canal was highly efficient. Whereas one wagon by road, could carry a 2-ton load, a single horse could pull a 24-ton barge along the Canal. However, another form of transport was 'gathering steam'— the Railways, and these, together with structural problems with the Canal, meant a decline in the use of water transport. Tonnage carried progressively dropped; in 1871 the general traffic level passing through Aberfan stood at 284,041 tons, but by 1897 it was a meagre 31,113 tons. In 1898 the section from Abercynon via Aberfan to Merthyr was closed, and by 1906 'had fallen into complete disuse, *(and) . . . not a vestige of a Canal boat was to be seen.'*

During its heyday the Glamorganshire Canal trade passing through Aberfan must have had a considerable impact. There is mention in the literature of 'The Red Cow Inn' being built in Aberfan, on the banks of the Canal just below Hafod Tanglwys Farm. I can imagine that such a hostelry must have served the needs of the bargees and Canal traders in their frequent journeys via Aberfan.

In 1886 the Rhymney Railway was built and this could have aided in the demise of the 'Red Cow Inn.' Its railtrack passed very close to the Canal near Hafod Tanglwys Farm and its construction might well have obliterated all traces of the Inn. But this is conjecture and I can recall no evidence of any building in that area that could have served as an Inn in times past.

Throughout my childhood the Canal was but a narrow waterway, at most two or three feet wide. The rest of the Canal was largely grassed over, and the raised towpath remained on the village side of the Canal. The 'Canal Bank' was a favourite summertime Sunday evening walk for courting couples and families, and the stretch up the valley to Troedyrhiw was an idyllic playground for village children making 'camps' in the trees around the old waterway. The 'Canal Bank' walk also continued in the opposite direction past Bryntaff and on to the remains of the lock at Perthygleision and the far end of the village.

I recall seeing a family of stoats on one childhood trip to the mountainside beyond 'Perthy', and the Canal itself was always a good source of frogs and of a most strange water creature with awesome jaws and upturned abdomen which I later discovered was the carnivorous larva of the Great Diving Beetle.

Another historical event which literally by-passed Aberfan was concerned with the journey of the famous Trevithick locomotive.

Tramroads were being built in Merthyr even before the Canal was opened. The main purpose was to link the Ironworks with the Canal and also to connect the limestone quarries with the Canal.

In 1802 a significant tramroad was built from Abercynon to Penydarren for horse-drawn wagons to convey goods to waiting barges. It was on this tramroad, on 21 February, 1804, that Richard Trevithick's steam locomotive travelled for 9.5 miles, pulling a 10 ton load plus 70 men in or on 5 wagons. The 500 guinea wager between Samuel Homphrey and Anthony Hill (or was it with Richard Crawshay?) is well documented and provided the spur—or should it be the 'spark'?—for *the novel application of steam by means of this truly valuable machine.*

A report of the great event in the "Cambrian" ends *It is not doubted that the number of horses in the kingdom will be considerably reduced, and the machine, in the hands of the present proprietors, will be made use of in a hundred instances never yet thought of for an instant.*

I don't know about the first prediction but certainly the use of steam power was, indeed, to have many future, unsuspected applications, not least that successfully pioneered by George Stevenson in the years ahead.

Trevithick, a fellow Celt, has, over the years, assumed the status of honorary Welshman, and there is no denying the importance of his innovative use of steam to haul passengers along a fixed track. Of course, his locomotive did not actually pass through Aberfan. The tramroad was laid through Merthyr Vale, the sister village on the other side of the Taff. But there can be little doubt that Aberfan residents witnessed the earth-shaking event and marvelled with all the other onlookers.

The old tramroad is still visible in places today in Merthyr Vale as it was in my youth and, no doubt, remains a calm and quiet walkway for local residents on balmy summer evenings. It also fulfils a similar function in nearby Edwardsville—significantly within sight of the modern Diesel railway track.

Later, and despite Trevithick's famous journey in 1804, it was the Canal that assumed the very greatest significance in transporting iron and other goods past Aberfan. In 1832 the combined output of Guest in Dowlais, Crawshay (Cyfarthfa), Thompson (Penydarren) and R. & A Hill (Plymouth) exceeded 263,000 tons of iron, and all of this was carried on the Canal.

But in that very year (1832) William Crawshay made a far-seeing prediction when he wrote *I believe Railways are better than Canals and will supersede them.*

Despite the powerful opposition of the Canal Company, the Taff Vale Railway Company Act received the Royal Assent in 1836 thus incorporating the first public railway of any commercial importance in the Principality. The pre-amble of the Act stated:

> " . . . the making of a Railway from Merthyr Tydfil to Cardiff . . . would be of great public convenience by opening an additional, certain and expeditious Means of Conveyance to the sea for the extensive Mineral and other Products (of the Iron works of Pen-y-darren, Dowlais and Plymouth and the Collieries of Lancaich (sic) and Dinas"), also for the Conveyance of passengers and Goods to and from the said towns of Merthyr Tydfil and Cardiff, and the several intermediate and adjacent Towns and Districts."

The main line was opened in 1841, and one of the *"several intermediate and adjacent Districts"* namely Merthyr Vale, had its own station on 1 June, 1883. Whoever was employed as Stationmaster (in my youth this was an Aberfan man) had to abide by the strictest rules—there were 800 of them—promulgated by the Taff Vale Company:

12. -Every person is to come on duty daily, clean in his person and clothes, shaved, and his shoes blacked.

26. -It is urgently requested every person . . . on Sundays and Holy Days, when he is not required on duty, that he will attend a place of worship; as it will be the means of promotion when vacancies occur.

40. -Not any instance of intoxication, singing, whistling or levity, while on duty will be overlooked.

277. -All persons, especially those in uniform, are to keep their hair cut.

428. -No person can become a Station Master . . . unless he is married.

The Taff Vale became amalgamated with the Great Western in 1922, and then became part of the Western Region of British Railways in 1948. In the late 90s it reverted to private ownership under the Government's Privatisation Initiative. The line (now a single track) still runs along the east bank of the Taff opposite Aberfan.

By 1854 the Rhymney Railway was incorporated and by 1886 connected Aberfan directly with Merthyr and Cardiff. By the 1930s 'bus travel increasingly attracted traffic away from the railways, and by the early 1950s the Rhymney line from Merthyr to Taffs Well via Aberfan was closed. My own memory of travelling on this Rhymney line is an affectionate one. From 1943 I caught the train, daily, from Aberfan (almost always frantically and breathlessly running up Station Hill in the mornings) to Quakers' Yard Upper Level Station, via the quaint and forlorn Pontygwaith Halt, en route to Secondary School. If I missed the train then there was the trek across the Park to catch the later, Lower Level train from Merthyr Vale.

During the war years the morning train from Aberfan was packed with factory workers travelling to produce munitions and other vital war-related products in the Treforest Trading Estate and other factories. Towards the end of my years in Quakers' Yard Secondary (later Grammar) School the journey to school from Aberfan was undertaken by Merthyr Corporation 'buses. This was a much less attractive mode of transport but it didn't entail that last-minute dash up Station Hill since the 'bus ran from Aberfan Square (on the flat!) and delivered us virtually at the school gates in Edwardsville.

Today the Aberfan Railway Station is derelict and the old track has become a walkway.

Whilst the coming of the Railways and the Canal might have contributed to the 19th Century growth of the Aberfan settlement, there is no doubt that it was the sinking of the pit which made a flourishing village of Aberfan.

John Nixon of Durham came to Wales in 1840 to make a mineral survey in the Merthyr area. He eventually selected a site in the valley bottom where the River Taff separated Aberfan and Merthyr Vale and began sinking Merthyr Vale Colliery on 23 August 1869.

After five and a half years, and with very many problems to overcome, the sinkers reached the four-foot seam; the first coal was raised on 4 December 1875.

However, there is evidence that coal was being obtained from the Aberfan area as early as 1842 from a level at Danyderi—a name which I associate only with a farm on the mountainside on the Troedyrhiw side of Merthyr Vale. There is also a record of 4000 tons of coal being raised in 1861 at Perthygleision Colliery, Aberfan, but I don't recall any mention of the existence of such a Colliery eighty or so years later.

Nixon's Merthyr Vale pit had a number of notable features, one being Nixon's own patent ventilator with three huge exhausting pistons removing 444,000 cubic feet of air per minute

74. Nixonville 1982. Through the gap and above the roofs of Aberfan Crescent, the Cemetery.

75. The Colliery, Merthyr Vale, 1908.

from the workings. Also, the large gas discharges from the coal seams were piped to the pit-top and used to heat boilers. This was a successful experiment devised by Colonel Gray (Colliery Agent) and Major Gray and which, reputedly, saved one hundred tons of coal, weekly. The No. 1 Pit winding engine was originally built for Her Majesty's Warship 'Gibraltar' but bought and adapted for use in Merthyr Vale by John Nixon.

A long, curved row of terraced houses was built opposite the pit entrance and aptly named Nixonville (Pic 74) to accommodate the ever-increasing workforce—over 1800 in 1892 and almost 3,500 by 1907. Coal output rose in these years from 536,631 tons to 852,418 tons, and as well as being highly productive, the pit had, for its time, a good safety record. (Pic 75).

John Nixon retired in 1894 and the new manager was Major W. Bell (the hill to the Railway Station in Merthyr Vale still bears his name) and under his guidance the pit became one of the largest in South Wales.

The growth of the sister villages of Aberfan and Merthyr Vale in the last quarter of the 19th Century is interestingly reflected in entries to be found in Worrall's Directory of 1875 and the Kelly's Directory of 1884 and 1895.

In the 1875 entry only a very brief mention is made of Merthyr Vale (*a rapidly rising village in Merthyr parish*), and none at all of Aberfan.

In 1884 Merthyr Vale's population is given as 3,605 and '*The church at Ynysowen (Merthyr Vale) is a stone building originally erected by Messrs Nixon & Co. Colliery proprietors, for the Presbyterians, but owing to the absence of any congregation, it has been temporarily lent to the Church of England.*' This building remained as a Church of England (later Church in Wales) place of worship until the disaster in 1966 after which a new building replaced it on the same site. Ynys-y-gored is mentioned as being one of the '*principal seats*', with John Bishop Esq JP listed alongside.

There was in 1884, also, a Board School (Mixed) at Merthyr Vale with E. Thomas, Master and A. B. C. Dunnett, Infants' Mistress. The Rev. Richard Morgan Williams, the curate-in-charge, was conducting services at Merthyr Vale C. of E. Church on Sundays at 11 a.m. and 6 p.m. and on Thursdays at 7.30 p.m. Various non-conformist chapels (Baptist, Calvinistic Methodist, Wesleyan and Congregational) had become established at this time in nearby Troedyrhiw, 2 miles away.

Although not mentioned in Kelly's 1884 entries, various chapels were, in fact, built in Aberfan before this date—notably Capel Aberfan (Welsh Independent Methodist) in 1876 and Smyrna (Welsh Baptist) in 1877.

Kelly's entries for 1885 are much fuller reflecting considerable growth in the Aberfan community. The Chapels listed now include Calvaria (Welsh Baptist) in Merthyr Vale, Aberfan Capel (Welsh Calvinistic Methodist), Merthyr Vale (English Calvinistic Methodist), Aberfan (English Congregationalist) and Bethania (Welsh Congregationalist). A Primitive Methodist (English) and also a Wesleyan Chapel are listed for Merthyr Vale.

The Church of England cause, Ynysowen (Merthyr Vale) had a new curate, the Rev. Henry Edward Thomas of St Aidan's.

Mr E. Thomas remained as headmaster of the Merthyr Vale (Mixed) Board School which had been built in 1879 for 700 children. However, the Infants' mistress was now Miss Margaret Edwards. The average attendance in 1895 was: Mixed 312, Infants 132. A new Infants' School had been built in Aberfan in 1891 for 200 children and four years later the average attendance was 100.

Both Railway Stations were fully functional, each with its own Stationmaster, Mr John Davies (Aberfan, Rhymney & Great Western) and Mr William Churchill (Merthyr Vale, Taff Vale)

The Glamorganshire Canal and its officers are also listed in Kelly's Directory for 1895. Nixon's Colliery output is given as being *"upwards of 13000 tons per week"*, and the following entry reflects local diversity in industrial enterprise: *"There is also an iron foundry and a small nail manufactory, and brewing and flannel weaving are also carried on here."*

A most revealing indicator of Aberfan's growth is to be seen in Kelly's list of Commercial establishments in the village. A mere twenty years after the first coal was raised there were over fifty shops and similar premises providing essential services to the expanding village population.

Nine butcher shops and eight grocers existed together with tailors, boot-makers, a baker, a teacher of music, a milliner, a china dealer, two hairdressers, three hoteliers, a (lady) tinsmith, an ironmonger, a gasworks manager, a timber and stone merchant, a stationer and paper-hanging dealer and two coffee tavern owners. In addition there was a physician and surgeon (shared with Troedyrhiw), a Police Sergeant, two Station Masters and a Sergeant-Instructor of the "3rd Vol. Batt. Welsh Reg. E. Co.", together with a Major and two Captains.

A number of farmers are listed with one doubling as sexton of the cemetery interestingly, the owner of nearby Hafod Tanglwys Isaf Farm.

76. Smyrna Chapel, Aberfan.

Of the shopkeepers listed in 1895 three names, in particular, were familiar to me in the village fifty years later. I recall a Mrs Maddock's shop still in existence in the 1940s and 50s, and Lewis James was still in the grocery business in Perthygleision. Llewellyn Jones' drapers' shop was the subject of many a household story in my youth. My mother often recalled details of the pre-war establishment; apparently, the owner, whenever a customer entered the shop, would summon one of her assistants to serve the newcomer with the words "Forward, Miss Shears!" I have a hazy memory of the long, dark shop where the "change hummed on wires," but that may be fanciful on my part!

Not surprisingly, there is a preponderance of Welsh names amongst the 'commercials'— Davies, Edwards, Evans, Hughes, Jenkins, Jones (5), Parry, Prosser, Rees and Williams; but in the years that followed, Aberfan was to experience an influx of English and other immigrants, including the Irish, Jews and Italians.

The main dichotomy was, of course, in the language of the residents of Aberfan. This is well illustrated by the establishment of local chapels; almost always an English denomination matched a Welsh one. The very first chapel seems to have been Capel Aberfan— the Welsh Independent Methodist Chapel which was built in 1876. This had a predominantly North Welsh congregation as late as the 1950s and I assume that the original founding fathers probably hailed from the 'Gogledd' (The North). Zion English Primitive Methodist Chapel came into being in 1889. This remained a modestly sized chapel throughout its life and was—and is—familiarly known as "Small's Chapel" because of its association with a respected local family which was the mainstay of that particular place of worship.

Literally next door to Zion stood the Church of Christ for many years, but alas, it no longer exists.

In 1877 Smyrna Welsh Baptist Chapel was built, a much larger extension being added in 1901. Smyrna holds a very special place in my affections; I was born beneath the Chapel. (Pic 76).

This needs an explanation.

My aunt at this time was the Chapel caretaker and lived in Smyrna Cottage which was sited, literally, beneath the original structure known as Smyrna Vestry. Evidently, my mother had a home confinement in Smyrna Cottage where her sister, my aunt, looked after her.

Having been born in such close association with Smyrna it is not surprising that I attended its Sunday School and became a baptised member of the church at the age of 16. Smyrna was a formative influence on my life as it and other chapels were for so many of my contemporaries. Chapels were a focal point for all sorts of cultural as well as religious activities in the village. Most had their own drama group and I well recall Smyrna's productions in the Aberfan Hall of *"The Passing of the Third Floor Back," "Yellow Sands"* and, that great favourite of amateur dramatic groups, *"The Monkey's Paw."*

The Sunday School movement played a vital part in community life throughout Wales during, and well before my time, of course, but I would want to identify its very profound part in my own upbringing. With portraits of the great Baptist preachers keeping us under their formidable and be-whiskered gaze, we Sunday School 'scholars' learned our Welsh alphabet, rejoiced in singing Welsh hymns and sat, spellbound, at great stories of missionary endeavour in darkest Affica. The story of Mary Jones and the Welsh Bible, that most favourite of Sunday School stories, was coupled with stories from the Bible which were used to inculcate in us the importance of good as opposed to bad behaviour and of the fundamental and absolute values of right and wrong. Sabbatarianism, too, was part of the

77. Brynhyfryd Chapel, Treharris, 1994.

package, and if ever I was tempted to buy ice-cream or sweets on a Sunday, my Sunday School teacher's entreaties were enough to make me desist or, at least, to feel guilty if I did succumb! This imperative stayed with me well into adult life and, to a certain extent, is still there.

Sunday School taught us Christian virtues and social skills. We saved diligently in the 'bank' and learned to recite and sing in public during the 'Anniversary' services just before the annual outing to Barry Island or to Porthcawl. As Sunday School Secretary I had the responsibility of securing the 'bus to take us to the sea-side and also of negotiating a menu and a price for a meal for all the scholars at the 'Merrie Friars' in Barry.

The 'Gymanfa Ganu' held each year in Brynhyfryd chapel, Treharris, brought together all the Welsh Baptists, adults and children, in the lower end of the Borough for a marvellous festival of singing. In my early childhood this event clashed with the very secular 'Fete & Gala' at Cyfarthfa Park on Whit Monday, but as the years went by there really was 'no contest' in my mind and I looked forward with great eagerness to the 'Gymanfa' as one of the highlights of the year. (Pic. 77).

There were also inter-denominational meetings within the village. During the war years (1939-45) Celebrity Concerts were held periodically—and always on a Sunday evening after the normal services of worship. Most of my memories are of packed congregations in the original Zion English Baptist Chapel. Here, predominantly local artists would entertain, but from time to time we were privileged to hear performances by visitors who were to become world-famous in later years. Kathleen Ferrier was one such distinguished visitor.

Chapels continued to play a vital part in village life late into the 20th Century, and history will record their important role, particularly at the time of the Disaster.

The Merthyr Tydfil Schools Board having come into being in 1871 had, as its first task, an assessment of the numbers of children currently living in the area. Only when this figure was accurately known could plans be drawn up for the provision of an appropriate number of schools.

In its Triennial Report of 1874 the need to provide school places for 10,434 children was identified:

> *"To meet this requirement there was accommodation in efficient elementary schools already existing, and in immediate contemplation, for 6,654, leaving a deficiency of 3,780 to be provided by the Board."*

By the late 1870s, so the Third Triennial Report confirms: *"Merthyr Vale has developed sufficiently to demand that school accommodation be provided there."* On land leased from Lord Windsor *"Substantial school buildings for the accommodation of 700 children in two departments, mixed and infants have been erected thereon."* The schools were opened on 31 October 1879. By the end of the year there were 377 children on the Registers and the average attendance was 77.18% (291 children).

In the Returns cited in the Fourth Triennial Report of 1883, of the 398 children on the Registers only 280 were *"in average attendance"*, that is a reduced percentage of 70.35 at Merthyr Vale Board school.

The Sixth Triennial Report of 1889 records *"A considerable number of houses have recently been built at Aberfan, and the Board . . . were urged to make school provision for the Infants there. As a temporary expedient, the Board obtained . . . sanction for the use of the Welsh Baptist (Smyrna) Chapel for the infants only on the Aberfan side of the River."* Places for 60 children were thus made available on 10 December 1889. In fact 58 children were on the Register but only 32, on average, actually attended (55.17%). The Merthyr Vale average attendance was 73.92% (394/533).

Schools were assessed by HMI for the Merit Grant as 'Excellent', 'Good' or 'Fair' and, happily, Merthyr Vale Mixed School received 'Excellent' grades for each of the years 1886, 1887 and 1888. The Infants' School was judged to be 'Good' in 1886 but 'Excellent' in the other two years. Around this time one report of the Infants' School states *"The children are under thorough control and the singing and marching are well executed. The . . . introduction of dual desks has proved a decided gain."* The Eighth Triennial Report of 1895 gives details of the opening of the new Infants' School at Aberfan (at a cost of £1,449) on 1st May 1893 to accommodate 200 children. *"The additional buildings for the Merthyr Vale district is now chiefly on the Aberfan side of the river, and the school is in consequence well attended."*

From 1891 to 1894 average attendance at Merthyr Vale Mixed School was also good, rising annually from 245 to 276 to 312. Merthyr Vale Infants' figures, however, were not so good, dropping from 153 to 136 and 132 by 1894.

The Tenth Triennial Report encompasses the end of the 19th Century and the start of the 20th Century. In 1901 it states: *"ABERFAN:—Owing to the growth of this district, further school accommodation becomes necessary.* **A site has been selected in the field between the Rhymney Railway and the Aberfan Road,** *on which may be placed a school to accommodate some 300 children."*

This decision was to have tragic consequences. This was the Pantglas School that was destroyed in the Disaster. The Aberfan Mixed School, as it was initially known, was built in the early 1900s on land leased from Messrs Wingfield and Mackintosh (their names being given to two of the side streets off the Aberfan Road).

"The school buildings (for 350 boys and girls)—a credit to all concerned—were formally opened on 8 June and the children received on the following morning." (Sites & Buildings Committee Report).

The population of the Merthyr District was growing by one thousand a year in the early part of the 20th Century and the rapid expansion of primary school provision included Pantglas Girls' and Infants' schools which were opened in 1908.

I can find no further evidence of new schools being built in Aberfan after this date (except for the one built on the Park after the Disaster), though I do recall the re-organisation of the two schools on the upper and lower Pantglas sites in August, 1940. Following the Hadow Report, the lower school at Pantglas (formerly the Girls & Infants' School) became a 'Modern' School to provide for Senior children who were not attending the selective school. It remained as a Secondary Modern School until the Disaster. The old Pantglas Boys' School became the Junior and Infants' School on the upper site. I recall that during the war children of all ages could attend the Secondary School canteen for lunch throughout the school holidays. Thick lentil soup and chunks of bread seem to have been standard fare, if my memory doesn't deceive me! I don't remember having any school meals at Pantglas Junior school (though I did have daily milk) so, no doubt, the catering facility for both schools was concentrated on the lower site.

78. Bryntaf Jazz Band rehearsing in Kingsley Terrace, Aberfan.
    Photo courtesy Mr. I. Conti.

311

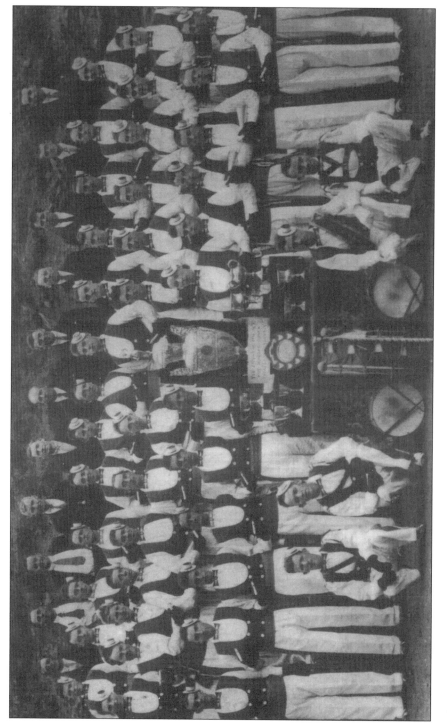

79. Aberfan Coons Jazz Band, British & Colonial Champion 1934.

Our family home at 15 Moy Road and later at 8 Moy Road was opposite the school at Pantglas and I have the happiest memories of my time in the Infants' class with Miss Morgan (although I never was chosen to ride the marvellous rocking horse!) and then in the Junior School under the concerned tutelage of 'Florrie' Havard, Tom Jenkins, Jack Evans and Idwal Evans. I recall two Headmasters, W. J. (Slogger) Williams, a formidable character who was also a deacon and precentor at Smyrna, and Arthur James.

Prior to starting my College Teacher Training course in 1953 I returned to Pantglas Junior School for a fortnight's teaching practice attachment. My direct memories of that school, therefore, are deep, varied and indelible.

For most of the 20th Century the coal mine was the centre around which Aberfan and Merthyr Vale grew. Coal production, population expansion and provision of schools were inextricably linked—and these factors came together in the tragic events of 1966.

By 1911 Merthyr Vale Colliery employed 3,421 men with an output in excess of 610,000 tons. This was typical of the wave of prosperity for collieries in the Merthyr area. It was a period of economic success reflecting substantial numbers in employment and large amounts of coal being mined. This growth was not sustained, however, and by 1920 there was a rapid decline in the coal industry. Many local collieries closed but the deeper and more modern collieries at Merthyr Vale and Treharris were able to survive until late in the 20th Century.

The General Strike of 1926 affected all miners' families throughout South Wales, and Aberfan had its share of hardship and poverty at this time. Huw Williams' article on the General Strike in the Merthyr Historian Volume 2 gives a penetrating account of the impact of *"this single most important event in the industrial history of Great Britain this century"* on the local community. The Strike which lasted from May to November was a *"story of jazz bands, summer sports and soup kitchens."* It was also a story of families 'on the Parish', of men scavenging for coal on the spoil heaps above the villages and of valiant attempts to maintain human dignity against overwhelming odds.

My parents often recalled the marvellously sunny weather in the summer of 1926. Spirits and morale were maintained by a programme of sports and entertainments on a massive scale. The Aberfan and Merthyr Vale Strike Committee at the end of May and under the auspices of the Rechabite Hall Comedy Party organised a comic football match between single and married teams for a remarkable prize—a faggots and peas supper! It seems that there was a surplus left and so a challenge was thrown out to other teams to play for this unusual trophy.

Another highlight (and there were many) was the August Carnival procession at Cyfarthfa Park—*"the best show of its kind ever seen in the town."* The mile-long procession was headed by the Merthyr Vale Silver Band and the Town Ward Band and, no doubt, many jazz bands. One of the most famous jazz bands (Pic. 78) came from Aberfan, being largely, if not entirely drawn from Bryntaf, a street with very strong community bonds. At the height of its fame, early in the 1930s, the band won a national trophy at Crystal Palace which was brought back to the village in triumph and proudly retained for a year. (Pic 79).

None of the jazz bands survived World War II though there was a resurgence of the Bryntaf jazz band for a while in the post-1945 era. Later jazz bands which developed in the Valleys were quite different in style and manner and were entirely female in composition. The social scene constantly changes and produces appropriately different responses, it seems. The Bryntaf jazz band in its time attained unsurpassed levels of excellence and its achievements still burn brightly in the Village memory.

After the General Strike the pits re-opened and by December 1926 hundreds of men were signing up for work, daily, at Merthyr Vale colliery and at nearby pits. There was a general decline in the coal industry, thereafter, but Merthyr Vale colliery survived, remaining in private hands (Powell Duffryn in my father's time at the pit) up to Nationalisation in 1947. It was finally closed in 1989.

Undeniably the main reason for Aberfan's existence *was* the pit, and in my childhood almost every household in the village had at least one member associated with it. My grandfather and father worked there for the 'P.D's' and they, together with other miners, held no great affection for many of the officials; the 'Overman', it seems, quite literally had power of life and death over people's lives. Specifically, the name 'Otto' (I believe he was the manager, at one time) was not a popular name in our household! Despite these justifiably unpleasant associations, there was a great camaraderie among the men of the village, sharing as they did, daily dangerous working conditions. Topics of conversation always seemed to centre on the pit and were about 'clearing stents', the shift you were working, what seam you were in (Gellideg was a familiar one), and whether or not you were working in water.

The sight of miners returning from their shift still in their dust-laden working clothes, some wearing 'Yorks', and all with tin 'jacks' and 'tommy boxes' was familiar to me, at least until the advent of the pit-head baths. The baths were housed in a brand new building at Merthyr Vale, next to the canteen.

Miners, when not at work, would often sit in a characteristic crouching position on the pavement outside their homes, chatting together in small groups. I believe this semi-sitting posture was familiar in other mining communities all over Britain; it probably was adopted as a consequence of working underground in low and difficult seams. Whatever the reason, it certainly was a very familiar sight in Aberfan in the 1930s and 40s.

Another all-too-familiar sight was that of men, old before their time, fighting for breath as they walked around the village. The hills were a particular and ever-present obstacle and necessitated many stops and pauses on their part. 'Dust' they would explain as passers-by offered a friendly word, and dust, coal dust was indeed the cause of the pneumoconiosis and silicosis that afflicted so many men of my grandfather's and father's generations. My grandfather died of silicosis having once worked in the silica-rich coal seams around his original home of Gwaen-Cae-Gurwen. Other and different sights were to become familiar in Aberfan following the rapid population expansion in the early decades of the 1920s.

Kelly's Directories for 1914, 1920 and 1926 document the development of commerce in the village which is a revealing indicator of the diverse needs of the growing community.

By 1914 Aberfan's population was 8,551; there were three schools, two railway stations and a *"mission room seating three hundred."* The Colliery's output was 16,000 tons per week and some of the smaller industries mentioned in Kelly's 1895 entry remained—an iron foundry and also brewing and flannel weaving. Significantly, there were branches of five banks, including Lloyds, and a Carnegie Library. The number of doctors had doubled to two! and a manager had been appointed for a new enterprise, the Picture Palace.

The 1895 Kelly list included around 50 shops and similar commercial outlets. By 1914 there were over 80 establishments selling a wide range of goods and services: boots, clothes, groceries, newspapers, greengrocery, hats, bread, confectionery, tobacco, timber, jewellery, furniture and watches. Numerically the largest groups were: Shopkeepers 15,

Grocers 11, Butchers 9 and Bootmakers and Repairers 8. Familiar names: Lewis James and Llywelyn Jones remain from the 1895 listing, with a new entry in the form of 'Wm James Hairdresser'. Mr Jarnes' shop was still a busy barber's shop whilst I lived in Aberfan, being run at that time by his son, Wayne James who also featured in some of the Smyrna dramatic society's productions in the 30s and 40s. Harry Stone's butchers shop, too, remained from 1914 and was familiar to me forty years later.

In 1914 there were significant 'immigrants' into the Aberfan commercial community. H. Cohen (Clothier), Samuel Silvergleit (Furniture) and Izzy Sonn (Watchmaker) had their establishments in Aberfan Crescent, the last two being next-door neighbours at numbers 20 and 21.

By 1920 these three tradesmen are no longer included in Kelly's Directory for Aberfan; I have no personal memory of any Jewish businesses in the village in the following decades.

There had been, in fact, a Jewish presence in Merthyr from the early 19th Century; a Synagogue was built in 1852 and another in 1872. A Jewish Cemetery was created and first used in Cefn Coed in 1870. After the Pogroms in Russia there was an increase in Jewish immigration to Merthyr with some 200 to 300 families domiciled in the town by the early 1900s. It is said that there were Jews living in every village from Treharris to Dowlais at this time and this seems to be substantiated by the names in the Kelly entry for Aberfan in 1914.

A different type of tradesman was to appear in South Wales, predominantly in Glamorgan, from 1871 onwards and Aberfan was to benefit from the newcomers' enterprise and industry.

I am speaking, of course, of the coming of the Italians.

There is a certain amount of debate concerning the identity of the very first Italian immigrants to Wales. There is a widely held view that the first three Italian 'pioneer' families were the Bracchis, the Bernis and the Rabaiottis. The last two families had a lengthy association with Aberfan and long after the Bernis had left, to be succeeded in ensuing years by Rabaiotti, Viazanni and Emmanuelli, my parents still referred to the Italian ice-cream shop and café on Aberfan square as 'Berni's'. In fact, throughout South Wales, the Ice-Cream Parlours were universally referred to as 'Brachi's' which was a familiar generic term used for all such establishments irrespective of the names of their current owners.

The growth of the Italian community in South Wales (1881-1945) is marvellously documented in Colin Hughes' (1991) book 'Lime, Lemon and Sarsaparilla.' Considerable assistance was given to the author by a well-known Treharris resident Ino Conti, and I am delighted to acknowledge the advice and help given to me by Mr Conti in respect of his Italian forebears in the local villages.

So, how did Aberfan benefit from the coming of the Italians?

By 1914 the Berni Brothers had set up Refreshment Rooms in Merthyr Vale and at 13 Aberfan Road. Coupled with the rise of the Temperance Movement, the establishment of Italian Cafes was to have a vital social function. Their Temperance Bars served as a much-needed alternative to the numerous Public Houses in the Valleys, They were warm, cosy and welcoming and the proprietors allowed customers to linger for as long as they pleased over a 'raspberry and ice' or a cup of coffee. The coffee was produced from an imposing, gleaming urn often topped by a silver eagle; hot water and steam was always available, night and day, and though we didn't know it as such at the time, it was the forerunner of the Espresso Machine.

80. Luigi Conti and his wife at the door of their double-fronted shop in Aberfan Crescent about 1920. Photo courtesy of Mr. I Conti.

Most favoured by the village youngsters, of course, was the genuine, home-made Italian ice-cream, sold in cornets and wafers. Nothing has ever equalled that distinctive creamy taste on a summer's afternoon. Hot Oxo, Bovril and Vimto were also great favourites, particularly on a cold winter's day in Troedyrhiw when the Welsh League football match reached half-time. Mrs Rossi's shop stood at the entrance to the ground (The Willows), and we young supporters would stream down for Mrs Rossi or Peter to serve us with a 'thawing' brew.

By 1920 L. Berni had taken over the sole ownership of the Refreshment Rooms at 13 Aberfan Road and by 1926 Luigi Conti had set up as a Confectioner in Aberfan Crescent whilst the Rabaiotti Brothers had taken over the Refreshment Rooms on Aberfan Square. Some time later Luigi Conti had progressed to a double-fronted establishment which, as the photograph shows (Pic. 80) was both a Greengrocers and a Temperance Bar. A billiards table was located in the back room with another practice table in the basement. I am reliably informed that the billiard cues in the basement were used more for killing cockroaches ('black pats') than for playing billiards! (Cockroaches were all too common in the pit villages of South Wales. It was supposed that the insects arrived in the imported wooden pit props used in the Collieries. The miners were given a periodic allocation of 'blocks' derived from these props, to use as fire-wood in their homes. In this way the cockroaches found a warm hearth awaiting them in which they could thrive).

The War Years were obviously difficult for the Italian community. Next-door to the Café on Aberfan Square (run at this time by Albert Viazanni) there was an Italian-owned fish and

81. George Martin's shop, 1982, still in business after trading for more than sixty years.

82. George Martin's shop had ceased trading by 1998 and was a private residence.

chip shop. Mr Luigi Belli, his wife Louise and sister Ann worked very hard to provide what was an essential service to the Aberfan populace. Sadly, the quiet, industrious Mr Belli was classed as an alien and was interned, leaving the two ladies to run the shop on their own. They did this in exemplary fashion. There was a brother, Guido, who had obviously become naturalised since he served as a private in the British Army.

In later years the Ice-cream parlour on the Square was taken over by the Emanuelli family. I was interested to see that in the Channel 4 documentary (Video Workshop Production) made 25 years after the Disaster, the name of Pino Emanuelli (the son of the original owner) appeared in the programme's credits (Archive BBC Wales). Whilst there were these unfamiliar and exotic names being added to the register of Aberfan residents the predominant names of business people in 1926 remained Welsh. By this time there were 13 shopkeepers, 9 butchers and 7 boot & shoe sellers together with 3 fried fish establishments, an undertaker, a dentist and two doctors plus almost 50 other shops. Of those places listed in Kelly's 1926 Directory the following were still flourishing when I was in my 'teens, well into the middle of the Century: Mr Roberts' shoe repair shop in Aberfan Crescent, (Mr) Richards-the-Jeweller, as he was familiarly known, and Mr H. Small, plumber of Mackintosh Street. (Small's Chapel has already been mentioned and one of Mr Small's descendants, June (later Mrs Cyril Vaughan) was to play a notable part in the religious life of the Aberfan community in later decades, as ordained minister of Bethania Chapel.). George Martin's newsagency in Aberfan Crescent, listed in 1926, passed on eventually to his son Lionel and then, finally, to grandson Terry who was still running it when I visited the shop in 1982. (Pic 81).

During the war the shop provided an accumulator-charging service. Heavy glass, acid-filled accumulators provided the power to run our radio sets in that pre-transistor era and from time to time it was necessary to recharge them, and Mr Martin's shop did this—for a small 'charge'!

Later, mains-powered radio sets superseded the accumulator-driven sets. (When I attended Quakers' Yard Secondary School in the 1940s I found that the school bells ran off a precursor of the accumulator, called Leclanché cells).

By 1997 Mr Martin's Shop had ceased trading and had become an ordinary domestic dwelling as the photograph shows (Pic. 82).

Another well-established, local newsagent was Mr Johnny Thomas at 36, Aberfan Road. In the 1940s my family moved from 15, Moy Road to 36, Aberfan Road where we lived, literally behind the shop. Johnny Thomas was a great raconteur who had a marvellous Bel-Canto tenor voice which we often heard from the back of the shop. The Carl Rosa Opera Company, so it was said, was very interested in Johnny Thomas, but for whatever reason (and it may well have been his small stature which prevented his translation to the Opera Stage) Johnny remained a newsagent.

Earlier, in the 1920 Kelly listing, one of Aberfan's two doctors was a formidable Scot, Dr Richardson White. I can still recall his visit to our home in 1942 when he diagnosed the yellow jaundice which prevented me from taking the 11+ exams for Quakers' Yard School, that year.

Mrs (Dr) White was regarded a 'real lady' and dispensed medicines from a room adjacent to the consulting room in the Nixonville surgery. No prior appointments were made in those days; patients simply turned up and took their places on the long wooden benches, moving along progressively until the doctor's door was reached. A significant entry in 1926 was in the list of Private Residents in Aberfan. At that time the name of Rev Rowland Williams

318

appears. He was Smyrna's 'beloved pastor' for very many years and he, together with his daughter, who was my Sunday School teacher, had a profound influence on me and many of my contemporaries as we grew up in the village.

Smyrna, I learned, had been registered for the conduct of marriages ahead of other Baptist chapels in the locality. My wife's parents travelled up from Treharris in 1926 to become the very first couple to be married by Rev Williams in Smyrna. Later, my own parents were also married by the same minister in the same chapel.

Our family's links with the chapel were deep and varied. My mother often said she 'loved every stone' in Smyrna. I have no doubt at all that this affection was due in no small measure to Rev Williams' ministry there.

Aberfan has been wonderfully served over many decades by all of its ministers, and many residents will be ever-thankful for the caring work of people such as Rev Stanley Lloyd of Bethania, Rev Kenneth Hayes of Zion English Baptist Church and Rev June Vaughan of Bethania, particularly at the time of the Disaster.

More personal memories

I was born in 1931 and my early schooling was at the Pantglas Infants' and Junior schools. My grandfather, father and uncles worked as colliers at Merthyr Vale pit, and my mother before her marriage ran the household, caring for her invalid mother and acting as mainstay for her brothers when they lived at home and worked in the pit. My maternal grandparents had emigrated from Gwaen-Cae-Gurwen, initially setting up home in Mount Pleasant (Black Lion), Merthyr Vale, before moving to Moy Road, Aberfan.

I can only imagine the hardships endured by my parents who were typical of so many local families in the '20s and '30s amidst strikes and general deprivation. I have to say that I was shielded from it to the extent that none of it left any scars on me. Like so many youngsters we formed 'gangs', played on the Canal bank and the mountainside. We even slid down the tips on pieces of 'belting' (discarded conveyer belt from the underground workings) and generally led a carefree life. We saw farmers delivering milk, bakers on their bread rounds, and 'ash carts' clearing rubbish—all drawn by horses. Very few cars were in evidence in the village in the pre-war era; funerals were led by a motorised hearse but followed by mourners on foot. The Council's ash carts and the large dray horses were kept for many years in a compound in Pantglas and I can almost smell the hay as I recall it!

By the time I entered Secondary school in 1943 the war was an accepted fact of life. The effects of rationing for us all were minimised by our resourceful, self-sacrificing mothers, so that the main childhood hardship was a relative scarcity of sweets. Even this was overcome by some modest trading (some would classify this as black marketeering!) in D (1 oz) and E (2 oz) coupons from the Ration books, which were traded for alternative items—sometimes even for money!

Air-Raid warnings came via the wailing sirens, but the threat of invasion was to be signalled by the Colliery 'hooter.'

Village adults, tied as they were to the pit, became members of the LDV (later the Home Guard) the ARP and the WVS. Fire Watching with stirrup pumps at the ready was undertaken on a regular rota but no alarms seem ever to have been raised in Aberfan. I believe a 'rogue' land mine exploded on the mountain above the village and everyone went to view the crater, but that was the extent of our threat from the air. Of course, we heard the nightly drone of German 'planes as they flew to bomb Cardiff and Swansea, and for a while we

83. Civil Defence Volunteers, Aberfan, World War Two.

would inhabit the 'cwtch' under the stairs in lieu of a proper air-raid shelter until the 'all clear' was sounded and we could wearily return to our much more comfortable beds. Picture 83 reminds us of the villagers who acted as Civil Defence Volunteers in those dark days.

One immensely sad episode remains with me from the war years. It was one which I witnessed from Aberfan Park on a beautifully sunny day—it may even have been a Bank Holiday since my memory is of lots of people on the Park.

We heard and saw three aeroplanes which we thought were Spitfires, coming up the valley from the Treharris direction. The leading 'plane, flying low, was followed by the two other 'fighters' side by side. As they approached Mount Pleasant the wing tips of the two rear 'planes collided and both plummeted to earth. The solitary leading 'plane, initially unaware of this tragedy, flew on, only to return a short while later to search for the two lost aircraft. Our young minds immediately empathised with the surviving pilot as he returned alone to look for his lost comrades.

Perhaps the most significant influence on the socio-cultural life of Aberfan in the war years can be attributed not to the Germans but to the evacuees.

Predominantly from London, the children brought an awareness of metropolitan attitudes and styles of behaviour previously unknown to the Valley children. Whilst their accents initially set them apart the evacuees soon found themselves absorbed into local activities to which they contributed with vigour and enterprise. We local children learned a great deal from our new school friends, and these city dwellers occasionally learned something of 'country' ways from us. One incident stands out. On a trip up the mountain above the village, my friends and I met up with a pair of evacuees. Apparently the London lads had been sent out on a wimberry-picking expedition and had been told that the berries grew high up on the hillside. They obviously thought that wimberries grew on trees and so had climbed all the available trees looking for the elusive fruit.

Some mothers were also evacuated and entered the life of the village in ways which did not always meet with universal approval. In the early forties the prevailing attitude amongst very many Aberfan residents was not favourable to women visiting public houses. Men could and did frequent pubs and clubs in the village, and this was accepted. But when the lady evacuees followed their normal social practice of going down to local public houses in the evenings, this was severely frowned upon by many of their Aberfan hosts!

No doubt our visitors had their own views about us, too!

In retrospect, all of this was a marvellous illustration of the way people's traditional attitudes, beliefs and values can be challenged—and accommodated. Certainly, things were never quite the same in Aberfan after the evacuee experience.

One of my final memories of the war concerns the events of VE Night. As soon as peace was declared we spontaneously marched in long 'crocodiles', singing and dancing along Aberfan Road. We were led by our minister's daughter brandishing the hand bell she used every week in Smyrna Sunday School!

Immediately after the war my focus increasingly centred on Quakers' Yard Secondary School. This school was actually built after World War I to provide a new secondary school at the lower end of the valley. (Merthyr's Cyfarthfa and Intermediate Schools were, it seems, very crowded). A temporary structure was brought to Edwardsville, consisting of 13 Army huts, purchased for £1300 and brought from Salisbury Plain to be re-erected by unemployed ex-servicemen. The school was ready to receive its first pupils in January, 1922, and temporary though the buildings were, remained fully functional until replaced by Afon Taff High School in Troedyrhiw on August 30 1967.

Quakers' Yard Grammar School, as it became known in consequence of the 1944 Education Act, received many youngsters from Aberfan and Merthyr Vale, and a fair proportion progressed to Further and Higher education. Many became school teachers whilst others entered a wide range of other professions.

Three former pupils from the two villages attained distinguished academic status. My long-time friend, Trefor Jenkins, became Professor and Head of the Department of Human Genetics at the South African Institute for Medical Research, in Johannesburg's University of the Witwatersrand. Professor Bernard John, after holding the Chair of Biology at Southampton University, progressed to become Head of the Research School of Biological Sciences at the Australian National University, Canberra. Thirdly, Merthyr Vale's Ronald Mason became Professor Sir Ronald Mason KCB FRS, and for a time was Chief Scientific Adviser at the Ministry of Defence in Whitehall.

No doubt the list could now be enlarged, but suffice to cite these contemporaries as an illustration of one kind of excellence stemming from the twin villages of Aberfan and Merthyr Vale.

My links with Aberfan became less regular after qualifying and moving away, firstly to complete National Service, and then to take up various teaching and lecturing posts in Dorset, Devon and West Africa.

It is not appropriate for me to write in any detail about the Aberfan Disaster. I was not there and I can't presume to offer any insight into the situation faced by the people who had

84. Central Café (left) formally owned by a succession of Italian traders. Still serving the community in 1998 as the Megabytes Café.

85. Smyrna Chapel, Aberfan.

to live through the dreadful events and their aftermath. Of course, I share in the grief; it is a miracle that the village has managed to emerge into the sunlight once more.

The release of documents from the Public Records Office in 1996 under the thirty year rule has, at last, revealed just how heartless and callous many of those in high office really were. The evidence is there, now, for all to see.

On 1 August 1997 an "Historic wrong" was put right when the Labour Government announced that the £150,000 wrongfully taken from the Disaster Fund to contribute to the removal of the tips was to be repaid.

After the Disaster the Coal Mine was never again to hold its pre-eminence in the lives of Aberfan people. The strikes of 1972, 1974 and in particular that of 1984 heralded the demise of Merthyr Vale Colliery; in 1989 the pit was finally closed.

Aberfan was born as a scattering of farms possibly 1500 years ago. In the 19th Century and within a span of 150 years it became part of the Industrial Revolution with the flourishing Glamorgan Canal traversing its boundaries. It was to share with Merthyr Vale two railways and one of the most productive coal mines in South Wales.

Now, as the Millennium approaches, there is little evidence that the Canal, the Aberfan Railway or the Colliery ever existed.

The village retains its chapels and shops. Significantly, the former Italian Café on the Square which served the social needs of the village for so long has now become the Megabytes café, a drop-in, counselling centre providing a continuity of service for the community (Pic. 84).

It has a new trunk road above the village. It has a Community Centre and a swimming pool. It has a Garden of Remembrance.

And Aberfan has its people with whom I am privileged to share a common heritage.

I am and shall remain Bachgen Bach o Aberfan, Erioed, Erioed.

Postscript

Historians require evidence of the use of 'primary sources' and I have done my best to refer to original documents wherever possible. However, this article also offers a personal view of the history of Aberfan, and this necessitates the calling up of subjective memories. Inevitably an individual's reminiscences may contain unintentional errors, and if this is the case here, then, of course, I offer my apologies. Distance, as we all know, does 'lend enchantment', but that is, after all, part of the attraction when we "summon up remembrance of things past." I don't apologise for that—it's all part of 'hiraeth'—which brings me back to "How Green Was My Valley"!

Acknowledgements

Thanks are recorded to Mr Roy Beynon for his valued assistance in preparing the photographs used in this article, and to Mr Ino Conti for providing useful background information on aspects of the Italian community in South Wales, and for permitting the use of his photographs. I am also grateful for the help given by long-term Aberfan residents Mrs Ethel Lloyd, Mrs Joan Bennett and the Rev June Vaughan in filling in some of the gaps in my memory of people and places.

Finally, I wish to thank my younger son, Alistair, for providing the impetus for the writing of this article and for allowing me to use much of the material he so painstakingly gathered whilst researching the history of Aberfan for himself.

Merthyr Tydfil: A Valley Community		Merthyr Teachers' Centre Group in association with D. Brown & Sons Ltd., Cowbridge, 1981
Merthyr Historian Volumes One To Eight		Merthyr Tydfil Historical Society 1976-present
Report Of The Tribunal Appointed To Inquire Into The Disaster At Aberfan		HMSO 1967
Lime, Lemon And Sarsaparilla	Colin Hughes	Seren Books, 1991
Aberfan: The Story Of A Disaster	Tony Austin	Hutchinson, 1967
Aberfan: A Disaster And Its Aftermath	Joan Miller	Constable, London, 1974
Is It Still Raining In Aberfan?	M. Doel & M. Dunkerton	Logaston Press, 1991
Canals Of The Welsh Valleys	D. D. & J. M. Gladwin	The Oakwood Press, 1974
The Taff Vale Railway	D. S. M. Barrie	The Oakwood Press Reprint, 1982
Kelly's Directories—various		Glamorgan Archive Service
Wild Wales	George Borrow	Collins, 1955 Edition
Aberfan	Edited by M. C. Harris	A. H. Stockwell Ltd., 1967
The History Of Merthyr Tydfil	C. Wilkins	Merthyr Tydfil, 1908